ALONG THE WAY

ALONG THE WAY

THE JOURNEY OF A FATHER AND SON

MARTIN SHEEN
AND EMILIO ESTEVEZ
WITH HOPE EDELMAN

THORNDIKE PRESS
A part of Gale, Cengage Learning

Detroit • New York • San Francisco • New Haven, Conn • Waterville, Maine • London

GALE
CENGAGE Learning®

LIBRARY OF CONGRESS CATALOGING-IN-PUBLICATION DATA

Sheen, Martin.
  Along the way : the journey of a father and son / by Martin Sheen and Emilio Estevez with Hope Edelman.
    pages ; cm. — (Thorndike Press large print biography)
    ISBN 978-1-4104-5033-3 (hardcover) — ISBN 1-4104-5033-3 (hardcover)
  1. Sheen, Martin. 2. Estevez, Emilio, 1962– 3. Motion picture actors—United States—Biography. 4. Fathers and sons—United States—Biography. 5. Large type books. I. Estevez, Emilio, 1962– II. Edelman, Hope. III. Title.
  PN2287.S3715A3 2012b
  791.4302'8092—dc23
  [B]   2012016997

Published in 2012 by arrangement with Free Press, a division of Simon & Schuster, Inc.

To Janet,
wife and mother,
and Ramon, Charlie, and Renée

CONTENTS

Prologue 9
St.-Jean-Pied-de-Port, France,
    September 2009: Emilio 15
1. Martin, 1940–1959 33
2. Martin, 1962–1968 69
3. Emilio, 1967–1969 130
4. Martin, 1969 164
5. Emilio, 1970–1972 184
Outside Pamplona, Spain, September
    2009: Martin 210
6. Emilio, 1972–1974 223
7. Martin, 1973–1976 251
8. Martin, 1976 285
9. Emilio, 1976 293
10. Martin, 1976 334
Haro, Spain, October 2009: Emilio . . 343
11. Emilio, 1976–1977 355
12. Martin, 1977–1979 384
13. Emilio, 1979–1980 412

14. Martin, 1981 446
15. Emilio, 1981 469
Burgos, Spain, October 2009:
    Emilio 476
16. Martin, 1981 494
17. Emilio, 1981–1983. 517
18. Emilio, 1983–1987. 552
19. Martin, 1984–1989 587
20. Emilio, 1990–1994. 605
21. Emilio, 2000–2012. 640
Santiago de Compostela, Spain,
    November 2009: Martin 656
Epilogue: Emilio: 2000–2012 665

ACKNOWLEDGMENTS 671

PROLOGUE

We never get over our fathers, and we're not required to.
— Old Irish saying

MARTIN

In the summer of 2010 I got a call from my oldest son, Emilio. He was calling from the editing room where he was working on *The Way,* our film about a father-and-son pilgrimage, written and directed by Emilio, in which I play his father. We'd spent forty days filming in southwest France and northern Spain along the Camino de Santiago, the thousand-year-old, 500-mile route leading to the cathedral in Santiago de Compostela, where the remains of Saint James the Apostle are believed to be interred.

The Camino de Santiago, also known as the Way of Saint James, is a sacred path for Christians and, in recent years, walking its length has become a spiritual endeavor for people of all religions and backgrounds. The Camino ends in Galicia, a region of northern Spain to which four generations of Estevez men are tied. My father, Francisco, was born and raised there and my grandson, Emilio's son Taylor, lives in Spain with his wife, Julia.

Working with Emilio on *The Way* was one of the most extraordinary and satisfying projects of my life, and I longed for another father-son adventure with him. And that day Emilio was calling with just such a project.

"Hey, listen," Emilio said. "Would you be interested in writing a dual memoir?"

"A memoir? You mean a book?"

"Yeah. A father-son memoir. Whatta ya say?"

I was intrigued. To my knowledge no such memoir had ever been published, at least not in our profession. Married couples have written books together, but not a father and son. The possibility began to excite me and I bombarded him with questions.

"Hold on!" he said. "I just want to know if you're interested."

"Of course I'm interested," I assured him. "I'd work with you on anything. Do you have an offer from a publisher?"

"Not exactly, but I have a meeting with a literary agent at my house this weekend.

We're going to have lunch, chat, and see if there are enough reasons to pursue this." Then he hung up.

I almost called him back to invite myself over for that lunch. After all, Emilio only lives a few hundred yards down the street from me and his mother, Janet. But I restrained myself and waited for him to report back.

EMILIO

That weekend, I sat on my outdoor patio with literary agent Scott Waxman and David Alexanian of Elixir Films, the producer for *The Way.* We were drinking wine that my partner Sonja and I had made and lunching on vegetables picked just two hours earlier from our backyard microfarm.

"Emil, maybe you should tell Scott about the kind of book you have in mind," David said.

I chewed on one of my homegrown cucumbers and stalled for time to come up with something pithy and meaningful.

"It's a father-son story," I said.

"Yes, that's what attracted me to it initially," Waxman said. "So it's not only about the filming and the experience?"

"Right. It's about how we got here, as men and as artists. Everyone thinks they already

11

know the story. Truth is most folks don't know the half of it."

Scott leaned forward. He was interested in those stories, too, he said.

So, here it is. These are the stories you thought you knew but didn't. Stories you can't find through a Google search, scenes that we've recreated from our memories, to the best of our abilities. In the course of our dual acting careers, we've been involved in more than 250 movies and television shows. It would be impossible to mention them all here, so we've highlighted only the ones that had the most impact on our relationship and on our emerging careers. As a result, we had to leave out some notable ones.

We joined forces with Hope Edelman, an accomplished memoirist in her own right, for the writing. Hope tolerated our madness, our impossible schedules, and our considerable distractions. She truly has the patience of Job and listened to our stories, the good ones and the bad, and pulled them together in our own voices. We showed our scars and our triumphs, and sometimes our asses. In many ways, the entire exercise was like a long, drawn-out therapy session with Hope as our trinity — counselor/confessor/writer.

We've chosen to be honest, even when it

was painful to do so, and even when a scene is less than flattering to one or both of us. We've done this in the hope that our story will inspire other fathers and sons to reflect on their journeys together and to inspire them to honor and give thanks for each other, in whatever way they can.

This is our journey on the metaphorical "road," the *camino* that *all* fathers and sons travel in some form or another. Our road sometimes gets a little bumpy, as roads often do. But on this road, nobody gets thrown under the bus while we're behind the wheel.

Let's go!

EMILIO

The fog in the French Pyrenees is so thick it's like driving straight into a cloud. A half hour ago, as we left the French Basque town of St.-Jean-Pied-de-Port, we saw hundreds of ivory sheep grazing the steep green slopes by the roadside. Then the fog rolled in. Now the sheep are concealed by the mist, but we can still hear their bells, faintly ringing out from somewhere beyond our reach.

My father and I are here on a Saturday morning to scout locations for our new movie, *The Way.* We've got the camera equipment, six magazines of Super 16 mm film, and a small crew in two pickup trucks we borrowed this morning. Our schedule says filming officially starts on Monday, but, if an opportunity presents itself today, we'll take it. With a tight budget and only forty days to shoot the film, we need all the co-operation and good luck that comes our way.

15

I'm sitting in the open bed of the first truck, wearing the orange windbreaker and brown hiking boots of my character, Daniel Avery. I'm playing a small role as a world traveler who dies on his first day out hiking the Camino de Santiago. My father, in a role I wrote specifically for him, is playing Daniel's father, Tom, a privileged country-club golfer and lapsed Catholic who decides to walk his son's ashes 500 miles to the cathedral in Santiago de Compostela. Along the way he becomes part of a small community of fellow travelers from all over the world, each of whom has a burden to carry.

With me in the truck today are my twenty-five-year-old son, Taylor, my assistant and associate producer on the film; Juanmi, our Spanish cinematographer; Tanya, who's in charge of props; and Anna, the wardrobe mistress. My father is up front in the cab with Jean-Jacques, the Basque inn owner who lent us his Toyota pickup this morning and then offered his services as a driver.

"I'll take you a back way here!" Jean-Jacques had shouted enthusiastically as he steered us out of St.-Jean. He knows the roads like the lifelong resident he is, and he's taking this one fast. Really fast. We're driving over rocks the size of a couch, hanging on to the edges of the truck bed as if

16

our lives depend on it. Which, come to think of it, they might.

My father doesn't like rough roads or dangerous driving and this definitely qualifies as both. I knock on the glass between us.

"How you doing up there, Ramon?" I shout.

Ramon is my father's given name. Ramon Antonio Gerard Estevez. He took the stage name Martin Sheen in 1959 when he moved to New York City from Dayton, Ohio. On location I call him either Ramon or Martin to keep from looking too familiar with him in front of the crew. It's also a way to remind them to treat him as one of the actors instead of as the director's father or as the Hollywood icon that he is. Other directors may look at him and think, "That's Captain Willard from *Apocalypse Now*!" or "That's President Josiah Bartlet from *The West Wing*!" but when we're on set together, I'm thinking, "That's Dad." This is my third time directing him, and it's always a balancing act between being his boss and being his son.

Inside the cab, my father waves back in an "I'm okay" motion. He's wearing a royal blue parka and the same hiking boots I am. Actually, they *are* my boots. We wear the same size and I bought a two-for-one in Madrid six weeks ago. This morning at the hotel in St.-Jean we traded boots when I realized he hadn't broken in his pair. I can't say I'd take the shoes off my feet for any actor, but that kind of thing happens when your leading man is also your dad.

In the course of six feature films I've directed dozens of actors, including screen legends like Sir Anthony Hopkins and Harry Belafonte; friends like Laurence Fishburne and Demi Moore; up-and-coming actors like Lindsay Lohan and Shia LaBeouf; and family members like my brother Charlie and my sister Renée. Even so, my father is my favorite actor to work with. He's incredibly talented and committed to his art. Also, as his son I don't give a damn that he's an icon. I know what he's capable of as an artist and I don't let him fall back on his regular bag of tricks, which I've come to know well over the years. I know exactly when and how to push him to get his best performance, and also when to back off.

The first time I directed him in a film was in 1995, for the Vietnam War–era drama *The War at Home,* based on a stage play by James Duff. It was the story of a young veteran, played by me, who returns from overseas to his family in Texas, where his domineering father — played by "Ramon" — can't and doesn't want to acknowledge the horrors the son has experienced.

We next worked together on my 2006 film *Bobby,* set in Los Angeles's Ambassador Hotel on the night Bobby Kennedy was assassinated there. My father played a stockbroker and Kennedy supporter married to a much younger woman, played by Helen Hunt. My dad was one of my biggest champions on that film, which took nearly seven years to make. When *The West Wing* was honored by the Robert F. Kennedy Foundation my father was given a bust of Kennedy as a gift. He put it on my writing desk to give me inspiration as I was shaping the script. It sits there to this day.

By now my father trusts me as a director. He knows I won't let him look foolish. I'll showcase his strengths and not his weaknesses. As the oldest of his four kids, I've always felt responsible for him, maybe even more responsible than he needs me to be. He was so young when I was born, only twenty-one, that in some ways we grew up together. When we're on set people say that sometimes it's easy to forget who's the father and who's the son.

That doesn't mean we always get along. We don't. We disagree, a lot. He's a devout and practicing Catholic, whereas I have my own ideas about spirituality and a strong connection to the earth. Where he's outgoing and impulsive, I'm introspective and cautious. He lives very much in each moment. I'm always living a year ahead. Case in point: He's in the truck right now mentally preparing for a location scout this morning. Me, I'm already in the theater, watching the film.

Nonetheless, we agree on one thing: that we have more in common than not. We both adore my mother, we love our children fiercely, and we take our art seriously. He's stubborn, I'm stubborn, and we can get angrier at each other than anyone would ever expect. Even when I got so furious that I took a swing at him in the Philippines and shouted at him in Paris and left him alone on a sidewalk, I always came back. I knew how much he loved us and that our family meant everything to him. Everything. Throughout it all, I understood his frustration and celebrated his triumphs the way a son does. Maybe the way only a son can.

Today he's not just my father, he's also one of my closest friends. He and my mother Janet still live in the same house in Malibu where they raised me, my brothers Ramon and Charlie, and my sister Renée. I live 200 yards up the street with my partner Sonja on an acre of land with a vineyard and gardens we planted in our front and back lawns. I know: My father is a famous recovering alcoholic and Sonja and I make wine. Go figure. He helps us harvest our grapes every fall. It's one of his favorite things to do. Despite our differences, the two of us now share a place of deep mutual acceptance and respect. But it wasn't always an easy road.

The pickup truck bounces and rattles as we climb the Pyreneees. Just beyond us are enormous, jagged limestone formations and beyond them, the low white farmhouses of Basque country, but we can barely see anything through the fog. Our producer David Alexanian is behind us somewhere, driving the other truck. David is one of my closest friends, but right now he's probably cursing me for having the brilliant idea to film today and is trying to come up with a plan B.

Me, I know I have to surrender to the moment. Sometimes as a filmmaker that's all you can do. That, and know when to get out of your own way. When I was in my twenties and first started directing, I wanted to control every aspect of my films. Now I know that's exactly how you overlook possibilities. You have to learn when to relinquish control. Otherwise, you miss all the gifts.

Fog, I think. *Okay. This is an opportunity. How can we make it work?*

No doubt, I am the only person in the vehicle with that thought in mind.

The most popular and well-trodden route on the Camino de Santiago is called the Camino Frances. It stretches from St.-Jean in the French Pyrenees to Santiago in the region of Galicia in northwest Spain. In ancient times, many pilgrims began the walk from their front doors. Others chose to assemble at Notre Dame Cathedral in Paris, where pilgrims would worship together before starting their treks. The plan was typically to walk to Santiago de Compostela and then to walk all the way back. Monasteries and hospices for pilgrims offered food and shelter along the way but the journey could be treacherous. If the wild animals didn't get you, the weather or the bandits often did.

Our plan for the film is to shoot the script in sequence, starting in St.-Jean and moving steadily west along the Camino Frances. We'll act like real pilgrims ourselves, picking up cast members along the way as Tom encounters them on his walk. As a result, this won't be the kind of production that cycles back to earlier sites to redo a scene. Once we leave a town we'll have left it for good, and whatever we didn't get on film the first time we'll have to do without. This means that whatever gets in our way, whatever surprises we encounter in terms of weather or townspeople or cast, has to become part of the film. A shoot like this is one part preparation, one part skill, and two parts faith that everything will work out in the end.

We have a forty-day journey ahead of us, but it was an even longer journey to get us here. In 2003, my father, his close friend and fellow actor Matt Clark, and my son, Taylor, saw the Camino for the first time when the three of them took a trip to Spain. My father was on hiatus from *The West Wing* and didn't have enough time to walk the Camino's length, so they drove along it for a few weeks instead. At an inn for pilgrims outside the city of Burgos, Taylor met and fell in love with the Spanish woman who would become his wife. Later that year he moved to Spain to be with her, and they live there to this day.

After that 2003 trip to Spain my father began to give me gentle nudges about making a film about the Camino — ideally, one that would feature him. He was always on the lookout for substantial film roles, and Spain exacted a strong pull on him as his paternal family's ancestral home.

Living 200 yards away from my father has both its advantages and its disadvantages. The advantage is that he can come knocking on my door at any time. The disadvantage is that he can come knocking on my door at any time. Especially when he has ideas about a film he wants me to write.

Knock knock.

"Yes, Dad?"

"I have a great idea. Write something for me set in Spain. A documentary."

"I don't do documentaries, Dad." When had I ever expressed an interest in directing a documentary? Besides, I was out pitching the script for *Bobby.* I didn't have time to start something new right then.

But my father didn't give up. He only regrouped.

Knock knock.

"Yes, Dad?"

"I have another idea. How about a story where two old guys go to Spain with a young guy who speaks the language and shepherds them along the way?"

Two old guys and a young guy traveling

together in Spain? Hmm. That sounded familiar. It also sounded like a small European movie with a very limited potential audience.

"What happens next?" I asked.

"That's for you to figure out. I'm busy with *West Wing.* Just write a script where I'm the guy. It'll be fun — you and me, in Spain!"

I sat with his idea for a while. Two old guys and a young guy walking the Camino . . . two old guys and a young guy walking the Camino . . . and then . . . *zzzz.* I couldn't find anywhere to go with this story, other than to sleep.

But since the beginning of time, every son in existence has wanted to please his father. From the painted macaroni cigar boxes he brings home in the first grade to the SAT scores in high school, the son is always angling for the father's attention. "Look at this," he says. "Look at *me.* Aren't you proud?" I was no exception. Even as an adult I still wanted to please my father. So after *Bobby* had been funded, filmed, and released, I returned to my father's idea. If I was going to invest a couple years' worth of time and energy in the project, I wanted it to be special for both of us. But I still didn't have a hook for the story.

When I started writing scripts in my teens and twenties, my mother would say, "Write what you know." What she meant was, "Don't write something so far out there it doesn't connect for you emotionally. Write movies that are thematically close to wherever you're coming from at that point in your life." I still have one of my early scripts for *Men at Work,* a film I wrote half my life ago, when I was twenty-five. *Men at Work* is about two garbagemen, played by me and my brother Charlie, who become involved in the murder cover-up of a local politician. What did I know about garbagemen? Not much. Murder cover-ups? Even less. My mother knew that, of course. She wrote a page of notes she attached to the script that said, "I'm reading this script and I don't know what it's about. It has nothing to do with who you are. I feel that your life experiences are limited and it's reflected in this screenplay."

She probably didn't know how much life experience I did have, much of it gained when I was fourteen and we spent five months in the Philippines during the shoot for *Apocalypse Now.* But as usual, she was right. I'd do better work if I wrote about what I understood.

What did I know about being an old guy

or a young guy walking in Spain? Nothing. But I knew what it felt like to lose a son to the Camino. That's what it had felt like after Taylor moved to Spain, and something in that theme felt right. This film needed to be about a father who loses a son.

But how would I get an American to the Camino? What could bring him there that wouldn't feel manufactured or contrived? Slowly, an idea came to me.

I pitched it to my father one day in the car, as we were driving north together on the 101 freeway. Right around the sand hills between Malibu and Ventura I explained, "I think it should be a father-son story. And I think the son is no longer with us. I think he died on the Camino and the father goes to pick up the body and decides he's not coming home and does the route himself."

My dad didn't even stop to think about it. "That's it," he said.

And so here we are two years later up in the French Pyrenees, in the freezing cold. In the last half hour the fog has become so thick we could walk right off the mountain and not even know until it was too late. Jean-Jacques tells us that's exactly what happened to a hiker in this same spot last year. As if on cue, half the crew walks right by us without even noticing we're there.

What if Tom's son Daniel got caught in a storm with a fog like this? It could happen.

"Wait a second!" I say. "This is where Daniel gets lost."

We break out the cameras and film me standing in the mountain fog, then walking away from the camera. Twenty feet ahead of me at the edge of an abrupt drop-off, a small wooden cross sticks out of the ground. It seems too coincidental but it's true: Someone has died here recently. The crew members share a moment of solemn respect when they realize what we're seeing. It's also a powerful reminder that we're onto something real. We don't know it yet, but this will be the first of many coincidences we'll encounter while making this film.

Five days later, we return to the same spot to film Tom Avery on his first day of his trek. The morning is sunny and clear this time. Half the crew, along with my mother, have already headed into Spain to prep for tomorrow's shoot in the small border village of Roncesvalles. The rest of us go up into the mountains and make a cross to mark the site where Daniel died. Tanya twists it down into a mound of dirt and drops fresh flowers at its base. My father drapes his rosary over the simple cross. He always carries a rosary. It comes in helpful today.

We shoot him heading uphill in his royal blue parka with a loaded pack on his back. He does yoga every morning and for a man of almost seventy he's extremely fit. But he's trudging uphill the first week of shooting with a nearly forty-pound pack on his back. It's twelve pounds more than the guidebooks recommend and he's adamant about carrying it full, just as he was adamant about not training with it in advance or training for the walk at all. The guidebooks about the Camino advise hikers to prepare for weeks before starting the trek, but he wasn't having any of it.

"Tom's not a young guy!" he insisted. "He's never carried anything before! He's a man of privilege. He wouldn't be prepared. Don't worry, I've got all this in hand."

I knew better than to get in the middle of that. Still, as I stand next to the camera and watch my dad charge uphill at 4,700 feet elevation with the pack strapped to his back, and then come back down and do it all over again, I'm not so sure about his choice. The director in me is grateful I have a leading man who wants to embody his character so fully. The son in me is worried that my father is going to seriously mess up his back.

"You've got to stop him!" our producer David says as we trail my father from the moving camera truck. "What are we gonna tell your mother?"

"Nothing," I say. "Tell her nothing. She'll see the movie and kill us both afterward."

This stretch from St.-Jean in France to Roncesvalles in Spain is the first, longest, and most difficult leg of the Camino Frances route, covering 25 kilometers (15.5 miles). Roncesvalles is where Tom spends his first night in a pilgrim shelter, arriving in the dark. We've been filming in the Pyrenees all day and now sunset is imminent. We still have to shoot Tom descending into Roncesvalles with a headlamp strapped to his forehead.

We pile the equipment back into the trucks and head down into the valley on another prehistoric road. Rocks and more rocks. *Huge* ones this time. The truck lists from side to side and comes down at nearly 45-degree angles. For the second time today, we're hanging on for our lives.

"Can you slow down, please?" my father shouts to Jean-Jacques, who cheerfully keeps up the pace.

My dad has had enough experience on sets to know that, just when you least expect it, just when you think someone else is in control and you become careless about your own safety, that's when accidents happen. He was on location in Mexico during the filming of *Catch-22* when John Jordan, a second unit director, fell out of a B-54 bomber to his death. He was also the only actor who stepped onto the navy patrol boat during the filming of *Apocalypse Now* and asked for a life jacket. There were so many people on that set in the Philippines, he's said, so much noise, so much action: helicopters, boats, weapons, fire. Somebody easily could have gotten killed, and he had a wife and four children. He didn't want it to be him.

I know what he's thinking up there right now. He's thinking that, pretty soon, one of these trucks is going to tip over and someone's going to be in the way. And that he's not going to stick around to watch that happen.

"Pull over!" he shouts.

Jean-Jacques brings the car to a neck-bending stop. My father slides out of the cab and takes off. We follow him but it's not easy. He's actually outpacing the truck on this road.

David watches all this unfold with awe. "That's an almost seventy-year-old man with a forty-pound pack on his back running at three thousand feet altitude in shoes that aren't made for running," he says. "Is he insane?"

Insane? Definitely not. Determined? Absolutely. He's trying to put as much distance as possible between himself and the truck, and he's succeeding. But as I watch him running ahead of us, his jacket now a blue smudge in the twilight, I see something else, too.

I'm his son. I know.

My father isn't just running away from us. He knows exactly where he's going. He's heading toward the border.

He's running toward Spain.

CHAPTER ONE:
MARTIN
1940–1959

My father, Francisco, once told me, "To be a man you have to do three things: have a son, kill a bull, and write a book."

"Well," I said. "You've got a lot to write about if you have a son and kill a bull."

My father never killed a bull or wrote a book but he raised nine sons and a daughter, and he did much of that work alone. My mother died suddenly of a cerebral hemorrhage at forty-eight in 1951, a few days before my eleventh birthday, and my father kept the family together on a modest working-class salary in Dayton, Ohio. Responsibility, honesty, and faith were the three pillars of his character. He was the kind of man who did the right thing simply because it was the right thing to do.

My father was a frugal man out of both upbringing and necessity. He had ten young mouths to feed and ten young minds to educate at Holy Trinity Catholic grade school and Chaminade High School. Family was the center of his orbit. He never thought about himself. His only jewelry was a watch and his wedding ring, his only personal luxuries a pipe for smoking and a glass of wine at Christmas. He owned one suit and two hats and ironed his own shirts. After my mother died, he shared a bedroom with me and my brother Alfonso until we both left home. Even when my brothers prodded him to buy new furniture or move us to a bigger house he stuck to his principles of austerity. He never owned a car, never even learned to drive. Instead he walked twenty-five minutes to and from his job at the National Cash Register company every day in every season. Years later I asked him why he chose our brick house on Brown Street in Dayton's working-class South Park neighborhood. He explained it was because from that house he could walk to work, he could walk to church, and he could walk to a hospital.

"I coulda carry you over there to the hospital, yes, no far away," he said in his deep, heavily accented English, still weighted with the cadences of Galicia. "I coulda carry you there."

I could carry you there. That was my father. Even in Dayton, Ohio, he lived with the rural sensibilities of northern Spain. Everything was about being responsible, about acting responsibly, about doing something responsible and productive with your life. In 1959, when I boarded a bus bound for New York City, nobody could have called pursuing a career as an actor "responsible." Least of all my father. Yet we grew to understand and respect each other for the different choices we made and we loved each other always, complicated as that love sometimes became.

The Irish have a saying: "We never get over our fathers, and we're not required to." The message is, "Don't even try. For good or ill, you won't get over that hurdle." We carry the image of that man we focus on most with us forever. And so to write about being a father, and even more so, to understand myself as a man, I have to begin with the source.

Francisco Estevez Martinez. He was a Galego, from the region of Galicia in the far northwest corner of Spain that sits on top of Portugal like a square hat. His family lived in the small farming parish of Parderrubias in the province of Pontevedra, five miles north of the Portuguese border. He was a child of auspicious beginnings, born on July 2, 1898, in the midst of the sixteen-week Spanish-American War. Whether his family received news of fighting that week, or even that month, is questionable. Today one village in the province blends right into the next, but in the early 1900s each town was self-sufficient, distinct, and relatively isolated from the rest of Spain. News didn't travel fast. Galegos have historically been seafarers, with their gazes and their hopes trained west — a smart choice given the state of Spanish infrastructure back then. I've been told the reason more Galegos headed for the New World than to Madrid, which was less than 300 miles away, was because both journeys took the same amount of time.

My father left Spain with two of his cousins in 1916 and landed in Cuba, where he found work in the sugarcane fields. Three years later, he entered the United States through Miami as a Cubano, and made his way to Ohio.

It's hard to imagine what those first few months in America in 1919 must have been like for my father. Though he spoke Galician, Spanish, and Portuguese, he knew very little English. I imagine him trying to gain a foothold in a country freshly out of World War I and in the midst of an influenza epidemic — tagged with the unfortunate nickname "the Spanish flu" — that would eventually claim more than 500,000 American lives, many of them women and children. In Galicia his family had its own vineyard, but, in the United States, Prohibition had just gone into effect. And women in America were poised to earn the right to vote. The Nineteenth Amendment would be ratified by Congress the following year. My father began the chapter of his American life during a momentous transition, a time of great victory and enormous grief.

He met my mother, Mary Ann Phelan, in Dayton, Ohio, a few years later. An Irishwoman from County Tipperary, she'd arrived at Ellis Island in 1921 at the age of eighteen. Her family owned a pub back in Borrisokane and had deep roots in the IRA, including her brother Michael, an Irish volunteer in the Irish War of Independence and the Irish Civil War. She spoke English and Gaelic, which was a tipoff to her family's Republican politics, and it's possible that she was used to run messages and goods in the IRA underground; British officers would not body search girls younger than fifteen. For sure her family sent her to live with cousins in Dayton because they knew civil war was coming in Ireland. She had every intention of returning home as soon as the fighting ended.

But in citizenship class in Dayton, she became intrigued by the handsome Spaniard with the glasses and the gentle smile who spoke hardly any English. He was quiet and shy, unlike her raucous, gregarious clan back home, and where she was feisty and stubborn he was steadfastly determined and reserved. They didn't share a common language but they were both devoutly Catholic and both had been shaped by the solid community ties of rural village life. Together they understood the daily challenges and small triumphs of being a foreigner in a new land. They began to study together for their citizenship exams, she taught him to speak English, and over time they fell in love. They married in 1927, when she was twenty-four and he was twenty-nine.

"The Spannerd," she would call him affectionately. "Go an' tell the Spannerd I need 'im."

Those two truly threw their lot in together. They'd left everything they knew behind. What hope they must have shared at first. But my mother lost her first pregnancy, and then my father's fluent Spanish landed him a job as a repairman with National Cash Register Company in Bogotá, Colombia. Living in the tropics was difficult for my mother's Irish blood, and she lost a second child in Colombia. When she became pregnant a third time she decided to return to Ireland to care for her ailing mother and deliver the child there.

My brother Manuel was born in Ireland in 1929. One year later, my father secured a transfer to Hamilton, Bermuda. The family reunited there and five more sons arrived in quick succession. The outbreak of World War II prompted the family's move back to Dayton, where my father took a job as a drill-press operator at NCR. I was born in 1940, the seventh son and the first child to survive birth in America. My sister Carmen and my brothers John and Joe followed, making our family an even dozen. As the oldest of the four American-born kids I was considered the leader of the Yanks in our family, a responsibility that has stuck with me to this day.

Growing up, I loved my name, Ramon, but my father was the only one who used it. To everyone else I was Raymond, or Ray, which was easier for Americans and especially my teachers to pronounce. *"Rrramon,"* my father would call me, with the endless rolled R's of Galicia. I couldn't hear it enough.

I can't remember the sound of my mother

saying my name, but I can recall her with great clarity. She was a large woman with the kind of enormous confidence that could have easily been mistaken for arrogance. We lived in precarious circumstances, in a very poor neighborhood, and yet she was so proud of who we were. Her whole presence conveyed an attitude of "And what is *wrong* with *that?*" She had a sense of dignity that even a child could recognize and admire, and she was terrifically proud of being Irish, particularly an Irish Republican. She was a real character, my mother. Often in the summer she would sit on our front porch on Brown Street and loudly sing the old IRA fight songs while she fanned herself and whacked at flies with the swatter she wielded in her right hand.

She also had great love, devotion, and faith. Every night after supper, wherever she happened to be sitting she'd pull out the beads and start reciting the family rosary. Whoever was home would gather around her and join in.

With ten children in the house, time alone with either of my parents was rare, especially rare with my father. There were so many of us, it was always a chore to get his attention for anything beyond the necessities. When I was about eight I was diagnosed with astigmatism in my left eye and had to wear glasses. The brothers would tease me and call me Four Eyes and I would immediately have to defend my honor. To keep me from taking swings at the other boys, my father took me hunting with him a handful of times early Saturday morning on the outskirts of town. Two sisters he knew from work lived on a farm where they would let him hunt their land for rabbits and birds. To get there we had to take the bus to the end of the line and then walk a few miles more. For me, these were precious and coveted days.

Memory is such an odd companion. Within its grip, we live simultaneously in the energy of the present and the deep emotional places of the past. A smell, a look, a feeling from long ago — sometimes one will come at you at the most peculiar time and a whole past world will awaken to you in the present. Of all my childhood memories, why does a single day of hunting with my father come back to me in such vivid detail now? Dramatic events are more likely to stick fast over the years — like the memory of my mother's funeral, where Alfonso and I served as altar boys — but when I conjure up my father, small, quiet scenes full of sensory images come to mind. Just simple, shared moments like this one:

We're waiting for the bus to the city limits. It's a cold fall Saturday morning before dawn. I'm eight years old. At home my mother and siblings are noisily coming down the stairs for breakfast. At the bus stop, my father and I share a comfortable silence. He rarely speaks outside the house. Shy by nature, he's uncomfortable with how he sounds when he speaks English. His accent is so thick you have to listen closely to understand what he says. When my father talks to strangers or even to people he knows at church or the grocery store, it's always, "Yes, ma'am" or "No, sir." Though he can talk up a blue streak at home, his public persona is that of a man of carefully selected words.

As we wait for the bus he puffs slowly on his cigar. Sweet pipe and cigar smoke cling to all his clothing. To me it's always been a comforting smell. We board the bus and take our seats. The cigar is still positioned between his index and middle fingers. Even at eight, I know this isn't allowed. Rules are rules and he always insists I follow them.

"Pop," I say. "There's no smoking on the bus."

Silence. I can't tell if he's heard me or not.

"Pop, you can't smoke on the bus."

More silence.

"Pop."

My father looks at me for a long, quiet moment and then holds up the cigar stub so I can see its doused-out tip.

"I'm notta smoking," he says with a small, sheepish smile. He's so frugal, he won't discard a mostly smoked cigar but saves the remainder for later.

He lights up as soon as we get off the bus and smokes as we walk to the farm, him toting his double-barrel shotgun in a case in one hand and his cigar in the other, me shuffling along beside him. Inside the farmhouse I'm in for a surprise. The sisters have a television, a luxury we can't afford at home. Theirs is a polished wooden box with a tiny screen on which grainy black-and-white Ohio State Buckeyes run from side to side. I badly want to watch the football game but the sisters have packed us a lunch and, after some small talk, my father is ready to leave. I don't dare not go with him, and I don't dare ask to stay behind. Many years later, I'll remember those simultaneous feelings of longing and frustration, that inner conflict of wanting two things so badly and so equally and not having the ability to choose.

In the field, my father strolls through the grass with purpose. I follow him as quickly as my short legs allow. It looks like an ordinary Ohio field to me — grass, trees, sun, the distant squeaks and calls of high-perched birds.

Suddenly, my father freezes in place.

"Rrramon," he whispers loudly. "Donna move!"

"What?" I say. Did something important just happen that I missed?

"Donna move!" Slowly, he raises the gun to his line of vision and . . . *kaboom!*

An earthquake erupts on the spot. The ground shakes. The air cracks. A loud scream escapes from my own mouth. In front of the bushes ahead, a rabbit appears out of nowhere and flails around on the ground.

"Shoot it again, Pop! It's still alive! Shoot it again!" I shout.

My father tips back his head and laughs. His great basso profundo voice echoes across the field. He picks the rabbit up by the ears and tosses it into a bag. A few more join it later in the day.

I've never been a fan of hunting, but I loved being out in that Ohio field with that man. He was such a mystery to me, my father, and I hold on to these small details

— an extinguished cigar, a double-barrel shotgun, a laugh that came from deep inside — for clues to who he was.

Sons absorb messages about manhood at their father's sides, much of it through osmosis, and I observed my father closely whenever I could. All of us lads did. There was such joy in just *being* with him. At night we would crowd into the house's single bathroom to watch him shave. He would talk to us and sing in Spanish as he sharpened his straight razor blade on a leather strop. As he sang he'd get a little rhythm going with the blade against the leather. I would sit on the edge of the tub and listen and watch. He was very tender in those moments. You'd ask him a question and he rarely gave a straight answer — I'd later come to recognize this as classically Galician — but he would lead you along in light and playful conversation the whole time.

"So, Pop," you'd say. "What about this?"

"Well, you know, *Rrramon,* that's the way itta is in here." He scraped the blade against the foam on his cheek as he talked. "I don't know-a 'bout thatta in there. But you know . . ."

It was a delicious kind of exchange and you knew it was going to last for the whole shave. I don't think my father ever realized how closely we watched him, what a powerful influence he was on us, or how much we adored him. Or maybe I'm wrong. Maybe he knew it all along.

Spain and Ireland were the twin enchantments of an Estevez childhood, distant lands that maintained an emotional pull on both my parents. My father had brothers in Cuba and Argentina by now and my siblings and I romanticized those countries, too — but Spain was our Golden Land. In European history class the Spanish Armada figured so prominently we felt a ripple of pride to be half Spanish ourselves. And again in U.S. history class, when we learned about the influence Spain had not just on the American southwest but also on Louisiana, Georgia, and Florida. We fancied ourselves descended from the great Spanish kings and queens. Of course, we were unaware of the horrible damage the conquistadors had done to native populations. We were taught to view Spain only as a glorious empire of the past.

As a result we had no great fondness for England, which had destroyed the Armada and, according to my mother, done a bad number on Ireland, too. "The wretched Brits," she called them. Ireland itself, the place that had birthed her and defined her in so many ways, was a great unknown to us. After she died we heard little about or from her family there, except for an occasional air mail letter that arrived with a black border, alerting us to news of a family member's death, sometimes months after the fact.

It wasn't until the mid-1950s that my father began to open up about his early years in Spain. My brother Carlos, three years ahead of me in school, won a medal for speaking and interpreting Spanish in a state-sponsored test. My father could not have been more proud. He and Carlos began speaking Spanish at home, and it was as if the language unlocked a store of memories that had been remote and inaccessible to him until then. He told us stories from his childhood in Parderrubias and dug out photos of himself with his brothers. It makes me realize, even in a house filled with children, how lonely it must have been for him to be cut off from the words and nuances of his culture and how difficult it may have been for him to share his feelings in a language he could never claim as his own.

I was already in high school by that point — at Chaminade High School, Catholic and all boys — and working as a golf caddy from early spring to late summer. Caddying at the exclusive Dayton Country Club was as much an expected part of an Estevez boy's heritage as serving as an altar boy and going to Catholic school. All my brothers before me had done it. I started at age nine. We would earn $4.25 for carrying two bags eighteen holes and get paid $5 or $6, which meant either a 75¢ or $1.75 tip, depending on the generosity of the golfer. At the end of a long work day, I'd head to the bus stop for the four-mile ride home with ten dollars in my pocket, twelve if I was lucky. Sometimes to save on bus fare, I'd walk.

The family needed the money we earned from caddying to pay for our school tuitions and books, that was true, but we never felt poor growing up. Or if we did, it didn't matter, because everyone in the neighborhood lived in circumstances similar to ours. Everybody was working class, everybody was struggling. Instead of begrudging those more fortunate or dwelling on what we didn't have, we innately realized how lucky we were to be part of a big family with such a great deal of love and fun. The brothers fought a lot but underneath it we were all like a bunch of clowns sitting around together on hot summer nights, laughing and smoking cigarettes, drinking three-two

Bürger beer from long-necked brown bottles, and playing poker at the kitchen table. In the winter, we spent long hours at the Boys Club after school, boxing, wrestling, playing basketball, and shooting pool.

More than anything, we knew we had a place where we all belonged. The cardinal, unspoken rules in our house on Brown Street were (1) you're not disposable and (2) we can't get along without you. There was no excuse for anyone ever having to stand outside. You would only have to open the door to be welcome. You didn't even have to knock. That was the kind of environment my father fostered and the kind of atmosphere that shaped us all.

On Sunday nights in the summer we would trickle home one by one from the country club after a long day's work in the sun. Sunday was the only night of the week that we didn't sit down for dinner together. In the kitchen, an elbow-deep pot of chili con carne would be warming on the stove and we'd each fill up a bowl. In the summer you could always count on a big pot of chili and in the winter a big pot of Spanish chicken and rice, my father's version of paella. He loved to feed people. He would make everyone who came into the house sit down and eat. That was his form of hospitality, no matter who you were.

"Come sitta down in here. You wanna somethin' to eat."

It was a statement, not a question. Even if you weren't hungry, protesting was useless. He would stand up and fill you a bowl. "You wanna somethin' to eat. I'd like-a to fix you somethin'. Sitta over there, *Rrramon.*"

Sunday mornings, of course, meant Mass, and there was no excuse for missing it. Not if you were an altar boy. Not if you were my father's son. If you were an altar boy *and* my father's son, forget it. No excuses whatsoever.

When Alfonso and I were in high school, we served the 7:00 a.m. mass at Holy Trinity Church every fourth or fifth week. That meant waking extra early every morning of that week. We'd see our names in the church weekly bulletin and think, *Oy. Again?* But to my father it was a responsibility we could not shirk.

After my mother died, the tradition of the family rosary went with her, but my father still attended Mass every Sunday. He would put an envelope in the collection basket for each of my brothers in the military, with their names written on the front. MANUEL. MIKE. CARLOS. FRANK. Even if he could only put a quarter or a dime in each envelope, he would.

The weeks that Alfonso and I had to serve weekday Mass, my father woke us both up before dawn. He made sure we were never late. His clock in the house was always set a half hour earlier than necessary because he couldn't tolerate being late himself.

"Alfonso! *Rrramon!* Come down here!" he would call to roust us out of bed.

I would roll over and glance at the window. Still dark. And in the winter, *cold.* Snow often blanketed the ground.

Alfonso and I never understood the point of us both getting up and walking the twelve blocks to the church in winter. The Mass didn't need two servers. If you tried to argue this with my father, he'd point to the parish bulletin defiantly. "Issa that your name inna there, Alfonso? Issa that your name, *Rrramon?* Then you must to going." Over time we learned how to take turns and cover for each other, but we both had to get out of bed anyway and go through the motions of breakfast to honor the ruse.

Downstairs, my father already would have made the coffee and sliced the thick Vienna bread from the local market. Our heads were foggy from waking so early when we slid into our chairs. In winter it was so cold it made your eyelids ache. My father sat across from us at the table and stared into the distance as he poured milk and sugar into his coffee. Then he began to stir.

Anyone who spent time with my father would quickly learn two things about him. First, he was a pacer. He paced from room to room whenever he needed to work through a problem in his mind. And second, his coffee stirring was endless. He swirled the spoon for so long and with such vigor it clinked loudly and rapidly against the side of his cup. This would drive Alfonso and me nuts first thing in the morning.

"You needa the money for the supper?" my father asked.

Clink, clink, clink.

"Yeah, it's my turn to cook, Pop," Alfonso said.

Clink, clink, clink.

"You buy-a the bread and the fish," my father instructed. He handed a few bills to Alfonso.

We sat for a while in silence. This early in the morning, you didn't dare say anything more. My father stared off into space, dipping a slice of bread into his coffee cup and lifting each bite to his mouth. Then he picked up his spoon and started stirring again.

Clink, clink, clink.

"You both needa the money for lunch atta school?"

Clink, clink, clink.

I stole a glance at Alfonso. He looked back at me. An invisible message passed between us: *If that spoon hits that cup one more time . . .*

"Yeah, Pop, we do," we said.

He handed us the coins to buy lunch. Then, without fail, he would pour his coffee into his saucer, lift it to his mouth, and slurp the liquid from the plate. He didn't waste a drop. I've never known anyone else to drink coffee this way. Why he did it I don't know, but for years I thought that's what a saucer was for.

When he finished he would clear his dishes, put on his hat, say good-bye, and walk out the door for work. My brother and I would rush to the window to watch him head down Brown Street. We already knew which one of us was going to serve Mass that day, but we always watched him disappear around the corner together.

"He's almost at the corner," I would say and then — *boom* — as soon as he rounded out of view one of us would run straight back up to bed.

High school was a time of dreams, when

everything felt possible and right on the brink of unfolding. It was also a time of strong community ties. At my school, in the neighborhood, at home, I knew I was part of something elemental and larger than myself, something solid and good. And yet during these years there was a sense of burgeoning separation as well. Every senior at Chaminade had to make up his mind: Was he going off to college, into the army, or into a local factory job?

Four of my six older brothers had joined the service, but a factory job would have been my lot. The military was out of the question for me. I had been injured at birth when the doctor pulled me out with forceps, crushing my shoulder blade and deforming my left arm, leaving it three inches shorter than my right. Though he never made much of it in front of me, my father felt that I had been crippled and he didn't think I could earn a living as a laborer. Unbeknownst to me until the end of my high school years, he had been setting money aside from every paycheck for me to go to the University of Dayton.

But I had no interest in going to college. My mind and my heart had already committed to another path. I wanted to become an actor.

No, that's not right. I *knew* I would become an actor.

No, that's not quite right either. I knew I *was* an actor. That explains it best.

Children know essential things about themselves at an early age. They may not be able to articulate the feelings until they gain more language and more experience, but even some very small children know who they are even if their parents don't yet. That was my experience. I understood something about myself that I couldn't articulate, a strange, circular sensation of knowing something important but not knowing what I knew. *Hmm, what is this about?* I would wonder whenever that odd feeling came up. And then, when I was about five or six, I started going to movies at the Sigma Theater, a second-run movie theater on Brown Street between a fire station and a bar. The people on the screen there felt familiar and comforting, and gradually it began to dawn on me: I was one of them. *That* was the feeling I'd always had about myself.

I was an actor.

If it's true that every creative person has a second date of birth, the one on which he or she discovers his or her true vocation, that afternoon of realization in a dark Dayton movie theater was mine. Knowing I was an actor flooded me with validation and a sweet sense of relief, and from that moment on I never wavered. I knew, for the rest of my childhood, that I would have to pursue this mystery that possessed me and that gave me possession of myself.

Once I had this knowledge, I then felt the responsibility to act on it. In high school I joined the drama club and started auditioning for plays. The first time I stepped on stage was during my freshman year to play the yeoman court stenographer in Herman Wouk's *The Caine Mutiny Court-Martial.* I had all of three lines but the experience of sitting on a stage and delivering them in front of an audience was one of the most thrilling moments of my life to that point. I felt like I was soaring. Before long I was earning larger roles in plays like *Arsenic and Old Lace,* in which I played Doctor Einstein. I became the guy who walked around in high school with copies of plays folded in half and tucked into his back pocket so everyone would know he was an actor preparing.

"Do you have play practice today?" a classmate would ask.

"I have *rehearsal,* thank you very much," I'd say.

And then, during my sophomore year of high school, I discovered an actor whose extraordinary talent and onscreen presence changed my life.

It was October 1955. The film was *East of Eden* and the actor, James Dean.

In downtown Dayton first-run movies cost $1.25, but at the Sigma Theater in our neighborhood, you could see second-run double features plus a newsreel and cartoons for 20 cents, so that's where my family and friends saw films. *East of Eden* had already been out for six months before I saw it and, tragically, Dean had been dead for a month by then. On screen, though, he was still a formidable presence and, from the moment he appeared I was riveted. Fascinated. Disarmed. I'd never seen anything like James Dean before. No one had. He completely turned cinema acting on its head. His onscreen persona was so effortless and natural it suggested he wasn't acting; he had transcended acting to a *behavior,* a way of existing in the world that spoke to a time and a place and a generation, and it introduced me to the idea that good acting drew from what an actor naturally possessed instead of just what he could mimic or learn. By taking his private pain public Dean offered an emotional refuge to a whole generation of young people. We knew he understood us.

When I was a boy, my favorite actors were Jimmy Cagney, Spencer Tracy, Humphrey Bogart, and Edward G. Robinson, in roughly that order. Growing up as an aspiring actor meant two things: one, if you were lucky you'd meet your favorite actors one day and, two, if you were really lucky you'd get to work with them. Sitting alone in the Sigma Theater that night I was overwhelmed not just by James Dean's incredible talent but also by the knowledge that, as I was discovering him, he was already gone. There would be no chance to meet him or to work with him, ever. Staring at the empty screen long after the double feature ended, I was left with an equal measure of inspiration and sadness.

I heard that James Dean had participated in the National Forensic League while in high school in Fairmount, Indiana, so I joined the NFL too during my senior year. My category was Dramatic Declaration, which meant I performed a monologue before judges at competitions around the city. I chose the salesman Hickey's monologue from Eugene O'Neill's *The Iceman Cometh,* in which the character tries to justify having murdered his wife just hours earlier by insisting he did it out of love. The monologue is loaded with passion and guilt and despair, a challenging choice for a seventeen-year-old, but I loved the character's vulnerability and the raw drama of the scene. Our NFL director and coach, Brother Thomas Corbett, edited down the monologue to a shorter, competitive version for me. *That last night I'd driven myself crazy trying to figure some way out for her. I went in the bedroom. I was going to tell her it was the end.*

I never did win a competition, though I usually came in second to a brilliant and beautiful young actress named Eunice Augsburger from Fairmount High School. She always took home the first-place trophy with her powerful monologue from George Bernard Shaw's *St. Joan.* We became close friends and remain so to this day. When she began her career in New York she chose the professional stage name Samantha Langevin. Both of our fathers worked at NCR, and in 1997 together she and I helped establish the Augsburger/Estevez Scholarship fund for the Theatre Arts department at Wright State University in Dayton, which continues to thrive.

I began playing larger roles at Chaminade as well as in an adult drama society called the Blackfriars and, soon, people in the neighborhood began to talk about my performances. Still, my father could never accept acting as a worthwhile career. To him it was a hobby, an afterschool activity that kept me busy and out of fights. My brothers came to see me perform in high school, but my father never did.

"I'm going to be doing another play soon," I would tell him. "You're coming to see me in the new play?"

"I to going inna there, *Rrramon*. I like-a to be inna there."

"Well, I'd have to get you a ticket now. We only play for four performances."

"Ah, don't warry. I to going inna there for you."

"Okay, Pop. I'm looking forward to it."

It was like a scripted dance, every time. I knew he would never show up. I also knew he wanted to come, but he didn't want to hurt my feelings by telling me he wouldn't. Going to our activities wasn't part of what he did. Maybe there were just too many of us. Maybe he was too shy to go out in public and sit among the other parents. He was in his early sixties by then and maybe he was just too tired. We all knew that he loved and supported us, but we didn't expect him to show up at our events. We accepted this as part of who he was.

Still, I would always invite him, just

because I so loved to hear him talk. His term of endearment for all of us, male or female, child or adult, was "honey." He pronounced the "h" with a guttural, throat-clearing, Germanic *"chh."* When he wasn't calling me *Rrramon,* he was calling me *chhoney,* and often I'd come up with an excuse to speak to him just to hear him say either one.

"Pop, you missed the play," I'd complain.

"Aw, *chhoney,* wasn't possible for me to going inna there," he'd respond.

As the clock ticked toward my high school graduation, our exchanges became increasingly more contentious. He was holding on to the idea that I might go to college, but in my mind, as soon as I had enough dough in my pocket I was out the door. Arguing was purely academic at this point, but still we went round and round.

"You've-a gotta go to school, do sommathing *responsible* with your life," my father would say. "You can't be offa having a fantasy. That'sa *nonsense.*"

One night we began arguing in front of the TV after dinner. It was our usual back and forth. As we bickered, a black-and-white Western flickered on the television screen. *Wagon Train.* Robert Horton ran across the screen in a storm to take shelter in a wooden farmhouse.

My father loved Westerns. Every night after dinner he'd plop down in front of the television and watch whichever one was on. *Gunsmoke, Maverick, Have Gun — Will Travel.* He watched them all. Evenings in our house were usually punctuated by the sounds of gunshots and hoofbeats emanating from the TV.

"Aw, *chhoney*." An almost pleading tone crept into my father's voice. "Why you wanna to go to New York to be an actor in a, what? You canta sing. You donna dance. You donna play the music. What you wanna to do over there?"

"Pop!" I said, exasperated. I pointed at the television. "You watch these shows. Every night there's another Western on and you love them all! Do you see anyone singing or dancing or playing a musical instrument?"

"Aw, *chhoney*," he said, swatting the air in front of him as if that settled the matter. "You canta ride a horse, either."

You can't ride a horse. That's exactly how he thought. So practical. Maybe he was trying to save me from disappointment. Maybe he just didn't want me to leave home. But at some level he must have known: My time in Dayton was drawing to a close. I spent the last months of high school looking out the window of my classroom at the Baltimore and Ohio Railroad roaring by. *I'm going to be on that train someday,* I thought as the teachers droned on. *I'm going to be on my way soon.*

Nothing could stand in my way. *Nothing.* Not even that man I adored above all, my father.

That's when Father Al stepped in.

Reverend Alfred Drapp, assistant pastor at Holy Trinity Church and School in Dayton. He'd come to our church, his first assignment, when I was fourteen, and he was still young himself, probably not more than twenty-five. He was shy, like my father, but also very energetic, and he made a positive impact on just about every family in our parish. I often served Mass for him, and he became my confessor.

Father Al understood my conflict with my father and he inserted himself between us in order to help us resolve our differences. When I flunked science my senior year, making me ineligible for graduation, my father was furious. I didn't care much either way — I wouldn't need formal schooling for what I planned to do — but Father Al gently convinced me to attend summer school so I could get my diploma. He also encouraged me to take the University of Dayton entry exams to appease my father. Begrudgingly, I did both, but I deliberately failed the college exam, scoring only three out of one hundred. My father got the message but still refused to give me his blessing.

That summer I auditioned for a local television show called *The Rising Generation*, which aired every Saturday night in Dayton. Essentially it was a local talent competition. Singers, dancers, musicians, magicians — all would perform live in front of the cameras, and the home audience would mail in postcards voting for their favorite act. I'd watched the show at home with my family and noticed that none of the contestants ever did dramatic readings. Other than playing golf, acting was the only real skill I had, so I figured I'd give it a try. The piece I chose was "The Creation" by James Weldon Johnson, a black minister who was known for dramatizing the Bible for his congregation. He'd shaped this piece from Genesis, and I was moved by its vivid imagery.

And God rolled the light around in His
   hands
Until He made the sun;

And He set that sun a-blazing in the
   heavens.
And the light that was left from making
   the sun
God gathered it up in a shining ball
And flung it against the darkness,
Spangling the night with the moon and
   stars. . . .

It was a fabulous piece to work with and I gave it all I had.

For the first time in the show's history, an actor won. A few months later I was invited back for the season finals and I won that, too. The grand prize was an all-expenses-paid, five-day trip to New York and an audition at CBS Television, an astonishing award for a teenage boy from Ohio. My father couldn't leave his job or the younger children for that long, so my oldest brother Manuel went with me. We flew on a TWA propeller plane, my first time in the air. The show put us up at the twenty-five-floor Sheraton-McAlpin Hotel in Herald Square, which was the most majestic hotel I'd seen up till then.

At the CBS headquarters on West Fifty-Seventh Street we were ushered into a studio. Robert Dale Martin, the casting director, was there to receive me. At the end of my audition he complimented me for having a beautiful baritone and regarded me thoughtfully. He must have seen some glint of promise in this Ohio kid standing in front of him because he gave me the first piece of solid professional advice I would receive.

"You won't be able to do much acting in Dayton," he said. "You ought to give New York some thought."

"I will," I said.

"Come see me again if you come back," Martin said as he shook my hand good-bye.

Back home I focused all my energy on earning enough money to return to New York. That fall I sold Christmas trees on a street corner and even hocked my high school class ring. I figured I needed a few hundred dollars to make a decent go of it in New York. I didn't have a trade or any prospects for immediate work and didn't know a soul in the whole city other than Robert Dale Martin. Yet at a very deep level, I understood this pursuit had to be mine and mine alone. And it had to cost me everything. If I'd felt I could go back home at any time I knew I wouldn't risk everything I had to be successful. I needed to know my next stop would be the street. At the same time, I didn't know how long I could last if

I ended up on the curb. Enough of my father's practicality had rubbed off on me to know I needed a cushion at the start.

Father Al understood the importance of pursuing one's calling. Careful not to offend my father, he loaned me $300 out of his pocket to get me started in New York. A few months later he sent me another $200. A $500 loan in 1958 was like giving someone $5,000 today. It was a tremendous amount of money for me at the time, more than two summers' full work as a caddy.

Had Father Al not stepped in, I don't know how long it would have taken me to raise enough cash. It would also have been much harder for me to leave home as I did. When Father Al gave me his blessing, it helped smooth the way with my father. It didn't override his concern or doubt, but it did allow him to let me go without a fight.

On Saturday, January 31, 1959, I boarded a Greyhound bus in Dayton, much as my father had boarded a ship out of Galicia bound for the New World. As the coach pulled out of the station, its tires crunching against the thin layer of ice and snow, I cleared the fog from the window with my coat sleeve and watched the city I'd known my whole life recede from view. Tomorrow, I knew, my father would add an envelope with the name RAMON on it to his stack for the church collection basket. Already, it all felt so far away.

The bus merged onto US-40 heading east and picked up speed. I laid my head back against the headrest and closed my eyes. Behind me lay family, community, history, comfort, home. Ahead lay my own version of the New World: New York City, Broadway, and — even sooner than I could have known — marriage, fatherhood, and all that they would bring.

CHAPTER TWO:
MARTIN
1962–1968

When a man becomes a father, the relationship with his own father changes forever. It's as if his boat leaves the shore. He can still see his father behind him and he knows he can reach back, but he has to take this journey to be independent and free of his father's influence. At the same time, the father is happy to see his son sail off because that's what he had to do when he had a child.

This is what happened between my father and me. We didn't disconnect, but I became independent in a whole new way when Emilio was born. And so even though Janet and I went on to have three more children, that first birth was the most defining event of my adult life, because that was the one that made me a father.

The night Emilio was born — Saturday, May 12, 1962 — I felt I could have stayed awake for weeks. Janet and I had sat up together all Friday night while she was in labor. When they finally wheeled her to the delivery room, I ran alongside the gurney, but the doctor stopped me at the final door.

"I can't let you go any farther," he told me.

"Why not? I have to be in there with her." I'd never seen a baby born, and besides, this was *my* baby being born.

"You're not trained for this," he said.

Wasn't that supposed to be *his* job? And what kind of training did I need other than to be at Janet's side?

"I must be in there," I repeated, but the doctor was adamant and Janet went into the delivery room alone.

In the waiting room, I fought to stay awake as each hour passed. What was happening in there? I had no idea. When the doctor finally pushed through the doors to tell me I had a healthy son, my exhaustion disappeared. I leapt to my feet and rushed to Janet, who looked as euphoric as I felt. Her hair was stuck to her face from the sweat and birthing effort but she was rosy and beaming, as beautiful as I had ever seen her. She was a mother now. Everything had changed.

We had a *son*. The word felt both completely ordinary and utterly foreign to say out loud. I had a *son*. It hardly seemed possible. I was still a boy myself, really, only twenty-one. Bursting with energy, crazy in love with my wife, hardly worried that most months we could barely make the rent. And yet here we were, a family. It seemed like a small miracle.

Jan and I met in the winter of 1960, not long after she arrived in New York. Her birthplace was Cincinnati, Ohio, just an hour's drive from Dayton. The only daughter of an unwed mother, she spent her first six years with her grandparents in Kentucky before moving to Cleveland, where she attended public schools and earned scholarships to both Western Reserve University and the Cleveland Institute of Art. When we met, she was on scholarship at the New School for Social Research, studying painting. Auburn haired and petite, a painter of enormous talent, she taught me about classical music, health food, and fine art. Through her, whole worlds opened up to me that had never revealed themselves back in Dayton. She was the most fascinating and cultured woman I'd ever met.

To be an aspiring actor in New York in the early 1960s meant signing up for a patchwork and hardscrabble life. You took whatever odd jobs you could get to feed yourself while trying to pursue your art. Since arriving in New York, I'd worked as a stock boy at American Express, theater usher, messenger boy, and part-time soda jerk while I pursued stage work. I'd landed in the city at a time when discrimination against Puerto Ricans was rampant, and a Spanish surname was no asset. I can't count how many conversations I had that went like this:

"Hello, I'm calling about the job you advertised."

"Your name, please?"

"Ramon Estevez. That's R-A-M . . ."

"I'm sorry. That job is no longer available."

Finding work as an actor was hard enough. Having a Spanish name became a double liability. So I made a purely commercial decision: My stage name would become Martin Sheen — Martin for the casting director Robert Dale Martin at CBS, and Sheen for Bishop Fulton J. Sheen, the auxiliary bishop of New York. His prime-time national television show, *Life Is Worth Living,* was a huge success during the 1950s, and he became popular as the first television evangelist. With his dramatic flair and striking presence, like a Shakespearean actor, he had a powerful charisma and I admired him greatly.

After ten months in New York, I landed a backstage job at the Living Theatre, the avant-garde theater group founded by Julian Beck and Judith Malina. At first I was a glorified curtain puller and janitor for $5 per week. I worked my way into the cast of the theater's hit *The Connection* when the original cast left to make the movie of the same name and got a pay bump to $30 per week. That's what I was doing when I met Janet, playing the role of Ernie, a wannabe jazz musician and junkie sitting in a Greenwich Village apartment crowded with other junkies waiting for their connection to arrive with a fix.

Janet and I moved in together in the fall of 1960. I think of us now as two crazy kids in New York moving from one apartment to another with a few sticks of furniture between us. Possessions, comfort, security — none of this felt like it mattered. All that mattered was making art, participating in art, and having a creative life. We took for granted that to be artists you had to live very frugally and suffer. Everyone we knew was barely scraping by, and we accepted this as our lot too, because we knew if we didn't pursue art we would never be happy. Thank

God we were young enough and foolish enough to believe in ourselves and our potential because we didn't have any input or support from either of our families. Thank God for that, too, because if they'd tried to influence our choices we wouldn't have been free to become ourselves.

I lived so deeply in the world of acting and theater that I didn't even notice when the weather turned cold and I needed a coat, or that it was time to wash my hair. Janet had to remind me and keep me grounded in these very simple endeavors.

In June of 1961 the Living Theatre was asked to represent the United States in the Festival du Théâtre des Nations in Paris and do a ten-city tour of Europe. I was asked to recreate the role of Ernie in *The Connection* for the tour and of course Janet joined me. We started in Rome and played at night, so days were free time for us to roam the city. Janet and I got tickets for the Wednesday audience with Pope John XXIII, who would soon usher in Vatican II and change things considerably for Catholics worldwide. We stood inside St. Peter's Basilica with a crowd of thousands to see him and receive his blessing. This was before the Popemobile, back when a pope would be carried through the crowd on a platform, almost like a throne. Until I was part of that crowd, I never understood why popes were carried like that. Then I realized: It's because that was the only way for him to see everyone in the crowd, and for everyone in the crowd to see him.

Somewhere in his remarks Pope John made a joke in his native Italian and the crowd had to wait while it was sequentially translated into different languages. Each time it was translated there would be laughter from the English section, then laughter from the Spanish section, and then the French section, and so forth. Each time the laughter rose up Pope John would raise both his hands in a thank-you gesture to the people in that section. It was an utterly human action, and it felt as if the barriers between the pope and the people were being relaxed just a bit as he recognized the humanity in everyone. I was excited to see it because I knew what this guy was up to. He was going to change the world.

Our little troupe from Greenwich Village won the Grand Prix award at the Paris festival and then moved on to Germany. By living very frugally, staying in pensions and scrimping on our meals, Janet and I managed to survive in Europe on $100 a week.

And yet despite all of our striving and

struggle just to make it from week to week, sometimes meal to meal, when we returned to New York and learned that Janet was pregnant there was never any panic. We never had any doubt. I'd come from such a big family that when a new baby arrived every year or two we all just slid over to make room. Even though Janet and I were both so incredibly young, starting a family seemed to make sense, as if this was what two people who loved each other naturally did next. We were married on December 23, 1961, in a fifteen-minute ceremony at the altar of the Church of St. Stephen on East Twenty-Eighth Street, sandwiched between an 8:00 a.m. Mass and a funeral. Afterward, we had an impromptu breakfast reception at a Jewish deli in the neighborhood with a dozen friends from the Living Theatre and three bottles of champagne. I couldn't have imagined a more perfect day.

After the birth, while Janet rested in her hospital room, I took the elevator down to the lobby pay phones and called the operator to place a collect call to my father in Ohio. I wanted him to be the first to hear the news.

"We had a boy!" I shouted when he picked up the phone.

"Wonnerful! Congratulations!" he shouted

back. I imagined him standing in the living room on Brown Street with the receiver pressed to his ear, motioning for my brothers to come into the room, and a wave of nostalgia swept through me. I could still picture every detail of that room.

Next I called our good friends Charlie Laughton and his wife, Penny Allen. He was an aspiring writer, poet, and actor, she a brilliant actress herself, and they were home waiting for my call.

"We had a boy!" I shouted for the second time when Charlie answered the phone.

"Congratulations! What are you going to name him?"

"Emilio," I told him.

"Ah, I like that," he said.

Emilio. We had a son. Emilio. We had a *son.* I had to say it to myself over and over again to believe it was true.

Late that night I rode the subway alone all the way from Sixty-Eighth Street up to our apartment on 203rd Street in the Bronx. I didn't know it yet, but back at the hospital one floor below Janet the abstract expressionist painter Franz Kline was hours from his death. Emilio had come into the world just as Kline was exiting. It seemed to represent a certain fateful symmetry. In Kline's family something had left that could never be brought back. For Janet and me something had just been added that could never be taken away.

The next morning was Mother's Day, and on the way back down to the hospital I stopped at a corner market to buy Janet a bag of her favorite cookies, Pepperidge Farm Milanos. We celebrated her first Mother's Day in the hospital room with Baby Emilio.

When Charlie and Penny walked into Janet's room during visiting hours he handed me a typed sheet of paper.

I looked at the single sheet. Free verse skipped across the page. While I'd been riding the subway back to the Bronx last night Charlie had been sitting at his desk composing a gift to mark the occasion. I was so moved I hardly knew what to say. He'd titled the poem "Emilio." I held up the page and read it out loud:

Emilio
many nights I would walk down that street
and look up to the rooftops —
and a voice would fall from somewhere
calling
E
    Mi

Li
                Oo oo oo oo oo!
(Emilio must have been a great bandit —
    A nocturnal gad-fly —
    A purple desperado —
    Yes, a bandit many times)

sometimes that voice would bring rain
and I'd put up my collar —
sometimes it would stop before I
reached the corner
and die on the face of a summer sky:
always it ran in ancient blood down my
    own veins

sometimes I'd hear it till I hit the big
    Ave —
till I turned the corner
and —
like a toy —
when the spring is sprung —
I sped!
shot zig-zag
    down the lights of the City:

and when I came home
I'd know that I too had only Emilio —
only the calling.

when I moved — just a suitcase —

I watched that voice
bequeath its last colors to the setting sun
and unlight the whole street.

I watched my hands go dark.

Charles Frank Laughton is an extraordinary poet who never received due praise for his talent. Thirty-four years later, when I was asked to participate in the audiobook *The Silver Lining: Twenty-Three of the World's Most Distinguished Actors Read Their Favorite Poems,* this was the one I chose to read.

To Janet and me, the poem was a heralding that welcomed Emilio into our circle of friends. For all of us, suffering for art meant making choices that had consequences, many of them difficult and some even severe. We weren't going to own a car, or at least not for a long time. We were going to miss a few meals. And forget about owning a suit. If you were a child joining this kind of community you had to be tough enough to handle it. You weren't going to be spoiled. You would have to sacrifice because everyone around you would be sacrificing, and you would probably grow up and look around and see that other people had it much better and wonder why you didn't. But you would be okay with that and you would grow from the experience. Someday, you might even be proud.

Somehow, from the start, we both knew Emilio would be tough enough to handle this kind of life. And he was. We took him with us everywhere. We'd go see shows in dingy little Off-Broadway theaters or movie houses and Janet would breastfeed him throughout the performance. Nobody seemed to mind. Bathing him made me nervous because he shrieked when he felt the water, but I changed his diapers and took him for walks and slowly got to know him as a person separate from Janet and me. And I began to recognize a presence in him that was strangely familiar. That's the very best way to explain it.

Throughout Janet's pregnancy I'd known a big transition was coming, a tremendous occasion that would last for all my life. Even as a child, I'd felt that somewhere beyond me was a measure of being that involved me but was larger than myself. It was one of those beliefs I couldn't articulate but knew to be true, like the one that had told me I was an actor. When Emilio was born, I felt that I had always known him. His presence was that comfortable. Holding him was like being reunited with a part of myself. I would look at him and think, *Oh! You're the one I've been waiting for. I didn't know what form you would take, but now I know it's you.* The part of this story that always astonishes me is that I hadn't known I'd been waiting for anyone until he arrived.

Years later I would do an interview with a journalist who said, "Tell me about your son, Emilio."

"Oh, Emilio . . ." I began. "I have known him all my life."

"Don't you mean all of *his* life?" the journalist asked.

"No," I said. "I meant what I said. I have known him all my life."

Soon after we brought Emilio home, a big square truck started coming by once a week to our apartment in the Bronx. We lived on the upper floor of a two-family home and the driver would pick up our pail of dirty diapers and carry a stack of fresh ones up to our door. Somehow Janet had known to set this up. She was far ahead of me on the parenting curve. I didn't even know a baby needed a bassinet. As it turned out, he also needed lots of clothes and bottles and a changing pad and . . . and . . . and. I'd had no idea that having a baby was so elaborate or so expensive. A crib? New *sheets?*

Me, I would have gotten everything from

the Salvation Army or Goodwill. We'd had no problem furnishing our apartments mostly from the curb. "A chair!" I'd shout when we saw one set out for morning trash pickup. "A couch!" I couldn't understand Janet's sudden interest in buying everything brand new. *He's a tough kid,* I thought. *He doesn't need all this stuff.* The truth is, all the spending made me nervous. I didn't have any work that summer and my residual payments from TV jobs that spring weren't going to last for long.

Fortunately, Actors' Equity offered support to struggling actors and their families. One of their programs, called the I Got Shoes Fund, allowed actors to qualify for a new pair of shoes every year or two because of all the shoe leather we burned going to auditions. I obtained several pairs of shoes that way. Another of their programs, called Bundles for Babies, collected used baby items from actors whose children had grown and handed them down to actors with newborns. Janet and I got a secondhand bassinet, crib, and stroller for Emilio this way. But the crib still needed a bumper and sheets, and Emilio needed clothing and formula, and for this we needed money.

One afternoon Janet went down to Macy's on Thirty-Fourth Street and got a store credit card. For a while it was our lifeline. We used it to buy baby clothes and also a black-and-white TV. Then we started eating at the restaurant in the store and using the card for groceries and formula. It was not, as my father would have said, "responsible," but that card was all we had.

When the bill came in the mail, I couldn't believe the amount. It was $600. How could we possibly have spent that much? In 1962 a loaf of bread cost 20¢ and a pair of shoes $3. A $600 bill was *staggering.* To this day, I still don't know how we paid it.

And then in July the truly unthinkable happened. I couldn't come up with the month's rent and we were evicted from the Bronx apartment.

There would be many moments to come that would test my courage as a father, moments that would require decision-making abilities I could only hope I possessed and moments that would literally bring me to my knees to ask for guidance or help. This was just the first. *Responsible.* The word had always felt like the opposite of free choice, but now it felt like a mission. Taking care of my new family was more than a task; it felt like a duty. I was my father's son, after all. And so he was the one I turned to when we had to leave our Bronx apartment and had nowhere else to go.

Janet and I packed what we could fit into suitcases and left everything else behind. We hitched a ride with Dick O'Reilly and Gerry Gellotti, two friends I'd grown up with in Dayton who'd driven out to visit us in New York and then brought us back with them to Ohio. Janet, Emilio, and I crowded into the backseat of their tiny car the whole way. We stayed in the house on Brown Street with my father and brothers while I borrowed money from Cal Mayne, the owner of the Dorothy Lane Market in Dayton and the sponsor of *The Rising Generation,* who'd become a friend over the years.

The plan was for Janet and Emilio to remain in Dayton with my father while I returned to New York to find us a new place to live. Manhattan was too expensive; New Jersey too far. We had friends on Staten Island, a working-class, family-oriented borough of neighborhoods that made me feel at home. I found a corner one-bedroom at the top of an art deco building at 30 Daniel Low Terrace, a twenty-minute uphill walk from the Staten Island Ferry. I signed the lease and started scouting around for furniture again.

"Another actor lived in this building years ago," the neighbors down the hall said when they saw me moving in. "You should be as lucky as him."

"Who was it?" I asked.

"Paul Newman," they said. He'd rented a furnished room in the basement of that same building for sixty dollars a month when he was starting out in the New York theater. Though he was long gone by the time we moved in, I hoped this was a good sign.

In September Janet and Emilio returned to New York and I finally felt some relief. We'd just suffered through a bout of pennilessness and homelessness and it hadn't felt like an artistic sacrifice. Not now, not with a baby. Mostly it had felt desperate and frightening. Sometimes suffering for one's art is just suffering, period.

The next day I would go out looking for a job and I would find one at the Bay Street Car Wash in the St. George neighborhood on Staten Island. It was honest, steady work that helped support us for the next six months until I started getting roles on television and stage. But today I was happy just to have Janet and Emilio back with me, in a place of our own. I led them out to the fire escape and held Emilio while Janet leaned over the railing. If you angled out far enough and looked north you could see the

Statue of Liberty, and just beyond her the buildings of Ellis Island, where my mother had landed forty-one years earlier. It was its own small form of welcome. For the next two years this building with that view would be our home.

When I went looking for someone to baptize Emilio that fall, the priest at the Eastern Orthodox church was gentle and kind. I didn't know much about the Eastern rites, but my lack of experience didn't seem to bother him. A father wanted his five-month-old son baptized; that was all he needed to know. I was grateful for his generosity. He was the only priest I could find in the neighborhood who was willing to perform the ceremony for a stranger.

He wasn't like any priest I'd encountered before. Eastern Orthodoxy allows married men to stay married after they're ordained, which explained the wife who greeted us warmly at their house. Our little group of four standing in the priest's home office consisted of Emilio, our neighbors Melinda and Gary Dodson, and me. Janet hadn't come, more because of lack of interest than displeasure. The idea that Emilio had been born tainted with original sin and needed to be cleansed to ensure his salvation was something she neither agreed with nor wanted to devote a Sunday afternoon to. Raised among Southern Baptists, she didn't have much interest in organized religion as an adult. She did have a highly calibrated radar for hypocrisy, and she zeroed in on mine right away.

"All of a sudden you're a Catholic?" she said. "Where the hell were you last year when we were living together in sin?"

She had a point. I certainly hadn't been a practicing Catholic when we met. I was more of a fringe Catholic, the kind who believed the spirit was willing but wasn't always able to follow up. Still, all my years of Catholic education and childhood practice made the idea of skipping a baptism too difficult to accept.

Janet agreed to the baptism if I took care of the whole procedure myself, so I asked our neighbors Melinda and Gary to accompany me. They were a young married couple like us, actors who couldn't afford to live in Manhattan. Melinda was Catholic and from the South, and I asked her to be Emilio's godmother. Gary stood in for my dear friend from high school, John Crane, who was my best man at our wedding and had agreed to be Emilio's godfather but was not available that day. Melinda and Gary stood by my side as I held Emilio in the priest's office and answered the required questions.

"What ees the baby's name?" the priest asked. He had an accent that could have been Russian, Greek, or maybe Armenian. I don't think I knew even then.

"Emilio Diogenes Estevez," I said.

"You can spell that, please?"

"Emilio," I said. "E-M-I-L-I-O." I waited for him to write it on the baptismal certificate. "Diogenes. D- . . ."

I paused and started again.

"D- . . ."

I looked at the priest. The priest looked at me. He didn't know how to spell it, either.

Janet and I had chosen Diogenes for Emilio's middle name after the Greek iconoclast who spoke out against corruption and carried a lantern through Athens searching for an honest man. The guy had courage and pluck. Emilio Diogenes Estevez: It was such a fine name. But it wasn't until that moment in the priest's office that I realized I didn't know how to spell it.

I glanced at the wall where I saw a picture of a saint who reminded me of Saint Dominic. Oh, why not.

"Dominic," I said. "D-O-M . . ."

"Ah, *Dom-in-eek,*" the priest said, nod-

89

ding. He spelled out D-O-M-I-N-I-C on the certificate and signed it with a flourish.

Inside the church, Melinda, Gary, and I waited by the front doors while the priest slipped on his vestments. His outer robe looked like an elaborate white tapestry cape. It was a striking contrast to the plain black robes I knew from the priests at Holy Trinity.

"Who will be speaking for the child today?" the priest asked.

"I will," I said.

"Face this way," he instructed us. We all made a quarter turn to the right. "Do you renounce Satan and all his angels and all his works and all his services and all his pride?"

"I do," I said.

"Do you accept for this child Christ, who is the light of the world?"

"I do," I said.

The priest made the sign of the cross over Emilio. Together we recited the Profession of Faith and then he handed me the baptismal candle to carry as our little group followed him to the altar. Small round bells hanging from his brass censor jingled as he swung it, chanting his way up the aisle. The smoke drifted out and around us.

Geez, this is getting a little out of hand, I

thought. At home they just sprinkled some water on the baby's head. Here, we were going for the full triple immersion. The baptismal font must have been at least two feet deep. Emilio started howling on cue when he saw it, as if he knew a dunking was imminent and was making his objection known.

The priest motioned for the baby and I handed him over, then watched him lift Emilio toward the ceiling and all the way down into the water — once for the Father, once for the Son, and once for the Holy Spirit. He came up the third time sputtering and blinking, with an expression of "What the heck was *that?*" When he was back in my arms I wrapped him in a dry blanket and held him to my chest. The priest took a dropper of oil and anointed Emilio's feet, hands, ears, and mouth in the sign of the cross.

The ceremony was sacred and beautiful and familiar and brand new to me all at the same time. Back in Dayton my father would be happy his grandson had been baptized. If Emilio wasn't going to be raised Catholic he would at least have this basic foundation. At least I'd have given him that.

We followed the priest single file as he circled the font three times and chanted some more. Then he snipped off three locks of Emilio's hair with a tiny pair of scissors, and we were done.

Twenty minutes from start to finish in an elaborate church with a priest, two friends, and no family members while Janet waited for us at home. It was as easy and as complicated as that.

After the doctor had blocked me from the delivery room the night of Emilio's birth, I vowed never to miss seeing another of our children born. Jan was an advocate of natural childbirth, and the process didn't seem all that complicated to me, so when she became pregnant again later that year we decided to deliver this baby at home, with the assistance of a professional midwife. Our second son was born on August 7, 1963, in the living room of our Staten Island apartment while Emilio stayed with the neighbors down the hall. Unfortunately, the midwife was unavailable due to a family illness and the baby was coming so fast we had no time to get to a hospital. We were left to deliver the baby alone.

It probably goes without saying that birthing a baby is a bloody, painful, messy business, but I didn't know the half of it. If not for the fear of leaving Janet to cope alone, I would have fainted before it was over. The delivery was complicated — the baby got stuck in the birth canal — and Janet started hemorrhaging. I called for an ambulance but the baby arrived first. At one point I started barking orders like a madman and instinctively rolled my forearm down hard against Janet's upper stomach to push the baby down. To my surprise, it worked.

While we were waiting for the medics a second baby started crowning. *My God.* I couldn't believe it. We were having twins.

"Janet, there's another one," I said, getting back into position.

"What?" Janet raised her head. "Where?"

"Coming out right now."

"No, you idiot!" she said. "That's the placenta!"

The ambulance transferred Janet and the baby to the hospital, where they were put under observation and pronounced fine. She gave the baby my name, Ramon, because I was courageous enough to stay the course during his birth. Despite his chaotic entry into the world he was a healthy and content newborn.

Sadly, another baby born that day was not. As I walked out of the hospital to retrieve Emilio from the neighbors the late editions of the New York newspapers were just hitting the stands.

"Extra! Extra!" the vendor at the corner shouted. "Jackie has a boy!"

Patrick Bouvier Kennedy, the president's second son, had been born earlier that day. Five weeks premature, he had a respiratory syndrome that made him unable to breathe on his own. Two days later he passed away. The president of the United States had access to the best doctors and medical care in America, yet he wound up losing the one thing he'd wanted most. Janet and I were just two crazy kids in a Staten Island living room with a bottle of alcohol and the Sunday *New York Times* and our baby had survived. I wouldn't have traded places with the president for anything that day, nor Janet with the first lady. Still, as we held our second son and understood what another family was mourning, it hardly seemed fair. We had no way of knowing, at the time, that in less than four months the president's family would be mourning another tragic loss, and that this time Janet and I and the whole world would join them.

New York City: early April 1964. Politically, culturally, socially — it was an incredibly turbulent time. President Kennedy had been assassinated the previous November,

American aircraft carriers were on their way to Vietnam, and the civil rights movement was about to peak.

In the midst of all this, *Funny Girl* opened at the Winter Garden Theatre on Broadway starring the wildly popular Barbra Streisand, who brought the country some much-needed good cheer. And two and a half blocks away at the Eugene O'Neill Theatre, I made my Broadway debut with a small part in the short-lived production of *Never Live Over a Pretzel Factory.* Directed by Albert Marre, it ran for only five previews and nine shows but earned me some positive attention and a few audition calls.

We closed on a Saturday night. After the audience filed out the cast and crew held a good-bye party on the stage. In the play, a band of five musicians follows a Hollywood star home to his apartment and plays a few songs, and the band performed for us at the party that night. Mitch Leigh, who'd composed a few pieces for the band to play, stood next to me on the stage holding a drink in his hand.

"What are you working on next?"

"Oh, I've auditioned for this play, a family drama," I said.

"What's it called?"

"It's this thing by Frank Gilroy called *The*

Subject Was Roses. What about you?"

"Well, I've written the music for a new show. Alby's going to direct it."

"Really?" I asked. "What's the name of it?"

"It's a take on the Spanish classic *Don Quixote.*"

It didn't sound very promising to me, but I didn't want to sound critical.

"Well, all the best," I said.

One year later I'd look back on that conversation and laugh. I got the role of Timmy Cleary in *The Subject Was Roses,* which became the biggest dramatic hit of 1964. Mitch's play was the biggest Broadway musical the following season. He called it *Man of La Mancha.*

With the steady work and $175-per-week paycheck that *Roses* provided, Janet and I were able to move the family back into Manhattan. We found a fifteenth-floor apartment on the Upper West Side a few blocks from Riverside Park with big windows overlooking Eighty-Sixth Street. When I came home from the theater late at night and looked out our living-room windows at the carpet of sparkling lights, it felt as if I were gazing down at the sky. A wife, two sons, and a costarring role in a Broadway hit: My life was as full as I'd ever imagined it would be. Sometimes it was hard to believe that only four and a half years ago I was selling Christmas trees on a street corner in Dayton.

Back home in Ohio, my father had worked his way up at National Cash Register to become an inspector and was ready to retire at age sixty-six. It had been his longtime dream to return to Parderrubias when his work in the United States was done, and now that my youngest brother Joe had finished high school, my father was ready to go "home." He hadn't been back to Spain since he'd left as a boy, but he'd been periodically mailing small amounts of money back to his brothers to build him a modest house on the family's land. "My castle," he called it. He bought a ticket on a ship from New Jersey to Spain in the summer of 1964.

"Rrramon."

I pick up the phone in our New York apartment to the sound of my father's voice. "I to coming a-there to visit you, on the train, and then I go onna the boat. You be-a there Sunday, *Rrramon?*"

"I'll be here, Pop," I say. I've got a role in the biggest dramatic hit on Broadway. I can't leave town. For sure I'll be home on a Sunday with Janet and the boys.

"You be-a there? Sunday? You sure?"

"Pop," I say. "We'll be here."

"I canna to stay with you, *Rrramon?*"

"You can stay with us, Pop."

"You sure?"

The plan is for my brother Mike, who now lives in Connecticut, to pick him up at Penn Station and bring him to our apartment for the week. I arrange for two tickets for him and Mike to come to the Tuesday show. Monday, I receive some serendipitous news. The first lady, Lady Bird Johnson, is coming to the Tuesday show with her two daughters, Lynda and Luci. This is terrific timing for Mike and my father and it'll be a memorable night for me, too: I'll be performing for both the first lady as well as my father, who has never seen me on stage before. I rush home from the theater Monday night to share the news.

"Pop, what luck!" I tell him when I get home. "The first lady is coming to the show tomorrow night and you'll be in the audience together. What do you think about that?"

"Oh, no." He shakes his head and starts turning away. "I no to going inna there."

"What? Pop, it's the first lady! Her daughters are coming with her. You should be there."

"I no to going inna there."

He's still so shy he can't bring himself to sit in a theater in the first lady's presence. He's still so stubborn that he won't even try. So I trade in the Tuesday tickets for Wednesday and he and Mike come to that evening's show instead.

The Subject Was Roses is a play about the emotional triangle between a Bronx husband, played in 1964 by Jack Albertson; his wife, played by Irene Dailey; and their adult son, Timmy, an ex-GI who returns home in 1946 after combat in Europe during World War II. At its core, it's the story of a son who keeps trying to save his parents' marriage and finally realizes he doesn't have that power.

In the play's final scene, the son decides to move out and the father shouts, "Go, and good riddance!" The son says, "No, I'm not leaving until you listen to me. When I was a boy I dreamed that you died and I went into the streets and somebody asked why I was crying. I said, 'Because my father's dead and he never said he loved me.' " The father in the play tries to cut him off but the son goes on, "It's true you've never said you loved me. But it's also true that I've never said those words to you. I say them now. I love you, Pop. *I love you.*" He puts his arms around his father, but his father holds off until the last minute, his stomach heaving as he tries to contain his emotion. Then he finally breaks and hugs his son back. The play ends there with the two of them in tears.

During rehearsals, I had had great difficulty with that scene. I knew the lines forward and back, but I couldn't find the right emotional pitch. Rehearsals took place in a warehouse on Fifty-First Street and one day, while we were working on that scene, Ulu Grosbard, the director, stopped rehearsal and pulled me aside.

"What's the problem?" he asked.

"I can't get this scene," I told him. "There's no reality here."

"What do you mean, no reality?"

"Boys don't tell their fathers they love them. That's just not done."

Ulu stared at me for a long moment.

"Have you ever told your father you loved him?" he asked me.

"No, I haven't," I said. *I've never even thought about that before,* I realized. *That possibility has never even occurred to me.*

"Neither have I," Ulu said. "Neither did Frank Gilroy. And that's why he wrote the play."

It was exactly what I needed to hear. I

walked back across the room to do the scene with Jack Albertson and I never had trouble with it again.

In fact, it becomes my favorite scene and, when we get to it Wednesday night, I play it squarely for my own father in the audience. I'm looking at Jack when I say my lines but the emotions I summon up come from that well of love, admiration, and frustration I feel toward the man I've called "Pop" all my life. I play the scene better than I've ever played it before, and by the time I get to "I love you, Pop. *I love you*," I'm weeping uncontrollably. Jack is weeping and I can hear some members of the audience weeping as well. It is the best performance of my life, before or since.

At the curtain call, we are greeted with thunderous applause, loud whistling, and repeated shouts of "Bravo!" I'm drained afterward but riding an emotional high. I head to my dressing room to wait for Mike and Pop.

I wait, and I wait. Then I decide to clean up and get dressed. Then I wait some more.

Finally, I look out in the hall. It's empty and quiet. Jack and Irene have left. It's been a half hour since the play ended, and nobody's around. I go downstairs.

"What are you still doing here?" the stage

manager asks.

"Waiting for my father," I say. "I don't know what's taking him so long."

It's odd he's not coming backstage to see me — surely he's coming back to see me — so I wait some more. Finally, I call home from the pay phone backstage.

"Oh, Pop's already here," Mike says.

"Why didn't you bring him backstage?"

"I couldn't," Mike says. "You know Pop."

I don't expect my father to offer congratulations or praise. He's never been the kind of father who offers it freely. Whenever he sees me on television he calls and jokes with me as if I'm still in character. "I dinna teach-a you to be doing that. Where did you learn thatta language? You beena drinking?" he'll say, and I'll laugh. That's his way of saying, "I saw you," but tonight I wanted him to really *see* me. I can't dance or sing or ride a horse, but I can *act,* and tonight I put everything I had into that performance for him. It's a *great* play. It will win the Tony Award for Best Play and the Drama Circle Critics Award next year and will win a Pulitzer Prize for Frank Gilroy. I'll earn a Tony nomination for my role, and Jack will take the Tony for Best Actor in a Play.

Why didn't he come backstage after the show?

By the time I return to our apartment, the boys are asleep and Janet and Mike are puttering around in the kitchen making late-night snacks. It's a heavy, hot August night and we don't have air-conditioning. The big windows facing Eighty-Sixth Street are wide open to encourage a breeze.

When I walk in my father is slowly pacing the apartment, waiting for his snack. Pacing is his form of meditation. He paced through the rooms in our house on Brown Street throughout my entire childhood, sometimes throughout family conversations. He would pace into a room, offer a few comments, and pace back out again.

As he paces across my New York living room, I want to know what he thought of the play, why he didn't come backstage, and what he thinks of my career choice now, but I don't dare ask. I'm exhausted from the show as I sit on the couch and rest my elbows on my knees, letting my forehead sink into my hands. Behind me I hear Janet's low laughter and the soft clinks of knives and plates in the kitchen. All I can see from this position are the straight planks of the wooden floor. If we're going to talk, my father will need to speak first.

I hear his feet in the living room before I see them. *Boom, boom, boom,* in a slow, rhythmic cadence. We don't have much furniture, just a couch and a few chairs, and his pacing takes him straight across the room to the windows. In my peripheral vision I see his shoes cross the hardwood floor and pause at the windows, then turn and head back to the kitchen. *Boom, boom, boom.* He goes in and out of the living room again. And again. I lose track of how many times he walks to and fro without a word.

Suddenly, the sound of his footsteps stops. I glance sideways toward the windows. He's not there. If he's not behind me and he's not over by the window, where . . .

He's right in front of me, I think. *What in heaven's name is he doing?*

I lift my head. He's looking at me like I'm someone he's never seen before in his life. Our eyes lock. My heart is pounding, but I don't dare say a word. It's as if he's trying, with great effort and determination, to figure out who I am.

And then, without a word, he paces out of the room and, a week later, he boards a ship for Spain. We never speak about the play before he leaves. I'm simply left to wonder.

The Parderrubias my father returned to in 1964 was remarkably similar to the one he'd left in 1916. Chickens still ran across his family's courtyard. The women still cooked over open fires. Each tree, each house had been perfectly preserved in his mind all these years and they were still in the same places. Only he had changed in the intervening years.

He settled into a "castle" far more rustic than the one he'd thought he was building. Watching Westerns on television was out of the question. The house didn't even have electricity. At night he carried an oil lamp to light his path to bed. I imagine him lying there under the blanket alone, enveloped by the kind of dense silence that never filled the house on Brown Street. In a darkness unbroken even by shadows he stared at the ceiling and thought, *This is notta working for me.* He'd returned to Galicia as an American citizen, a man accustomed to modern conveniences. Plus, he missed his children more than he'd anticipated. All the years he'd been raising us alone, he'd dreamed of the simple, quiet life of Spain. Now that he had it back, he discovered that the good-natured chaos of Brown Street was where he belonged.

He lasted six months in Parderrubias. That winter he returned to Dayton and bought a little house in the Kettering section of town. Three of the brothers moved in to keep him company.

In *The Zoo Story,* the playwright Edward Albee observes that, sometimes, we have to go a long distance out of the way in order to come back a short distance correctly. He might have been talking about my father.

Performing on Broadway meant working six-day weeks, eight shows per week, with only one day off. I spent every day off I could with Janet and the boys. One Sunday afternoon that summer, Frank Gilroy invited the entire *Roses* company for a picnic at his home in upstate New York. Janet and I welcomed the chance to be outside in the country and let the boys run free.

Frank Gilroy and his wife Ruth had three sons: Tony, the oldest, and five-year-old twins, Dan and John. I loved being in Frank's company. He was and still is one of the most positive, talented, compassionate, generous people I've ever known. This was a man who'd seen heavy combat in Europe during World War II and helped liberate one of the concentration camps. He'd witnessed true brutality and horrible examples of man's inhumanity to man, and yet he was always upbeat. In the months leading up to the debut of *Roses,* he worked relentlessly to patch together the financing to open the show, and later to keep it running. At our lowest moments when we would all be thinking, *We're going to get the ax here. This show is not going to survive,* he'd lift us back up with his infectious energy and sense of humor. I've carried that lesson with me to this day, to always look for a bright spot even in the darkest of times.

That Sunday afternoon he and I sat together on a picnic bench and watched our five boys run around together across the lawn. One twin chased Emilio, who ran after the other twin, while Ramon, who'd only recently learned to walk, toddled good-naturedly behind them. Their play was so innocent and uninhibited, it was a joy just to sit in the warm sun and watch them.

"Do you think our kids will be friends when they grow up?" Frank asked me.

"I'm sure they will, if they still know one another."

"No," he said. "I mean, do you think our own kids will be friends with one another?"

What an odd question, I thought. I'd grown up in a house packed with siblings and, while some of us were closer than others and nearly all of us fought, we always had one another's back. We loved one another without question and without reservation. But did we all consider one another friends?

"I never thought about that," I told Frank. "I wonder about it sometimes," he said. "You know, it's not always a given."

When I looked at Emilio and Ramon playing together on the grass, I couldn't imagine a time would ever come when my children wouldn't seek out each other's company or rush to each other's aid. They were brothers, and family is the most important tie we have.

Janet gave birth to our third son, Charlie, on September 3, 1965, just five days before we began the nine-month national road tour of *Roses,* which continued its run on Broadway with a replacement cast. Meanwhile, Martha Scott joined Jack and me as we opened *Roses* in Los Angeles to start the tour.

Looking back, I'm amazed by how little actual planning I did during those years. I never had a life plan that was more detailed than being an actor, husband, and father. Whenever a new opportunity or challenge came along, I'd just figure out how to make it work in real time. *Let's see if we can get these two things to come together,* I'd think. *Okay. Yeah. That'll work. I can handle that. Let's do that!*

The benefit of living this way is you become flexible and resourceful. The downside is that the line between spontaneity and stupidity can be very thin. You often wind up making the most ridiculous choices and the dumbest mistakes, and then you have to find your way back out. But you learn best from personal experiences, and making peace with your mistakes is a measure of maturity.

We went on the road with *Roses* in September 1965 with three children under the age of four. The tour was among the last of the traveling road shows and put us on the move frequently. In Los Angeles, we set up house for three weeks in the Montecito Apartments, a beautiful 1930s-era Art Deco building right in the heart of Hollywood. I would walk to and from the theater every night as the late-summer heat started to cool. I would have been perfectly happy to keep the show in Los Angeles, but our next stop was a month-long run in San Francisco. Then came Denver, and next we headed to the Midwest for shorter runs. Our train would pull into a city at odd hours, we'd do a few shows, and then we'd pack up and move on to the next town. Split weeks like these were brutal with three kids because we had to unpack and pack and uproot and unpack again in such short bursts.

Somehow Janet managed to keep us all together by feeding and clothing three small boys, one of them a newborn, for seven months while I performed for rooms full of strangers in cities like Kansas City, Des Moines, Milwaukee, Chicago, Boston, and Washington, D.C. Charlie spent most of the first year of his life carried around the country in a wicker basket. Chicago was so cold in January, if you spit on the sidewalk it would turn to ice before hitting the ground. Janet had to keep the kids inside the whole time. One night we pulled into Cleveland well past midnight and had to wake up the sleeping boys. I had to maneuver Emilio and Ramon off the train with them literally hanging on to my legs as we went slurping through the depot.

In the cold early spring of 1966 we rolled into Boston for a three-week run. Back on the East Coast, closer to home and near the end of the tour, our spirits lifted. We took the boys to the Boston Public Garden and watched the swan boats float by on the lagoon. One Sunday I went to Mass at a beautiful old church downtown. I hadn't been to Mass in years. Vatican II had occurred in the meantime and I was astonished by the changes it had ushered in. Growing up in Dayton, I'd served countless

Masses where the priest faced the altar and said the Mass in Latin. This priest was facing the congregation and he kept looking up nervously, as if he were self-conscious about suddenly being exposed. And he was saying the Mass in English. Everyone could participate and for the first time I understood everything that was going on. *Oh, my God,* I thought. *This is extraordinary.* It made all the difference to feel like I was on the inside of the Mass instead of feeling like an observer on the perimeter.

We ended the nine-month *Roses* tour with a long run at the National Theatre in Washington, D.C. Emilio was about to turn four by then, and one night I asked Janet to bring him to the play. He had come backstage before, but this would be the first time he was old enough to sit in an audience and watch me perform. Before the show I peeked through the curtain and saw the two of them sitting up in a box, his little blond head barely peeking over the railing.

That night I played my heart out for him. When I said the final line — "I love you, Pop" — I imagined Emilio as an adult saying it to me. When an actor reaches down into his emotional well and pulls up a deeply personal response, the audience can sense something special is going on. They may not know exactly what they're seeing, but they recognize it as authentic. I felt grateful that Emilio was there to see it happen on this night. Even if he didn't understand it right then, maybe the scene would somehow lodge itself in his memory. One day, maybe, he'd remember the image of his father on a stage saying, *I love you,* and realize how important it was for fathers and sons to say those words to each other.

After the play, I waited backstage for Janet and Emilio, but they never came. I walked back to the hotel to find Janet reading in bed while the boys slept.

"What happened?" I asked. "I looked for you two after the show."

"Oh, he fell asleep during the first act," she said. "I had to bring him home."

Oh well, I thought. *Like grandfather, like grandson.*

As challenging as it was to travel with an entourage of three children, I much preferred it to traveling alone, because I didn't do well by myself on the road. Despite the success of *Roses* and the Tony nomination, I was back to living from job to job, struggling to pay the monthly bills. I was talented and I worked hard. So why wasn't I getting more work, or being celebrated the way I thought I deserved? And when I got into that self-pitying frame of mind, usually I drank.

Growing up in a working-class Irish neighborhood of Dayton, drinking had been an accepted social activity. We got drunk at weddings. We got drunk at funerals. We got drunk on front porches, in kitchens, and at neighborhood poker games in Dick O'Reilly's living room. Only after I started working at the Living Theatre and dating Janet, though, did I start going to bars to drink. By my mid-twenties I knew I should avoid being alone whenever I could and that I had better avoid alcohol altogether.

On April 2, 1967, our daughter Renée was born in New York City. Janet had been hoping, and I had been praying, for a girl. What a special blessing! Once again, we all moved over to make room for a new addition to the family. And yet everything changed with a baby girl in the house as we started all over again, this time with pink clothing and fluffy toys.

In the fall, I landed a guest-starring role on the television series *FBI*. All the storylines on *FBI* were based on real-life cases, and Efrem Zimbalist Jr. played the inspector who investigated them. Ed Asner and I were hired to play an uncle-nephew team that kidnaps the youngest son of a prominent family and hits up his older brother for ransom. The older son was played by Russell Johnson, fresh from a three-year run as the Professor on *Gilligan's Island.*

The episode was shooting on the Warner Bros. lot in Burbank for two weeks. Janet and the kids couldn't accompany me, especially with a new infant in the house. Even with my sister Carmen now helping with the kids, managing four children under the age of six was often more than a two-person job. I convinced Emilio, who was five, to travel with me to California ostensibly to ease the load on the women, but really so I wouldn't have to travel alone.

Today, it's unusual for an actor to show up on set with a five-year-old son in tow, but 1967 was a different era of television production. "Bring him along!" the producers said. They even helped find a preschool nearby that would take him during the day while I was working.

I didn't know how to drive, so the show put us up in a motel in Burbank, walking distance from the set. The first day of shooting, I woke Emilio at 5:30 a.m., helped him dress, and walked him the few blocks to the school. The buildings in Los Angeles were lower than the ones he was accustomed to in New York and the streets weren't as noisy or as crowded, but the place was unfamiliar to him and he held on tightly to my hand.

Oh, no, I realized as we headed toward the preschool. Kids needed to bring lunch to school, didn't they? This was the kind of thing Janet would have remembered, but not me. I'd forgotten to pack a lunch for Emilio.

At that hour, only a Bob's Big Boy burger place was open. Out front it featured a larger-than-life-size statue of a chubby guy with a pompadour and checkered overalls, brandishing a fake plate with a fake burger above his head. It was exactly the kind of food Janet would never feed our kids. I said a fast and silent prayer that she wouldn't know, and if she did find out, she'd understand and forgive me. The food would be cold and soggy by Emilio's lunchtime, but I didn't have another choice. I ordered him a hamburger-and-fries combo for eighty cents to go.

When we got to the preschool, Emilio wouldn't let go of my hand. Trying to ease the separation, the teacher introduced us to the resident mynah bird.

"Good morning, Albert!" the bird said as we approached his cage. "Good morning, Albert!" His name must have been Albert, and he was repeating the children's greetings he heard. Emilio was so fascinated by the bird I was able to slip away without incident.

That week we slid into an easy routine. In the mornings I would get Emilio a donut and an orange juice and walk him to school on my way to the studio. He would race over to the mynah bird and I would leave for work. After school, drivers for the show would pick up Emilio and bring him back to me, because we often shot until 6:00 or 7:00 p.m. The drivers wore Brooks Brothers suits and dark sunglasses and drove squared-off black Ford sedans. For most of grade school Emilio believed the real FBI had picked him up from preschool every day in L.A.

One afternoon Ed Asner and I were filming a scene in the studio that ran into late afternoon. Ed's character had me digging a hole that was going to become my grave, but my character didn't know it yet. In the Warner Bros. studio the floorboards could open and you could dig in the space underneath them. I was down about four feet in the ground going at it with a shovel, dirt flying up in the air, when I looked up to see Emilio's little blond head peering down at me.

"Pop?" he said. He sounded small and

unsure. "Pop?" Much later he would admit he thought Ed Asner was trying to kill me that afternoon.

"Emilio!" I said. I leaned casually against the shovel and tried to look as normal as possible, given the fact that I was standing in a grave I'd just dug for myself. "How was school today?"

He pointed to a gold star affixed to his shirt.

"Because I listened to them," he said.

Because I listened to them. The sentence cracked open a place deep inside my chest. I had to lean harder on the shovel to stay steady. I'd been so focused on doing my job and just making sure Emilio had a place to spend the days that I hadn't stopped to think about the emotional toll it took a five-year-old to fly across the country to a city far from home and go to an unfamiliar school alone for a week. He did it all so eagerly, just to please me. I'd leveraged his love and dependence to get him to come with me so I wouldn't have to travel alone, and then I'd left him there with a soggy lunch in a room full of strangers. And he hadn't complained. He'd been such a good sport about it he'd even been rewarded.

I was twenty-seven years old and already the father of four, but it wasn't until this moment, when I looked up at my five-year-old son from the depth of a grave I'd dug, that I fully understood how much his love and trust and dependence meant to me.

He peered down at me in the hole, waiting for my response. I knew how important a father's praise is to a son.

"That's great, Emilio! I'm so proud of you!" I said.

As attached as he was to me, so I was to him. Our dependence was mutual. I didn't want to take this journey or any future journeys alone. And thanks to him, I didn't have to.

Playing Timothy Cleary in the 1968 film version of *The Subject Was Roses* was significant for several reasons. First, it gave me my first costarring role in a studio feature film and earned me a Golden Globe nomination for best supporting actor. Second, it allowed me to work again with Jack Albertson (who won an Oscar for this role) and this time with celebrated actress Patricia Neal. Third, but not least, it required me to learn how to drive. We'd never had a family car in Dayton, so I'd taken buses or walked wherever I needed to go. New York's buses and subways had suited me just fine. But to film a scene where Timmy and his father travel back from the family's lake cabin, I needed to drive a car, so, at the age of twenty-seven I finally got a license to drive.

In the spring of 1968, Jan and I took the kids to visit her mother and stepfather in North Benton, Ohio, at their house near Berlin Lake. On Tuesday night, June 4, I borrowed my father-in-law's car to take the kids to a drive-in. After the movie, the fog coming off the lake was so thick I could hardly see the road. We crept back slowly. It was a relief to reach the house safely.

After we put the kids to bed, Jan and I checked the news on television. In the California and South Dakota primaries that night, Robert Kennedy and Eugene McCarthy were battling it out for the Democratic nomination for president. Kennedy supporters, we had seen his recent loss to McCarthy in Oregon. The news in Ohio that night declared him a winner in South Dakota, but if Kennedy didn't win California he would drop out of the race. In California it was only 9:00 p.m., but preliminary poll figures showed Bobby well in the lead.

I'd been following Bobby Kennedy's career since his days as attorney general in his brother's administration. His commitment to protect the Freedom Riders, who rode desegregated buses through the South in 1961, moved me deeply, and I considered him a decent, honest, hopeful man with enormous compassion and humanity. I had volunteered for his campaign in 1964 when he'd run for the United States Senate in New York and celebrated when he won. On April 5, 1968, the day after Martin Luther King Jr. was shot, Bobby spoke to a crowd in Cleveland, Ohio, with a speech that left a lasting impression on me. "Whenever we tear at the fabric of life which another man has painfully and clumsily woven for himself and his children," he said, "the whole nation is degraded."

Clumsily. That's the word Bobby used. We *clumsily* go about weaving the fabric of our lives. It's a beautiful sentence because it's so true. We never know in advance what our next step will be. We just take a step, even if it's a clumsy, stumbling one. Sometimes we have to admit, "That wasn't a very good move. I'll try this instead." Or "Oops, I didn't realize how expensive that was going to be." Or "Oh, dear, I didn't realize that you loved me." But through it all we keep walking. We keep living. I didn't become an actor because I was organized to become one. I became an actor because it was my clumsy attempt to become myself. We, all of us, just keep engaging in these clumsy attempts to realize ourselves. It's such a perfect expression of what it is to be human.

"He's going to win," Janet predicted that night in Ohio, "but it's going to take too long. Let's go to bed."

Six hours later, I wake in my parents-in-law's guest room to a small hand pressing against my left shoulder. I open one eye to see Emilio standing at the side of the bed. Sunlight streams in through the window behind him, giving his blond hair the aura of a halo.

"Pop," he says. "Wake up. Pop. Bobby Kennedy was shot."

I close my eye. "Go back to sleep," I say. "It's just a dream."

Pop. He pushes my shoulder again, this time with urgency. "Bobby Kennedy was shot. It's on TV."

I open both eyes now. What? Just six hours ago Bobby was about to win the California primary. Jan and I went to sleep certain we'd wake to good news.

"He was shot? On TV?" I say. "Where?" In Los Angeles? At the hotel?

"In the head," Emilio says. "It's on TV."

In the head? *Oh, Jesus, don't make this*

121

true. I throw back the covers. *This can't be true. We just got through Reverend King. Please don't make this be true.*

"What is it?" Janet asks.

"Emilio says Bobby Kennedy was shot. He saw it on TV."

"Oh, my God," she says, rushing down the stairs behind us.

All the television channels are choked with special reports and updates. Oh God, Emilio was right. What *happened* while we slept? I flip through the dial. Nobody seems to know anything, but everyone is acting like they do. Shot in the head, hospital, surgery. Is he going to live? Please God, let him live. I pick up the phone to call my friend Matt Clark in Los Angeles. He'll know what's going on. It's three in the morning there, but he's one of my closest friends. He'll understand my need to know.

"Pop?" Emilio says. His voice is tiny and unsure, his expression grave. He's six years old, barely knows who Bobby Kennedy is or what he stands for, but he knows how important this news is to me.

"It's okay," I say. "It's going to be okay," but the words are as much for myself as they are for him.

Matt's telephone rings once, twice. Bobby Kennedy. Shot in the head. Please God, no.

The news is too horrific to imagine. What kind of lunatic would do such a thing?

I once sat with Bobby for two hours on a stage in New York City, as close to him as Emilio is to me now. It was a Sunday afternoon, October 4, 1964, a month before Election Day. He was running for a U.S. Senate seat from New York. Politicians and political hopefuls from all over the state had shown up that day at the old Madison Square Garden on Eighth Avenue and Fiftieth Street to rally against the closing of the Brooklyn Navy Yard. Nearly sixteen thousand shipyard workers and their families packed the arena. The roster of speakers competing for their votes was staggering: Nelson Rockefeller, the governor of New York; Robert Wagner, the city's mayor; both U.S. senators and ten U.S. representatives from New York; the Brooklyn and Bronx borough presidents; and Robert Kennedy, who was facing the incumbent Republican Kenneth Keating in the Senate race.

A small group of Broadway actors had been asked to show their support for the Kennedy campaign, including Buddy Hackett, who was appearing in *I Had a Ball;* Rudy Vallee from that season's big musical hit *How to Succeed in Business Without Really Trying;* Jack Albertson and me. I said I'd go if Janet and I could meet Bobby. At the Garden one of his contacts met us backstage and escorted us onto the stage, just a platform with rows of wooden folding chairs. A tremendous banner with a picture of the shipyard and the admonition DON'T GIVE UP hung behind the stage. We took two empty seats and waited. Senator Keating got up and delivered a long prepared speech. "You've been stabbed in the back by Navy Department policies!" he shouted, and the room exploded in a cheer.

I heard a rustling noise just offstage, and suddenly Bobby emerged with a small entourage and walked up to the platform. A year after his brother's death the toll of the loss was obvious. His hair had started to gray and his movements were careful and measured. He was still the handsome young heroic figure we'd come to admire as attorney general just a year before, but he'd become introverted and reflective. His disarming smile was less frequent and his sharp Irish wit was more tempered now.

He was still a man in mourning and the crowd seemed to sense his vulnerability and fragility and treated him with utmost respect. Everyone on stage stood up to let him through. He took a seat in front of us, at the very side of the stage, and when his contact murmured something in his ear he turned around to face Janet and me and extended his hand.

"Mister Kennedy, we're honored to meet you," I whispered, and he smiled and nodded in response as he shook my hand.

"Thanks for coming," he said, and shook Janet's hand as well.

Politician after politician spoke that afternoon while Bobby waited with his legs crossed and his chin resting in his hand. I couldn't take my eyes off him. Every few minutes he'd reach into his pocket for a pen and paper, scribble something down, and motion for an aide, who retrieved it and then scurried away on an errand. We sat like this for nearly two hours. The crowd chanted loudly between speakers. I began to feel uncomfortable for Bobby — *Why were they making him wait so long?* I wondered. *How dare they do this to him?* He was the most important one in the arena, the only one who made any sense amidst all this political claptrap, and they were making him sit for hours and wait his turn.

Finally he was introduced, and when he rose to speak, he held the microphone for no more than five minutes. His speech was brief, humble, and to the point.

"I don't think it's an easy problem," he

said, "and I'd be wrong to come to you and say that I do. But I think a major effort by all of us — all of us on this platform — I think that we can make a difference." After all of the political jockeying and promises of the past two hours, it was almost startling to be spoken to in such a straightforward, honest manner. "I think what should guide all of us is not the fact that the struggle is so difficult," he concluded, "but what really should guide us is what George Bernard Shaw once said: 'Some men see things as they are and say, Why?; I dream things that never were and say, Why not?' "

He gave a little wave to the crowd and stepped down from the podium. The stadium erupted with cheers and whistles. The crowd just went mad for him.

It's hard to convey to anyone who didn't live through that era exactly what kind of emotion Bobby inspired. To many of us, he was the brother we wanted, the son we hoped for, the father we wished we'd had. He was the first rock-star politician my generation had known, with a magnetism that was awe-inspiring to witness. And I realized then that the reason he'd been held for last was because he was the one everyone wanted to see and hear. That was the only way to keep everyone in the building until the rally came to an end.

That's when I knew he would win. A month later he beat Keating by more than 700,000 votes. It would be hard to stop him if he ever ran for president.

In Los Angeles, in the early morning of June 5, 1968, Matt Clark answers his phone.

"Matt? It's Martin. We're out here in Ohio. The news is saying Bobby Kennedy was shot. What's going on?"

In the brief moment of silence that stretches between us, I get my answer.

"It happened last night," Matt says. "At the Ambassador Hotel."

The news that day was grim. One bullet lodged near his brain, one in his neck, one through his chest. All day I prayed for a miracle. I told myself that, if Bobby was in the hospital, he was still alive, and if he was alive, there was still a chance he'd pull through. I went to a local grocery store to shop, then took the kids to a nearby park and tried all day to stay focused. This was Mahoning County, Ohio, rural and conservative. There were no prayer services, no public displays of concern, and when Bobby died the next morning, Janet and I wept alone.

The memorial service and requiem Mass for Bobby were held at St. Patrick's Cathedral in New York City on Saturday, June 8. I had to leave Ohio and travel to New York that day to begin rehearsals for *Romeo and Juliet* at Joseph Papp's Shakespeare in the Park. I kissed Janet and the kids good-bye at the train station. Settled in my seat, I pressed a little transistor radio tight against my ear. The smokestacks of Youngstown streamed past the window as I strained to hear the ceremony broadcast from St. Patrick's. I could not even imagine the depth of Ethel Kennedy's sorrow, pregnant with her eleventh child, or that of the ten other children who had just lost their father. As we sped toward Pittsburgh, Ted Kennedy stepped up to the altar in New York to eulogize his brother.

"My brother need not be idealized, or enlarged in death beyond what he was in life," Teddy said, "to be remembered simply as a good and decent man, who saw wrong and tried to right it, saw suffering and tried to heal it, saw war and tried to stop it."

He was burying the last of his three older brothers, a loss almost unbearable to witness. Though I did not know it yet, in less than three months I would be heading back to Ohio for the funeral of my own brother, Manuel, the oldest, a husband and father of two who would die of a heart attack at the young age of thirty-nine.

At 1:00 p.m. the train carrying Bobby's casket and his family left New York for Washington, D.C. He would be buried in Arlington National Cemetery not far from his brother's eternal flame. What should have been a four-hour journey from New York to Washington took twice as long because so many mourners lined the tracks all the way through New Jersey and Pennsylvania to pay their final respects.

My train sped on into the night, unimpeded. It would take me a long time — another thirteen years — to discover that Bobby had been right: Every life, even the clumsiest one, is a life of honor.

It would take me even longer — thirty-five years — to discover what Bobby's death had meant to Emilio, and for him to transform the events of that night into an artistic expression with his film *Bobby*.

CHAPTER THREE:
EMILIO
1967–1969

New York was sirens and hot dog steam in the summer, sirens and the smell of roasting chestnuts in the winter. Soft pretzels all year long. Two dimes, a nickel, and a penny bought you a can of cream soda and a hot dog with sauerkraut and mustard from Frankie the hot dog vendor at the end of our block. I ordered the same thing every time.

We were living on the fifteenth floor of a brick prewar apartment building in New York City the day my father gave me twenty-six cents to go down to Frankie for a hot dog and a soda. It was the summer of 1967 and I was only five, but this was a different New York than New York today. Five-year-olds could take an elevator down to the street and walk to the corner alone without cause for worry. We thought they could, at least.

On the sidewalk outside our building, two

of my friends balanced on their bikes, watching pedestrians rush by. I said hello and stood with them for a while. Before long, two older kids, middle schoolers maybe, swaggered up to us. They had the kind of tough attitude I already identified as street smart. I knew this would not turn out well. My friends knew it, too, and took off on their bicycles, leaving me there alone without an exit strategy.

The older kids looked down at me.

"Your money or your life," the bigger one said.

Something flashed quick and silver near my face. A knife. Not a big knife, but big enough. Not that size mattered. I was five. A knife was a knife.

Okay, I thought. *What do I do now?* They wanted my money. I'd have to give them some. I slowly took the coins from my pocket and started dividing them up.

A dime for them, a dime for me . . .

Even in kindergarten, I was already looking for parity, aiming for equality. Both of which would later become major themes in my life.

A nickel for them . . .

Smack. One of the kids hit my hand from underneath. The change flew up and scattered across the sidewalk. The kids pounced

131

on the coins and took off running down the street.

I couldn't understand what had just happened. I was going to *give* them what they wanted. I thought it had been obvious I was going to share.

I was crying when I entered our building. "What happened?" the elevator operator asked.

"I got robbed," I said.

He escorted me up to our apartment. "What happened?" my father asked when he opened the door.

"Two boys . . ." I said.

"What? Where?" my father demanded. *"How?"* He led me back to the elevator by my arm. "Let's go down there."

He looked angry, maybe even dangerous. I didn't know what he might do if he caught those kids. Suddenly, I wasn't sure that telling him about it had been a good idea.

On the street, everyone was going about business as usual. It was already ten minutes after the incident. The boys were nowhere to be seen. Even I knew they were long gone by then.

"Which way?" my father asked, twisting his head from left to right. I'd seen him get angry like this before, except this time it was directed at strangers. That part was new. "Which way did they go?"

I pointed to the right. He took off like he was running a hundred-yard dash. The only line missing from this scene was "Follow that cab!"

Forty years later my father would remember this day and how bad he'd felt for me, how he'd known that such an incident could steal a child's innocence and make him afraid to leave the house again. Taking off at high speed wasn't an attempt to catch the kids — he knew they'd already disappeared — but it was the only action he could take at that moment to help him feel he was righting the wrong for his son and demonstrating that he cared.

While I waited for him to return, my two friends cycled back around the block on their bikes. They tried to act nonchalant, as if they hadn't just bailed on me during a crisis.

"Where did you *go?*" I asked. They shrugged but stayed by my side. I knew if I stood there long enough, my father would come back down the sidewalk. That was something I knew I could count on. My father always came back.

When you grow up the son of an actor, you get used to seeing your father come and go. Really, that's all I ever knew. During rehearsals he'd be out of the house all day and home in time for dinner. When a show went up, he'd be home all morning, leave before dinner, and I'd see him at breakfast the following day. Sometimes he flew to California or Hawaii for several days at a time to shoot episodes of TV shows. At home, my constants were my mother and my siblings. Ramon, Charlie, Renée, and I were so close in age we were playmates as well as siblings. The four of us shared one bedroom until well into my grade school years.

When my father was coming and going it meant he had work. Those were good months. When work was scarce, he was home most of the time. I wouldn't say we were poor in those years, but we often lived close to the edge. The feeling when I was born, my parents have told me, was that it was the three of us against the world. Being the oldest I was probably witness to more of their early struggles than Ramon, Charlie, and Renée were. I understood they were vulnerable both financially and emotionally, without support from the extended family, and I grew up wanting to make sure that someone had their backs, even if that meant me. They had each other's backs, but it seemed like no other adults had them covered, not for a long time.

When you grow up the son of an actor you also learn when you're pretty young how to distinguish between what's real and what's art. Watching my father on stage and occasionally on TV helped me understand and appreciate what he did. When I saw the actors backstage after a show and was allowed to walk out on the stage myself afterward, I understood the difference between an actor's work and private life. In January 1968, when I was five and a half, I saw my father play Hamlet in Joseph Papp's Public Theater rock-and-roll version of the play, called *Hamlet as a Happening,* which also became known as *The Naked Hamlet.* Papp took Shakespeare's original text and rearranged it around the five main monologues of the play. Galt MacDermot, who'd written the music for *Hair,* composed the songs. The characters appeared on stage dressed as soldiers with flashlights, or in their underwear, or like garbage collectors. In one scene they threw popcorn at one another. Each time my father appeared on stage he was in a different guise. When he delivered the "To Be, or Not to Be" soliloquy, he walked out as a young Puerto Rican janitor, and when he spoke I heard my grandfather's Spanish accent in Ohio coming at me from a New York stage.

Papp showed audiences that Shakespeare's words could be just as relevant in 1968 New York as they'd been in Elizabethan England. Who else would have thought to have the "To Be, or Not to Be" soliloquy coming from the mouth of a Puerto Rican kid? Before the end of the monologue, people around me in the audience were crying. I didn't understand why, but it gave me a very early lesson in how art could make people react in ways you would never expect.

The *New York Times* panned the show by calling it "jejune nonsense," but to me it was outrageous and exciting and inspiring. In one scene Hamlet walked up and down the aisles handing out peanuts and balloons. When my father handed me a balloon I understood that I shouldn't shout hello. And the next morning, when I woke up and walked into the kitchen, I knew I wouldn't find Hamlet there. It would just be Dad.

New York to a kid in the 1960s was rumbling from the subways, gray snow in winter, *The Flintstones* on Channel 5. My godfather, John Crane, who'd been my father's best friend in high school, had also wound up in New York. So New York to me also meant weekends with John Crane. A towering

African-American man, skinny as a pole, John spent his days working for the postal service and his nights reading books and listening to opera. He was one of the most cultured men I've ever known. His apartment didn't have a television but it was lined with full bookshelves, and he loved classical music. On weekends he took me to the opera and the ballet. These were the last places in the world you'd want to sit as a six-year-old, but you have to give the guy credit for trying.

At home, our pleasures were simple and cheap. While our basic needs were met, I understood that we didn't have money for extras, and I tried not to ask for more than what was essential. But when I was five or six I became obsessed with a pair of construction boots I had seen another boy wearing. I already had shoes, as my mother pointed out, but I didn't just *want* those construction boots, I had to have them, desperately *needed* to have them, and I begged my parents to buy me a pair. When they finally gave in I wore those boots every day, even after my feet grew and the boots became too tight. For weeks I didn't tell anyone my feet hurt because I didn't want my parents to have to spend money they couldn't spare to buy me a new pair.

Even when times were tough, my parents still put education first. I was an extremely curious child, and to give me a proper start at school they decided to send me to kindergarten at a private French lycée. All the students had to wear uniforms, which weren't cheap, and nobody was excited about buying me a suit I'd soon grow out of, but somehow they rallied up the money for the cause.

The school was tightly structured. The students lined up for everything. Every day we had to sing in French. I lasted from September until March 17, the day of New York City's big St. Patrick's Day parade. The school was on East Seventy-Second Street, just off Fifth Avenue, only a half block from the parade route. Knowing that I was related to Ireland on my father's side, I loved that parade, the marching bands and the oversized shamrocks. But on St. Paddy's Day that year, there I was at 11:00 a.m. stuck in a stupid French school, wearing a stupid suit, not allowed to go outside. I was sitting in the class just miserable, listening to everyone around me count in French. Finally I said the five-year-old equivalent of "The hell with this!" and got up and walked out the door.

What does a kid know about danger? I'd

been to parades before and knew what to expect. There would be people standing three deep on the sidewalk, colorful, loud bands marching by, elaborate floats. None of it seemed treacherous to me. I walked to the corner and angled my way through the crowd to the curb so I could have a good view.

Nobody saw me leave the school and it took the teacher a while to figure out I was gone. When she did everyone flew into a panic — "Where is he? We've lost one!" The school immediately called my parents, who rushed across town and into the street to look for me. My aunt Carmen lived in the neighborhood, and she headed out, too. She was the one who found me, standing on the curb in my little suit, minding my own business as the parade marched by.

"What the hell are you doing out here?" she shouted.

"They wouldn't let me watch the parade," I explained.

"Everyone in the family's out looking for you!"

I hadn't considered that part. I'd just figured I'd watch the parade and go back to school when it was over, an arrangement that had seemed perfectly fair and reasonable to me. The school took care of my return. My parents were told I wasn't to come back, which was fine with me. I transferred over to PS 166 a few blocks from our apartment, a five-story Gothic-style building with mini-turrets at the entrance. The place had academic cachet as the former elementary school of J. D. Salinger and Jonas Salk, but it just looked like a castle to me.

That's where I was going to school in 1969 when my father was cast in *Catch-22*. The film is director Mike Nichols's adaptation of Joseph Heller's novel, the story of Captain John Yossarian, a World War II fighter pilot stationed on an island off the coast of Italy who requests to be released from his remaining missions. That's when he discovers the army's "catch-22": that a pilot who keeps flying missions must be crazy, but any pilot who asks for a release from combat must be sane and therefore has to keep flying. Alan Arkin was hired to play Yossarian, and the actors who played the band of jaded, corrupt, and naïve pilots, officers, and nurses in his unit read like a roster of screen icons past and future: Orson Welles, Martin Balsam, Bob Newhart, Charles Grodin, Buck Henry, Anthony Perkins, Paula Prentiss, Richard Benjamin, Art Garfunkel, Jon Voight. And Martin

Sheen, although in 1969 he wasn't yet widely known outside of New York.

The shoot was scheduled for eight months in California, Italy, and Mexico, where Nichols and his art director recreated a U.S. Army World War II B-25 bomber base in the middle of the Sonoran Desert. They hoped that the area near Guaymas, Mexico, would pass as a Mediterranean island on the screen. The Mexico portion of the shoot would take four months, so my parents decided we'd all go down there together. Afterward we'd travel to California, where my father would shoot more scenes, but this time we'd stay there. My father was starting to get steady television and film work in Hollywood, and some of his good friends from New York were already heading west to live.

As much as we'd traveled around the United States for *The Subject Was Roses* tour, I'd never been to a foreign country before. I had no preconceived images of Mexico. The idea of picking up and leaving New York was foreign enough to me. I couldn't imagine living anywhere without hot dogs from Frankie at the corner, skating in Riverside Park, or *The Flintstones* on Channel 5. On my last day of school, my first grade teacher asked me to go to the

141

front of the room. "I'd like everyone to take turns coming up to say farewell to Emilio," she said. "He's moving away."

One by one, my classmates came up to hug me and say goodbye. I stood in front of the blackboard staring out at the class, weeping. I felt as if I were being ripped from the only home I'd ever known. New York was my whole world. I never wanted to leave.

We couldn't afford to ship anything to Mexico so we took only what we could carry, leaving behind all the furniture and nearly all of our toys and books. My aunt Carmen was in charge of selling everything that would generate money my parents could use, but Carmen learned about a needy family in New Jersey and gave everything to them instead. Somewhere in an antique store in Newark you can probably find our whole bedroom full of toys circa 1969. That sounds nostalgic now but was pretty upsetting for a kid back then.

We arrived in Guaymas in January 1969 with one suitcase each and a small trunk of household items. Most of the cast and crew were being put up at the Hotel Playa de Cortés in town, but it was too expensive to house a six-person family there for long. After a week we moved into a house about ten miles away in the rural village of San Carlos, on a peninsula that jutted out into the Sea of Cortez. By now San Carlos has been eaten up by developers but back then it was just the local fishermen and some American families associated with the NASA Manned Space Flight tracking station about 15 miles away.

To a city kid, Mexico was vast and hot and dry. The desert seemed to stretch on forever. I'd never seen so much empty space in one place. The beach was made of fine white sand, and we could walk down to the bay barefoot every morning and watch the fishermen head out into the water. Our house was simple and efficient, two floors of cinderblocks with big, square orange Saltillo tiles on all the floors. My mother was vigilant about checking behind all the furniture and inspecting our sheets before we got into bed every night. She knew a bite from a yellow bark scorpion could kill one of us, especially Renée, who was still a toddler.

The duplex was close to a slaughterhouse, and at certain times of day, we could hear the animals as they were killed by hand. We must have gotten the place for a good price. Still, it had running water and electricity, both of which were luxuries available only for Americans. The local families that lived in the shantytown behind the slaughterhouse had to haul their water in from a communal pump.

My father's role in *Catch-22* — Lieutenant Dobbs — was a minor one, and in our four months in Mexico he only needed to be on set for a total of about twelve days. It was a long and difficult production with a large cast on a remote location that included many old World War II B-25 bombers and the pilots and crew to fly them. The weather often didn't cooperate and sometimes the cast would sit around for days waiting to shoot a single scene. All this meant my father was with us in San Carlos much more than he was on set, and our family became as much a part of the local community as we could. Ramon and I went to a local Catholic school where classes were held in Spanish and I stood out as the only towhead in my class. One of the fishermen who lived nearby had eight or nine children, and after school the eight of them and the four of us would kick around on the beach or run through the dust together. The oldest, Manuel, was twelve and took a special interest in our family. Ramon and I would bring him and his brothers and sisters to our house for dinner and my mother would make big pots of beef stew and vegetables and serve it up in bowls with tortillas for everyone. Anyone who was hungry was welcome. Sometimes fifteen kids filled our house at dinnertime.

One morning we woke up and went down to the beach to watch the fishing boats load up and head out. It was a typical San Carlos morning: dry, salty air, navy blue ocean, a hot sun pressing down on the tops of our heads, except . . . as I ran onto the sand I stopped short. Something had gone horribly wrong. Hundreds of enormous gray fish, some as long as ten feet, were lying on the beach while children darted around them and men bent over the carcasses making fast, deep incisions with their knives.

"*¡Mira! ¡Mira!*" the littlest kids were pointing and hopping. "*¡Delfin! ¡Tiburón!*"

It took a moment for my mind to process what I was seeing. Dolphins, porpoises, hammerhead sharks — I'd never seen so much sea life up close and definitely never out of the water. Fish out of water meant fish must be dead; that simple equation came to me in a rush. Groups of older kids were using their bare hands to push and drag the fish and mammals up onto the sand where their fathers tore into the flesh. At eight in the morning already the smell was oppressive.

The first movie I ever saw in New York was Jacques Cousteau's *World Without Sun,* and I'd been fascinated by the sharks. Now I saw a small posse of kids rolling a dead hammerhead away from the water's edge, and I ran down into ankle-deep water to help them push it onto the dry sand. When we finished, I crouched down close to the head and inspected the shark's eye closely. It was wide and beady and much whiter than I would have imagined. Its other eye was positioned directly on the other side of its head, so far away from the other I couldn't imagine how this could actually result in sight.

We must have been witness to a red tide that morning, when the water is robbed of oxygen and fish in shallow water suffocate and wash up on shore. At the time it was just one of many episodes in Mexico where, faced with something entirely new and unfamiliar, I accepted it without question, in the way that's easy to do only when you're a kid. Kids don't always stop to judge or analyze an unusual experience unless the adults around them react strongly. Otherwise, they just take in the experience and move on to the next one. When I walked onto the San Carlos beach that morning, I registered the sight of a hundred 300-pound fish scattered along the shoreline, recognized that something different was happening, something very wrong, but the adults on the beach didn't seem troubled by the situation. They seemed to have it under control. So I ran down to the shoreline and very soon the physicality of the sun and the seawater, the sand crystals adhering to the shark's tough, rubbery skin, took precedence. Activity. Motion. Experience. For an inquisitive seven-year-old boy that was the gold standard for a good day.

At age seven I was old enough to understand time and distance to a point where I knew it was possible to get on an airplane at home in the middle of winter and get off somewhere else very far away in the middle of summer, but for my younger siblings the move to Mexico was harder. Of the four of us, Charlie was the one who had the most difficult time adjusting. He was only three and the inconsistency of going from snowsuits on a city street to shorts and flip-flops in a desert, where we couldn't understand the language spoken around us, seemed to hit him harder than it did the rest of us.

Somehow when we were in Mexico, Charlie also came to the realization that everyone has to die. Maybe it was because we lived near the slaughterhouse, or maybe it was something he dreamed about or saw on TV. Whatever it was, most kids learn about the concept of death slowly by losing a pet or a grandparent and gradually accepting their own mortality. For Charlie it all came in a single, terrifying rush and it happened that winter in San Carlos.

Almost every morning my father would wake up early and go upstairs to the kitchen to make pancakes for everyone's breakfast while we slept. And almost every morning, as my father remembers it, Charlie would walk upstairs into the kitchen, clutching his blanket and screaming, "What day is it?"

"It's Tuesday," my father would say.

"What time is it?"

"It's eight o'clock."

"Where are we?" Charlie hadn't learned the days of the week yet and didn't know how to read a clock, but he demanded to know these details as if they were his only source of safety and security in the world, the only buffer between him and annihilation.

Being the children of a successful actor would mean that this type of disorientation and dislocation would become so common that we'd eventually come to accept it as normal. Mexico was only the first of many temporary moves we'd make over the next seven years, the first episode of what I'd later come to think of as the gypsy traveling circus of my childhood. We'd come to town, set up the tent, put on the show, and then pack it all up and go home until the next time. Between *Catch-22* in Mexico in 1969 and *Apocalypse Now* in the Philippines in 1976, our family would go on location together no less than seven times to different places around the world. Film roles are often offered on short notice and it became our norm to quickly load up the car or board a plane and stay on location for weeks or even months at a time. I learned how to quickly adapt to new languages, new schools, and to navigate everything from a tractor in eastern Colorado to the subway system in Rome to martial law in Manila. Up until our time in the Philippines, when it became critical for the kids in the family to have a say in where we were going and what we'd be exposed to, we never questioned the moves, even if it meant picking up and leaving in the middle of a school year. We were a family, and families stuck together. It was a given that, when Dad traveled for work, we all went, too.

When *Catch-22* finished filming in Mexico,

we packed up the duplex in San Carlos and boarded a train to Hermosillo, Mexico. From there we took another train to Nogales, where we walked across the border checkpoint. My almost seven years in New York and another four months in Mexico had been reduced to the single suitcase I dragged out of Mexico and into the United States. Among the six of us, we carried everything we now owned.

Just on the other side of customs, in Nogales, Arizona, my father rented a car to drive us all the way to Los Angeles. This would have been a good plan if he had actually known how to drive on an interstate. All of his driving hours to that point had been logged in small towns where turn signals were optional and fast lanes nonexistent. The 550 miles from Nogales to Los Angeles in June of 1969 have etched themselves into family memory as one of the most uncomfortable, disastrous family road trips we ever made. My father didn't know what high beams were or how to pass another car so we plodded along in the right lane the whole way. We weren't allowed to turn on the air-conditioning because he was afraid it would make the car overheat or explode. Exit? Merge? Not a chance. What should have been an eight-and-a-half-hour trip through western Arizona and southeastern California took more like twelve. With four kids crammed in the backseat it felt more like twenty.

"Dad, we need a bathroom."

"Don't talk to me. I have to focus on the road!"

"Martin, the kids are hungry."

"Don't talk to me. I have to focus on the road!"

We must have driven straight through the night. I don't remember stopping at a motel. As the traffic thickened and the buildings of downtown Los Angeles appeared in the distance against the backdrop of the purple San Gabriel Mountains it was already midmorning. Charlie, Ramon, Renée, and I lay sprawled across the backseat and floor — this was still years before seat belt laws — while my mother spread the map of L.A. across the dashboard and directed my father to the Vermont Avenue exit. He gripped the steering wheel tightly, braved the turn signal, and glided us off the freeway.

After the vast expanses of the Mexico and Arizona deserts, the cinderblocks and concrete of Los Angeles were disconcerting. I'd been out of New York for only four months, but it hadn't taken long for me to get accustomed to Sonora's panoramic mountain vistas and fine white sand. There were beaches in California too, I knew, but when I looked out the window all I saw were stretches of asphalt, cars, used car lots, and liquor stores. I felt sudden pangs of nostalgia for Riverside Park and San Carlos Bay.

My father pointed the rental car north on Vermont Avenue. A motel room was waiting for us ten miles up the freeway but Dad had a more immediate goal.

First stop: 3400 Wilshire Boulevard.

Destination: the Ambassador Hotel.

It says something important about my father that, when he relocated his family to Los Angeles, the first place he took us was not the Pacific Ocean or the Hollywood sign or any number of tourist or natural attractions that draw visitors every day. Instead he took us to the place where Robert Kennedy had been shot so we could bear witness together. As we walked into the lobby of the five-hundred-room hotel and saw the square gilded columns and the shallow alabaster fountain, my mother held Renée and my father grasped Charlie's hand. Ramon and I trailed along behind.

Outside, we'd seen the entrance to the Cocoanut Grove nightclub, where Judy Garland, Frank Sinatra, and Barbra Streisand had all performed. Two years before our visit, the hotel lobby had been used in *The Graduate* as the site of the rendezvous between Benjamin Braddock and Mrs. Robinson, played by Dustin Hoffman and Anne Bancroft. For a hotel built in 1921 on the site of a former dairy farm, the place packed some serious history. The ornate architecture and the way the thick brown-and-pink carpet muted conversation told me we were someplace solemn and it would be in my best interest to behave. Fresh from four months in rural Mexico we must have looked like quintessential hippies to the out-of-town guests and tourists hoping for a fading glimpse of Hollywood splendor. They sure didn't find it in us.

My father led us to the Embassy Ballroom, where Bobby Kennedy had delivered his final victory speech. It was the largest indoor room I'd ever seen, bigger even than the gym at PS 166. Cavernous. The ceiling arched above us, with coffered panels that looked like rows of squares had been cut into the sky. On our right was the podium area where Kennedy had stood in front of five hundred supporters just after midnight on June 5, 1968, after winning the California primary. "We are a great country," he'd said that night, "an unselfish country, and a compassionate country, and I intend to make that my basis for running."

Behind the podium was the door to the pantry where Bobby was escorted after his speech, and where the fatal shots were fired. I remembered waking up that morning in Ohio and turning on the television in my grandmother's living room. I'd known to run upstairs to wake my father because the newscasters were saying something he'd want to hear, even though I didn't understand the full meaning of the message. In the ballroom that day, I didn't understand all the implications, either, but I could sense that coming to this place was an important pilgrimage for my father. I stood quietly by his side.

He looked at the empty wall with what seemed like a blend of sadness and reverence.

"Kids," he said. "A great man, Bobby Kennedy, once spoke here."

He *had* been a great man. I was beginning to understand that was a noble goal, and not an easy one to achieve. We stood there together for a few more seconds, thinking about it all.

And that's how our life as a family in California began.

■ ■ ■ ■

Pico Boulevard is a busy main thoroughfare slicing right through West L.A. When you turn off Pico onto Castello Avenue, you enter a sudden, quiet lull. Low cement-and-stone houses, empty sidewalks, sumac trees that drop red berries every fall lining both sides of the street — this was where my mother found us a furnished house to rent just one block from where the Museum of Tolerance now stands. The house had a small front yard and a grassy spot in back where we could play. With rosebushes, manicured lawns, and the sweet scent of night-blooming jasmine before we went to bed, it was a small suburban pocket in the middle of a city. All we needed to add were two sets of bunk beds that my father set up in the second bedroom. Ramon and I, as the oldest and most agile, immediately claimed the top beds.

I finished the first grade at Canfield Elementary School less than a mile from our house, and then it was summer and we had months to spare. The *Catch-22* set was moving to Rome for a few weeks to film the characters' R&R break on the mainland. My father was needed for just a few scenes, mainly one at an outdoor café on the Piazza Navona with Alan Arkin and Art Garfunkel. He wouldn't need to spend much time on the set, but Nichols wanted him in Rome the whole time. My mother didn't want to uproot the family again for such a short shoot, so my father decided to take just Ramon and me to Rome. Through an American actor who lived there, he arranged a short-term furnished apartment for us in the Gianicolo neighborhood and a house-keeper who'd watch Ramon and me during the days. There would be one week when my father wouldn't be needed on the set at all, and he decided he would take us on a side trip to his father's village in Spain to visit the family we'd never met.

My father had a Kodak Brownie camera, and on that trip he took more than two hundred snapshots, more photos in those three weeks than I think he's taken in the forty years since. For some reason he got the idea of running ahead of us and then spinning around and catching Ramon and me in motion as we raced toward him. My sister Renée has been working alongside my mother organizing all our family photos, and, when I look at the ones they've archived from Rome in 1969, I see black-and-white shot after shot of two little boys running through the streets of Rome in their jeans and striped shirts, chasing each other up flights of marble stairs, sitting on a concrete wall eating ice cream on a stick from Café Gelate nearby.

The apartment we rented was large and stuffy. The furniture had gold tassels hanging from the upholstery, floor-to-ceiling curtains, and floor-length tablecloths on all the tables. Every evening you could trace your name onto any exposed wooden surfaces in just that day's dust.

My memories of visiting the sights that summer are sketchy. Goofing around at the Fontana di Trevi. Standing at the foot of Michelangelo's *Pietà* in the Basilica of St. Peter at the Vatican and staring up at the body of Jesus lying sprawled across his mother's lap. And then the flight to Spain and the long, long train ride from Madrid to the Galician city of Tui, the nearest railroad stop to Parderrubias and the Estevez family home.

We had left Madrid midmorning for the nine-hour trip. At lunchtime my father brought us into the dining car, which looked like an elegant restaurant in New York: white tablecloths, cloth napkins, china plates. A big, heavyset Spaniard with dark hair and a beard sat down alone at the table across from ours. He picked up his napkin, shook it out, and tucked it into his collar. When his food arrived he ate carefully and slowly, relishing each bite. He held the stem of his wineglass between his thumb and forefinger and swirled its contents before drinking. I couldn't take my eyes off of him. In northern Spain it wasn't, and still isn't, uncommon to sit down at the table at 2:00 p.m. and not get up until 5:00, but I'd never seen evidence of this kind of luxuriousness at the table before. Until that point, food had never been more than basic, practical nourishment to me, something you had to put in your body three times a day to keep from being hungry. To watch the Spaniard treat his meal as if it were a celebration was completely new to me and stirred something deep inside. One day I'd be growing my own food and sitting down to a meal from my own garden with the same reverence I observed in the Spaniard.

We arrived at my grandfather's village late at night in a light rain. Galicia is famous for its constant drizzle: Parderrubias gets an average of more than 60 inches of precipitation and upward of one hundred rainy days each year. Through the taxi window, all I could see was darkness — there were no streetlights — and the rain dripping against the glass. When I tilted my face up, I saw a perfect, glowing full moon.

The taxi dropped us off in front of a high wall made of tall granite slabs that were connected by thick vertical stripes of cement. This was where our relatives lived? This was where my grandfather came from? It looked more like the ruins we'd seen in Rome.

My father banged on a wooden gate. He waited for a minute or two with his hands shoved in his pockets and then pounded on the gate again. We stood in the rain and hoped someone heard us. Where would we go for the night if no one was home? No one was expecting us because they hadn't known we were coming. Without telephone or electricity, there would have been no easy way to alert them.

It was difficult to imagine my grandfather Francisco, who lived in a regular house in Dayton, ever living in a place like this. When we visited him in Dayton he rushed around in his modern kitchen and liked to spend evenings in front of the TV. Still, I thought of him as mostly strict, serious, and humorless. His accent was so thick I could barely understand a word he said. He regarded us with curiosity and sometimes with a puzzled confusion. My parents were raising Ramon,

Charlie, Renée, and me in a very progressive atmosphere, where sexuality was considered normal and body parts were not taboo. "It's just a body part," my mother would say. "Stop being so silly about it!" When I was about four and just becoming aware of what made a boy a boy and a girl a girl, we went to visit my grandfather in Dayton. One afternoon I was sitting on his lap in his house and was suddenly overcome by a great need to know if men as old as he was had parts similar to mine.

"Grandpa, do you have a penis?" I asked him matter-of-factly.

He stared at me with a funny expression on his face but didn't say anything in response. So I asked again.

"Grandpa, do you have a penis?"

"No, Emilio," he finally said. "I donna to have inny peanuts."

That night in Spain, his brother Matias answered the gate and greeted us exuberantly when he realized who we were. Matias lived in the family compound with his wife Juaquina and his brother Lorenzo, three old folks who could still have been living in the nineteenth century by American standards. Juaquina cooked over an open fire and carried buckets of water into the house from a well in the courtyard. Out in the pasture the family had a single cow for milk and cheese. Whatever Spanish I'd picked up in Mexico was useless here, where everyone spoke Galician. We got by with nodding and pointing and smiling.

It was summer, but *cold.* I knew cold from winters in New York and the *Roses* tour stop in Chicago, but I'd never known true bone-chilling cold until I spent a night in a cottage with stone walls and stone floors in the mountains of Galicia. We could see our breath inside the house. At night my father, brother, and I slept in our clothes in the bed where my grandfather had been born, curled up together like kittens against the chill.

The family's land was a child's paradise. Ramon and I were allowed to run freely through the garden and the pasture. We chased the chickens that ran through the courtyard and poked at the cow when she was brought back at the end of the day. I was fascinated by the garden and all the vegetables that were bursting through the soil. I'd never given much thought to where vegetables came from before. In New York you got them from the supermarket, and in Mexico you found them in large mounds on tables at the weekly farmer's market. June in Galicia meant nearly everything was ready to harvest. My father had also brought a little Super 8 movie camera along on the trip, and he filmed my aunt Juaquina and uncle Matias digging potatoes out of the ground. Potatoes, beans, tomatoes, onions — between the vegetables they grew, the chickens they raised for slaughter, and the cow that produced milk for drinking and for cheese, the family was nearly self-sufficient on just two acres of land.

They also cultivated a small vineyard to make their own wine. Of the many photos my father took that week is one of me standing in the family vineyard, wearing a pair of muddy Converse gym shoes, jeans worn and faded at the knees, and a long-sleeved, striped polo shirt. At seven I was still very blond and I was standing almost in profile, midstep, casting a sideways glance in my father's direction as if I were looking for permission to step into the vineyard. Behind me, neat rows of grapevines planted by the family extend to the edges of the photograph, and beyond.

My partner Sonja and I use that photo now on the home page of our own vineyard's website, CasaDumetzWines.com and on the labels of our new vintages of 2010 Syrah and Grenache. I like knowing that, even at age seven, among all the options on the family farm in Spain, at that moment the vineyard was where I chose to be. But what always strikes me most about that photo is how tall the grapevines are behind me. Or rather, how little I am in comparison. I remember the woodsy, smoky smells of wet earth and open fires when that photo was taken, and the slight, damp chill in the air, and the way my father shouted, "Emilio! Over here!" as he positioned the Brownie camera in front of his face. I remember all of that. I just don't remember ever being that small in the world.

CHAPTER FOUR: MARTIN

At the railroad station in Tui, the taxi driver who picked us up looked at the piece of paper with the address my father had given me and then stared me in the eye. I'd hoped it would be self-explanatory, because my Spanish wasn't going to get us very far and my Galician was nonexistent.

Fortunately, the cab driver knew some English.

"Estevez?" he said, looking again from the paper to me. "Is Paco?"

Paco is a common nickname for Francisco in Latin culture and was my father's boyhood name. Was the driver confusing me with my father?

"I'm the son of Paco," I said. "From America."

"Ah, Paco!" His rugged face broke into a friendly grin. "Your father, I know him when I was a boy."

As he pulled out of the train station and

headed up into the mountains, the driver told us he had also grown up in Parderrubias, which is one of seven parishes in the municipality of Salceda de Caselas, in the province of Pontevedra. Each of those names means something specific to the residents of each area. It's like saying I live in the city of Malibu, which is part of metro Los Angeles, which is in Los Angeles County. About 8,000 people live in Salceda today, where the parishes have expanded until they all run into one another, but when we visited in 1969 they were still isolated villages that had been clinging to mountainsides for centuries. Parderrubias and my father's family's house were out in the wilderness and the roads were rough and few. You couldn't even rightly call them roads. They were more like wide paths that frequently washed out in the rain. You really had to know your way around to find my family's place. It was a remarkable stroke of luck to find a driver who not only remembered my father from fifty years ago but also knew exactly how to find the family's home.

After a half hour's drive on pitch-dark back roads, the cab pulled up in front of a tall stone fence with a plain, locked wooden door. "Here," the driver said. The boys and I walked up to the gate. It was close to

10:00 p.m. The comforting smell of wood smoke filled the air and a bright full moon made the granite slabs glow a ghostly gray. This area of Galicia was known for its wine and stone. A rock quarry in nearby Budiño supplied the village with granite blocks to build houses and fences, and to support the grapevines in the vineyards.

I banged hard on the gate.

No answer.

I banged again.

My father had sent a letter in advance of our trip telling the relatives we might come in the next month or two, but there was no telling when or if it had arrived. If the roads were any indicator of the postal service's speed, the letter was probably still halfway back to Madrid. And now it was getting close to midnight and the boys needed a place to sleep.

I pounded on the door again.

"*¡Ola! ¿Quen é?*" A muffled voice came from the other side.

"Hello! It's Ramon!" I shouted back. I wasn't sure if he could hear or understand me. "The son of Francisco! I'm here with my boys for a visit!"

Then came the sound of a heavy lock scraping against wood and the door swung open.

My uncle Matias, my father's younger brother, stood before us in the moonlight. I recognized him right away from the photos my father had shown me as a boy. *Oh, my God,* I thought. I'd never met a member of my father's family before and Tio Matias looked so much like my father it was startling: small, thin, with a gently rounded face just like my father's, and bald on top like him, too. Except Matias's head seemed to be two-toned, shiny and white on top and brown from the forehead down. He blinked hard at us. From his nightclothes and his expression, I could tell we'd woken him up.

"*¿Quen . . . ?*" he said, as he looked from me to the boys. A slow recognition crept over his face. "*¿Do meu irmán . . . Paco . . . ?*"

I showed him the letter of introduction my father had written but Matias didn't need it. He'd seen photos of me, too. He just hadn't expected me to show up on his doorstep near midnight on a random June night in the rain with two small boys hanging from my legs.

"*¡Ay yi!*" he shouted as he motioned us through the gate and hugged me. He let loose with a stream of Galician I couldn't understand, but it didn't matter. His joy upon meeting us was palpable and didn't need words to express.

In 1969, Spain had been in the authoritarian grip of General Francisco Franco — also a Galician — for thirty-three years. As I would later learn, the uncle standing before me in his nightclothes was a liberal who'd taken part in an uprising against Franco in a heavily conservative region of Spain. He paid dearly for his heroic actions with a year of imprisonment in a concentration camp on an island off the coast and then three more years in Franco's mountaintop jail outside of Pamplona.

Matias led us across a dirt courtyard and into the family's stone house, where his wife Juaquina came into the kitchen to check on the commotion. Well fed, with ruddy cheeks and a long graying braid, she fussed over the children and insisted on making us a meal. While we sat in the kitchen she went into the courtyard, chased a chicken around, brought it back to the kitchen, and broke its neck in front of us. Then she plucked it, threw it into some boiling water, and cooked it. All this while she kept chattering at us and saying who knew what in Galician. The boys stared at her, astonished. That was surely something we hadn't seen in New York, or even in Mexico, for that matter.

Juaquina's stove was a large stone about

the width of a single bed and six feet long, with an open fire and a chimney that led up and out of the house. She cooked with a tripod, putting the pot on top and constantly feeding little sticks into the fire beneath it to keep it burning. Her ruddy cheeks came from spending so much time each day leaning over an open fire. Electricity had come to Parderrubias only a few months earlier and the house's single, naked lightbulb hung from the center of the kitchen ceiling. The walls of the kitchen were black from decades of accumulated soot from the cooking fire. A running joke in that region of Galicia was that, once electricity arrived, everyone saw how badly their houses needed indoor paint jobs.

Juaquina talked over her shoulder to everyone as she cooked, as effortlessly as if she were working on a modern range. I loved listening to her voice and I adored her from the moment we met. I could tell right away that she had a strong, generous character.

Within an hour after our arrival, we were eating the chicken and some vegetables from the family's garden. I tried to explain about filming in Rome, to send regards from my father and brothers, to explain that my wife and two other children were back in

California, but we were limited to smiles and nods, gestures, and the few words of Spanish the boys and I had picked up in Mexico.

Past midnight, Juaquina led us by candlelight down a corridor to a bedroom where the bed, if I understood her correctly, was the one in which my father was born. It was so cold that night the boys and I slept in our clothing, huddled together for warmth. It was an extraordinary feeling, to know that I was lying with my two boys in the bed where my father had come into the world, as if three generations of us were sharing the space together.

In the morning, I woke before the boys and looked around the room. I hadn't been able to see much of it at night. Sunlight shone in through the windows and cast bright squares on the stone walls and floor. And then, directly across from the bed, I saw the poster from *The Subject Was Roses* hanging on the wall. I'd given it to my father when he'd visited us in New York in 1964. The image of Jack Albertson, Irene Dailey, and me smiling out from the bedroom wall in Parderrubias hit me right between the eyes. I'd forgotten that my father had taken it with him when he'd sailed to Spain, thinking he was going home to stay. I thought back to the night he'd paced back and forth across our living room floor, and the way he'd looked at me as if he were seeing me for the first time.

In this bedroom in Galicia, an entire ocean away from Eighty-Sixth Street, this poster would have been the first thing my father saw every morning when he woke. He had never mentioned hanging it here but I understood what its presence meant. It was his way of showing he was proud of me, even if he couldn't bring himself to say it out loud.

The neighborhood where I grew up in Dayton had been populated mostly by Italian, Polish, and Irish immigrants, and as a result I always had felt most connected to the Irish side of my heritage. Spain had existed only in photos and intermittent stories, as vague to me as a twenty-nine-year-old father as it had been when I was a twelve-year-old boy. But that morning on the Estevez family's farm, my Spanish heritage suddenly came alive in vivid, four-color, living detail. Chickens squawked across the dirt courtyard. A mild-mannered cow chewed its cud and slowly ambled along as Juaquina untethered it from a post and led it out to pasture. The ripe scents of wet earth and fresh wood smoke hung in the air. The homestead was simple and rustic, constructed from stone blocks and wood.

My childhood daydreams of Spain had involved kings and castles and galleons, explorer's maps and royal decrees, not suppers cooked on open fires and chickens pecking at my shoes. My father had tried to tell me what to expect before I arrived. "Donna to expect the conveniences," he'd said. "There issa no toaster. No TV. You'll do the walking to go places and the rain, itta rains a lot. But you will enjoy. Therra good people. And you'll-a be well fed." He was right, but his descriptions couldn't come close to standing in the middle of the genuine article. The village was much more basic and rural than I could possibly have imagined, almost like traveling back in time a hundred years. I felt as if I'd stepped into a scene from *Fiddler on the Roof,* minus all the daughters and the tsar. I could see why my father had loved his home so much but also why, after forty-eight years in America, it had been impossible for him to return for good.

I breathed in deeply. My lungs loved the sweet, fresh air. The air in this part of Galicia was so clean, free of the pollution and diesel exhaust that permeated the big European cities at the time. All the smells in Parderrubias — cooking smoke, animal droppings, vegetation wet from recent rain — were created because they were necessary for daily existence. And it was so *quiet* here compared to anyplace I'd ever lived. There were no cars on the road, no motorcycles revving by, no noise from automatic anything. Occasionally a bird would call out or the cow would moo, and the chickens were constantly complaining about something, but these were all natural noises that blended seamlessly into the background of a rural existence. I could have spent the better part of that morning standing in that courtyard breathing that clean air into my lungs, exhaling, and doing it all over again.

"Good morning!" Matias said, joining me in the courtyard. He clutched a mug of strong coffee against his chest. A black beret fit snugly on top of his head and I realized why his skin had looked two-tone the night before. The beret lined up perfectly with his tan line. He must have worn it all day, every day, out in the fields.

When I started going to Central America in the 1980s I was reminded of Galicia in the 1960s. Parderrubias in 1969 was third world for all intents and purposes. Our family there were, for the most part, subsistence farmers who lived off their own patch of land. This wasn't unusual for the place or time. The whole community was similarly struggling along.

To them, the boys and I looked like creatures of plenty. Back in America, we were still living hand-to-mouth financially, but nonetheless we had modern appliances in our rental house, running water in our bathrooms, and electrical outlets in every room. I sensed a slight discomfort from the relatives as they showed us our sleeping quarters and fed us meals, as if they were embarrassed by their poverty and ashamed they couldn't offer us better.

"I'm sorry," Juaquina said as she served us breakfast.

"It isn't much," Matias apologized as we walked through the garden.

I suspect this was especially pronounced because my father had sent them photos and magazine articles about me, which made me a celebrity of sorts in their eyes. Even though I hardly thought of myself this way, I was moved by their humility and by their pure generosity and integrity. Compared to many families I knew in the States, my relatives in Spain were the fortunate ones. They had family, community, tradition, a sense of humor, graciousness, hospitality, humanity, joyfulness, and a natural spirituality. They were the rich ones, not us.

"I'm sorry," Juaquina said again when she served us a delicious lunch of rice and chicken.

"Are you kidding? I'm delighted to be here," I said. I hoped they could understand my passion if not my words. I wanted them to know that I would sleep anywhere, and eat anything, without complaint, just for the simple joy of being in their presence.

That first day in Parderrubias we also met Tio Lorenzo, another of my father's brothers who lived there with Matias and Juaquina. Like the family I grew up in, my father's had been a gang of brothers with a single sister — Maximillian, Alfonso, Francisco, Matias, Lorenzo, and Dolores. Lorenzo had also left Spain for the New World, settling in Argentina, where he worked as an embassy cook before returning home after his retirement. A lifelong bachelor, Lorenzo still dressed like a South American gentleman even in a rural setting, in shirtsleeves and a sweater vest. Like all the men I saw that day, Lorenzo also wore a black beret and carried an umbrella wherever he went. Everyone was always expecting rain.

Shoe leather was the main mode of transportation in Parderrubias. I don't think I even saw a bicycle while we were there. To go on an outing that afternoon — I wanted to get a gift for the family to show my gratitude — I needed to get a ride from my cousin Camilo, who had access to a car. My cousin took us back to Tui, the small city where we'd gotten off the train. Tui sits on a gentle hill along the River Miño, just on the Spanish side of the border with Portugal. On the other side of the river is the Portuguese city of Valença, connected to Tui by an international bridge whose construction was overseen by Gustave Eiffel of Eiffel Tower fame.

My cousin led us through the narrow stone streets of the medieval old city and up to the very top of the hill to see Tui's source of architectural pride, its castle cathedral. The presence of a cathedral, rather than a basilica, gave Tui its "city" status. Like most of the ancient towns in Spain, or anywhere really, the tallest structure was always the church. Nobody dared build anything taller than a monument to God. In our modern-day cities, the tallest buildings are the skyscrapers owned by banks and insurance companies, the false deities of our era. It's a pleasure to step back in time in a town like Tui, where the narrow cobblestone streets and squat medieval buildings retain a simple, practical charm.

Tui's cathedral was consecrated in 1225 during the reign of King Alfonso IX and took more than a century to build. The carvings inside the portico — which were the first example of Gothic art in Spain — were magnificent. Representations of Saint John the Baptist, Saint Peter, Isaiah, and Moses were perched on pedestals, and above them were elaborately carved representations of the adoration of the Magi and the birth of Christ. Inside the courtyard, the vaulted cloisters were a testament to precise proportion. A small adjoining chapel built in the sixteenth century housed the relics of Peter Gonzalez, also known as San Telmo or St. Elmo, the patron saint of Spanish and Portuguese sailors and fisherman and also patron of Tui.

The boys ran joyously through the cloisters and I marveled at all the man hours and manpower that went into creating such a monument to faith. Only a week ago, I might have been in awe of the grandeur and beauty, but, after meeting my Spanish relatives, I now also thought about the construction itself. A hundred years of labor. Had any of my ancestors cut the stone or lifted the blocks to build the cathedral? Carved the reliefs in the portico? Had they considered it their duty to God or to their king? It was impossible to know, but I still felt a sense of pride in being descended — not from royalty, as I'd fantasized as a child — but from the good, honest, hardworking folks of the region. Were they not royalty in their own way? They were my people, and I was theirs.

Earlier that morning I'd noticed Matias and Juaquina owned a single, treasured radio that was battered and old. In the newer section of Tui, I found a modern model for them with enough batteries to last for a few months. This way if the electricity went off, as it often did in Parderrubias, my aunt and uncles could still listen to the radio. At the cash register, I waited while my cousin bought a lottery ticket. The state lottery was a big event in this region, a source of both hope and entertainment, which was why the radio was so important to the family. It was how everyone learned about the winning lottery numbers. I added a handful of lottery tickets to my purchase and gave them to Juaquina as a special gift. Maybe I'd bring her some luck.

■ ■ ■ ■

After the dusty apartment in Rome and the crowded train up from Madrid, the boys were thrilled to have open space to play in and ran through the wet grass all afternoon. The small farm was a perfect place to let boys be boys, where nature was both accommodating and forgiving. Juaquina and Matias's daughter was already grown and they seemed pleased to have the voices and energy of young children back on their land.

In the village, Juaquina was regarded with a combination of respect and scorn. She was the local matchmaker, the *bruja,* the seer. In Galicia, the local term for witch is *meiga,* and that's what she was known as. Galicians have an ambivalent relationship with their witches, who have been part of the fabric of their culture for centuries. A popular local saying is *"Eu non creo nas meigas, pero habelas hainas,"* which roughly translates to "I don't believe in witches, but they exist." That pretty much captures the contradiction. I never saw evidence of Juaquina's mystical powers during our short time there unless you include getting the boys to eat food they'd never tried before. Juaquina appeared to be a hardworking, loving, strong-willed farmer's wife who enjoyed cooking and feeding guests. My father had been right. We did eat well.

Every day, for breakfast and dinner, I helped Juaquina spread the red-checkered tablecloth across the top of the wooden table. Then we positioned bottles of wine and *orujo* on top. *"Orujo"* roughly translates to "remains of the grapes" and is a popular strong liqueur Galicians have been making since the 1600s. Every family has its own secret recipe. The *orujo* maker takes the residue left over from winemaking — the stems, skins, and seeds — and ferments it all in a vat, then distills it in a copper pot heated over an open fire. The result is a clear liquid that makes you gasp for breath. The first swig I took of Matias's *orujo* made my eyes sting. It was nearly 50 proof alcohol but the relatives seemed immune to its effects.

Food staples at the farm were rice, chicken, vegetables, eggs, fruit, and meat. Flour, sugar, and coffee had to be purchased in town and were literally kept under lock and key. Before every meal Juaquina reached into her apron pocket, took out a large, antique key, and unlocked a high cabinet in the kitchen where she kept the family's most precious possessions. In our honor, she would take down the good silverware and china plates. Then she took the sugar and flour from the same cabinet. I tried to understand what this meant. My aunt and uncles never seemed to lock their doors and didn't exhibit any distrust. They were very gracious to one another and seemed to share everything. Yet they locked up their flour and sugar? Maybe there was a baking thief in the neighborhood. Truly, I didn't know.

Before we sat down for dinner one evening I asked the relatives to pose for a photo. The three of them lined up in front of the table, each one holding a different piece of tableware: a china plate, a coffeepot, a silver serving spoon. As I lifted the Brownie camera to my eye they displayed their articles of finery and aimed broad smiles at the camera. They were posing with the family treasures, perhaps to impress the relatives in America they still had yet to meet. They didn't understand that possessions didn't matter a bit to Janet or me. She would have been as thrilled as I was just to be in their presence.

On our last day in Parderrubias, Matias walked us over to the nearby cemetery so I could pay respect to the ancestors. Most of the names were familiar to me. As I walked through the rows of aging gravestones, I could see how synonymous our family had been with the community, and for how long. There was the grave of Manuel Estevez, my father's father, my grandfather. Next to him, Dolores Martinez, my father's mother, my grandmother. I sank down to my knees in the wet dirt in front of my grandmother's grave, suddenly overwhelmed by emotion. This was the woman who had birthed the son who had given life to me, so that I could give it to my four children, whom I loved more than I had ever thought possible. If not for my grandmother Dolores and my grandfather Manuel, put to rest in this earth beneath me, my children and I would not exist.

Everywhere I looked in the cemetery, there was an Estevez. A Martinez. Estevez. Estevez. Martinez. Estevez. At Calvary Cemetery in Dayton only two graves bore the name Estevez: one for my mother and one for my brother Manuel. My father's generation had dispersed from Parderrubias to the New World, settling in South America, Cuba, and the United States. Some of them had returned to the ancestral homeland, but others had stayed overseas. And the next generation, my siblings and cousins and I, were scattered across America and the rest of the globe.

I looked over at Emilio and Ramon, running through the wet grass between the graves. Like my father and his brothers, we had embarked on a westward voyage together and California was where we would stay for good. Like true homesteaders we would embrace the culture and traditions of our new home. Janet would start cooking macrobiotic. I would buy a used Ford station wagon and learn how to merge. A year later we would move up the coast to Malibu, an unincorporated beachfront community of twelve thousand people stretching one mile wide and twenty-seven miles long. In 1973 we bought our first house there, which became our family homestead. Thirty-nine years later, we still call it home.

CHAPTER FIVE:
EMILIO
1970–1972

If you travel west on the Pacific Coast Highway all the way up to Point Dume, you'll pass the Pacific View Nursery on your right. At the end of its long driveway lined with one- and five-gallon containers with succulents for sale, you'll see a white farmhouse. In the 1970s, that farmhouse was red, and it was the first place our family landed in Malibu after leaving the house on Castello Avenue in West L.A.

After a year of city living, my parents wanted to move us into a more natural setting, mostly for better air quality. Cars were running on leaded gasoline in 1970, and Los Angeles, land of the car, had serious air pollution. We considered moving to Topanga Canyon, a mountain enclave up the coast populated by musicians, artists, and hippies, where my parents' friends lived, or to Ojai, a town with a similar vibe up near Santa Barbara. Eventually we settled on

Malibu. The red farmhouse for rent on the Pacific Coast Highway became ours, unfurnished, for four hundred dollars a month.

The name "Malibu" automatically inspires images of surfers and celebrities and multimillion-dollar beachfront homes. It was also a surfer's paradise in 1970, but with much more of a rural, small-town feel than it has today. Horses. Hippies. Farmers. Lots of people growing pot in their backyards. The place was basically a mix of working- and middle-class locals who'd been there for decades; a handful of successful actors, directors, and studio heads; and new families like us looking for an alternative to city life. The summer we moved there, the for-sale section of the *Malibu Times* was advertising trail horses and tractors. Articles like "Rabid Skunks Again Found in Malibu Area" made front page news. President Nixon was in the White House and the war in Vietnam was going full-tilt boogie, but the news in Malibu in 1970 was more likely to be about the 4-H Club's Twelfth Annual Horse Show and Safety Fair and the number of fatal car accidents on the Pacific Coast Highway — where the maximum speed limit was an astonishing 75 miles per hour.

Our new house was bigger than anyplace

we'd lived before. And empty. All we owned were the two bunk beds, which my father set up again in a second bedroom, and our clothes and toys. Just as in Mexico, we were starting all over again. We stuck a picnic table in our dining room and shopped garage sales for everything else. My parents found a king-size bed and two dressers for a hundred dollars and a red vinyl couch for the living room. For a while that was pretty much all we had. The farmhouse came with a detached garage and my mother put all our toys and books in there to use it as a playroom when the weather was bad, which wasn't often. Most of the time, you would find the four of us kids outside on the ten-acre front yard.

Ten acres is an enormous amount of space for a kid who spent his first seven years in Manhattan apartments. The grassy fields surrounding the house were filled with mustard plants and wild oats that grew rampant and had to be cut back every spring. It wasn't the kind of yard where we would go out and play ball. It was the kind of yard where we could have dirt-clod fights or hunt for arrowheads and, between March and September, we had to watch out for rattlesnakes. Because we had so much outdoor space, we started inheriting animals from people who needed a place to park them. At one point we were hosting ducks, geese, two or three dogs, and a couple of cats. Almost overnight we'd gone from a very urban environment to country living, with all the eco-trimmings.

I loved it.

My mother was way ahead of her time in eating organic food. Her friend in Topanga, the actress Collin Wilcox Paxton — best known for her role as Mayella Violet Ewell in *To Kill a Mockingbird* — was cooking macrobiotic, and that year my mother followed Collin's lead and put us all on a macrobiotic diet. We ate mostly vegetables cut into matchsticks, brown rice, homemade bread, some fish — a very healthy diet, but limited. Our birthday cakes were apple-raisin pies with no sugar. Most people at the time rolled their eyes at the lengths my mother went to in order to make sure we all ate well, but I recognize it now as a gift she gave us even though we objected, frequently, to the meals. The defining smells of my childhood are fresh-baked bread, steamed brown rice, and nori, a dried seaweed product, which filled the kitchens of every house we lived in.

Hoping to grow her own produce, my mother planted a garden on our land, but the soil had too much clay and the veg-etables didn't get very far. My father would go out in the back yard and hoe up the dirt, hoping to help her along, but then he'd get a job and go off and leave the plot untended until it needed to be hoed again. I started my own small two-by-four-foot garden plot outside, just a little patch of soil with two stalks of corn and some carrots, watching them grow. I was fascinated by the sprouts that pushed through the earth and wiggled their way up and out into plants. I felt the desire within me to have a bigger, more complete connection with nature and, for a short time, imagined myself becoming a farmer like my Spanish uncles, but the yard and my friends were a bigger draw.

That fall I joined the ranks of 2,300 school kids in Malibu when my mother enrolled me, Ramon, and Charlie at Juan Cabrillo Elementary School. On September 25, a few weeks after school started, a three-day wildfire erupted, the largest Malibu had seen in years. My parents, Ramon, and I were down in Santa Monica when it started and Charlie and Renée were up in Malibu with our next-door neighbors, the Beatty family. We tried to get back to them but our car was turned away. It was a terrifying two days before the flames were put out, the roads reopened, and we could be reunited again.

My father was getting work here and there, but nothing steady yet. *Catch-22* had been released in June of 1970 to good reviews — Vincent Canby of the *New York Times* called it "quite simply, the best American film I've seen this year" — but much of the public attention for a war film had already been diverted to a March release about the Korean War called *M*A*S*H*. *Catch-22* was a critical but not a commercial success, and Hollywood has always liked numbers. Critics' darlings are good for dinner-party discussions, but if you want to keep working you have to bring in box-office receipts. After *Catch-22* my father did mostly guest spots on TV shows like *Hawaii Five-O* and *Ironside,* and he played a Civil War captain in the TV version of the play *The Andersonville Trial,* about the war crimes trial of Henry Wirz, commander of the Confederate POW camp in Andersonville, Georgia, directed by George C. Scott. His earnings were enough to keep the family going, but barely. Money was always tight.

One day my mom needed to go grocery shopping. She checked inside her purse. Nothing there.

"Can I have some dough?" she asked my father.

He looked at her blankly. "I thought *you* had the money," he said. That's how he said it: "the money." As if everything they had at any moment was stored either in his wallet or her purse. Probably it was. They didn't have a savings account. I don't think they even had a checking account. We survived on a purely cash economy, living week to week.

"I thought *you* had the money," my mother said.

They started searching through their pockets. They searched through drawers. They even looked behind the cushions on the red vinyl couch. All of their efforts produced a single dime. One dime! At least that old joke about not having a dime between them didn't apply. I imagine it was a very sobering moment for them both.

When the mail arrived later that day, my mother opened an envelope addressed to her and my father. It was from a friend in New York who'd borrowed money from them months ago. Inside the envelope was a thank-you card and the ten dollars returned in cash. That's what we used for groceries. At Malibu's Trancas Market in 1970, you could get a dozen eggs for thirty-nine cents and four cantaloupes for a dollar, so my mother managed to buy enough food to last us a few days until my father's next paycheck arrived. If I were to put this scene in a movie, viewers would say, "Bullshit. Not buying it!" but the truth really can be better than imagination. Sometimes the universe does step up and say, "Got you covered."

Third grade was also the year I started thinking of myself as a writer. I was an avid reader, especially of science fiction. I belonged to a sci-fi Book of the Month Club for kids and every month I'd sit by the mailbox and wait for the next package to arrive. One of my favorite television shows was *Rod Serling's Night Gallery,* his follow-up to *The Twilight Zone,* in which he told horror stories that were depicted in paintings on the wall behind him. *Night Gallery* was where you could stay up way past bedtime on a Wednesday night and see stories about a survivor of the *Titanic* getting rescued decades after the ship sank or about dead people whose shadows refused to die. The stories were spooky but not very elaborate, and they didn't seem that hard to invent.

So that winter I decided to write an episode for *Night Gallery.* My uncle Alfonso had told me a ghost story that I used as a basis for an episode. I wrote it out in pencil on notebook paper, really more of a summary than a script. I didn't have any idea yet how to write a screenplay and had only had glimpses of those my father brought home. Then I got an address for Rod Serling's office from somewhere and mailed it off.

A few weeks later, my notebook pages came back in the mail clipped to a form letter. *Thank you very much for the submission. We are unable to accept unsolicited manuscripts at this time.*

That kind of impersonal rejection didn't discourage me. Instead it made me determined to figure out what "unsolicited manuscript" meant and not make the same mistake again.

At 6:01 a.m. on a Wednesday morning, February 9, 1971, I woke to a freight train rumbling through my room.

"Ramon?" I called out in the dark. "Charlie! Renée!" My brothers and sister were still sound asleep. The wooden ladder on my bunk bed was banging hard against the frame. What the heck was going on? I lay in bed for a few seconds until my mind cleared and I realized it was an earthquake.

I steadied the ladder, climbed down, and ran to my parents' bedroom. By the time I got there the shaking had stopped.

"Mom! Dad! It's an earthquake!" I said, pushing against my mother's arm.

My mother rolled over. "It's probably just a truck driving by," she mumbled and went back to sleep.

I walked back to my room and climbed up into my bed. *A truck? Was that possible?* I wondered about this as I stared at the ceiling from the top bunk. Did minds play tricks on us to that magnitude? We'd done earthquake drills at school and they'd told us what to expect. Then again, they'd also told us to duck and cover under a table with our heads between our knees and our hands on the backs of our necks, and instead I'd bolted for my parents' room to make sure they were safe. I fell back into a fitful sleep, uncertain about what else might happen before daylight.

What I'd just experienced soon became known as the Sylmar earthquake of 1971, which registered 6.6 on the Richter scale. It claimed sixty-five lives and caused half a billion dollars in damage. In Malibu the impact was minimal — a strong rattling, nothing more. I was the only one in the house who'd woken up.

It's no surprise that my parents began to call me the family alarm system. After the morning of Bobby Kennedy's assassination, I had fallen into the family role of alerting everyone to danger, a role I took seriously, partly because, as the oldest child, I felt responsible for the others, but also partly because it's in my nature to be cautious. That probably comes from my mother, whose nature is to be careful, too, but she also had to take that position in order to keep the family balanced. My father has always been more of a happy-go-lucky character, the kind of person who walks through fire safely, shaking peoples' hands along the way, while the city collapses behind him. He'll say, "No, no! I'm aware!" but the situations he willingly puts himself into can be mind-boggling to those of us who watch from the sidelines. My mother and I sometimes joke that it's our job to run along behind him with a broom and dustpan while he obliviously charges ahead. And yet he always manages to emerge safely from every episode. He leads a charmed existence that way.

Growing up, I positioned myself between my parents' two extremes and kept a watchful eye on everyone. At eighteen, I was the first person in the family to put an earthquake survival kit in my car. I also made sure one was accessible in the house and learned how to use a firearm to make sure I could get us out of any situation. Even at a young age, I was preoccupied with safety and survival. Sometimes it felt like a burden, but it was never something I was unwilling to do, to keep the family safe.

Nineteen seventy-one was a momentous news year by anyone's standard and a tumultuous one for me. Between January and December we saw Idi Amin go mental in Uganda; ongoing violence between Northern Ireland and Britain; a riot at Attica Prison in upstate New York that left 39 dead; and Charles Manson's conviction and death sentence for murder. On the other hand, Walt Disney World opened in Florida and *The Electric Company* debuted on PBS, making it more of an up year for kids.

Throughout all this, war was ongoing in Southeast Asia and any American with a television in the house could tell the situation there was still bad. U.S. forces were by now bombing Cambodia and Laos in addition to Vietnam. The war had been going on for as long as I could remember, and to me it had started to feel like a war without end. By 1971, 60 percent of all Americans opposed it and half considered it morally wrong, including my parents. My father wasn't as politically active then as he is now, but as a family we were definitely politically aware. My parents talked about Robert McNamara, secretary of defense, who was pushing the domino theory, the idea that, if Vietnam fell, all of Asia might follow. The idea that the conflict could spread to other countries and keep going on and on sounded ominous to me.

Watching television with my mother in our living room that August, we saw a man on the screen rotate a plastic drum and pull out a red capsule with a slip of paper inside it. Then he turned a different drum and pulled out a green capsule that held another piece of paper. He read the writing on them both out loud. It looked a little like Bingo but it wasn't any game. This was the televised draft lottery for men born in 1952, to determine their order of induction.

My mother bit her lip as we watched. President Nixon was already withdrawing troops by then, but boys were still being drafted. More than 94,000 would be inducted in 1971, down from about 163,000 in 1970.

"December fourth," the man on the television said. "One."

I was both fascinated and frightened by the lottery. In Malibu we lived in a protective bubble and war was far away. But my father's older brother, my uncle John, had been a navy medic in Vietnam in the 1960s, and his youngest brother, my uncle Joe, was going in and out of Vietnam on a naval supply ship, giving our family a firsthand connection to the war.

"May twelfth," the man on the television said.

My birthday. I whipped my head around and looked at my mother. She looked startled, too. He pulled out the second capsule. "Fifty-two," he said.

Fifty-two? Out of 366? That sounded awfully low.

It may not have been my birth year that was being drafted, but I felt a certain sense of ownership of my birth date. I knew that if I'd been born on the same day ten years earlier I'd be getting ready to pack my bags now. *This war looks like it's gotten out of hand,* I thought. *I could be next.*

"If this continues, we're going to move," my mother said. She wasn't going to take chances with any of her sons for a war she didn't support.

Four years later, Saigon fell to North Vietnam, marking the end of the war. I escaped the compulsory draft but the memories of the Vietnam War years would stick with me forever. The inner struggles between duty and conscience, between responsibility and free will, between meeting others' expectations and pursuing one's own path would become themes I'd soon struggle with on a personal level and would later choose to explore on screen.

By early 1972 we'd moved to another rental house in Malibu, this one on Point Dume, a small triangle of land that juts out into the Pacific Ocean. This house had floor-to-ceiling windows, white walls, and a pale yellow carpet. "Shoes off at the door," my mother would say. How she kept that place clean with four very active kids running around remains a mystery to me to this day.

We lived more minimally there than we ever had before, even in Mexico. This time it was deliberate. We left the bunk beds behind but Ramon, Charlie, Renée, and I still shared a room, sleeping four on the floor in sleeping bags like caterpillars. Making our beds in the morning was easy: just roll 'em up and stick 'em in the closet. Our living room furniture consisted of bean bag chairs we could sprawl across to watch TV. Our dining room table was low and Japanese style, made out of rattan, and we sat around it on pillows on the floor with our legs crossed. We were still eating macrobiotic, so the aesthetic fit.

We felt no embarrassment over what we did or didn't have, or any shame. We didn't have rich friends to compare ourselves to, or if we did we didn't know they were rich. Hardly anyone on Point Dume back then could have been considered wealthy. We were living in Malibu because it had good public schools and was still a relatively cheap place to raise a family. Our neighborhood had no streetlights. No sidewalks. No fences, no gates. Horses and dogs roamed across the yards. Today the most prevalent sounds on Point Dume are construction and leaf blowers, but in 1972 they were dogs barking and children playing.

Our family lived simply, ate simply, and dressed simply. The boys in my grade wore a new brand of jeans called Toughskins that you could buy at Sears. They had built-in kneepads to keep kids from wearing out the cloth, and for that reason mothers loved them. They were stiff and horrible to wear but they were *indestructible.* My mother would take all of us clothes shopping at Sears in Santa Monica a few times a year. Getting from west Malibu to Santa Monica today is an ordeal down the Pacific Coast Highway with more than a dozen traffic lights and perpetually slow traffic, but in 1972 you could drive all the way there in fifteen or twenty minutes and see *maybe* a half-dozen cars the whole way. Coming back at night you might not see any at all.

My father was getting more regular work by now, guest spots on TV series and also larger roles on made-for-TV movies. Although his career was starting to get traction, it wasn't yet up to the measure of success that some of his New York peers had started to achieve. And I think he probably felt like the big roles were passing him by. He was thirty-two and physically looked younger, but he wasn't getting the meaty roles he knew he was ready for and felt he deserved.

This was a time when my father must have needed his faith, but he couldn't find his way back to it yet. During this period I didn't think about God or religion at all, though my parents fought endlessly about religion in the 1970s. My father desperately wanted the four of us to be raised Catholic and to go to Catholic school and learn the rituals. My mother said, in so many words, "Over my dead body. Not going to happen." She'd been raised a Southern Baptist and never had freedom of choice as a child or the ability to question or express her true self. She wanted us to be able to discover religion on our own. Religion had caused my parents enough trouble already. My mother's mother thought she'd married the devil by marrying a Catholic and refused to go to their wedding, and my father's father had been horrified he *hadn't* married a Catholic. Frankly, I was relieved that I didn't have to choose. A religious upbringing would have given me a type of discipline, but I had my own inner discipline. Growing up, I didn't feel any lack.

The closest we ever came to prayer in our house was a song we sang together before dinner, influenced by my mother's friends in Topanga Canyon and used by Yogi Bhajan at the end of his yoga disciplines and classes. We would all hold hands around the table and sing:

May the longtime sun shine upon you,
All love surround you,
And the pure light within you guide your
   way on.
Peace.

That was our equivalent of grace before dinner every night, whether we were at home or in a restaurant. My father insisted on singing it, and loudly. Imagine being ten and doing this with your friends at the table, and nobody in the family eating meat. Not always so easy to explain.

There was no "amen" at the end of our prayer. Instead there was "peace." Nixon was pulling troops out of Vietnam but the world somehow seemed more godless and chaotic than ever. To my father, our dinner song was a compromise, serving as some measure of acceptable group prayer during troubled times.

That April he packed us all into his 1966 Ford Country Squire station wagon with the faux wood paneling for a ninety-minute drive to the town of Ojai to hear the Indian spiritual teacher J. Krishnamurti deliver a public talk. When I tell people that I heard Krishnamurti speak in person in 1972, they ask, "What did he say?" in a kind of breathless whisper. He's revered now and I suppose he was back then, too. But when you're almost ten years old and sitting in a hot auditorium listening to a boring old guy going on and on in a high-pitched monotone about the nature of disorder and the need for psychological revolution to save mankind, while your father sits next to you listening in rapt attention . . . well, it's not exactly an occasion for awe. At some point my father finally gave up and set us free outside. If you listen to that public talk on-line now you can hear the distant shouts of children in the background. One of them might have been me.

My dad was listening that day for some route to inner peace. About this time, he started doing yoga and meditating, too, but it wasn't enough. His frustration over work and himself escalated and led to resentment and sometimes rage, which, more and more frequently, he directed at us, leading to spankings. He never used a belt, but when we kids would fight a lot, or complain, he'd shout, "I'll knock your heads together if you don't stop!" and occasionally he followed through. It was very painful. Somehow this was considered permissible in the 1970s. We had neighbors whose father used to beat them with a shovel, awful child abuse by today's standards. In our house it was usually done by hand.

If my father had been able to connect with his Catholic faith in a meaningful way back then, would he have acted differently? Was being estranged from something that was vital to him part of his rage? If he'd had the outlet of his faith, would the family have been spared some of that madness? Ulti-mately Mass, Communion, confession — they're all forms of meditation and grace.

But if they are absent from your life, where do you turn?

My mother was open to the search herself and in those years was even more spiritually connected than my father. She was always looking for the answer to the great mystery, always striving to guide us toward pure and healthy states of body and mind. As a result, various gurus came in and out of our lives. My mother would plug into somebody and learn what she could from him — for instance, Bikram Choudhury, who was a huge presence in our house before he became a yoga franchise king. He is still revered with great affection in our family.

Even as a child, I was aware that my father was struggling spiritually, and it helped me feel compassion for him. I knew that was why he raged. I understood that. And even when I felt so angry at him and wanted to rage in response, I still wanted to earn his love and approval. I always found a way to forgive. Underneath it all, he loved the five of us with everything he had. I knew that. But he was hurting, and I hated that I had no way to make it better for him.

About that time, my father landed a role in a movie about a military gas leak that kills a rancher's sheep and also his son. It was based on the true story of an incident in Utah in 1968 where thousands of sheep were allegedly killed by the U.S. Army's chemical warfare tests. The movie was called *Rage.* The six-week shoot was taking place in Tucson, so once again we packed up, said good-bye to our classmates, and hit the road. *Rage* was the directorial debut of George C. Scott, a celebrated actor and my father's friend from our New York days. Scott also played the rancher, and my father played Major Holliford, a military doctor who lies to the rancher and keeps him sequestered while studying the effects of nerve gas on humans.

Tucson was hot and dry, with fine sand and cactus in every front yard. Instead of renting a house, we lived in a motel, and there wasn't much to do during the day, so my mother went down to the local elementary school and enrolled us for what she — but not they — knew would be only a few weeks. She had to lie about Renée's age to get her enrolled in kindergarten. I guess in 1972 when a mother walked into a school office and said, "My kids need to go to school," it wasn't hard to convince anyone to take them. Scenes like this would repeat themselves many times over the years as my father's career took off. I wouldn't spend a full school year in one place until the tenth grade.

On May 12, 1972, I turned ten. My father was out of town on a job and couldn't attend the birthday party my mother threw for me, but she gave me presents from both of them, and my grandmother in Ohio sent me a card with five dollars. My mother also gave me two letters she and my father had handwritten the day before on yellow legal paper. I read them on my birthday and saved them to this day.

May 11, 1972

Emilio,
Ten years ago tonight you wiggled into the world and into my heart. My first words to you were, "Look, isn't he beautiful!" We have grown together over these long and so short years. It seems like yesterday.

Many times you could have tried the patience of a rock but equally as many and even more you have given great joy.

We've both made mistakes and have shed tears at times but if I could change my life I would not — since you might not have been a part of it any other way.

You are still my treasure and great joy

206

and you will be all the days of your life.

Happy Birthday — *know* that you are loved and *be* happy.

Love,
Mom

May 11, 1972

My Dearest Emilio,

How very sorry I am not to be able to be with you today and celebrate the day, ten years ago today, that you came into our lives.

I just want to say, however, that I could not have wished for a more perfect son and dearest friend than yourself. I love you so much — Happy birthday little friend and welcome to the double figures.

Love & Peace
Dad

Birthday wishes almost always lean toward the positive and these were no different, but when I read these letters now I'm reminded of how honest my parents always were with me, especially my mother. The letters offer proof that, as young as I was, and as young as they still were, we all understood we were on a remarkable journey together.

That November my father starred with Hal Holbrook in a movie of the week called *That Certain Summer.* It was about a gay middle-aged divorced man living in San Francisco with his younger lover and the events that unfold when his fourteen-year-old son comes to visit for the summer and learns his father is gay. My father played the lover. A script about a well-adjusted gay couple living like married partners was so controversial for the time that NBC executives turned it down, but Barry Diller at ABC was willing to take a stand and green-light the project.

Watching the movie now is like time traveling back to the early 70s — long Beatles-style haircuts, ribbed turtleneck sweaters, tight jeans — but it was ground-breaking for the time, the first television movie to depict a gay male couple with sympathy and humanity. Until that point, homosexuality had been at best hinted at on television and at worst depicted as a psychological illness. Many gay viewers at the time described watching *That Certain Summer* as "life changing."

It was a risky role for my father to take, but I don't remember him laboring over the choice. He liked the script because, instead of preaching or advocating a lifestyle, it focused on the relationship between two individuals who cared deeply about each other. When a journalist later asked if he'd been afraid that the role would stigmatize his career, he answered, "I'd robbed banks and kidnapped children and raped women and murdered people, you know, in any number of shows. Now I was going to play a gay guy and that was like considered a career ender? Oh, for Christ's sake! What kind of culture do we live in?"

Touché.

Martin

The water level in the River Arga is higher today, and the current is moving fast. Yesterday, when we scouted this location, the river was a mellow stream, too mellow for our purposes. Emilio and David, our producer, went upriver to talk with the operator of a nearby dam and convinced him to release more water for the filming.

Today's sequence calls for Tom to accidentally knock his backpack off an ancient Roman bridge when he pauses to rest between Roncesvalles and Pamplona. The bag holds everything Tom needs for his journey but above all his son's ashes, so when he sees it fall into the river and get swept away he heads into the water to retrieve it. Yesterday's knee-deep water level wouldn't have conveyed the risk Tom is willing to take to get the bag back.

Still, I wasn't exactly bargaining for a whitewater situation today.

"Whoa," I say softly. "Whose idea was this?"

Emilio casts me a sideways glance. He doesn't have to answer. We both know who came knocking on his front door with this one.

"I have an idea!" I announced as I charged into Emilio's living room that day, caught up in my own excitement. "The bag falls in the river!"

"Okay," he said calmly, closing the front door behind me. "The bag falls in the river. Then what?"

"Then it gets caught up in the current and Tom jumps in after it. He rolls this way and that . . ." I acted out the motions for him as I spoke.

"That sounds kind of dangerous," Emilio said. "You're really going to jump in the water?"

"Sure! Why not? You can tie a rope around my waist for safety."

He looked at me for a long moment. "So after a fifty-year acting career, now you want to become an action hero?"

We both laughed. "If I can work it in organically, I will," he said.

The river scene comes after Tom has dismissed a gregarious Dutchman, played by Yorick van Wageningen, and turned his back on a bitter Canadian pilgrim, played by Deborah Kara Unger in a role Emilio describes as "the only angry Canadian in the history of film." By the time Tom reaches the old stone bridge to rest he has committed to walking the Camino alone. I was trying to show, and Emilio concurred: *You can do this journey, mister, but you're going to face more obstacles than you can anticipate, and you'd be better off as part of a community.*

When the backpack falls in the river, Tom is faced with two choices: let it float away and abandon his pilgrimage, or risk his life trying to save it. He chooses the latter. In Tom's mind, his son is drowning, so there's no question he has to jump in and save him.

I also wanted the backpack to be its own character in the film. Generally, pilgrims on the Camino have fascinating relationships with their backpacks. At the start they pack everything they think they'll need, and then some. After walking a while on the Camino, however, they begin to lighten their loads little by little. The *refugios,* or pilgrims' inns, become repositories for extra pairs of shoes, books, cosmetics, and all the other personal items everyone thinks they need at the outset of a trip, before they learn simply to trust. As the pilgrims lighten their physical loads, they often start to lighten their inner loads as well. But Tom's bag is Daniel's bag, and he's not willing to shed any item that Daniel carried to his death.

Before we left for Spain, Janet and I went down to a sporting goods store in Santa Monica to try out hiking boots and backpacks. I was such an inexperienced hiker, I didn't even know that a backpack straps across the chest and around the waist or how that would affect my balance.

Also, I didn't train for the walk in advance. "You have to get in shape," Emilio kept urging me, weeks before we left for Spain. "You've got to start walking with a backpack."

Even if I'd had the time to train, which I didn't, would I have used it for that purpose? Probably not. Tom didn't have time to get in shape. He arrived in France to retrieve his son's body, not planning to take a 500-mile trek with his son's forty-pound backpack. He wouldn't have been prepared for all that walking, and so I thought it better for me to be unprepared as well.

In every role, actors have to find the right balance between personally identifying with a character and identifying too much, which can impose our own feelings and idiosyncrasies onto the role. For the past week Emilio has been reminding me of all the ways that

Tom and I are different. When I ad lib a farewell or ask for a *café con leche* on camera, Emilio takes me aside.

"You have to stop playing Martin!" he says. "Remember, you're Tom. You can't throw in 'God bless and all the best!' when you say good-bye to someone. Martin might do that, but Tom wouldn't. And you can't speak Spanish."

"But I live in California," I argue. "I'd speak some Spanish if I was from California."

"Maybe," Emilio says. "Chances are you'd know a few words if you talked to your gardener. But I don't think this guy speaks to his gardener. I don't think he even sees him."

"Well, in Starbucks I ask for a *grande latte*," I insist.

"That's Italian."

"*Grande* is a Spanish word, too."

"You don't speak Spanish!" Emilio says. "Maybe later you can say a few words. But at this point, you've only been in Spain for a couple of days. You're still a stranger in a strange land." Then he really drives the issue home. "Remember: You belong to a private country club. You're a Republican. You never would have voted for Jed Bartlet, your own character on *The West Wing*."

Point well taken. Tom and I do have differences, after all. And a big one right now is that Tom is willing to jump in the river after his backpack. Martin, however, isn't so sure.

Fortunately, David has found a Spanish stuntman, Jorge, who can pass as me from a distance. He will do the more treacherous shots in the water and leave the close-ups for me.

A big, strapping guy with a full head of hair, Jorge reminds us of Johnny Weissmuller, the Olympic swimmer and actor who played Tarzan. He went in the knee-deep river yesterday without a hitch but today he eyes the chest-deep water suspiciously.

When the cameras are ready, I lean back against the edge of the stone bridge and unsnap the buckles on the backpack. I rest it against the ledge and stretch my back, which accidentally knocks the bag over the edge. It hits the water with a big, resounding splash and takes off downstream.

Jorge starts running along the riverbank, tracking the backpack as it floats along. Juanmi, our cinematographer, is in a red boat on the river shooting Jorge from a distance as he plunges into the water and starts swimming toward the backpack.

Emilio and I watch as Jorge flails and then catches hold of the bag, gripping it to his chest. The expression on his face is a cross between surprise and a grimace. Except we're not supposed to see that.

"He's looking at us," I say.

"I know," Emilio answers. "We can't use it."

Rule number one for a stunt double: Never look at the camera. The whole idea is to trick viewers into thinking the double is the actor.

Jorge stumbles out of the river dragging the backpack, and crew members rush to wrap him in towels. Back up on the bridge, he peels all the wet layers off his upper body.

"How was the footing?" I ask. I'll need to go into the river later for the close-up shots and I want to know what to expect. "Was it slippery?"

"*¿Escurridizo?*" my grandson Taylor translates for me.

"*Muy, muy escurridizo,*" Jorge says, nodding. "*Sí, sí. Y muy peligroso.*"

"Slippery and dangerous," Taylor says.

We'll need Jorge to go back in the water and do another take. Emilio explains the situation and asks him to enter the river downstream next time, where the rapids are faster.

Jorge calmly shakes his head no. *"Muy peligroso,"* he says again. "My thing is horses, not swimming," he explains through Taylor as he leaves.

We don't know exactly how to proceed so we break for lunch. Shooting the script in sequence as the characters move along the Camino means we have to get the river shots today, because this evening we're moving the crew on to Pamplona. But now we're suddenly minus a stuntman, and there's no time to find another. We either get the river shots today or Emilio will be forced to cut the whole river sequence from the film. Nobody wants that to happen. David has already invested time and money into getting several boats with safety crews on the river. The lifeguards are on set in their red life vests and red helmets, waiting to pluck Tom from the water as soon as the cameras stop rolling.

The only solution is for me to go into the river myself, but I'm apprehensive. I didn't learn to swim until the age of thirty-six for *Apocalypse Now* but even then I was *on* the river in the navy patrol boat, not in it. I've never done a scene that has required me to swim and I've never filmed in rapids. Also, I haven't been swimming in . . . I can't even remember how long.

"Aw, you big sissy," Taylor chides me during lunch. "I'll do it in my skivvies, if you want, to show you how safe it is."

Taylor and I have an exceptionally close relationship. I have adored him all his life. We joke around endlessly, and I know he's only trying to pump up my confidence now. Even so, I don't know if I should let a twenty-five-year-old with professional lifeguard training be the benchmark for what I can accomplish in the river.

"We'll be right downstream," Taylor assures me. A rope has been extended across the river for me to grab on to, he explains, to keep me from getting too close to the waterfall fifty meters downriver.

A waterfall? That's the first time I've heard of a waterfall.

"Four lifeguards are out there in two separate boats, ready to pull you out," Taylor says.

I make my choice: I have to go in. We need to get this scene. And the whole thing was my idea in the first place.

Emilio and I stand together on the bridge while Juanmi readies the camera on the river. Emilio talks me through the backpack's fall to improve upon the last take of that shot.

"You took it off last time and then it

looked like it got out of control," he says. "It looked like the weight of it pulled you back."

"Right, on the left side," I agree. "Okay." I know how to fix that.

Emilio leans over the bridge's thick stone ledge and shouts down to Juanmi in the boat below. "Okay, Martin's gonna go in the water now!"

First, the camera operator on the bridge shoots me as Tom leaning back against the edge, unhooking the bag and accidentally letting it fall over the edge. This time I maintain better control over the bag. After it hits the water I run off the bridge and down a gentle grassy slope to the riverbank, where I see the bag passing by. I quickly run to the next clearing on the bank. I have to time my entry into the water just right, making sure I leave enough time to reach the bag before the current carries it away.

I see the bag heading this way, almost in line with me. I can't hesitate. I run into the water.

Jorge was right; the bottom of the river is slippery. I stumble a little going in and enter face first. The water is *freezing,* colder than I possibly could have imagined, the shock of it indescribable. All the breath is sucked out of me. My limbs become blocks of ice and my hiking boots are cement bricks dragging me down. I raise one arm over the other and do a quick crawl stroke toward the bag but I don't know if I'll make it in time. My blue parka fills with air between my shoulder blades — I didn't expect that — and drags against the water, slowing me down even more.

I have a desperate few seconds in the water when the bag nearly passes me by, but I manage to grab a strap and pull it toward me. I cling to the bag while the force of the current flips me over onto my back, and then back onto my stomach. The buoyancy of the bag acts like a little life raft and gives me a moment to catch my breath. No sooner do I feel relief to be holding the bag than I have to deal with the current. The bag and I are speeding downriver and I don't know where we're heading. The word "waterfall" lodges uncomfortably in my mind.

A little cluster of low trees sits in the middle of the river just ahead of me. Everything's happening quickly yet I still have time to think, *If you miss that little island, I don't know where you'll end up.* As the water carries me close I instinctively reach out with my right hand and grab a branch. It's wet and mossy and slips away from me, but

I manage to hold on to the next one.

"Cut!" Emilio yells. A red safety boat motors over and the lifeguards help me onto the bank of the little island. I shiver and smile with relief as I make the sign of the cross and thump my chest in gratitude.

Then I look down at my hiking boot, where a big, four-pronged fishhook, a relic from some long-ago fishing adventure, is lodged in the sole. The boots weighed me down considerably in the water but thank God I wore them. I wouldn't have wanted that hook to catch me in the foot, or anywhere else.

We pry the hook out of my shoe, motor me to shore, dry me off, and get me back into wardrobe to do a second take. This time, I know I can grab the branches on the island, but I'm afraid of missing the bag if I enter the water too fast. Still, Juanmi gets some good shots and in post-production frames from both takes will be edited together to create a tight, convincing scene.

Afterward, we all assemble near the bridge while I towel off my face and hair.

"And now," I announce, brandishing the towel like a matador's red cape and swirling it theatrically through the air, "I want to go into bullfighting."

The crew laughs. The tension of the day is

221

broken. Together, as a team, we've proven that a sixty-nine-year-old man without training, who's been on the Camino for only two days, is capable of running into a raging river and retrieving an errant backpack to save his son's ashes. As we pack up and head on to Pamplona I'm feeling content. Not because I, Martin, dove into the river to catch the backpack and made it safely back to shore — well, maybe just a little — but also because today the little community we've created here on the Camino made it look like Tom could do it on his own.

CHAPTER SIX:
EMILIO
1972–1974

In the summer of 1972 our family relocated to La Junta, Colorado, in the southeastern part of the state. Far off to the west, you could see the outline of mountains, but southeast Colorado was farmland, ranch-land, rolling miles of short-grass prairie and sagebrush. We befriended a local family that lived outside of town, and one of the sons taught me how to drive their flatbed truck, an enormous piece of machinery when you're ten years old, especially when you're the one behind the wheel.

A few days after my first lesson, I was somehow considered qualified to drive a truck full of kids and friends and hippies to the soybean field across the eighty-acre spread our friends, the Cranstons, owned and farmed. "Let Emilio drive!" one of the kids had said.

All right, I figured. *I'd better get behind the wheel.*

Poised on the driver's seat, I couldn't believe I was taking workers into the fields. Driving! My friends back in Malibu wouldn't believe it if I told them. I could barely believe it myself. I looked back over my shoulder through the rear window to make sure what I was seeing was real. One of the workers gave me a two-finger wave.

I couldn't believe how cool this was. I was *driving.*

"Watch it!" someone shouted as the truck started veering off the road. The Cranston boy next to me grabbed the wheel and yanked the truck back toward the center.

"Easy," he drawled. "Eyes on the road."

I'd almost run into an irrigation ditch. If I'd run us off the road, people would have sailed off the back of the truck. For sure some would have gotten hurt. Letting a ten-year-old drive a truck is one level of madness. Letting him be responsible for the safety of a dozen other people is another. I got off easy that day. I'd never take the responsibility of driving lightly ever again.

Our family had come here for the summer so my father could shoot a film called *Badlands,* the directorial debut of a twenty-eight-year-old philosophy student and former Rhodes Scholar named Terrence Malick. The film told the story of a rebellious twenty-five-year-old South Dakota greaser and his teenage girlfriend who take off on a shooting spree across the upper Midwest. Loosely based on the real-life eight-day killing rampage of Charles Starkweather and his girlfriend Caril Ann Fugate in 1958, the film cast an unknown actress named Sissy Spacek in the role of fifteen-year-old Holly Sargis and my father as the aimless greaser Kit Carruthers.

Remorseless and cocky, Kit was a latter-day James Dean, which was a good fit for my father. A veritable who's who of up-and-coming actors had auditioned for the role: Richard Dreyfuss, Robert De Niro, Don Johnson. As my father would later tell the story, he knew when Terry Malick offered him the part that he was being given the chance of a lifetime. On the way home from receiving the offer, my dad pulled over to the side of the road in his car and started weeping because someone had faith enough in him to give him this chance. And so in early July we packed our bags, climbed into our Ford station wagon, and headed out to Colorado for the four-month shoot.

We left Malibu in early July to make the long, hot drive to La Junta — 1,100 miles and two full days on the road. On road trips I liked to sit in the very rear of the car tucked in among the luggage with a book, usually science fiction. That summer on the way to Colorado I read Michael Crichton's *The Andromeda Strain,* the story of a lethal alien virus that arrives on earth and the scientists who race to stop its spread. I read the book cover to cover three times. The film had come out in 1971, directed by Robert Wise of *West Side Story* and *The Sound of Music* fame. I saw it ten times. The actor Ramon Bieri, who played Major Manchek in *The Andromeda Strain,* also had a role in *Badlands,* giving me an early lesson in the inner workings of Hollywood. From the outside it looks large and impenetrable but once you're on the inside you quickly learn it's really a very small group of people coming together, breaking apart, and coming together in different configurations, over and over again. If you liked working with someone in the past, chances are you'll find yourself working with him or her again before long — maybe even two or three times.

In Colorado we rented a house across the street from a big park, met the neighbors, got to know the local kids. La Junta was a tiny town, maybe seven thousand people, along the Arkansas River about an hour east of Pueblo. We could walk downtown to the grocery store and to the Fox Theater for movies, and it didn't take long for us to meet many of the people who lived there.

My father said living in La Junta was just like growing up in his boyhood neighborhood in Dayton. To me, it was like stepping into the Wild West. Ranchers would come into town in their Stetsons and cowboy boots. Our next-door neighbors were an elderly couple who claimed to have migrated west to Colorado in a covered wagon. Every morning the wife would come across our lawn shouting, "Yoo hoo! Yoo hoo!" to catch my mother's attention and they would spend the day cooking together and swapping stories. For my father's birthday in early August, my mother paid each of us kids fifty cents to sit for half an hour while she painted our portraits, then gave them to him as a gift. They still hang in the hall of my parents' house today.

Malick was brilliant on that set and pulled stellar performances from his cast, many of whom revere him to this day. He was fond of using whatever assets he had available on location because the movie was being shot on such a low budget.

My brother Ramon and I both made our acting debuts in *Badlands,* in a brief shot where Holly looks out of her bedroom window at night and sees two boys playing in the light of a streetlamp. Terry had asked if we'd step in, but when we showed up on set the evening of the shoot, he froze in place and stared at us. Immediately, I could tell that we were not what he'd had in mind. *Badlands* was set in the clean-cut crew-cut era of 1959, but Ramon and I were kids of the scruffy '70s with hair down to our collars.

I didn't want to cut my hair and I didn't particularly want to be in the movie, so that was fine with me, but Dona Baldwin, who was doing hair and makeup and who also played a small part in the film as a deaf maid, assured Terry, "Give me a minute with both of them, okay?" She sat us in the makeup chair and smoothed our hair with Brylcreem. Then she pinned it up and under with bobby pins.

I'd never felt so humiliated in my life. Pinning my hair up like a *girl's?*

It worked, though. When we returned to the set, Terry was pleased. What the grease didn't accomplish, the bobby pins took care of, and the shot was in the dark and from so far away that nobody could tell our hair was a good six inches longer than it looked in the scene.

Soon after arriving in Colorado we became friendly with the Cranstons, the farmers who had eight kids. They gave my mother goat's milk and she learned how to make ice cream. I liked to run around with one of their sons who was about my age and, when harvest time arrived, the family invited me to stay with them for a while. I moved onto their farm for three weeks to help harvest corn, to bale the hay, and pick soybeans and melons. For them harvesting was a predictable annual event but for me it was like spending time at farm camp. School started in Malibu that month but I was getting a better fourth-grade education on the land than I ever could have gotten in a classroom by the beach.

The set of *Badlands* could get turbulent at times: crew members would leave for other jobs or get fired; the film went past schedule and over budget in hundred-degree heat with thunderstorms every afternoon; and a special-effects man was badly burned during a fire scene. But over on the farm, operations proceeded in smooth, easy, lockstep motions. If we had extreme heat and daily thunderstorms I don't remember them. I was so caught up in the work of a farmhand, it would have taken a tornado to distract me, and maybe not even that. Every day was a different harvest — one day soybeans, another day lettuce, then melons. We'd go out into the field till late afternoon and come back to grind our own wheat and make our own bread. While my father pretended to shoot victims at close range for the camera, I was learning how to milk goats and churn butter. Even my mother with her macrobiotic cooking hadn't gone *that* far.

In summertime, the Cranston kids slept in old boxcars on the property that were rodent-proof and used for storing grain. At the top of each boxcar was a hatch and we'd lift it and climb down into a space that held mattresses and sleeping bags and pillows. Charlie was seven at the time and became curious about what I was doing on the farm, so my parents let him come out and spend a night with me. In the morning we woke up before everyone else and climbed down the side of the boxcar. The fields stretched out in front of us as far as we could see. Eighty acres is a lot of land.

"I'm hungry," Charlie said. "What do you do for food here?"

"Follow me," I said.

I led him into the nearest field, where watermelons and cantaloupe were ready for harvest.

"Here," I said.

Charlie picked up a melon and stared at it. "How do we open these things?" he asked.

I felt around in the pockets of my Toughskins and found a quarter. By digging deep stripes into the melon I was able to cut it open. We tore it apart with our hands and ate until the juice ran down our chins. That was breakfast. Charlie didn't care much for that kind of living — it didn't speak to him the way it spoke to me — but I loved it. The communal lifestyle, the freedom, the responsibility, the gratification of a long day out on the land, all of it. I didn't ever want to go home.

Back in Malibu that autumn, my driving privileges were quickly and wisely revoked. My father was zipping around town in a little orange Mazda he'd come home in one day after an impulse buy — *Orange?* we all said — and my mother drove the Ford station wagon, but I was back to biking around to get anywhere. My prized possession that year was a new white Raleigh ten-speed I'd seen at a bike shop in Malibu. It cost $109. "If you want that bicycle, you're going to have to earn the money and buy it yourself," my folks had said. It took me a whole year to save up enough, earning a dollar a week from my parents for feeding the dogs and making all four of our lunches every morning before school. My grandmother in Ohio would send five dollars for my birthdays and that helped, too. Working for so long to get the bicycle felt like an ordeal but it makes a difference to earn something as a child instead of having it handed to you outright. I treasured that bicycle like I treasured nothing else during those years, because I'd earned it myself.

Our local Point Dume Plaza had a coffee shop, bank, pharmacy, hardware store, bakery, dry cleaners, and health food store, as well as the Mayfair Market, our local grocery store, with Malibu's first recycling center newly installed out back. "Ecology" was a buzzword of the early 1970s — that and "littering." Kids at my school were encouraged to collect newspapers and tin cans and TV dinner trays and participate in a massive recycling drive on the school lot. As a country we were just starting to gain a consciousness of humanity's long-term impact on the environment and the legacy that would be left to us kids if we didn't start turning the damage around.

Most of my friends in the neighborhood would bike over to Point Dume Plaza when a new comic book or new edition of *Mad* magazine came out. Every week I'd ride over to buy the new issue of *TV Guide*. I'd stand in the parking lot flipping past the opening articles and then pore through it page by page to see what shows my dad was going to appear in that week and how he was billed. Was he listed as the first guest star, which meant better than second guest star? Did the movie or episode appear inside a little box, which meant it was a highlight? And if not, why wasn't his show being highlighted? He may not have known this at the time, but I was a big fan, proud of what he did for a living and proud of him.

I'd dog-ear every *TV Guide* page he appeared on to make sure we could all stay up and watch him on screen. His shows were Event TV for our family. We might have already seen some of the movies at private studio screenings, but it was still special to watch them together in our living room. My father would watch with us and sometimes he'd criticize his performance. "What was I thinking?" he'd laugh, or "That's an awful angle," he'd say. "I look terrible!" We watched the shows critically, wanting him to have gotten the best exposure possible. We also appreciated the work it took to put a movie together. We would often have spent time on the set and when we watched together certain scenes would resonate with us because we had seen them being shot. I knew what city I'd been standing in as I watched the cameras roll, but when I saw the finished product I could almost believe I'd been standing somewhere else entirely. I was amazed by the way filmmakers could make audiences believe that what they were seeing was real. To a kid it seemed like a unique type of science fiction.

We had only three network channels back then. If you were lucky you could also get PBS. Ramon or Charlie or I would have to jockey the rabbit ears into just the right position to get reception and sometimes we'd have to hold on to them to keep the signal. Despite the progressive stance some parents took toward television in those years, meaning flat-out banning it, my parents never did. It was obviously what Dad did or wanted to do, so it wasn't looked at as an evil. Neither was it considered a pacifier or a babysitter. Because there weren't any restrictions on it, it didn't become something we wanted more than life itself, which often happens when you put limits on something for children. We did have restrictions on certain foods like milk and sugar, which meant I'd go to a friend's house and gorge myself on chocolate milk and Pop-Tarts because I knew I'd never get them at home. Maybe because in Southern California we had so many good-weather months to play outside, television wasn't a big draw. It wasn't even something a lot of my friends' fathers worked in at the time. The father of one of my friends played bass for Crosby, Stills, and Nash but otherwise our neighborhood was full of therapists, accountants, police officers, firemen — as mixed a bag of middle-class professions as you'd find in any other suburb in America.

In the spring of 1973, just before my eleventh birthday, my father did a Canadian commercial for Texaco that gave him a sizable paycheck. For the first time he had a chunk of money in the bank. Property values were starting to go up in Malibu and this gave my parents an idea.

"Enough of this renting," my father said. "We're going to buy a house."

He and my mother made a down payment on a sprawling ranch house a few blocks away from our rental. It had three bathrooms, which was a first for us, and four bedrooms, which made it seem like a palace compared to the places we'd lived in before. We four kids didn't have to share a single room anymore and we had gotten to the ages when we didn't want to. Ramon and I decided to bunk together. We took the bedroom at the end of the hall with a big window that gave us a view of the front lawn, but more important, it was the only kids' bedroom with its own bathroom. Charlie and Renée had their own private bedrooms, but with no bathrooms.

Our new backyard was a big, open flat space with patchy grass and lots of weeds. A little old corral had been built to house a pony. Nobody fenced in their land back then so you could pass without interruption through a straight string of backyards to get to your friends. Point Dume was a real community. If you lived there you knew every family, and if you were a kid you knew every kid in that family. Your arm would get tired waving to people when you walked, drove, or rode your bike up and down the street.

Some of the neighborhood kids would become well known in later years, with names moviegoers and TV watchers would recognize: Sean and Chris Penn, Rob and Chad Lowe, Robert Downey Jr. The place was a crucible for young male talent but we didn't know it then. We were just a bunch of scrappy kids riding around on bikes in our Toughskins jeans, learning fractions, watching *The Godfather,* and wondering what it took to become a Pacino or a Brando one day.

We'd lived in the new house for only a few weeks, not even long enough to unpack, when my father was cast in an *ITV Saturday Night Theatre* movie called *Catholics*. It was based on a novella about a futuristic Catholic Church where most of the old rituals had been banned. An older monk, played by Trevor Howard, was still leading Mass in Latin on a remote island and had attracted an international following. My father played a young priest dispatched from Rome to rural Ireland to bring the monk and his followers back into line. The priest my father played never had to say Mass or hear confessions or wear the Roman collar, which was probably a good thing because my dad wasn't a practicing Catholic and didn't have a very keen interest in the religious themes in the script. He'd been attracted to the story of the monks struggling to hold on to tradition in a wild, remote land, and also by the adventure of shooting in Ireland and bringing us all along.

The shoot started in England for a few days and then hopped over to Ireland for three weeks, moving from County Clare to County Tipperary to Skibbereen on the south coast, and then out to Sherkin Island off the extreme southern tip of Ireland. Sherkin Island was tiny — just three miles long by a half mile wide — untamed and remote, with a population of only about a hundred residents. It also had a fifteenth-century friary built from stone, which was the big draw for the film's location scout. The island's perpetual cold and wind chilled us all to the bone even in May but added to the austere effect the film was going for.

We moved into a small hunter's cottage my father found for us near the little town of Cahir. It was also remote and surrounded by farmland. Every now and then a bull would appear in our yard and snort at my father when he did his morning calisthenics. This was enough to drive him back inside to exercise. The cottage had no heater and was so cold at night we had to stuff newspapers into the window cracks and sleep with hot water bottles. We were all furious with my dad for insisting that we have an authentic Irish experience, deprivation and wind chill included, when the rest of the film's cast was staying at a warm hotel with all the modern amenities.

One day when he wasn't needed on set he rented a little car and we drove to see the towering Cliffs of Moher near Connemara in western Ireland. It was a perfect, rare

May day, with the sun shining brightly and birds swooping above the 500-foot vertical cliffs and out over the Atlantic Ocean.

Before we'd left the States, my folks had bought a new 8-millimeter movie camera to bring with us to Ireland and an 8-millimeter projector for us to play the movies on when we got back home. Before long I commandeered the camera in Ireland and started making little movies with my brothers to pass the time. I called one of them *Falling* and made everything in the movie fall down, whether it was a tree or a person. We didn't have any means to edit the film so I'd have to say, "Okay, that's the shot I want. Hold it right there! That's the close-up I want! Don't move!" and I'd cut the film as I shot it. It taught me great discipline from the start because there couldn't be any waste. Then again, I was eleven. What did I know? I thought this was how films were made.

That day at the cliffs I filmed a bunch of seagulls near the ocean. I held the camera up to my eye and followed the birds moving across the sky. It felt completely natural to look at the world through a lens like that, as natural as riding a bike. I held the camera steady and let the birds fly across the screen. If I stood still long enough, some would float by in one direction and others would return in another. A roll of 8-millimeter film was about four minutes long. I finished one and started a second. I filmed more seagulls and some more seagulls, seagulls here and seagulls there. The folks really had no idea what I was doing: They were probably relieved that I'd found a way to occupy myself.

We didn't get any of my footage developed in Ireland. We just accumulated rolls of exposed film and brought them all home. At the time, 8-millimeter film was very expensive to buy and to process, about ten dollars to develop one roll. When we got back home to Malibu we dropped off all our film. When it was ready we sat down together as a family to watch the footage from our family trip. My father threaded the first reel on the projector and sat down with us to watch.

A seagull floated across the screen, swooped down, and arced back up. Then another. In fact, the whole first reel was footage of seagulls.

The second reel was seagulls, too.

Reel three? Seagulls.

The group became increasingly more frustrated and, by the end of the fourth roll of seagulls, ultimately angry because of how expensive it had been to process all this footage of birds.

"Emilio!" my mother said. "We gave you this camera so you could shoot pictures of *human beings*. How could you shoot all this footage of seagulls?"

I think, even though I was so young when I'd been on the set of *Badlands,* that I'd been influenced by Terry Malick. As a director he pays very close attention to light and weather conditions and the contours of the land. He closely observes nature and works it into his films, sometimes focusing more on the natural world than on human beings. This was very clear in his most recent film, *The Tree of Life,* and it was already evident on the set of *Badlands.* One day in Colorado some crew members watched him shoot a spider in a fruit jar for several hours until he felt he'd gotten the angle just right.

That's what I was going for with the seagulls: the perfect shot. At eleven I'd started emulating the filmmakers I'd been lucky enough to observe, and working with Terry had profoundly affected just about everyone on that film.

Badlands premiered at the New York Film Festival in October 1973 and went into wider release the following year to — once again — uniform critical acclaim but only modest box office receipts. Over time it has developed almost a cult following, but in 1974 the film was considered too quirky and provocative to attract mainstream appeal. While it put my father's name in more people's mouths it didn't propel his career into the stratosphere as many people had expected it would. Six months later, he was still doing TV movies, although now he was more likely to land leading roles.

Sometimes I would stand at the kitchen doors that led to our backyard and watch as he took out his frustration on our lawn. He'd grab a screwdriver and go out there for hours, with his shirt off, tearing at the weeds. I could feel his anger and his disappointment and I shared it. I wanted him to succeed almost as much as he wanted it himself. I knew what he was capable of and couldn't understand why other people didn't recognize his talent and give him the acclaim he deserved. He needed that recognition, and not just for his self-esteem. Like it or not, film actors are in an industry where key people need to recognize you to make things happen. You need benefactors. You need the right people to believe in you and get behind you. They need to believe in your potential to help you get to the next phase where you can be recognized by many others.

At the same time, this is a fickle business with desires that change with the seasons. You have to be pretty solid in knowing who you are and what you stand for or you can get thrown off balance and wind up chasing other people's ideas of what you should be. My father had confidence in his talent and knew who he was, but that wasn't enough. He didn't have the support of the industry yet, and he didn't like to fake friendships for his own personal gain. He wasn't comfortable socializing with executives or ingratiating himself with the men in suits. Very few of our family friends during those years were people who could further his career. None of them were wealthy and none were players in Hollywood even though that was often the way to get deals made. To my parents' credit, they chose friends who were loyal, trustworthy, creative people, many of whom were struggling to survive themselves. My folks couldn't tolerate dishonesty or phoniness in others, but my father also suffered for being unwilling to play the Hollywood game.

"This guy invited you to be his friend!" my mother would tell him. "That guy's the producer of that show!"

"Well, that'll be about the last time I talk

to him," my father would laugh. He never wanted anyone to think he was offering friendship because they could give him a job. If he went out for supper with someone powerful or famous he would always grab the check and pay for both meals to make sure his dinner partner didn't feel taken advantage of. He was a lot like his own father that way. A man of *scrupulous* integrity. Admirable, maybe, but also potentially lethal in an industry that thrives on the compliment and the back pat and the occasional back stab.

It's not a big surprise that these were the years when his drinking began to escalate. My uncle Al would come over on the weekends with the big 18-ounce cans of Coors, and I knew when the ice chest came out the twelve-packs of Coors would go in and they'd start drinking on the patio outside. After a couple of beers my dad would start getting hammered. His eyes would roll back in his head and his voice would get louder. Before long they'd become a bunch of drunks sitting around, babbling incoherently about how they were going to change the world.

Watching my father drink was like watching weather patterns blow across the backyard. Alcohol first made him sentimental, then it made him self-pitying, and then he'd get angry. And self-righteous and arrogant. "What did you just say?" he'd shout at us. "How dare you! What was that? Oh, you think so?"

My mom would stand there and roll her eyes. We'd seen it too many times before. Sometimes my uncle Al would rage and laugh and carry on and then pass out on the floor for hours. My mother banned him from the house at one point to protect us kids from seeing that. Several of my uncles got so stupid and juvenile when they drank. My father, too. When he drank he needed attention and if he didn't get it he'd demand it. He acted as though alcohol gave him license to misbehave, when instead it made him unreasonable. It didn't make him stronger in my eyes. It made him look weak.

Even as I continued to admire him and want his admiration, I also started to become more irritated and fed up. He would drink to get rid of his insecurities but the alcohol only amplified his self-pity, so then he would drink more. And before long, the worst of him would come out. The whole process seemed like an endless, exhausting loop. You didn't have to be an adult to figure that out.

■ ■ ■ ■

In the winter of 1973–1974 my father began filming a made-for-TV movie for NBC. It was called *The Execution of Private Slovik* and told the true story of Eddie Slovik, a World War II army private and the only U.S. soldier to be court-martialed and executed for desertion since the Civil War. (If you're noticing a distinct military theme among the roles my father played you'd be correct, though I think that probably says more about what was being produced in the '70s than the kind of roles that appealed to him most.)

The script was cowritten by Richard Levinson and William Link and directed by Lamont Johnson, the same team that had been responsible for *That Certain Summer*. *Private Slovik* was shot almost like a dramatic documentary, in *Citizen Kane* fashion with cuts back and forth between the present and the past. Gary Busey and Ned Beatty played supporting roles, as did Matt Clark, my father's buddy from the Living Theatre in New York who had also moved to Malibu and whom we frequently saw at home. Filming took place in Canada and California with the court-martial scene filmed in the Grand Ballroom aboard the *Queen Mary* cruise ship docked in Long Beach. When shooting was local our family was often welcome on set. *Private Slovik* also marked Charlie's television debut when Johnson needed a kid to appear in a wedding scene. One by one, we kids were starting to appear on screen.

As Private Slovik, my father delivered a devastating performance that became known as one of the best of his career. In real life, Eddie Slovik was an ex-con and something of a born loser but my father managed to portray him with both toughness and compassion. The movie's most famous scene, when Slovik recites back-to-back Hail Marys with the military chaplain as he's being strapped to the execution post and the black cloth hood is being fitted over his head, still wipes me out every time I see it. The Hail Marys were my father's idea.

The Execution of Private Slovik won a Peabody Award for NBC and collected eight Emmy nominations, including Best Directing, Best Writing, Best Art Direction, and Best Lead Actor in a Drama. It was my father's first Emmy nomination and he had heady competition in the category: Alan Alda, Laurence Olivier, Dick Van Dyke, and Hal Holbrook.

But it wasn't going to be a simple contest, not for my dad.

In the spring of 1974 he was being touted as front-runner for the Lead Actor Emmy, and rightly so. But George C. Scott was a big influence on my father, and Scott believed that actors shouldn't compete. He'd called the Academy Awards a popularity contest with little artistic significance and brought public attention to the political and social pressures that went into voters' selections. Scott was nominated for an Academy Award for his starring role in *Patton,* which he won. But he refused to accept it. Influenced by Scott's artistic courage and honesty, and to our dismay, my father withdrew his name from the Emmy competition.

There was a great deal of communication between him and his agent and Universal Pictures about this. Of course they didn't want him to withdraw, but my father was adamant. While his justification for withdrawing was admirable, still it occurred to me that all this might be the result of his own fear. I think he wanted to win but was scared he might lose. All the polite applause you often see nominees giving at award ceremonies when someone else wins is good sportsmanship. Nobody goes there to lose. So was it really that my father wanted to publicly support George C. Scott's position, or was it that he wanted to go so far the other way that he remained anonymous and immune from competition? If so, why do the film in the first place? Why not take a supporting role instead of the lead?

Or was it the years of Catholic teaching that you shouldn't be prideful? I didn't understand what was wrong with being prideful.

Watching my father give up the chance to achieve what I'd thought he always wanted — appreciation, celebration, acclaim — was confusing to say the least. I wish now that my father had been able to be honest with himself. That he'd said, "You know what? I want the careers of my contemporaries." He was still a struggling actor, rarely number one on anyone's list. I think a lot of his rage derived from waiting for the phone to ring, waiting for the agent to call with the offer, not getting the job he wanted and having to take one that he had to accept to feed the family he was deeply involved with. My father would take big chances but he wouldn't devote himself exclusively to his career because we would suffer. He always put family first. But he paid a price for this choice and so did we. The spankings and the rage we endured — where was that coming from? From frustration at not being honest, I think. At not being honest with himself. It would be almost twenty years before my father was nominated for an Emmy again, this time for a guest spot on the TV series *Murphy Brown,* and he would win. By then he was ready to accept it. For whatever reasons, in 1974 he wasn't.

He probably didn't realize it, but I was watching him. I was watching him closely and learning from him, all the time. Both good lessons and others.

CHAPTER SEVEN: MARTIN
1973–1976

Badlands was filmed in 1972 but only those of us who made the movie associate it with that year. Everyone else places it in 1974, the year it was released. That's an odd discontinuity of being a film actor. Your memories of a film refer to your time on location, not to the date when it enters public discourse. In the gap between filming and release, only the actors know how the material changed them and what capacity it has to change others. I didn't know if *Badlands* would be a commercial success when we filmed it, but I knew it was an extraordinary artistic venture that would move people deeply and alter many viewers' image of American cinema, thanks to its brilliant screenwriter and director Terrence Malick. But I had to wait two years for everyone else to discover it, and a lot of life happened to me in between.

The trip to Ireland in 1973 for *Catholics* was more than a job and a vacation. It was also my first opportunity to meet the Irish side of my family. My mother's hometown of Borrisokane was only sixty miles from the house we'd rented in Cahir, so on my first weekend off we piled into a little rented car to tour around Ireland, with the plan to end up in Borrisokane to meet the family. My father, who knew the names and addresses of the Irish relatives, had tried to alert them of our trip by mail. But just like the relatives in Spain, our Irish family didn't have telephones, and my job in Ireland had come up so suddenly I didn't know if my father's letter had reached them in time.

Our rental car was tiny, just a front and a back. The four kids crammed themselves into the backseat, a situation that made fighting difficult and to be avoided. This was the first time I'd driven on the left side of the road, which was an adventure for us all. We drove up to see the Cliffs of Moher along Ireland's west coast first. The hour-long trip to the Atlantic Ocean, my driving skills notwithstanding, was a spectacular route through gently rolling pastures and past the brightly painted small pubs along the main street of Ennistimon, a small town near the midpoint of our trip.

Out near the cliffs the weather was so beautiful I pulled over by the side of the road so we could all get out and enjoy the view of the sea. A bucolic green field stretched out in front of us, with birds swooping far in the distance.

The kids opened the back doors and out they went, running across the field like puppies set free. Emilio took with him the little 8-millimeter camera we'd brought along on the trip.

"Look at them," I said to Janet, admiring their lack of inhibition. "Isn't that great?"

"Martin," she said quickly. "I don't see a fence."

I was out of the car as fast as you could say "catch them." *"Whoa!"* I shouted as I took off across the field. *"Whoa!"* I was very fit from jogging and daily calisthenics, and I overtook them with an added dose of adrenaline. Thank God I did. You couldn't tell from the car, but we were at land's end. The field was the top of a sheer drop-off into the ocean.

When the four of them stopped short in front of me, I leaned over to catch my breath. We stared at the 300-foot plunge into waves below. I'd arrived just in time to stop them from sailing over the edge.

From the cliffs we headed east toward County Tipperary past Lough Derg, the third-largest lake in Ireland, to the village of Borrisokane. As we drove into the town in early evening I looked at the simple gray stone houses surrounded by fields and thought, *My God. It looks so much like Spain.* I had the relatives' names and addresses from my father and knew the name of the family pub. In such a small town it wasn't hard to track them down.

My mother's brother Michael, an IRA soldier, died in 1952, and his widow had been left to raise their nine children, most of them girls. These were all my first cousins. Most of Michael's children had since moved to London to find work but three still lived in Ireland. Sean Phelan lived in Borrisokane and was the first one we found. He lived with his wife and child just around the corner from the house where my mother grew up.

Sean and his family lived in such poverty it was hard to witness, especially having just moved into our own four-bedroom house in Malibu. Their stone house was tiny, almost like a child's playhouse, with just a bedroom and a toilet. Sean made us biscuits and tea and insisted on sharing what little they had. And yet there was nothing at all sad about him or his family or any of the other cousins we met on that trip. They were filled with a unique zest for life, with great humor and joy. "How y'keepin'?" they asked us. "How long y'home for?" It was the most extraordinary welcome we could have imagined.

Sean brought us to meet his brother Liam, a pharmacist in the nearby village of Roscrea, and also his sister Theresa who lived out in the country with her husband and thirteen of the sixteen children she'd eventually bear. She and her husband had some acreage and eighty head of cattle. I felt a deep sense of connection to the place — not only because these were blood relatives, but because the Celtic nature of the tribe reminded me of my father's family in Galicia. They were both big families, deeply loyal to their countries, fiercely independent, and very poor. The places even smelled the same: wet and green, with houses permeated by the smoke of open fires. In Borrisokane, huge indoor stoves burned local peat and stayed warm all day long.

Most of all, both sets of my relatives had a strong Catholic faith and coveted land. If you had land you could have livestock, and if you had livestock and land you could survive. The Celtic influence on Galicia has been disputed, but after I'd stood in Parderrubias and then in Borrisokane, it wasn't hard to see the same fingerprints on both.

That Saturday we spent the night at Liam's house, which was the largest and least crowded of the three. The next morning I accompanied him to Mass at a church in Roscrea. As we stepped outside afterward we were approached by a group of young men selling blood-red poppies and collecting donations in a tin can.

"What are these guys, veterans?" I asked Liam.

"Oh, no, sure," he said. "They're the lads."

"The who?"

"The lads, you know."

"Who's that?"

"We'll talk," he said. Later, in the car he explained, "They're IRA."

These would have been members of the Provisional IRA, not the old IRA that had been in existence pre–Civil War when my mother had lived there. May 1973 was only a year and a half after the Bloody Sunday shootings in Derry, Northern Ireland, when British paratroopers gunned down fourteen unarmed Catholic demonstrators, seven of them teenage boys. Support from brethren in the Republic was helping to sustain the new IRA in Northern Ireland, where the Troubles were about to begin. We all knew it would get worse before it got better and Borrisokane had enough sympathizers to provide support for the new "lads."

If I'd been raising my boys in Ireland, would they have joined the fight for the cause? Sometimes I could see that fire and determination burning in them. If my mother had raised her children there in Ireland instead of Dayton, among family that had long supported the IRA, would I have joined the cause as well? It was impossible to know.

We adored the cousins and they adored us and they practically tripped over themselves to make us comfortable. At first I thought it was the hospitality of kinship but I soon realized it was more than that. In Theresa's house a picture of my father hung prominently on the wall.

"My father?" I said. "What's his picture doing here?" They'd never met, I was sure of that, since my father had never been to Ireland.

That's when I learned that my father had been helping to support Michael's widow and her children in Ireland all this time. As little as he earned at NCR, and as many children as he'd had at home, he was still sending small amounts of money every month to both my mother's family in Ireland and his in Spain, and he'd never mentioned this to us. We were poor in Dayton, it's true, but the European relatives were far worse off. In my father's mind, there was no question. This was what you do. You take care of the needy, especially those in your family. I thought of the criticism my father had received from his sons as we grew up, especially the older boys. "Why don't we have better furniture?" they'd ask. "A bigger house? A car?" They just hadn't had a clue who this man really was. I hadn't, either, but when I looked at the portrait of my father hanging on the wall of my cousin's house in Borrisokane, I gained a new admiration for him, and a new understanding of honor.

When filming wrapped on *Catholics,* we flew to London and then on to Spain. Charlie, Renée, and Janet had not met my father's relatives, and by now my sister Carmen was living and teaching in Madrid. She traveled up to Galicia to join us and became our interpreter as well.

Matias, Lorenzo, and Juaquina had built a new, modern house for themselves on their property with money my father had been sending every month. For sixty years, the homestead had hardly changed, and then enormous change had come in the past four. We used Emilio's little movie camera to shoot footage of the family and their new house and sent it to my father when we got back home.

At the time, I was trying to stay fit by doing daily yoga sessions. One evening the family was setting up for dinner down in the vineyard near the old house. We were staying up in the new house and I hadn't done my yoga postures yet that day.

I told everyone, "I'm going to take this time to do my yoga."

My session went on for a while and worked its way up to a posture where I stood on my head. That was exactly when Juaquina arrived at the house to summon me down for supper. I could see her upside down in the doorway, her ruddy face inverted underneath her worn apron and sensible shoes.

She walked into the room and broke into applause.

"Bravo!" she cried. "Bravo!"

I flipped myself back to a standing position and rubbed my hands against my thighs. The blood rushed down from my face. "Thank you," I told her. "I'll be right down."

When I walked into the vineyard and joined the family at the table, they all started laughing, with Carmen chief among them.

"Carmen, *what* is so funny?" I asked.

She gasped for breath and sputtered, "Juaquina has been wondering all these years since she met you, and for the years she was hearing about you before then, about what you did for a living."

"Oh, really?" I said. I didn't have any idea what she was talking about.

"Yes," Carmen said. "She saw you up there and now she knows. She's convinced you're in the circus."

In the fifteen years since I'd left Dayton, I'd been able to see my father only about a dozen times: once soon after I left home, the next time with Janet after Emilio was born, then when he made that trip to New York after he retired, and once when he visited me on a set in West Virginia. Otherwise I would see him only when I could route a flight through Ohio on my way to or from a job in New York. That averages out to less than once a year, which doesn't sound like a lot, but it wasn't unusual for an adult in the early '70s who'd moved away from home and started his own family. Not many of my siblings had the time or the money to travel across the country for visits other than for holidays and special occasions, even when we wished we could go home more.

My father was living with my brothers Mike, Conrad, and Al in the little house he'd bought after he returned from Spain. On my stopover flights in Dayton I'd rent a car and stay at the house for a day or two with him and the boys, where it was easy to slip right back into the family life and join in on the jokes my brothers had going with him. They were like a bunch of rowdies, and he was so responsible that their constant banter was like watching the Marx Brothers engaging with their straight woman, Margaret Dumont. The brothers would poke fun at my father's tendency to elongate chores — it could take him weeks to paint the outside of the house because he so enjoyed the pure pleasure of the labor — but they'd also take care of him and make sure he got around town safely.

"Do you want a ride?" someone was always asking him.

"Oh, I donna wanta to trouble you," he'd object. It was like a little dance he did with us, every time.

"Come on, Pop, let me give you a ride," one of the brothers would insist.

"Oh, thanks," he'd say. "Nice of you."

Nice of you — the formality was one of his trademark phrases. When I came to town I'd give him a lift to Mass or to the grocery store and he'd always say, "Thanks, *Rrra-mon*. Nice of you." His gratitude was so simple and so sweet.

On one of my visits to Dayton I recruited my brother Mike as co-conspirator in a plan. I wanted to get my father on tape and have his voice for posterity. I'd brought a tape recorder with me, but I knew he'd never agree to speak into it. He was so shy he would have left the room or even the house if he'd seen it, so we had to record him clandestinely. The best time to do it, we figured, was when he was absorbed in a chore. He could never sit still, always had to be doing something, and he loved to talk while he did his tasks.

One night after supper in the kitchen, he was washing the dishes and drying them endlessly. Mike and I were sitting at the table while Pop was standing at the sink, and we seized the opportunity. We buried the microphone under a napkin and took turns yelling out questions so he could hear us over the running water.

"Pop, how did that happen?" I shouted, in reference to an incident from his childhood. Then Mike would make a comment about what we were talking about so we'd remember when we listened to the recording later.

I still have the tape. I played it for Emilio recently, and he was astonished. He hadn't remembered my father having such a strong Spanish accent. We could hear the noise in the background while he puttered around the kitchen, drying the dishes and putting them away. I'm grateful to have that tape now. That evening in the kitchen was one of the last times I heard my father talk.

The phone call came from my brother Frank on October 26, 1974. Janet took it on our kitchen wall phone. It was a Saturday afternoon and I wasn't home. When I walked through the door later that day, she broke the news to me gently.

My father had died? He'd *died?* It didn't seem possible. I'd seen him only three weeks earlier. He'd been admitted to the hospital with a heart problem but he hadn't seemed to be in crisis.

"Hey, you're looking good," I'd told him as I walked into his hospital room. It was the truth.

"Oh, *chhoney*, no," he said, flapping his hand against the air. "I'm notta feel well, because in here I to do this and I canta do that." He looked normal, sounded normal, and still had his spirit and his energy. No one had expected him to die.

When I said good-bye to him that day, I leaned down and kissed him on the head. "I love you, Pop," I said. It was the only time I ever kissed him or told him that privately. Three weeks later, I was glad I had.

I called Frank back in Dayton for the details. Four of the brothers — Al, Mike, Joe, and I — were now living in California and I started planning how to get us all home to Ohio for the funeral. At this time in our family, I was the one who had accepted the responsibility and had the means to step forward and bring us all together in emergencies. The rest of the family knew they could depend on me and I took the responsibility seriously. Even when I was drinking I had that sense of duty in tough situations. Maybe that was one of my father's legacies to me.

The plan was for the four of us to ride in the same car to the airport, get the airline tickets, and fly home to Dayton. On the day of our departure, the phone in our house rang again. This time it was Donna Lopez, one of my sister Carmen's oldest and dearest friends from childhood, who now lived in New York. Carmen was set to fly to Dayton for the funeral by way of New York, but she'd had a medical emergency on the airplane from Madrid and had been taken straight from JFK to a hospital in Queens. The doctors thought it might be food poisoning, but nobody knew for sure.

The gears in my mind starting turning in the opposite direction. No more Dayton — now I had to figure out how to get to New York. "You stay with her tonight and I'll be there tomorrow," I told Donna.

I changed my airline ticket and sent the brothers to Ohio without me. I would go to New York to look after Carmen and then meet up with everyone else in Dayton in time for the funeral. It wasn't an optimal plan, but it was a plan. And this was a family emergency.

By the time I got to New York, Carmen was out of intensive care but was still weak. She'd been diagnosed with a tubular pregnancy and had lost a lot of blood. She was so relieved to see me that I knew I had to stay with her. I found a hotel room walking distance from the hospital and settled in.

Every day, I'd call home to Ohio. "How's it going over there?" I'd ask.

"How's it going over *there?*" they'd say.

The brothers were delaying the funeral for me and Carmen to attend, but it was becoming clear that Carmen wouldn't be well enough to go. After a few more days it became clear that I wouldn't be able to, either.

"You guys should go on with the funeral without us," I said. As much as it pained me to miss it, we all had to get back to our respective homes and jobs. Further delay wasn't practical. Funerals are for the living, not the dead. We'd already lost my father, but Carmen was still in need.

A few days after the funeral, Mike and Al flew to New York. I left Carmen in their care and returned home to California. Seeing Janet and the kids so healthy and vibrant after I'd been dealing with a death in the family and a medical emergency made me grateful for all we had. Still, I cannot deny that missing the funeral left a giant hole in my heart. I didn't get to mourn my father or grieve with my siblings or to say a proper good-bye as the casket was lowered into the ground. I was left with an angst that, once I reentered the fray of work and the routine of family life in California, I had no chance to explore.

■ ■ ■ ■

My father never got to see *Badlands,* which went into wide release about the time he was admitted to the hospital and passed away. I would have liked for him to see my performance, which I've always felt was one of the best of my career. I know he would have been proud.

The critical response to *Badlands* was overwhelmingly positive. Terry Malick was heralded as a genius, and rightly so; the film was lauded as a hauntingly beautiful, warped fairy tale. The *New York Times* called Sissy Spacek and me "splendid" in our roles. Still, opportunities did not immediately come pounding on the front door. At thirty-four I was starting to feel like my time to break out of the pack was passing. Other actors, the ones I admired most and thought were the most talented of my generation had all advanced careerwise; I felt I was equally talented and, while I confess to a large measure of envy at times, I was far more confused and left to wonder, *Why can't I get the big jobs?*

That's a big reason why I drank. Alcohol allowed me to feel and do things I didn't have the courage to feel and do when I was sober. Often when I got a few in me I would get in people's faces, get self-righteous and accuse them of dishonesty, when in reality I was the one who couldn't be honest with myself. Or I'd go off on an arrogant tangent that became increasingly heightened and absurd. When I drank, I was an angry, terrible bore.

Thank God for Janet. The kids could always trust her to be honest and reliable.

There was one great benefit to drinking that I wasn't ready to give up. Back at the Living Theatre in New York, I'd discovered that I could use alcohol to help me draw on the range of emotions that actors need to feel. When I was drunk, I was more sensitive and less inhibited, more open to this abundant pool of sense memories. I would weep a lot when I drank and feel sorry for myself, and this became an easy ticket to the emotional well when I needed to get there on stage or on camera. Sometimes I went on stage after a few drinks, but I knew how much I could drink before I lost it, and I kept enough control to always stay on the safe side of that self-imposed limit. Or at least I thought I did.

When I was in character, this felt acceptable, as if alcohol were a legitimate professional aid, but off stage and at home my drinking only fed my insecurities and self-pity. It fed right into my sense of "poor me" and I thought it gave me license to misbehave. It was so easy to make excuses for myself to myself, like *Oh, hell, I'm drunk. They'll understand.* Sometimes they did. More often they didn't.

Fortunately, I took acting too seriously to ever let drinking get in the way of my work. In 1974 and 1975, I acted steadily in some very fine television movies. I played an army deserter with a death sentence in *The Execution of Private Slovik,* a Robin-Hood style bank robber in *The Story of Pretty Boy Floyd,* a hot-rodding vigilante in *The California Kid,* Attorney General Robert Kennedy in *The Missiles of October,* and an escaped mental patient who kidnaps Linda Blair in *Sweet Hostage.* Then in early 1976 I was cast in *The Cassandra Crossing,* an ensemble film produced by Carlo Ponti. It was scheduled to shoot for three months in Europe. Janet and I took the kids out of school in January and headed to the first location in Basel, Switzerland, for one very cold week and then to Rome for three months. We rented an apartment in the Pinciano district north of the city, a short drive from Cinecittà Studios in southeast Rome where all of the interiors were shot.

Among the last of the 1970s disaster flicks, *The Cassandra Crossing* was in the spirit of *The Towering Inferno, The Poseidon Adventure,* and *Earthquake.* It told the story of a deadly virus introduced onto a train full of innocent people traveling across Europe and of the passengers' mad rush to save themselves before a U.S. government agency could destroy the train. My character was the younger lover of a wealthy German diva played by Ava Gardner. He was also, as it was revealed late in the film, a heroin smuggler being pursued by O. J. Simpson, who played a U.S. narcotics agent disguised as a priest. My character got to trade blows with O.J.'s before flying off the side of a moving train to his death. And that wasn't the half of it, for that film.

The Cassandra Crossing may not have been one of the best movies ever made but it was the most fun I'd ever had on a set and one of the most talented casts I've worked with. In addition to Ava and O.J., there were also Richard Harris, Burt Lancaster, Lee Strasberg, and, in the role of heroine, Carlo Ponti's wife — the legendary Sophia Loren. The kids would come onto the set and not recognize anyone except O.J., who was still playing football for the

Buffalo Bills at the time. Ava Gardner took a special liking to them. She didn't have children of her own but she loved spending time with ours, and they responded to her almost as a special aunt. She developed a close bond with Ramon that lasted until her death in 1990.

Rome's Cinecittà Studios lived up to its name. Cinema City was the crucible of Italian filmmaking and a draw for American filmmakers as well. *Roman Holiday, La Dolce Vita, Ben-Hur,* and *Cleopatra* had all been filmed there. With twenty-two stages on nearly a hundred acres, multiple movies would always be shooting at the same time. While we were doing *The Cassandra Crossing,* Federico Fellini was a few sound stages over shooting *Casanova* with Donald Sutherland in the lead role. Emilio would meet me for lunch at the commissary and Sutherland would be there outfitted in a long powdered wig and the ruffles and buckles of an eighteenth-century Venetian dandy. Max von Sydow would show up in military uniform shooting *The Desert of the Tartars* and we'd sit with Sophia Loren in full makeup and O. J. Simpson wearing the black-and-white Roman collar. Just eating lunch at Cinecittà was like being inside a Fellini film.

The Cassandra Crossing was set to wrap on schedule in April, right after Easter. One weeknight before Good Friday, our apartment phone started ringing in the black dead of night. I rolled over and looked at the clock: 3:00 a.m.

I stumbled out of bed and into the living room, which held the apartment's only telephone. The line crackled with the static of an international connection.

"Hello?" I said.

"Please hold for a call from the United States," a voice said.

Then — "Marty? Fred Roos calling."

I rubbed my eyes to wake myself up. Fred Roos was a producer who worked with Francis Ford Coppola.

I'd met Coppola briefly in New York in 1968 when he was making *The Rain People.* I was one of a group of up-and-coming New York actors he was trying to get to know. I'd seen him again in February 1971, this time with Roos, when I did a screen test for *The Godfather.* I was in the middle of shooting a TV movie in L.A. that had been shut down by the Sylmar earthquake. The shutdown gave me a few days to fly to New York for the screen test, but I couldn't cut my hair or shave my mustache, which I would need when filming resumed, so I did the screen test playing Michael Corleone with long, scruffy hair and a mustache. I knew immediately that I was wrong for the part but I knew someone else who'd be an exact fit.

"You know, my friend Al Pacino is perfect for this role," I told Coppola. "If you don't use him for Michael it'd be like benching DiMaggio in his prime."

"I know," Coppola agreed. "I want Al but the studio doesn't. That's where I'm at."

I don't know how they resolved that difference, but one Academy Award and two sequels later, Pacino proved to be the best choice by far.

Coppola was now in Southeast Asia making *Apocalypse Now,* a film about the Vietnam War. I'd heard that Steve McQueen, Al Pacino, and James Caan had all turned down roles. It seemed that nobody wanted to go to the Philippines for four months. They must have known something I didn't.

Harvey Keitel ultimately was cast in the lead role of Captain Benjamin Willard, the army captain sent up the Nung River to assassinate Colonel Kurtz, a Special Forces operative who'd gone rogue. Filming had started in the Philippines months ago, but now Roos was calling me in Italy, in the middle of the night. How had he even gotten my number at the apartment?

"Listen, Francis would like to see you. What's your schedule?" he asked.

He didn't say what Coppola wanted, but when the director of *The Godfather* asked for a meeting, it was in your best interest to take it.

"As a matter of fact, I've got Good Friday, Saturday, and Easter Sunday off," I said.

"All right," Roos said, and that was it.

When I got back to the bedroom, Janet was awake. "Who was it?" she asked.

"Fred Roos."

"What did he want?"

"They want me to come to the Philippines and do *Apocalypse Now*." I don't know where that knowledge came from. Roos hadn't said anything of the kind, but nonetheless those words came tumbling out into the darkness of our bedroom.

"He said that?" Janet asked.

"No," I said. "But I know that's what it's about."

Sure enough, Roos called back the next day. "We can arrange a ticket to Los Angeles," he said. "Can you come?"

"I will," I said. I figured I could fly back to Los Angeles, stay in Malibu for Easter weekend, and then turn around and return to Rome for the last few days of filming the following week.

I got on a plane two days later — me and the four giant duffel bags I was lugging home for the family. In Basel we'd bought ski clothing for all of the kids, and as I prepared to leave Rome Janet said, "As long as you're going home, I'll pack up the kids' heavy stuff and you can bring it all back. That'll save us from having to take everything with us when we leave next week."

"Good idea," I agreed. So we bagged up four enormous duffels full of winter clothes. I checked them at the airport in Rome, retrieved them from the carousel at LAX, and dragged them over to the customs line. My instructions were to meet Fred Roos outside of customs and then he'd take me to the Philippine Airlines lounge, where Coppola would be waiting to meet me before his return flight boarded for Manila.

The customs officer looked at my forms and motioned me to a side table. He opened the bags and pawed through the piles of children's winter clothing.

"Are you opening a haberdashery?" he said.

"No, of course not," I said.

"Then what are you doing with all this clothing?"

"These are my children's clothes," I said.

"Where are your children?" he asked.

"They're still in Rome. I'm traveling alone."

With that, the officer escorted me into a small room where an interrogation began. I couldn't believe it. Did they *really* think I was trying to sneak in used kids' clothing from Europe to sell in the United States without declaring them to customs?

The answer, it became evident, was yes.

I answered all their questions, but it didn't seem to matter what I said. An hour and a half passed. I couldn't get out of customs, and if you can't get out of customs you can't get into the country. Meanwhile, Coppola was sitting in the Philippine Airlines lounge with his own clock ticking. His flight would be boarding in thirty minutes.

"Look," I said. "The clothes aren't even new. They've already been worn." I opened a bag and pulled out a sweater with a small hole in it, and a pair of pants streaked with stubborn dirt. "If you want to keep the clothes you can keep them all. I don't care."

That finally convinced the officer, who released me from the room. I lurched out of customs dragging my four gigantic bags of children's clothing and practically collided with Fred Roos in the receiving area.

"Francis is up in the lounge," he said,

ushering me along. "The driver will stay with the bags. We have to run!"

We took off toward the Philippine Airlines lounge. If we'd had the kind of airport security then that we have now, I never would have made it in time. I still had the collar-length hair of a heroin-smuggling lothario and by then I'd played any number of bank robbers, kidnappers, and degenerates on the run from the law. But this was real life — no cameras, no lights, no mics. Just me and Fred Roos racing across the international terminal of LAX hoping to make it to a meeting that could potentially change the course of my life and most certainly my career.

Like action heroes, we burst through the doors of the Philippine Airlines lounge. And there was Francis, sitting calmly in an armchair across the room.

"I've been waiting for you," he said.

"I'm sorry," I said, trying to catch my breath. "I got stuck —"

"Yeah, I know," he said, cutting me off. "Look, I just wanted to see you. You know I'm in the Philippines and I'm doing this film. We're having some problems. When are you finished in Rome?"

"Next week. Just a few more days of shooting, that's all." I'd heard his film was regrouping but beyond that, I didn't have a clue what was going on.

We made some small talk and then he said, "Okay. We'll be in touch." And he left.

That was it. The whole meeting lasted fifteen minutes tops, and he was on his way back to Manila. I didn't know what to make of any of it.

I turned to Fred Roos. "I have a script for you," he said, "and I want you to read it as soon as you can. Okay?"

"Okay," I said. Fred gave me the script and said, "I'll be in touch."

Then he left and the driver took me and my four duffel bags back to our house in Malibu. My body was still on Italy time, exhausted but too revved up to fall asleep. I sat in the backyard and read the script. I still hadn't been told what part I was being considered for, but I had a suspicion that it might be for Captain Willard.

I put the pages down on the table and thought about all this. I was thirty-five and in reasonably good shape despite a two-pack-a-day smoking habit, but I was still more than a decade older than kids in their twenties who'd been in Vietnam. Though I'd played soldiers before — in *Catch-22* and *The Execution of Private Slovik* — I'd never played a soldier in active combat. My younger brother John had been a Marine Corps medic, but I didn't know the first thing about an M16 or a .45, both of which the script called for the character to use as effortlessly as a third arm. The role was an enormous opportunity I knew I couldn't pass up, but I honestly didn't know if I could pull it off convincingly.

Roos called me at home the next day. "Did you read it?" he said.

"I did."

"Would you like to do it?"

"Of course." There was still no confirmation of the role, but I knew. It was Willard. It *had* to be Willard.

"We'll call you in Rome," Roos said.

The next day, Easter Sunday, I boarded a return flight to Rome with the first-class ticket Coppola's production company had bought for me. On the plane I sat down next to the actor Martin Balsam. We knew each other from *Catch-22* and we talked all the way to Italy.

"There's a chance I'll be going to the Philippines in a few days to work on Coppola's current movie," I said.

"Really?" he asked. The film's production woes had been covered in the U.S. press for the past few months, but I hadn't seen any of it in Italy. Marty probably knew more about the film than I did at that point.

At the airport I met up with our Italian driver, Carlo, who brought me down to the seacoast. The family was staying in a little cottage there on the beach for Easter week.

"How'd it go?" Janet asked when I arrived.

"Well, I don't know," I said. "We'll see."

Roos called again the next day, just after we returned to Rome. "Can you be in the Philippines this Friday to start shooting?" he asked. He confirmed that Keitel had been let go and they wanted me to replace him. This meant some scenes would have to be reshot and the production was already running over schedule. I was asked to commit to sixteen weeks in the Philippines, which would bring us right to the end of summer.

"I'm not too old for the part?" I asked.

"The guy's a captain. He'd be older than the rest of the soldiers. We don't want someone who looks twenty-one."

Good point, I thought. Maybe I could be a convincing captain, but I still didn't know if I could endure the physical rigors of sixteen weeks of shooting in the jungle.

"I finish here on Wednesday," I said.

"We'll have to speak with your agent to work out the deal."

That's when things got complicated.

Francis was asking for either five-year personal contracts or a commitment of seven movies with his company from his principal actors in *Apocalypse Now,* with the right to use us in future films for a predetermined salary. Later Francis told me this was because his films had turned a good number of unknown actors into major stars and when he wanted to work with them again he couldn't get them signed without breaking the bank.

"You're going to be a star after this," he told me, "and I don't want to have to go through hoops or go broke to get you to work in another film. I'm just protecting myself."

Most of the young actors on the film had already agreed to this deal, but it didn't make sense to me. Why should an actor my age, with a large family, agree to such a deal? On the other hand, this was the opportunity of a lifetime. Francis Ford Coppola was the most brilliant and successful director on the planet.

"Okay," I said. "We'll make a deal."

I would have been honored to work for Francis anywhere, at any time, on any film, and would have considered myself fortunate to have had such an opportunity, but I simply could not feel forced to do so. My agent negotiated throughout the entire filming period and even long after filming concluded, but we just could not reach a mutually satisfactory agreement. Consequently, I never signed a contract for *Apocalypse Now,* not even to this day.

Meanwhile, back in Rome, shooting wrapped on *The Cassandra Crossing* and Janet and I went to the Rome airport together and said our good-byes. Everything had happened so fast we didn't have a plan beyond me heading to the Philippines and her heading back to Malibu with the kids. I boarded a plane to Bangkok with a connecting flight to Manila, and she and the kids boarded theirs to Los Angeles.

A day and a half later I landed in Manila, where Ferdinand Marcos, a corrupt and crafty dictator, was in power and martial law had been in effect for nearly four years. Soldiers with M16s slung across their shoulders patrolled the airport. The city was under curfew from midnight to 4:00 a.m. every day. But the heat, the extreme poverty, and the pollution made the biggest impression on me as I rode from the airport to the high-rise Manila hotel.

That first evening I placed a call to Janet to let her know I'd arrived safely. In 1976 you had to call the operator to request an overseas line and then wait for her to call back with a connection. When Janet answered the phone, it was the middle of the previous night in Malibu, and the phone woke her.

I'd never placed this much time or distance between me and the family before and it was unnerving to know we wouldn't even be sharing the same day on the calendar for a while.

"What's it like over there?" Janet asked.

"It's very hot, so we won't need any of those winter clothes for the kids," I joked.

The next day, April 26, 1976, I boarded a small private jet with Francis for a twenty-minute flight to Baler, a coastal village 140 miles northwest of Manila on the Philippines's main island of Luzon, and began the most extraordinary and challenging adventure of my life. If I had known what lay ahead for me in the coming year, I would surely have "let this cup pass." Yet life is a progression in a series of mysterious and personal choices that invite us to accept the cup as offered, not altered, although I could not have articulated it this way at the time. All I knew was that I had to embrace whatever was coming if I was ever going to become my true self. I just didn't know how much *Apocalypse Now* was going to speed up that process.

CHAPTER EIGHT: MARTIN

PHILIPPINE ISLANDS AND MALIBU, CALIFORNIA
1976

The very first scene I filmed for *Apocalypse Now* took place in Baler, when I hopped out of a Huey helicopter with actors Sam Bottoms and Fred Forrest. With M16 rifles in hand, we ran along the beach tracking after Robert Duvall. It was the middle portion of the most memorable sequence in the movie, sandwiched between an air cavalry assault and a napalm drop on a tiny Vietnamese seaside village, all to accommodate an ideal surfing opportunity for Duvall's Lieutenant Colonel Kilgore and his "boys."

The scene on the beach was organized chaos, with Hueys taking off, landing, and kicking up sand as they deposited swarms of GIs; loud incoming mortar rounds exploding regularly all over the beach; thick multicolored flare smoke drifting through the action; oppressive heat from the fires, the choppers, and the sun; and several hundred Vietnamese men, women, and children streaming up and down the sand playing captured Vietcong and North Vietnamese regulars and displaced refugees. The noise was deafening, visibility was limited, and acting was impossible. In fact, no acting was required. We only had to show up and be engulfed in the intensity of the situation that surrounded us.

On the very first take of the scene, while racing along that beach under those circumstances, I stumbled over my own combat boots and fell face first into the sand, embedding the sight of the M16 into my left cheek.

This is not starting off very well, I thought.

A number of similar complex combat action scenes are spliced throughout the film, but that first one is paramount, at least for me, because it set the tone and defined the boundaries of my life for the next year.

Janet joined me in Baler, but soon afterward the vicious Typhoon Didang struck Luzon, wreaking havoc. We waited out the storm in Manila as it pushed out into the South China Sea. Then we drove to Iba on the west coast of Luzon with the rest of the cast and crew to resume production. Suddenly, and unexpectedly, Didang (now known internationally as Typhoon Olga) reversed course and slammed back into Luzon with 115-mile-an-hour winds and three solid days of torrential rain. Tragically, the storm took more than two hundred Filipino lives, caused disastrous flooding, and left many thousands homeless. Most of the film sets were destroyed as well, so Francis shut down production for two months and sent everyone home.

The film was now six weeks behind schedule and $2 million over budget, and it was becoming clear that the sixteen weeks I had signed up for were going to extend, by necessity, far longer. How much longer, nobody knew. But I was relieved to be getting a break from the storm and the intensity of the whole situation. I now had a much better idea of how huge the scope of this film was, and no amount of training or planning could have prepared me for what I'd found. Some valuable time at home would help me acquire at least the basic skills I needed to return. Janet, too, had been ill prepared, but now she had a clear idea of what we needed to bring back with us next time given the possibility of natural disasters, and especially if we wanted to return with the kids. Our game plan, not necessarily in this order, was:

- Order sixty cases of bottled water and

have it shipped to the Philippines ahead of us.

- Ship sixteen boxes full of spaghetti, oatmeal, Cream of Wheat, parmesan cheese, and other nonperishable foods that were hard to find over there. (We must have spent nearly all I'd earned so far sending boxes of food and cases of Evian and Perrier into the Philippine jungle, but it was worth it.)
- Learn what a soldier did in Vietnam, how he did it, and why. I had to get proficient with all the weapons. Just the sight of them made me nervous.
- Above all, learn how to swim.

That last one was crucial, given that most of my scenes took place on a boat. The first day we'd filmed on the navy patrol boat, I'd stepped on board, looked around, and asked, "Where are the life jackets?"

Some of the crew members laughed, thinking I was making a joke, but they didn't realize I didn't know how to swim. The boat would get top heavy with so many people and cameras on board, and the diesel engine broke down all the time. Nothing about that boat felt safe.

Back in Malibu, I hired Rob LeMond, the local swim instructor who'd taught the kids how to swim, and he started taking me out in the ocean with an inner tube for lessons. Francis also hired a Vietnam veteran to train me as a soldier. I opened the door one day to a dark-haired, broad-shouldered former airborne ranger with a handsome Irish mug and a New York accent standing on my front step.

"Hi, I'm Joe Lowry," he said. "Nice to meet you."

I led him through the house and out into our backyard to show him where our training could take place. It was a big, flat open space facing north with the Santa Monica Mountains barely visible in the distance.

"Oh God," he said. "This looks just like where I got shot."

Thus began one of the great friendships of my adult life. Born in Boston and raised in Brooklyn, Joe was a meticulously precise, fiercely loyal, and scrupulously honest aspiring actor and musician who'd been wounded very badly during his tour in Vietnam. His eleven-member unit had been out on patrol when they walked into an ambush. Only two survived. Joe was shot up his right side from his calf to his face. It took several years of surgery and convalescence before he was able to walk again.

For the next four weeks of private boot

camp in our backyard, Joe taught me how to hurl a six-inch bowie knife into a tree trunk from a distance of thirty feet and how to throw a hand grenade with equal accuracy. He taught me how to break down an M16 and a .45 automatic pistol, how to shoot them — without live rounds, of course — and how to use an M79, a small grenade launcher I had to fire in the film. I learned how to oil, load, and reload each weapon without a flaw. By the time Joe was done with me, I could take the .45 apart and put all nine pieces back together in under two minutes.

"You're an officer and I'm going to be your sergeant," Joe Lowry told me. "So you call me Sergeant, I'll call you Captain, and I'll show you how to be a soldier in the ranks and what to do in the field, starting with the morning report."

Every morning when he arrived he greeted me with a "Good morning, Captain." Then he brought his hand up to his forehead in a crisp half salute.

"Good morning," I would answer.

"No, no," he would say, "Good morning, *Sergeant*. And you have to return my salute. If you don't I have to stand here with my hand up like this until you return it or until you leave. That's standard military procedure."

Eventually I got the hang of it. Good morning, Captain, Joe's half salute, Good morning, Sergeant, my full salute, then Joe would complete his salute and we could get down to the business of that day.

This was June of 1976. The kids were just finishing up their school year and our plan was to take them back to the Philippines with us when shooting resumed at the end of July. There was some slight hesitation from all four of them but Emilio in particular was concerned about being back in time for the start of the new school year in September. A conscientious student and an athlete with a close-knit group of friends, he didn't want to miss any of the ninth grade.

"Dad," he said. "Please promise me we'll be back in time."

"You'll be home when school starts," I said.

I wasn't lying. I also wasn't in a position to promise anything of the kind. The shooting schedule was far out of my control. Once we touched ground in the Philippines, it was going to take however long it took to finish the film. *What if it becomes twenty weeks of shooting instead of sixteen?* I thought. *So what? What's another month?*

"Give me your word that I'll be back in time to start school," Emilio pleaded. He was so serious, and it meant so much to him. I didn't want to disappoint him.

So I gave him my word. What else could I do? I just didn't realize how hard it would be to keep it.

CHAPTER NINE:
EMILIO
PHILIPPINE ISLANDS
1976

The flight from Los Angeles to the Philippines seemed eternal, eighteen hours inside the tube of a Philippine Airlines DC-10 with a layover in Hawaii. When the six of us finally landed in Manila the calendar date was two days after we'd left. Crossing the international date line, a whole day had vanished. Just like that: gone.

The driver who met us at Manila International Airport loaded us and all our bags into the car for the two-hour trip south. We were headed to the town of Pagsanjan, where the production had moved its headquarters and where many of *Apocalypse Now*'s major sequences would be shot. On the way to Pagsanjan we passed rice paddies, roadside stands made from palm fronds, water buffalos grazing, and countless small fires burning in nearby fields. Some looked like garbage piles that had been set ablaze. In other places, mounds of freshly cut brush crackled with flame. In the middle of the ride, I opened the car window and the smell of fresh smoke filled the air.

Our driver took us up a mountain road and then to the shore of a lake. The film company had set us up at a resort on the other side. We took a short motorboat ride to get across and got out to survey our new temporary home. We'd been to Hawaii for vacation and this place had the same kind of tropical vibe: dense vegetation, high humidity, buildings with thatched roofs. The communal dining hall was a big open-air structure where the incongruous "Rocky Mountain High" played on an endless Muzak loop. *They must really like John Denver here,* I thought. Our cabana had a living space and two small bedrooms with bunk beds for us kids. The place wasn't elegant but it was beautiful and comfortable and more than adequate for a fourteen-year-old boy.

As the rest of the family settled into the cabana I headed outside to explore. White orchids, red hibiscus, and coconut palm trees decorated the lawns. Another boy my age, an actor in the film, was also staying at the resort. His name was Laurence Fishburne — he was going by Larry then — and he was there with his mother, Hattie. He was playing the part of Tyrone "Mr. Clean" Miller, the youngest crew member on the navy patrol boat (PBR) that takes Captain Willard, my father's character, up the river. Fishburne, or "Fish" as I came to call him, was a tall, skinny, fast-talking city kid dressed in the uniform of fourteen-year-old boys nationwide: T-shirt, jeans, and white Pumas with a red swipe. He was smart and hilarious and right on it and reminded me of kids I'd gone to school with in New York. I immediately felt a kinship with him.

Checking out the resort together we discovered little motorboats that guests could use for bass fishing and touring the lake.

"Let's take one," we decided.

Being two kids from New York City and L.A., we didn't know much about motorboats, but the outboard engine seemed straightforward enough. Pull the cord and start it; doesn't get easier than that. We cruised out into the middle of the lake and kept going. Near the other side some reeds were sticking out of shallow water, and that was where the boat slid into a thick patch of mud and the engine stalled.

We tried the pull-start to get it going again. It choked a little but didn't catch.

We tried again. Still nothing.

"I'll get out and push us back to the middle of the lake," I offered. "Maybe we can get it started there."

The water didn't look deep so I jumped over the side. Very bad plan. I hadn't considered how deep or how thick the mud at the bottom might be. My ankles immediately started sinking, and the suction was so strong I couldn't pull either foot out. I slowly sank deeper. It was like quicksand.

I'm in trouble, I thought, as I grabbed on to the rim of the boat. *I'm going to drown.*

Laurence peered over the side. We'd known each other all of thirty minutes and now he was going to be the sole witness to my demise.

"I don't know, man," I said. "I'm going down."

So fast there wasn't even time to think about it, Laurence reached behind me with one arm, grabbed me with every ounce of strength in his 120-pound frame, and pulled me up and into the boat. I couldn't believe how strong he was and how fast and sharp his survival instincts were. He may actually have saved my life that day. That experience bonded us forever, resulting in a friendship that's lasted more than thirty-five years.

After a few days, my mother decided that

ferrying four kids back and forth across a lake to get to and from the set had reached its limit. About ten minutes away on the shore of a picturesque volcanic lake, Lake Caliraya, was a gated summer community, a private retreat for the Philippine rich and elite, with modernized cabanas and immaculate grounds. Marcos himself stayed there sometimes. The film's producer, Gray Frederickson, had a cabana there as would Marlon Brando, who was scheduled to arrive in early September. Marlon was the big name in the film but my father was the leading man, and my mother pulled whatever strings she could and probably a few more to get us into the same place as Marlon.

As my father says, "Tell Janet no, and she'll find a way."

Thanks to my mother's persistence we wound up with two adjacent cabanas down near the lake, one for me, Ramon, and Charlie, and one across the porch that Renée shared with my parents. On the outside, the cabanas looked like authentic native huts but inside they had most of the comforts of home. We converted one bathroom into a makeshift kitchen and laundry facility. Every few days a woman would come to wash our clothes and lay them outside to dry. We'd come home from the set to find our shorts and T-shirts stretched across the grass like colorful two-dimensional lawn ornaments.

Soon after we'd moved into the new place, my mother's provisions arrived from the States. I went out to the road to help shuttle the boxes across the lawn. Twenty of the sixty cases of water had gone missing — broken or stolen, we never did find out. That left fifty-six boxes in the truck. I was awed by the amount of stuff my mother had managed to ship 7,000 miles across the Pacific. *How did she organize this?* I wondered, grabbing a box and hoisting it onto my shoulder. Even at fourteen I could appreciate the logistical effort it took to bring a family of six to a developing nation for the summer.

Just then the sky opened up and it started to *pour.*

This was the end of July, still monsoon season in the Philippines. I'd never seen rain come down so hard. The raindrops were enormous and hit the ground with force. Even more remarkable was how the locals kept going about their regular business in the downpour. The truck drivers kept shuttling boxes from the back of the truck across the lawn to our cabanas as if they barely even noticed the rain.

I swung my box down onto the porch of our cabana and headed back to the truck. The lawn was already so saturated at that time of year that it started flooding almost immediately. Back and forth between the truck and the cabanas, the drivers and I sloshed across the grass with boxes balanced on our shoulders, drenched straight through our clothes, until all of the boxes had been safely delivered.

On August 3, a Tuesday morning, a partial crew assembled in downtown Pagsanjan. Set designers had converted an upstairs room of a two-story gray courthouse to resemble a room in the Saigon Hotel for what became the opening scene of *Apocalypse Now*. In this scene, Captain Willard has returned to Vietnam after a brief and turbulent visit to the States and has holed up in his hotel room, smoking and drinking himself into near oblivion while he waits for his next assignment.

The day and night of filming there has since become the stuff of legend. It was my father's thirty-sixth birthday and he started drinking that morning to celebrate. By midday he had become so drunk that he miscalculated a punch in front of a mirror and broke the glass at close range, tearing open his thumb. He'd gone so deep inside his character that he had retreated to a place where no one could reach him. Francis tried to stop the cameras but my father insisted they keep running, intent on publicly purging whatever demons he was confronting in that room. You can see the raw footage in *Hearts of Darkness,* the documentary about the making of *Apocalypse Now.* It's a brutal five minutes of film.

Earlier that same day my mother and I had been on set to watch another scene being filmed, in which two servicemen knock on Captain Willard's hotel room door with his orders to report to Nha Trang for a briefing. Finding him drunk and disoriented, the GIs drag him into the shower to clean him up. In the film that scene appears after Willard punches the mirror, but the shooting schedule that day called for it to be shot first.

My mother and I stood behind the camera operators to watch the filming. The actor who handed Willard the letter from COM-SEC headquarters was nervous. In each take, every time he pulled out the letter his hand would shake uncontrollably. You can actually see it in the finished film.

Why is this guy so nervous? I wondered. *What is there to be so nervous about?* I had a lot of time to wonder that day. The edited version of a movie always looks like nonstop action, but the majority of time on set is spent standing around. There'll be a fast flurry of activity, followed by more waiting, followed by another setup and another take of the exact same shot, and then more waiting. Years later I would work with a first assistant director who described it perfectly when he said, "It's not the time that it takes to take the take, it's the time in between the takes that takes the time." (Try to say that ten times fast.)

The hotel room set that day was small, crowded, and humid. The lighting equipment made the room unbearably hot. After a few hours of watching everyone else do their jobs, my mother and I got restless and headed into town to do some shopping. Toward the end of the afternoon we received word from one of the film's producers that we needed to get back to the set. My dad was in a bad way, the producer said.

He didn't say what he meant, but I could guess.

I can see myself now, a blond fourteen-year-old boy rushing across town with his mother, darting between the three-wheeled motorcycles, scooters, and bicycles, coughing from the dust and smoke that hangs thick in the air. I follow her into the court-house and up the polished wooden staircase, around the corner and see —

What had been a semipristine hotel room set that morning is now a disaster zone. Bloodied sheets lie twisted across the bed, exposing the bare mattress. Empty alcohol bottles are scattered everywhere. My father is lying naked in the center of the bed. He seems to be holding himself together but then I notice a heavyset Filipino nurse bandaging his hand. Francis and his wife Eleanor are standing at the side of the bed with producer Gray Frederickson and some members of the filming crew. Whatever happened in here while I was gone wasn't good.

"All right, everybody!" my father shouts. His voice is husky. Loud, and slurred. "Let's sing again! 'Amazing Grace.' Let's sing 'Amazing Grace'!"

I know that voice. He's hammered.

"I'm tired of singing 'Amazing Grace,' Martin," Francis says. He manages to sound both patient and irritated at the same time. "We're not singing 'Amazing Grace' anymore."

My father looks up, sees me and my mother, and immediately changes his strategy. "Okay, then. Let's everybody hold hands and pray!" he shouts. "We need to confess our fears."

Those of us standing around the bed look at one another. I shrug. We take one another's hands. What else can we do? And so here we are — me, my mother, my father, Francis, his wife Ellie, the producer, and the Filipina nurse — holding hands around the bed while my father prays and leads us in song. The nurse prays out loud with him.

"Jesus loves you, Marty," she says.

None of this is nearly as charming to the rest of us as it seems to be to him. My mother and I have been called back to get him out of the room. We have a job to do.

"All right," my mother announces to him. "We're wrapping it up here." We pull my father from the bed and with no small amount of effort, guide his arms into a bathrobe. We get the belt tied around his waist.

I've seen my father hammered and out of control before. This isn't even the worst I've seen him. My mother and I manage to stay calm and deal with him. As we do.

Once we have him vertical, we're all faced with the challenge of getting him down the stairs and into the car without incident. There is no elevator, just the wide, public staircase of a government building. As we carefully lead him down, we can hear night court in session through an open door on the ground floor.

"I've got to go in there!" my father shouts, lunging for the doorway. I move fast and pull him back. As if this whole thing wasn't embarrassing enough, now we're going to interrupt a legal proceeding?

"I've got to go in there!" he shouts. He struggles against me, but with my mother on his other side, we're able to hold him back. "I've got to go in there!"

"Martin!" Francis says. "Why? *Why* do you have to go in there?"

"I've got to speak my piece! I've got to protest! If I don't, some poor son of a bitch is going to end up in front of a firing squad!"

"You're not going in there, Martin," Francis says.

Somehow we all get him onto the street and into the waiting car. More than an hour has passed since my mother and I arrived at the room. It's nighttime by now, and raining. Francis climbs into the car behind us, and our caravan takes off. Within minutes we're outside of town, enveloped by jungle on both sides of the road. The windshield wipers go back and forth, back and forth in the light rain.

Fishburne's mother Hattie has prepared a birthday dinner for my father, so Ramon,

Charlie, Renée, and Laurence are waiting for us at her house. I imagine them sitting around a table piled high with food, wondering what's taking us so long.

A few miles down the road, my father motions for the driver to stop. "I've got to take a pee," he announces. We pull to the side of the road. The jungle is dense, dark, forbidding. I hope he's quick about it. He gets out of the car and walks toward the trees but, instead of stopping at the jungle's rim, he spins around to face us.

"Ha-ha!" he shouts gleefully. Then he throws off his robe and takes off naked into the trees.

In seconds we're out of the cars and chasing him into the jungle. It takes half an hour to corral him and coax him back to the car. We stuff him into the backseat. The driver takes off for a second time. The wipers start swishing back and forth again.

Two miles down the road: "Pull over! I've got to take a pee!"

"You know what, Martin?" my mother says. She's exasperated, and who can blame her? We're all exasperated by now. "Piss in your hat."

Finally, we roll up to Hattie's house and herd him into the party. He bursts through the cabana door in his bathrobe, grabs a chicken leg from the table, and takes a huge bite. "Ha-ha!" he laughs through a mouthful of meat. He is ravenous. He has no interest in going to sleep or sobering up. I'll never forget the looks on my brothers' and sister's faces, or on Hattie's and Laurence's, as they realized what was going on.

What happened that night was embarrassing and humiliating for me as a son, but today as an adult and as a filmmaker I can understand it. Aided by alcohol, my father had gone so deep inside his own pain that he connected with a source of universal suffering. There, weeping and bloodied, he found the broken places that existed inside of Willard. For those few hours, he and Willard merged and, by journeying into the darkness of his own soul, he discovered the madman inside us all. When Francis tried to stop the cameras, my father insisted on exploring that place. He had traveled into a realm beyond self and other, beyond reality and illusion, beyond duality. My father wasn't the first actor to get hammered and have a breakdown on set, and he won't be the last. He was, however, one of the few who had the courage to insist that his be filmed.

Francis and his wife Eleanor also had

brought their kids to the Philippines, and we got to know them well. Their oldest son, Gio, was a year younger than I was, Roman was eleven, and Sofia five. All of us kids were welcome on set for the scenes filmed on land, but there was either no room or no safe place for us on the boat or in scenes with helicopters. My father had an intense daily schedule with an 8:00 a.m. pickup time, and we didn't see him much during the first week of filming, unless we were on set. Standing around between takes, we became friendly with many of the crew members. Charlie developed an interest in special effects and makeup. Freddy Blau was one of the best makeup artists in the business. Some days he was responsible for making up hundreds of faces before a morning shoot. That summer he often let Charlie observe his work and even try it out. Charlie was particularly fascinated by how wounds were made. He would come back to the cabana at night with a big gash in his cheek or one eye hanging out of its socket. It was outrageous.

Francis wanted Gio to play a GI in the Do Lung Bridge sequence, which started rehearsing in early August. Gio asked if I'd like to be an extra, too.

Was he serious? Of course I did.

307

Back home at Malibu Park Junior High, I'd joined the drama club and done some small productions. I knew I wanted to act, and the chance to appear in a major Hollywood film directed by the most celebrated director in the world wasn't something to pass up. Also, standing around a set without anything to do gets boring, fast.

The Do Lung Bridge scenes appear at about the film's halfway point, when Willard and his PBR crew come upon a bridge under bombardment at night. It's the last U.S. Army outpost on the Nung River, a trippy, anarchic place full of spaced-out GIs with seemingly no one in charge. Strings of lights span the river as the boat approaches and pyrotechnics go off constantly throughout the sequence. To get the eight and a half minutes of footage used in the film required an arsenal of more than 500 smoke bombs; 1,200 gallons of gasoline; 2,000 rockets, flares, and tracers; and 5,000 feet of detonating cord.

We shot the scenes at a remote location along the Magdapio River outside Pagsanjan. A bridge had once been there before the Japanese blew it up in World War II, and the old concrete pilings were used as anchors for the bridge built on our set. Hundreds of extras were recruited, mostly

American expats living in Manila and some Vietnam veterans living off their military pensions in the Philippines. Students from the American School in Manila who were the sons of businessmen and diplomats were also brought in.

Every morning twenty of us in uniform would pile into the back of a military personnel carrier to be transported to the set. Glenn Walken, Christopher Walken's brother, was there, and so was an actor named Jack Thibeau, who would later appear with me in 1982's *Tex*. Riding over that first day, I noticed something unusual. Some of the extras were actors who were already done filming their scenes — actors who would have been able to find work back home — but they'd chosen to stay on as extras for twenty-five dollars a day. They hadn't wanted to leave.

Jimmy Keane was one of those actors. He'd played Robert Duvall's machine gunner in the beach attack filmed in Baler back in April. When Captain Kilgore steps into a chopper and asks, "How you feeling, Jimmy?" Keane yells back, "Like a mean motherfucker, *sir!*" which became one of the most recognizable lines of the film. Jimmy and my father became good friends on set, and he often came by our cabana for dinner.

Back in the 1970s and 1980s actors routinely committed to two or three weeks of rehearsal, sometimes without pay, before filming began. Now, however, it's more common for an actor to show up the day before shooting. For the Do Lung Bridge sequence even the extras had weeks of intensive training. Real drill sergeants on set taught us how to dig trenches and crouch in them, how to use automatic rifles, and how to wear our battle gear properly. We even went out on night maneuvers and staged night firefights using live blanks. An enormous amount of time and resources were put into making the sequence look authentic.

Back home, being fourteen meant playing soccer, learning geometry, trying to get a girl you liked to notice you were alive. There was a structure to each day and expectations were clearly defined. In the Philippines, a different set of rules applied, if you could call them rules at all. I'd just turned fourteen in May, which made me closer to thirteen than to fifteen, but in the Philippines I was treated like a man. After rehearsals we'd have to check our M16s with props but we'd wear our wardrobes home. Going to the bars in Pagsanjan with the other actors after work meant walking down the street in full battle gear. I was only about five foot six and wearing a uniform at least one size too big, but to the locals I looked like an occupier. "Hey, Joe! Hey, Joe!" they would shout, as if I were a serviceman from down in Subic Bay. That month, I learned how to drink like one, too.

Sometimes I'd come back to the cabana in military uniform and my mother would stop in her tracks.

"All these years I never wanted to see you go off to war, and now here you are," she would say. "Do you know how much this terrifies me?"

By the time shooting began, Gio and I had fully integrated into the group of extras, who treated us just like two of the guys. Very few of them knew I was related to Martin or that Gio was Francis's son. We were both trying to downplay the connections, wanting to blend in.

When the time came to film our scene, I was completely wired and ready to go. We shot at night, close to 2:00 a.m. Some nights we went almost till dawn, but I was never tired. Even if I had been, the flares soaring overhead and the explosions in the water would have kept me awake and edgy.

The set was a beehive of activity. Hundreds of extras and crew members swarmed in all directions among all the trucks and lights and cords. Luciano, the lighting gaffer, shouted instructions in Italian over a megaphone to his lighting crew. The air was heavy with humidity; hordes of insects buzzed around the light towers. Every now and then someone on the special effects crew fired a test flare and the whole set brightened for a second or two, then went dark again.

First assistant director Jerry Ziesmer walked over and started giving everyone instructions for the scene.

"Okay," he said to our little group in the trench. "I'm going to have you guys over here and" — he motioned to one of the extras — "you're on the machine gun. Some guy's going to get shot" — he motioned to Gio — "near you" — he motioned to me — "and I want you to scream, 'Medic!' just as Marty passes by."

"Okay," I said, nodding. It was perfect. My first film role had just been bumped up to a speaking part.

Ziesmer moved on to the next group of extras. A little while later, as we got closer to filming, I walked up to him. I wanted to be sure I had the instructions right. I didn't want to mess up my first speaking role.

"So when my dad runs past me, that's when you want me to scream for a medic, right?" I asked.

"Your dad?" Ziesmer said. "What are you talking about?"

"Well, Martin is —"

"You're kidding me!" he said. "What are you *doing* here?"

"I wanted to get my hands dirty. I wanted to play with you guys."

"Oh, for God's sake," he said. "Yeah. When your *dad* runs past you is when I want you to yell, 'Medic!' "

We got into position, someone yelled, 'Action!' and the cameras started to roll. The bridge was ablaze with white light-bulbs, and the special effects men and lighting technicians hovered way above us on platforms, swinging huge arc lights above the trenches. I looked up and saw my father run past at ground level. That was my cue.

"Medic! Medic!" I yelled. I yelled it once, twice, three times, for each take we did and redid.

This is so cool, I thought. *I'm going to be in this movie.*

Except . . . I'm not. If you watch that sequence in the film you won't see me or Gio in it anywhere. Nobody shouts for a medic in the final cut. My first speaking role, left lying on the editing room floor.

It happens. The real value was in the experience, and that's what remains over time.

By the time the Do Lung Bridge sequence finished, we were well into the second half of August. At home, school would be starting up again after Labor Day. I was beginning to wonder how I'd get back in time. Even I could tell that a lot of filming still remained. But my father had promised he'd have me back for school. He knew how much being there meant to me.

I *loved* school. I loved the ritual of it, the structure and the predictability. I loved studying and I loved reading. I wasn't getting any of that intellectual depth in the Philippines. Before we left Malibu I'd been writing for the school newspaper, involved in the drama club, playing on the soccer team, and making honor roll. Most important, that past June I'd been elected boy's vice president of the student body and I had an obligation to the school for the coming year. I'd already missed most of the spring semester when we'd been in Rome. I didn't want to miss even a day of ninth grade.

By the end of August, I thought, *Okay,*

this has been fun. This has been an experience. But now I'm ready to go home.

"Yeah, yeah, soon," my father said, when I asked about it.

"We'll be finished before long. Not to worry," he said when I asked again.

He held our tickets and passports. I couldn't go anywhere without them. It was an enormously frustrating position to be in. And a strange one, too. On set, I was surrounded by actors who couldn't get enough of the action in the Philippines and there I was, just wanting to get the hell out.

Then, on the last day of August, Marlon Brando arrived.

Here, too, the story of the film's production slides nearly into myth. Marlon showed up so overweight that the character of Colonel Kurtz, the rogue army captain who had set up his own violent, lawless compound in the Cambodian jungle, had to be reconceived. Francis spent days reading Joseph Conrad's *Heart of Darkness* out loud to him because it served as a template for the film and Marlon was supposed to have read it in advance but hadn't. He brilliantly ad-libbed most of his lines, but his tight three-week shooting schedule for a $3 million paycheck almost forced Francis into a state of scheduling and financial crisis. Having seen Marlon's work in *The Godfather,* which was practically required viewing for teenage boys back home, I knew that he was a legend. I also knew he was the guy who'd sent Sacheen Littlefeather up to refuse his Oscar for *The Godfather* in 1973.

Everyone on set treated him carefully, as a fragile Hollywood star, but to our family, he was just a kind, gentle actor staying in one of the cabanas up the hill. At dinnertime he would come down to our porch when he smelled my mother's chicken or beef on the grill. He probably came down as much for the company as for the food. "Where are you from?" "What are you doing here?" my brothers and sister would ask him, and we'd all sit around joking and sharing stories late into the night. He would light a single cigarette after eating, hold it aloft, and confess, "This is the only time I smoke. One a day."

When he fell ill, my parents sent him a case of Evian and a case of Perrier from our stash. They knew the local water could make you sick. "No one else thought of that," he said, which endeared my mother to him forever. He made sure a lei of fresh flowers was sent down to her every day.

With Marlon's arrival, the filming location shifted to Kurtz's compound on the river.

Production designer Dean Tavoularis and his team, along with six hundred Filipino laborers, had constructed the immense temple ruins from the ground up out of 300-pound dried adobe blocks. They used photos of Angkor Wat for inspiration and created a gorgeous, mysterious imaginary world. I loved everything about that set.

Kurtz's army of native Montagnards were played by more than 250 Ifugao tribespeople who'd been brought down from the rice terraces of a northern province. They were related to the real-life Montagnard forces that American forces had encountered in Vietnam. Within days they set up stilt houses with bamboo floors and created a temporary village adjacent to the set, complete with their own pigs. They helped build props for the film, like the cage in which Willard is imprisoned by Kurtz's loyal followers, and made handicrafts to sell. Their ingenuity using the jungle resources was completely natural to them but remarkable to me.

I was there the night they sacrificed a water buffalo by hacking off its head with four brutal blows, images that were used in the movie's final cut. Most viewers think the slaughter was orchestrated for filming purposes but it wasn't. The Ifugao themselves chose to do this tribal ritual, led by their native priest, and the cameramen spontaneously decided to capture it on film. I saw the whole thing. The animal went down in minutes and several tribespeople stripped and gutted it right away. They scooped the blood from the carcass into a yellow plastic bucket and gave the tail to the children to play with. It was horrifying and fascinating at the same time, primitive yet reverent, painful to watch but impossible to turn my eyes away from.

When you spend weeks on a single set, whether it's the Do Lung Bridge, Kurtz's compound, or any other location, you dig in for a while. It becomes your home base and the cast and crew form a temporary family. The longer the filming takes, the more apparent this becomes. We were at the temple ruins for almost a month. After a while, everyone on set talked freely around me, as if I were one of the team. The crew was having difficulties with Marlon's weight and the delays on set that resulted while he and Francis sat together fine-tuning his lines. "We're trying to figure out how to shoot him," I'd hear, or "We're waiting for the same light as yesterday to reshoot the scene." I was privy to some of the crew's decision making and watched how they solved problems on the spot, and I absorbed it all. It was an extraordinary film education for a junior-high-school kid to receive.

Still, I would rather have been back home, at school.

"Yeah, yeah," my father said when I asked again in mid-September. Gio and Roman had already flown back to San Francisco to start their school year on time. Mine was starting that week in Malibu without me. "We're getting around to that. Not to worry," he said.

Many of the compound scenes were rehearsed and shot during the day, leaving the actors with free time at night. By then, everyone was settled in and knew they'd be there for a while. The crew was staying at a hotel in downtown Pagsanjan, where they held Ping-Pong tournaments at night. Charlie and I entered, and I held my own for a while but a sound mixer named Nate Boxer was an amazing Ping-Pong player and always beat the hell out of everyone.

The demands of my father's role and the logistics of family life in a jungle were stressful, and my parents were trying hard to hold everything together. Between the emotional pressures of playing Willard and the plentiful alcohol, my father was trying to stay alive, and my mother was trying to keep him alive; that's no exaggeration. As a result, I went unsupervised much of the time. Looking back, I can see how this might make them look like neglectful parents, but I never felt that was the situation. Because I was the oldest and most independent of their four kids, they trusted me to be responsible.

On his nights off, Fishburne and I would sometimes take off for Manila by ourselves. We'd catch a ride in a jeepney, a form of local public transportation that's like a cross between an army jeep and a psychedelic Guatemalan chicken bus. In the capital we'd check into the Manila Hilton for the night, eat dinner at Pizza Hut, and drink beer without being asked for ID. Then we'd wander around and wind up racing back to the hotel at 11:59 p.m. to beat the midnight curfew imposed by martial law. You didn't want to get caught out on the street after curfew by a grim-faced soldier with a machine gun strapped across his back. And yet none of this felt dangerous or even risky. It had actually started to feel normal, which reveals just how crazy the situation was at the time.

The Manila Hilton was the only place where I could get an outside line to make telephone calls to the States. I'd have to ring the operator to request an international call.

"Hold on, sir, I'll call you back when I have the connection."

I'd go to sleep and the phone would ring two or three hours later in the middle of the night.

"Please hold. I have your call to the United States, sir."

"What's going on?" I'd say groggily, when I heard a friend's voice. "Remember me? I'm still alive." They were sixteen hours behind me, still living in my yesterday, but I was the one missing out on everything. The calls were expensive and I had to keep them short. A minute, two minutes, that was all we could talk.

On the nights we didn't go to Manila, Fishburne and I often could be found together in Pagsanjan. He and his mother lived in an apartment there with two bedrooms where I was always invited to sleep over. It was easier to go there from the set than back to our cabana at the lake.

One night Fishburne and I went out for dinner at the crew's hotel in Pagsanjan. We were joined by Dennis Hopper and an Asian journalist he was trying to seduce. Hopper had arrived just a week or two earlier. He was a force unto himself, like a frenzied molecule bouncing off everyone who stood near him, and he injected a big dose of hilarity and playfulness onto the set. Hopper was there to play the manic American photojournalist who runs down the steps to greet Willard and his remaining PBR crew when they glide up to Kurtz's compound. He became notorious for not knowing his lines and making some of them up. His ad-libbed scenes with Willard, in which he describes Kurtz as a brilliant madman, show traces of his own mad genius.

"You can't travel in space, you can't go out into *space,* you know, without like, you know, with fractions," he tells Willard when the captain is being held inside Kurtz's compound. "What are you going to land on? One-quarter, three-eighths? What are you going to do when you go from here to Venus or something? That's dialectic physics. Dialectic logic is there's only love and hate. You either love somebody or you *hate* 'em."

That night at dinner, the four of us — Hopper, Fishburne, the journalist, and I — are sitting in an outside dining area eating our food. Suddenly, and out of nowhere, two well-dressed men climb over the fence between the garden and the restaurant and walk up to our table. One of them is balancing a wooden board with cheese, crackers, fruit, and an enormous knife on top. The other is holding a bottle of wine.

What? I think. *Who* are *these guys?* They're totally incongruous with the surroundings, more like a pair you'd see at a wine tasting in Napa.

One man is very blond, the other dark haired. Of course they recognize Dennis right away.

"I'm John from America," the blond man introduces himself. "Mind if we join you?" They sit down without waiting for an answer.

Now it's the six of us. I look at the two men. I feel the distinct energy of something weird about to go down, but I can't get a grasp on what it will be. The scene is too confusing. Dennis is trying to get it on with the journalist and Fishburne starts talking to the dark-haired man when, apropos of nothing, the blond man announces that he's an assassin.

What?

He calmly turns to Dennis. "I'm an assassin," he repeates, "and I've been sent here to kill you."

A long pause settles over the table. I glance at the enormous knife lying on the cheeseboard. I'm fourteen, Fishburne is fifteen, and Hopper is . . . Hopper. He's sitting there in his photojournalist costume, with the knotted red-cloth headband and the olive-green shirt and pants and all those beaded necklaces. He hasn't taken it off the whole time he's been here, and by now it stinks. Still, why the hell would anyone want to kill Dennis Hopper?

Dennis breaks the silence with a laugh. "Yeah, yeah," he says. "Whatever, man." He turns his attention back to the journalist.

It's clear this wasn't the response the American was expecting. It only makes him more insistent. Dennis acts even less interested, if that's possible. Then the woman excuses herself to use the restroom, and Dennis gets up and follows her.

The dark-haired guy tosses his napkin on the table and stands up. He's not going to let Dennis out of his sight.

Great. Now it's me, Fishburne, and this blond man, John from America, who may or may not be an assassin. Either way, he's crazy. He has to be. You don't just announce out loud in a restaurant that you're an assassin, and you definitely don't announce it to the guy you want to kill.

Fishburne turns to the blond man. "Listen, man," he says, in a calm, measured tone. "I'm not letting you kill Dennis Hopper."

I feel my eyes go a little wider. Fishburne's from a tough neighborhood in Brooklyn. He's probably no stranger to confrontation or men with weapons. Still. He's *fifteen.*

"I have this knife," the blond man says. I glance at the long blade. He does, in fact, have that knife. "And I can do it if I want."

What the hell am I doing here? I think. *This is all going so sideways.* The skin on the back of my neck starts to crawl. Night maneuvers for the Do Lung Bridge scenes were nothing compared to this.

Fishburne and the blond man go back and forth for a while: "You're not killing Dennis Hopper." "I can do whatever I want." *"You're not killing Dennis Hopper."* "Oh, yes. I am."

Where did Hopper *go?* Not that he was a help, but there might be some safety in numbers.

Finally, Fishburne looks the blond guy right in the eye. He breathes in, and out. "You can take that knife and you can stick it in my heart," he says. "Or we can be friends."

Wow. The two of them sit there face to face, eight inches apart, their eyes locked. It's a showdown. I don't know who's going to win.

The guy sizes up Fishburne and realizes he's serious.

"Let's be friends," he says.

And that was it. I couldn't believe Fishburne had defused the situation that fast. Whatever admiration I already felt for him increased sixfold that night.

The story should end there, with Fishburne's heroic gesture, but it doesn't. The next day, while the rest of the family is on an outing, Charlie and I are hanging around together outside the cabana. We notice a man at the end of the dock where the boats come in. He's throwing a knife into the wood at his feet. It looks like he's doing a practice maneuver. Throw the knife, *boom,* pull it out, throw it again, *boom,* pull it out. The blade pierces the wood perfectly, sticking upright each time. The man knows how to handle a knife. I'm watching him, not quite understanding, and then he looks up.

It's John from America.

I know that guy, I think. *I know that knife. We've got to get him out of here.*

I quickly tell Charlie what happened the night before. He's only eleven, but he gets it. He completely freaks out. Now we both know this guy could be dangerous.

If I turn him in, I wonder, will that make me a target as well? Does it mean he'll come back and try to get all of us in the middle of the night? My mind clicks through the options. Isn't it better for the police to deal with him now rather than me having to deal with him in the middle of the night? There's no security at the compound. Anyone can walk right up to our cabana, at any time.

"The hell with it," I tell Charlie. "We're calling the cops."

I call the front desk from our room. "There's a strange man who says he's an assassin here to kill Dennis Hopper and he's on the dock throwing a knife," I say. I can tell how ridiculous it sounds, but I can't take any chances. Marlon is staying in the compound, too, and this blond guy is a threat.

Ten minutes later, the police show up and take him away. I heard they detained him for questioning and then let him go. It turned out he was a banker with a strange story about being on our dock. Maybe he was having a psychotic episode in the jungle. Or maybe he really was an assassin, an operative, or mercenary. Really, he could have been anyone. He was mysterious, ambiguous, unhinged. He could have stepped right out of Francis's script.

Seven hundred kids were enrolled at Malibu Park Junior High that fall. Six hundred and ninety-eight of them had shown up when

327

the school year started. The other two, Ramon and me, were stuck here in this jungle. September was almost over, and by now I'd missed two weeks of the ninth grade. My worry started turning to panic.

"You *promised*," I reminded my father.

"Yeah, yeah," he said. "We're getting to that."

Fishburne's mother, Hattie, tried to homeschool us so we wouldn't fall behind, but our little school failed, through no fault of hers. I didn't want to do lessons in the Philippines, I wanted to do them back in Malibu with my friends. And there were too many distractions pulling my focus away from school. A couple nights a week I was going out with crew members to a house called Dampa in Pagsanjan. "Dampa" means "hovel" in Tagalog, and this place fit the bill. It was a toilet, literally: The bathroom had a drain that ran right through the center of the restaurant. Downstairs was warm San Miguel beer, Boz Scaggs singing "Lowdown" on the jukebox, and local girls who worked as prostitutes sidling up to the Americans at the bar. That's where I'd spend some of my weeknights, drinking warm beer, smelling urine, and doing what everyone else was doing upstairs. It was madness, and I knew it.

I didn't even care anymore if the family came back to Malibu with me. I'd go alone if I had to.

"Yeah, yeah. Sure, sure. We're getting to that. Soon."

What was it going to take to be heard?

As September turned into October, I felt my worry turning to anger. *Enough already,* I thought. I'd spent most of my childhood following my father to locations, leaving my friends behind, having to adjust and readjust to school after months away on the road. I understood my father's desire to keep the family together at all costs. I truly did. But I had obligations back home. Didn't he realize that?

Equally important, I had started getting scared of what might happen if I stayed. My behavior had gotten reckless and crazy and I didn't feel grounded anymore. The jungle had started getting to people and not in a good way. Days earlier the prop guy had taken my mother aside and said, "Get your children out of here," because it had started to feel as if anything might happen. People were drinking heavily and doing drugs. An exhilarating form of darkness seemed to have penetrated everyone on set. The heat, the drugs, the pressure, the chaos — it felt like our own little Vietnam. Jimmy Keane took some photos of me at that time, and at fourteen I already looked like a tired old man. Miserable and unhappy. A part of me had started thinking I might die there in the jungle if left to my own devices for much longer. I needed to get out, to save myself.

By the middle of October, a month into the school year, I'm ready to make my move. My father comes back from the Kurtz compound set one night. I'm waiting in the cabana to confront him.

"Not to worry . . ." he begins, but I'm not taking that for an answer. Not anymore.

"You're a liar!" I explode at him. "You promised I'd be back for school and the clock's ticking. This isn't just about you! I've got to get home!"

"But I can't do anything about it," he protests, his voice rising to match mine. "I'm not in control of —"

"You gave me your word!" I shout.

"I'm not in control of the schedule! Can't you see this from my point of view? I'm carrying the weight of this enormous —"

"You gave me your word!" Helpless and furious, I'm weeping and screaming. I drag my arm up across my eyes to wipe away the tears.

"What the hell's the *matter* with you?" he yells. "For God's sake, can't you be a good sport about this?"

A good sport? A good *sport?* He lied to me and he won't even admit it. He lied to me *and* he's being dishonest. I don't know which is worse.

"I'm *out of here!*" I shout defiantly. I don't know how I'm going to leave on my own, but I'll find a way. I'm going home. That's all I know.

"You're not going anywhere! You're staying right here!" he hollers back.

When my father rages, he can *shout.* But I've been holding my rage in for a long time, and tonight the lid is off. His rage doesn't compare to mine. Not even close.

"You lied!" I roar. "You lied!" I charge at him in a blind fury. He grabs me in a restraining hold, and suddenly — *thwack* — we're both down hard on the wood floor, wrestling for our lives. He's strong, but I am, too. We kick and roll around, giving it everything we've got. My head knocks against a plank on the floor. I throw him off me and tackle him again.

"You lied!" I shout.

Coming from behind us, I hear a rapping sound, knuckles against wood. Someone's at the door? Then more knocking, louder this time.

"What's going on here?" a low, calm voice

asks. "Is everything all right?"

We look up from the floor. It's Marlon peering in through the door screen. Shit. He heard us. I notice all the cabana's windows are open, covered only by thin screens. *Shit.* That means *everyone* in the compound has heard us.

My father and I both rise slowly, brushing dirt from our clothes. "It's fine," my father tells Marlon. "Everything's fine."

Our fight that night remains one of the lowest points in our relationship. It was the only time we ever came to blows. The explosion was terrible but in retrospect, necessary. It showed me how determined and how strong I was as an individual. It also helped my father understand I was no longer a son who would quietly follow him everywhere he needed to go. I had a life that extended beyond the family now and a right to participate in it.

A son's struggle to free himself from a father's influence can be a messy job. He has to push against the father's authority to come into his own. The father's struggle is no less difficult, but his is an internal one. He has to be willing to let the son separate and become his own man. Trying to hold on only stifles the relationship. It doesn't give it a chance to grow. But the son doesn't love or respect his father less for letting go of him. He winds up loving and respecting him more.

With my mother's help, my father realized the time had come. As much as he wanted to keep the family together, as much as he wanted to hold on to me for longer, he knew he had to let me leave. I said my good-byes to Laurence, to Jimmy Keane, and to Renée, Charlie, and Ramon. Within a week, I was on a plane bound for home.

CHAPTER TEN:
MARTIN
1976

Emilio was right. I had no intention of letting him leave the Philippines before production ended. Every time he asked me about leaving I offered up a vague excuse. I was stalling for time, and he knew it.

What were the options? I felt as if I were trapped inside an impossible dilemma. I couldn't go back to California with him in the middle of the shoot, everyone knew that. No one, me especially, had thought we'd be filming in the Philippines for this long. Now there was even talk about breaking for Christmas and returning in January with a smaller crew for the final sequences. That meant we wouldn't be done until next spring, possibly. For better or worse, I had an Old World belief that the kids were better off with me, wherever I was. If something went wrong with one of them I'd be there, and if something happened to me, they'd be there. *We're a family,* I told myself. *We have to stick together through this.*

But mostly, I would have done almost anything to avoid being in the Philippines alone. I was afraid that, if I let Emilio go, the other kids would want to follow, and then Janet would have to go with them. I'd been so unprepared for the experience on every level, from the abrupt departure from Rome to the physicality of playing the part to the realities of daily life in the jungle. It was an enormous film and I felt I had to carry the weight of it emotionally while all my weaknesses were exposed. And then there was my drinking, and my constant anxiety. It was a very risky situation for me and I couldn't trust myself to resist the temptation to drink and misbehave if I'd found myself alone. But I also knew it wasn't fair to expect Janet and the kids to stay just to keep me in check.

Emilio was right about this, too: It wasn't just about me anymore. When he shouted at me in the cabana, I knew he'd seen right through me. By focusing so tightly on myself I'd been ignoring him. I hadn't re-alized how much his routine had been disrupted and how much he needed to get back to his own life. I had such a singular focus on myself and my career, I just as-sumed the kids would adjust and make friends in whatever new environment we brought them to. I didn't pay much attention to how they were getting along or if they were unhappy. I just assumed that as long as they were with Janet and me, they were fine. Again, I didn't make any plans. And this time, it showed.

Instead of being honest with Emilio about going home I kept pushing his needs aside as if they were less important than mine. When the ego gets involved to that degree, the outcome is rarely good. It's no wonder we came to blows that night. Emilio was blaming me, I was blaming him, and there was nowhere else for us to go. When he couldn't convince me to listen, he had to get my attention somehow. Taking a swing at me worked. It was an act born of frustration and desperation. He couldn't get me to notice his distress any other way.

It was so strange to find myself rolling around on the floor, wrestling with my oldest son. It's never a good idea to engage your children physically when they're angry and emotional, but Emilio was wailing and weeping, and I was trying to control him, to keep us both safe. We weren't punching each other and I wasn't trying to hurt him or conquer him. I was just trying to contain him. Then Marlon came down from his cabana at the top of the hill, asking, "What's going on here? Is everything all right?" He feigned innocence, but he was a father as well and knew exactly what was going on.

I was so embarrassed to be seen by Marlon in such a compromising situation that I stood up and ended the struggle immediately. If he hadn't materialized with his gentle inquiries, I don't know where we might have ended up. We were both so angry and out of control it took someone from the outside to break it up. Marlon never even came into the room. He didn't have to. Just seeing him at the door brought us to our senses.

Not long ago, at my oldest grandchild's graduation party, I saw a father in the audience interacting with his two young sons. The older one was about thirteen and the younger maybe ten. The older son had been playfully taunting his father all afternoon. He was brushing against him, swatting at him, and pulling on his shirt. "What do you want?" the father would ask, and the son would say, "Nothing." Then a few minutes later he'd start playfully swatting his father again. The father was a good sport about it, but eventually he started getting annoyed.

And I thought, *Oh dear, no. Just receive your boy.*

Boys who have good relationships with their fathers at that age challenge the fathers in many subtle ways — emotionally, intellectually, and sometimes physically. It's not an affront to the father because he's always going to win a physical contest. But the boy has to know the father is receptive to this kind of play. It helps him come into his own as a man and to start exerting his independence from the father. It's almost a tribal rite of passage, part of the initiation by which a boy becomes a man.

The physical part of this relationship is important. Fathers and sons need to brush up against each other, whether it shows up as a friendly slap instead of a high five, or the son choosing to tackle the father during a football game instead of tagging him. It's personal, it's direct, and it's meaningful for both males. I received this from all three of my sons at one time or another during their adolescence. For example, on the basketball court they would slam into me unprovoked. I would see it coming and brace myself. It always carried a sense of, *Look out! It won't be long before you won't be able to whoop me!*

The thirteen-year-old boy at the graduation who was swatting at his father was doing it out of affection. He was saying, *Give me my attention as a man now. I'm no longer a little boy. You used to pick me up and hold me. Now I just want to be able to playfully challenge you and know that it's okay.*

Because the father is the last line of authority before the son goes out into the world, the son has to learn from him that he's capable of dealing with other male adults with confidence on every level. If he doesn't have that confidence, everyone notices that he's psychologically wounded. All his insecurities, all his imperfections become apparent. Such men project their darkest fear-based secrets when they go out into the world and their weaknesses are clearly visible. Bullies who persecute weaker kids have often been bullied or persecuted themselves, usually by a male head of the family. The message the bully has received is "This is what you have to do to get along in the world," and he does unto others as has been done unto him. But if a boy is allowed to be physically playful with the father without fear, to trade punches with him, to arm wrestle with him, to bang into him on the basketball court or roughhouse around without being punished, to have no fear of physical contact with a male authority figure — this helps create a healthy child who doesn't become aggressive. On the contrary, he becomes compassionate and confident. That unique type of male physical attention is necessary to foster confidence and growth in a boy, but it can happen only if the father is aware of this and able to respond.

In my thirties, as the boys were coming into their teens, I was still primarily focused on my career and my own needs. The night when Emilio came at me in the Philippines was a startling revelation. He had discovered how dishonest I could be and how hurtful that was. He made me realize he'd reached an age where he needed something different from me. He didn't need my approval or my protection the same way he once had. Now he needed my blessing. He needed me to allow him to separate and stay connected at the same time. And he needed my honesty. He needed me to be empathetic, just, and fair.

Unfortunately, his needs came at me at the most vulnerable period of my life. It's difficult to convey what it was like performing in that film, at that time, in that place, to travel emotionally deeper and deeper into the heart and mind of an assassin and to do it under the pressure of being over schedule, over budget, and at the breaking point of physical endurance. At some level, I suppose, art became life and life became art and I started losing sight of which was which.

All of us did, I think. That was part of the brilliance of the film, no doubt, but it came at a great cost to those of us involved. In 1978, when *Apocalypse Now* was screened at the Cannes Film Festival, where it shared the prestigious Palme d'Or prize, Francis told the audience, "My film is not a movie. My film is not about Vietnam. It *is* Vietnam. It's what it was really like. It was crazy. The way we made it was very much like the way the Americans were in Vietnam. We were in the jungle, there were too many of us, we had access to too much money, too much equipment, and little by little we went insane."

When you lose a sense of the border between reality and illusion, you enter a different state of being. I would retreat into the mindspace of Willard for days or even weeks at a time, and I know that had a negative effect on everyone I loved at home. I think especially of the impact it had on the three boys, who were moving into and through their teen years right then. A son who doesn't get the special blessing he needs from his father, that he can get only from his father or father figure, will go looking for that validation elsewhere. He'll have to go outside the family to learn he's a worthy individual, that he's cherished and loved. I got that blessing from my father through actions rather than through words. Still, I got it. Did my three sons get it from me? And what about Renée, the youngest and the only girl? What was her inner reaction to all that went on and what were her needs? Only they could answer those questions, and I had to allow them to do so, in their own time. But if they were going to challenge me in the same manner as Emilio, I had better be more prepared.

Passport photo of
Francisco Estevez

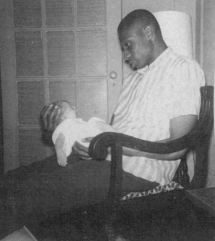

John Crane, the best man
at Janet and Martin's wedding
and godfather to Emilio and
Ramon, 1962, New York City.
Photo by Janet Sheen.

Christmas with Martin and
Emilio, New York City, 1966.
Photo by Janet Sheen.

Emilio, Charlie, Ramon, and Martin, at Janet's mother's house in North Benton, Ohio, 1968.
Photo by Janet Sheen.

Martin, Emilio, Ramon, and Charlie on the set of *Catch-22,* Guaymas, Sonora, Mexico, 1969.
Photo by Janet Sheen.

Emilio and Ramon, running toward the camera, on location for *Catch-22* in Rome, Italy, 1969.
Photo by Martin Sheen.

Emilio in Uncle Matias's
vineyard, Galicia, Spain, 1969.
Photo by Martin Sheen.

Emilio, Uncle Lorenzo, and
Ramon, Galicia, Spain, 1969.
Photo by Martin Sheen.

Cross-country trip, Emilio
sleeping in the back of
the Ford Wagon, Charlie
looking into the camera,
1970. Photo by Janet Sheen.

Emilio and friend,
grade school,
Tucson, Arizona,
on location for the
movie *Rage*, 1972.
Photo by Janet Sheen.

Gomby the Tiger
and Martin outside
Martin's on-set hut
for *Apocalypse Now,*
the Philippines, 1976.
Photo by Janet Sheen.

Martin with PBR crew:
Frederic Forrest,
Laurence Fishburne, Sam
Bottoms, and Albert Hall,
Apocalypse Now, 1976.
Photo by Janet Sheen.

Emilio and Martin on location
in the base camp hut,
Apocalypse Now, 1976.
Photo by Janet Sheen.

Martin with Ifugao
tribespeople,
Apocalypse Now, 1976.
Photo by Janet Sheen.

Laurence Fishburne throwing a
baseball, *Apocalypse Now,* 1976.
Photo by Janet Sheen.

Denah Harris, ACSW, New York,
family therapist and lifelong
friend, New York City, 1977.
Photo by Janet Sheen.

Martin and Emilio,
Hotel Plaza Athénée,
Paris, France, 1977.
Photo by Janet Sheen.

Martin in India, location
of the film *Gandhi,* 1981.
Photo by Emilio Estevez.

Martin and Uncle Matias
in Galicia, during the third visit
to Martin's father's home, 1983.
Photo by Ramon Estevez.

Martin at a nuclear testing
protest in Nevada, 1987.
Photo by Renée Estevez.

Emilio with daughter Paloma
in Malibu, California, 1988.
Photo by Janet Sheen.

Emilio with son Taylor
in Malibu, California, 1988.
Photo by Janet Sheen.

Martin, Charlie, and Ramon on the set of the movie *Cadence,* in Kamloops, Canada, 1989. Photo by Martin Sheen on timer.

Emilio and Martin on the set of *The War at Home* in Austin, Texas, 1995. Photo by Janet Sheen.

Martin, Taylor Estevez, and Paloma Estevez in costume on the set of *Bobby,* Los Angeles, California, 2005. Photo by Janet Sheen.

Emilio and Taylor
on the set of *The
Way,* Spain, 2009.
Photo by David Alexanian.

Martin and Emilio on
location for *The Way,*
Muxia, Spain, 2009
(the final scene).
Photo by David Alexanian.

EMILIO

When we announced that we'd be shooting in northern Spain for forty days in September and October, ten out of ten Spaniards told us we were out of our minds.

"It won't rain frequently," they warned us. "It'll rain *every day.* And if it doesn't rain every day, it'll rain twice a day." They told us we'd be lucky to get half our filming done in that time. "Make the film next summer," they said. "Make it next spring," but we couldn't wait till then. We already had everyone on board for the fall, and we had to do it then, rain or shine.

Since leaving St.-Jean-Pied-de-Port three weeks ago we've been moving steadily west along the Camino, and so far we've had only one day of rain. Taylor says it's the driest autumn he's seen in his six years in Spain. The Spanish crew says this weather is a minor miracle. Even more providential is that the day it rained we were scheduled to film an interior scene. We never had to go outside.

Today's forecast also calls for rain but the sun is shining brightly when we arrive at our location. We're filming in the town of Haro, in the northern province of La Rioja, known for its wine production. Haro is a few kilometers off of the Camino and for today's shoot we've chosen a *bodega* — the local word for winery — that frequently attracts pilgrims. Bodega Cune dates back to 1879 and has buildings and wine cellars positioned around a courtyard. The layout is reminiscent of a small town square, which is the look we're going for. The sequence calls for Tom and his small band of fellow travelers to stop at the *bodega* for a few bottles of wine, where Tom gets drunk and airs his grievances against the others. He becomes so loud and disruptive that the local police cart him away.

At this point in the film Tom is traveling with the three pilgrims who'll accompany him for the rest of his journey: Joost the Dutchman; Sarah the Canadian; and, most recently, Jack the Irish journalist who suffers from writer's block, played by the Irish actor Jimmy Nesbitt. I modeled the character after the author Jack Hitt, whose deeply insightful and hilarious 1994 book about walking the Camino, *Off the Road: A Modern-Day Walk Down the Pilgrim's Route into Spain,* was my inspiration as I wrote *The Way.*

We take some time setting up to shoot in the *bodega*'s courtyard, where Tom and Sarah have a scene at an old grape press. Deborah and my dad rehearse their lines and then nail the scene for the cameras. The next sequence calls for the whole group to sit together at a table in the courtyard, where relations between them start to get tense. We're just about to begin filming when the sky opens up and rain comes pouring down.

We chose this *bodega* also because it has partial cover, a feature that turns out to be useful. We move the shoot to a table on an open-air patio with a tiled roof, protecting us from the rain.

A director may wish to have a $100 million budget or six months to spend on location, but that's not usually the case. Instead he has to assess his situation realistically. "What are our resources? Who are the players? What are they capable of? Where is the setting? How many days do we have to shoot? Do we have a chance of making it work?" Independent filmmaking is a zero-sum proposition, which requires creativity.

After thirty years in the business I like that I can look at a scene and say, "On this budget, on this schedule, there's no way we can do it without sacrificing something else." The question then becomes, "If the scene is important to include, what are we willing to sacrifice to make it happen?" Directing a film is a series of constant compromises. Every day on set I have to ask, "What will this choice cost us?" Not necessarily in a financial sense, but what will it cost us in the long term, given our ultimate goal? My most important role as a director is to make sure the film's original vision isn't compromised.

So far, our experience with *The Way* has been different from any film I've made. It seems that every obstacle we've encountered somehow opens new and better doors. Maybe it's because this is the first time I've looked at events that can be considered an inconvenience and instead thought, *This could be an opportunity.* For example, we'd originally planned to film Tom arriving in Spain by airplane, but we couldn't get access to an actual plane. The only airplane offered to us looked like a shabby version of a 1970s Aeroflot jet and rented for 20,000 euros a day — the equivalent of $30,000 in

2009. There was no way we could make that work.

Thinking about other options, I realized it didn't matter whether we showed Tom arriving in Madrid by airplane or arriving in the Pyrenees by train, so we filmed the scene on a train coming into St.-Jean instead. The camera rolled as the train passed through a tunnel and captured beautiful footage of Tom's face emerging from the darkness and becoming bathed in sunlight. Then at the railway station in St.-Jean we were able to film real pilgrims getting off the train to start their journeys. We never would have gotten those images if we'd stuck with our original airplane plan.

Today at the *bodega,* our new and accidental set under the tiled overhang works even better than the setup on the grassy courtyard. On the patio, the four travelers have to sit in closer proximity, which makes for a more intimate exchange. For this scene my father, who hasn't had a drop of alcohol in twenty years, has to transform himself into a belligerent drunk. I can tell this scene reminds him of how he used to behave after having a few, and he's not happy about having to do it.

"Do we really have to do another take?" he asks. "It's so uncomfortable, and I'm so embarrassed. I just hate going there."

We need him to get the tenor of the scene just right, so I make him do another take. This is the only big, showy scene Tom has in the film, and I want him to nail it. The rest of his performance is so phenomenally restrained, it hardly looks like he's acting. When the dailies come back from Madrid each day, I see how much quiet dignity he injects into the role. The other actors have noticed it, too.

"Working with Martin is like taking a master class in subtlety," Jimmy Nesbitt says nearly every day. "It's a master class in not showing your work."

Of the four actors sitting at the *bodega* table, Yorick van Wageningen is the one who seems most like his character, the affable Joost. Joost's biggest downfall is food; he's walking the Camino to lose weight, but his quests for the perfect goat cheese and an exquisite plate of roast lamb keep getting in his way. Joost is actually modeled after a friend of mine, a boisterous winemaker from the Netherlands who has said some of the lines I gave to Joost, such as "We Dutch are always looking for the quickest way to get to the next party" and "If it ain't Dutch, it ain't much."

When David and I were casting for Joost,

we wanted to find a middle-aged Dutchman for the role. There wasn't a deep bench to choose from. Eight days before we were scheduled to start shooting in the Pyrenees we still didn't have a Joost, who, because he's the first fellow pilgrim Tom meets, needed to appear on our second day of filming. Dave and I were sweating about this in our hotel in Madrid, trying to figure out what to do.

"I found five guys on the Internet," he said at one point. "It's down to this. Pick one."

I looked at the options. "I like this guy a lot," I say, pointing to a photo of Yorick, who had a long résumé of film and TV work in the Netherlands. "Let's bring him in."

We made the arrangements for Yorick to meet us in Madrid the next day, where we waited for him at the hotel. Hours passed. No Yorick.

Then his agent called, apologizing. "We're so sorry," he said. "We thought you were in Barcelona. He can be in Madrid tomorrow. Please don't leave yet. Stay and meet him."

"All right," we agreed. Really, what else could we do at that point? We were now six days from shooting, and we still didn't have a Joost.

Yorick showed up in Madrid the next day, exhausted, disheveled, and contrite, dragging his suitcase across the plaza. Dave and I looked at each other. *Oh, no,* we thought. This didn't look good.

"Guys, I'm so sorry," Yorick said. "My gosh, I'm so sorry, the screwup. But it wasn't a total loss."

"Really?" Dave asked. "How so?"

"I had the most amazing lamb dish in Barcelona."

This time Dave and I looked at each other and smiled. We had our Joost.

In the *bodega* scene, Joost sits with Sarah and Tom while Jack stands at the head of the table, pontificating about the virtues of the "true pilgrim," one who lives off the land and eschews creature comforts. Tom, who by then has had one glass of wine too many, lays into Jack about being a "true fraud" on the Camino with his wallet full of credit cards. "Fraud!" Tom shouts hoarsely to the two police officers lounging across the street, "Police! Over here, gentlemen! Arrest this man for being a fraud!" As Tom becomes louder and more disruptive he slips and falls. The police officers rush over and, when Tom takes a swing at one of them, they cart him off to the station.

The police officers on film are real police officers from the nearby city of Logroño. They show up on set in their black and yellow Policía Local uniforms with the caveat that they can film only until noon because they go back on duty at 1:00 p.m. As skilled as they are at their jobs and as official as they look, it becomes clear that they don't know how to stage-fight, so my dad and I demonstrate how to duck a wild punch on screen. On duty, the officers probably would have used a baton against any pilgrim who tried to hit them, so teaching actual police officers how to avoid getting hit by my dad was an education in itself.

We get the shots of the officers lifting Tom from the ground, of him taking a wide swing that misses one officer's head, and of them leading him away. Then we move the set to the main police station in Logroño to film the officers bringing Tom in while Joost, Sarah, and Jack hurry behind them. The camera crew follows the actors through an archway and down the street while Tom, hands cuffed behind his back, struggles against the policemen as they lead him to the station. "I speak American!" he shouts. "God bless America! Call the American embassy! Tell them I'm being kidnapped on the Camino!" He breaks into a loud rendition of "God Bless America" as the officers force him through the station doors.

Townspeople and members of the local

press have lined up on the other side of the street to watch the commotion. They recognize my father from his role as President Bartlet in *The West Wing,* which began airing in Spain in 2003 as *El Ala Oeste de la Casa Blanca.* A local newspaper photographer snaps some shots of the policemen pulling my father down the street.

The next day's paper in Logroño features a photo of my father being led away in handcuffs under a headline in Spanish that says, "The President Is Arrested." We all get a good laugh from that one.

Seeing my father get hauled off to jail isn't uncommon for me. In real life he's been arrested sixty-seven times for demonstrating nonviolently for social justice and environmental causes. From his first arrest in 1986, when he demonstrated against President Reagan's so-called Star Wars program, which proposed putting nuclear weapons in space as a defensive shield, to the most recent one at Vandenberg Air Force Base in 2002, his presence has often turned an event into a news story. My mother and I would often see him on television, loudly reciting the Lord's Prayer or shouting the lines to Tagore's poem "Where the Heart Is Without Fear" as the police hauled him away. Many times he'd look like a complete lunatic, a man possessed, and at first I felt embarrassed to see him like that. I would shake my head, but over the years, as I watched him get arrested again and again, I started admiring him, not totally understanding and yet understanding at the same time. I came to realize that shouting those lines as he was being pushed into the back of a paddy wagon was an expression of both his commitment and his fear.

I participated in the grape boycott of the 1980s and I've come out for various environmental and social justice causes, but never to the extent my father has. By giving Tom this arrest scene in *The Way* I wanted to show a scene where an American who behaves badly in Spain, the typical Ugly American, gets his comeuppance. The scene offers instant karma when Tom emotionally levels his companions by telling them exactly what he thinks of each of them, only to be humbled almost immediately by the embarrassing arrest. The people he just railed against become the ones who bail him out of jail. In that moment, everyone realizes how much they need one another to complete their personal journeys.

This is a common story on the Camino: Many pilgrims encounter people they can't seem to get away from, but by the time they all reach Santiago de Compostela they've discovered the lessons they needed to teach one another along the way. From Sarah, Tom learns compassion; from Jack he learns honesty; and from Joost, kindness and tolerance. My father already has these personal qualities, and shedding them to play Tom, and then trying to acquire them anew for the camera, has been one of his biggest challenges in this role.

The rain stopped long ago and the sun hangs low in the sky. This day of shooting is drawing to an end. We don't know it yet, but this will be the last day of rain we'll encounter on this shoot. Forty days and forty nights in northern Spain in September and October with only two days of rain. If I didn't believe in miracles before, I would have to believe in them now.

CHAPTER ELEVEN:
EMILIO
1976–1977

When I returned home from the Philippines in October 1976, Mr. Thacker welcomed me back into the drama club. A slim man with short-cropped dark hair, some days he'd walk into our drama class in a dark suit with a white shirt and a tie. The next day he'd show up in casual slacks with Converse gym shoes and a floppy white hat. His first name was William and his wife was a home economics teacher: That was all we knew about his personal life, but he could get four ninth graders at Malibu Park Junior High to transform into completely different people using only an empty stage and two folding chairs for props. It was like magic to watch.

While I'd been gone, a ninth grader named Jeff Lucas, a wiry guy with wavy brown hair and a long, thin neck, had emerged as the most talented actor in our class. Like a throwback to another era, he was a master of physical comedy in the vein of Charlie Chaplin or Stan Laurel of Laurel and Hardy. In 1976, the year of Sylvester Stallone and Robert De Niro, Jeff's favorite actor was Rudolph Valentino. For Halloween, he dressed as Clark Gable. In ninth grade he was getting cast in every play, and I knew I could learn from working with him.

"Hey," I said to him at school one day. "I heard you're the actor guy here. Do you want to read some plays together?"

That was drama-class speak for "Let's play around with some characters, run lines, put something together for the stage." Mr. Thacker encouraged students to pick their own material, believing we'd have as much or even more passion for projects we chose as for ones that had been chosen for us. *Mad* magazine was wildly popular at the time and some of the drama students created parodies of films to perform on stage, but Jeff and I were more interested in classic and contemporary plays. My parents kept a stack of playbooks in the house from plays my father had done and ones they'd seen together, and I would leaf through them looking for scenes that Jeff and I could practice.

My mother had arranged for a woman named Mary Arnold to stay with me at the house until the rest of the family returned for Christmas. Peripherally connected to *Apocalypse Now,* Mary was the girlfriend of an assistant film editor and also the sister of Sam Bottoms's wife. She was only nominally in charge at the house, since there wasn't much to do other than cooking dinner. The school bus picked me up every morning and brought me back every afternoon and I spent weekends at the beach or making short films with my parents' camera and my neighborhood friends. The arrangement at home worked out well enough and after a few weeks my parents decided to send Ramon back to Malibu, too. That autumn we lived in our shared bedroom, did our homework, and watched television at night.

I was relieved to be home though of course I missed the rest of the family. I was right on the cusp of independence, functionally able to care for myself but still in need of minimal guidance and protection. The week I returned to school a girl I'd had a crush on in eighth grade — and still did — saw that I had hair growing on my chin.

"That looks terrible," she told me. "You've got to shave."

I hadn't even realized it was noticeable. Later that afternoon I found one of my dad's old razors in his bathroom and taught myself how to shave. Afterward, I rubbed the smooth skin of my chin. It seemed this was the kind of thing a father should teach a son but my father had never been the kind of dad who made a show of walking me through male rites of passage. We never talked about girls, never had the sex conversation or did a driving lesson together, though he did try to teach me — several times, without success — how to tie a tie. I wonder now if he was unable to hand down his knowledge effectively or if he was still very much a kid, like me. Somebody would have had to tell him, "It's time to have that sex talk now with your son," and he would have woken up and said, "Oh, I guess that's . . . is that my job?" Luckily I had my mother. Whatever keys to manhood I received during those years I either got from her or figured out on my own.

That's not to say my father wasn't affectionate. He was, greatly so, and much more than other fathers I knew. I once saw Steve McQueen drop his son Chad off in front of school. When they said good-bye, they shook hands. I stood on the sidewalk and cocked my head to one side. It seemed like such a disconnected, formal good-bye. That never would have happened in our family. My father would have hugged *and* kissed me. On the mouth. He didn't come from a family that showed physical affection, but when he was in high school he saw his friend's dad hug and kiss him good-bye and thought, *When I have children I'm going to always hug and kiss them. I'm going to make sure they know they're loved.* That year my father was 7,000 miles away from me, whenever I saw a father and son give each other a formal good-bye I would miss my bear-hugging dad powerfully.

We'd all hoped that *Apocalypse Now* would wrap before the holidays but by November it was clear that wouldn't be the case. The new plan was to break for Christmas and New Year's and then go back to the Philippines with a smaller crew. For the holidays we all met up in Hawaii, on the island of Maui. My parents, Charlie, and Renée flew in from Manila and Ramon and I flew in from Los Angeles and we all stayed in Hana for a week. Freed from the pressures of school and set, we could focus exclusively on being a family for the first time since we'd left for Rome nearly a year before. We stayed at the Hana Maui resort, which is a high-end destination now, though back then it was ramshackle and affordable and gorgeous, with bunk beds in the guest rooms and communal meals. Guests had to eat at designated times or they'd miss being served, and every day we'd come running from far-flung corners of the property, laughing, and scramble to get a table so we wouldn't overshoot the meal. My father remembers that vacation as one of the great weeks of his life, to be reunited with all of us in such natural beauty and to have such fun.

After Hawaii and a few weeks back in Malibu, my parents headed back to the Philippines in January for the third leg of filming. Figuring it would be for just another month or so, they decided all four of us kids should stay home and go to school. Joe Lowry and Jimmy Keane were also back in Los Angeles and they were recruited to help Mary take care of us at the house. From a one-adult, two kid household we'd now grown to a three-adult, four-kid mini commune. Advantage: kids. No doubt the adults started losing their minds trying to keep us all in line until my parents returned, whenever that would be.

That winter I immersed myself in drama club, appearing in the musical *Bye Bye Birdie* and other smaller productions. One afternoon at home I was looking through the stack of my parents' plays, searching for something Jeff and I could perform. I pulled a book of two Harold Pinter plays off the shelf, *The Caretaker* and *The Dumb Waiter.* A piece of paper fluttered to the floor. It had been tucked into the back of the book. *Dear Miss Templeton,* it began. It was a thank-you note from the actor Donald Pleasence to my mother. In 1961 she'd written him a fan letter after she and my father saw him star in *The Caretaker.* I thought, *Well, this must be a sign.* Settling on the couch, I flipped through the book.

The Caretaker was a three-act, three-character play about a mentally disabled man who lives with his brother and the homeless man he brings back to their house. *The Dumb Waiter* was a one-act, two-man play about two hit men waiting in a basement for their next assignment. That one had potential for me and Jeff. Before long, I was absorbed in the story of Ben and Gus, arguing in a basement while a dumbwaiter in the back of the room mysteriously kept sending food orders down to them.

The next day at school I sought out Jeff Lucas. "This Pinter play, *The Dumb Waiter,* it's a two-hander," I told him. "A small production. We wouldn't have to burden anyone. We could just put it on together."

"Great," he said.

Jeff took the role of Ben, the older, experienced hit man. I would play Gus, the younger protégé who annoys Ben with his running stream of questions. The play was quintessential Pinter: an absurdist plot with few characters set in a sparsely furnished room. It would be an easy one to stage.

For the next couple of weeks we rehearsed at Jeff's house. We rehearsed at my house. We ran lines during lunchtime at school. With only two characters carrying the action we had to memorize long passages of rapid back-and-forth dialogue. We rehearsed that play more than any other production I'd rehearsed to that point. We rehearsed it until I could practically recite Pinter's lines in my sleep.

During the day, the auditorium at Malibu Park Junior High functioned as both cafeteria and assembly room. At night it became a stage with audience seating for five hundred and a better than adequate sound system. It was an impressive venue for its time.

The Friday night that *The Dumb Waiter* premiered, I watched the students and their parents filter into the room and take their seats. Almost everyone I knew from school was there to see Jeff and me perform. I peeked through the curtain and saw Mr.

Thacker sitting proudly in the front row. Every Sunday when my parents called home from the Philippines, I'd talk with them about the play and how much I liked the language. They would want to hear a blow-by-blow of the performance. In two days I'd give them the full report.

Backstage, Jeff and I looked at each other and nodded. We were ready to go. We knew the play forward and backward by then, but still, my palms were sweating. The lights in the theater went down, and Jeff and I took our places on stage. Curtain went up, stage lights came on. And then it was just the two of us in a basement room, with Pinter's carefully scripted stage directions.

Jeff, as Ben, is lying on a bed, reading a paper. As Gus, I'm sitting on a second bed, unlacing my shoes. My character is supposed to be bothering him with the activity, and Jeff/Ben rustles the paper to show his annoyance. The audience sits quietly, watching us begin the scene without words. I walk off stage, and the audience hears the sound of a toilet trying to flush. When I return Jeff slams his newspaper down hard on the bed.

"Kaw!" he says. He picks up the paper again. "What about this? Listen to this! A man of eighty-seven wanted to cross the road but there was a lot of traffic, see? He couldn't see how he was going to squeeze through. So he crawled under a lorry."

"What?" I say. The correct next line is supposed to be "He what?" but I fumble it. Jeff doesn't seem to notice.

"He crawled under a lorry. A stationary lorry," Jeff says.

"No?"

"The lorry started and ran over him," Jeff says.

"Really?"

Ouch. That's not supposed to be my next line, but . . . what *is* my next line? This time, Jeff cocks his head slightly. He can tell that something is up.

"That's what it says here," he continues.

"Really?" I say. Wrong again.

What's going on with me? This never happened during our rehearsals. This morning I knew every line in this play.

"It's enough to make you want to puke, isn't it?" Jeff says.

I open my mouth to say my next line . . . and my mind goes completely blank. *Completely* blank. This time I don't have a clue what comes next.

Jeff sits on the other bed, waiting. The audience waits, too. The theater is completely silent while everyone waits for me to say something. Anything.

I frantically flip through the last few lines in my head, hoping they'll offer a trigger. Nothing. It's like all memory of the play has been siphoned out of my brain. Now my palms are really sweating. I wipe them against my pants. *What the hell is wrong with me?* Pinter is famous for using silence for effect but this brings dead air to a whole new level of absurdity. I carefully avoid looking at Mr. Thacker in the front row. I don't think I can bear seeing his face right now.

"I wonder who advised him to do a thing like that?" Jeff says. Right. That was my next line. Jeff is trying to save me, God bless him. Unfortunately, I'm beyond salvation by now.

"A man of eighty-seven, crawling under a lorry!" Jeff continues. That's his next line. Maybe the audience won't notice that he's doing both speaking parts. Oh, who am I kidding? Of course they're going to notice.

What the hell is happening to my brain?

"It's unbelievable . . ." Jeff says, shaking his head in mock empathy. He says it in character as if it's been scripted, when it's actually the start of my next line. He's trying to feed it to me without giving himself away. My God, this guy is good.

Somehow we stumble through the rest of the play. We cut ahead, we cut back, I ad-lib, and after a certain point we don't even care where we are or whether the lines are correct, we're just trying to get ourselves to the end. At one point the audience sits through, no exaggeration, four or five minutes of dead silence while I stare at the floor, wishing it would swallow me whole. I feel like I'm in the middle of one of those dreams where you show up at school naked or arrive just in time for a test you didn't study for and didn't know was scheduled. Except this is no dream and several hundred real people are witness to my humiliation.

Afterward, my friends and teachers generously try to offer some form of praise. "I thought you were taking a moment," one of the fathers says. "I thought that was a real actor's moment."

Really? I want to say. *Five minutes of silence, you thought that was scripted?* but instead I shake his hand and thank him for coming. Then I walk away.

I don't know what I'm going to tell my parents on Sunday when they call. I can't decide which is worse, having to get through this night without them or how I'd feel if they had seen me on stage. It's a tie.

Next time, I vow, I'll pick a play that's less challenging. I won't pick material that's over my head.

Even now, thirty-five years later, the act of

remembering that night brings back all the emotions I felt on stage. The humiliation, the anxiety, even the sweaty palms. But what strikes me most is not that I managed to survive the experience intact, or that I survived it at all, but that even as I walked away I was already thinking about the next time. Despite what had just happened on stage, I never doubted there would be a next time. I knew I wanted to act. A night of public humiliation wasn't going to stand in my way.

When I told my father about what happened that night, he shared a similar story with me about having once forgotten his own lines on stage. It was an actor's rite of passage, it seemed, which made me feel better. Sort of.

Monday morning, the seventh of March. I'm walking out of English class, heading for my locker, when a kid I barely know walks up to me.

"Hey, I heard something on the news about your dad," he says.

"What do you mean?" I say. I have no clue what he's talking about.

"Yeah, he got sick or something. My parents heard it on KNX this morning."

Something's wrong with my dad? My

parents hadn't called home on Sunday, but that wasn't unprecedented. Normally they'd go down to Manila for the weekend to stay in the city, eat in restaurants, and use the phone to call home, but sometimes my father had to work weekends and couldn't leave the set. Still, I knew that if he was sick enough to make the news, somebody would have called to let us know.

At lunchtime, another kid walked up. "Sorry about your dad," he said. And again in science class: "Bad news about your dad's heart attack."

Heart attack? *What?*

When the next bell rang I headed straight to the school office. "I need to use the phone," I told the secretary. "I've heard something's going on. I need to call home."

Jimmy and Joe were at the house, and both of them got on the phone.

"What's going on?" I asked.

"Your dad's in the hospital in Manila," Joe explained.

"He has heat exhaustion," Jimmy added.

Heat exhaustion? Having been in the oppressive heat of the Philippines for four months, knowing how much my father was drinking, heat exhaustion made sense. *I can see that happening,* I thought. It wasn't a life-threatening condition. So I went along with my day.

"Heard about your father's heart attack," a kid in my next class said. Word must have been spreading quickly.

"No, it was heat exhaustion," I said.

"Sorry to hear about your dad," my PE teacher said.

"He got heat exhaustion," I said.

All afternoon, classmates and teachers kept saying "heart attack." I pushed back with "heat exhaustion." When I got home, Jimmy and Joe were sticking to the heat exhaustion story, but their grim expressions made me suspicious. Why such serious faces for something as fixable as overheating? Unless . . .

"All right, guys," I said. "Is it what you tell me or is it what's on the news?"

Jimmy looked at Joe. Joe looked at Jimmy. Finally, Joe confessed. "It was a heart attack. He's in the hospital in Manila." My mother had called home with the news right away. She'd spoken only with Jimmy and Joe, to discuss the situation among the adults first.

"A heart attack? What?"

"They want all of you guys to go back there," Jimmy said.

Back to the Philippines? I'd barely had time to digest that my father had suffered a heart attack. Now I was learning I'd be leaving school for who knew how long. Heart attack? Hospital? The Philippines, again?

Later that night, lying in bed, I tried to piece together the day's events. I knew how crazy the shoot was in the Philippines. It was hard to be surprised by anything that happened over there. But a heart attack? Heart attacks were something that struck grandparents, not thirty-six-year-old men in their prime. My father was young and very fit. A heart attack didn't make any sense at all.

I didn't learn the details of what had happened until much later, how my father woke up with chest pains in the dark early on a Saturday morning while my mother was away in Manila; how he crawled alone for a mile through the jungle to get to the main road; how he was picked up by a bus and airlifted to Manila, where he was given last rites by a priest who didn't speak English and so couldn't hear his confession. To those who knew how he'd spent the previous few days, a heart attack made sense. He'd sat wet and dirty in a cage as a prisoner at Kurtz's compound, had snakes crawling across his legs, and was dragged upside down through the mud by the Ifugao tribesmen, scenes that taxed him

370

physically and mentally. I think he reached a kind of invisible, inner threshold that only he could recognize. When asked years later about what he thought caused the heart attack, my father would explain, "I call it fragmentation. There was a lot of responsibility on me that I was unable to carry. I was divided spiritually. I was almost non-existent, not in touch with my spirit at all. I was not in command of my own life."

It's hard to re-create the week that followed with any clarity. Everything happened so fast. I went through another round of good-byes at school, another transpacific flight on a DC-10. Someone must have flown over with the four of us, but I can't remember who. Unlike the last trip over, when we hadn't known what to expect or how to prepare, this time we knew the place. We knew the players. My father's condition was the only unknown, but it was a big one. We knew his condition was serious, but nobody had said he was dying. This gave us reason to be both scared and hopeful on the long flight overseas.

By the time we arrived in the Philippines, my dad had spent three weeks in the hospital. My mother had not left his side for a moment. She and her former therapist, Denah Harris, a psychiatric social worker in

New York, spoke by phone once or more a day, unraveling my father's fears. My mother refused to let anyone but friends into his room. No producers, no studio heads, no Francis. She also kept the doctors at bay, refusing all medication and exploratory surgery, relying instead on therapy with Denah and food of her choice from the hospital kitchen. She must have appeared totally insane.

On March 18, the two of them were awakened by a massive magnitude 7 earthquake that sent the entire hospital staff scurrying under their desks. My father yelled to my mother to bring his boots so he could lead the rescue down the nine floors to the street. Instead, they huddled together until the shaking subsided.

Denah had suggested a healing technique that Norman Cousins had written about based on his own experience: laughter. Cousins had been diagnosed with a terminal spine condition and checked himself out of a hospital and into a hotel room with a stack of Marx Brothers films. As he describes in *Anatomy of an Illness,* he laughed so hard when he watched them he activated chemicals in his body that helped him heal. So my mother requested some funny films, and the production office sent a 16-millimeter movie projector and a projectionist over to the hospital one evening, along with the 1942 comedy *To Be or Not to Be,* starring Jack Benny and Carole Lombard.

Near the end of the first reel the Filipino projectionist began to feel ill. My father called the nurse, who took the man down to the emergency room. A few minutes later they returned. The nurse announced that the man was having a heart attack but had no money for admission. My mother grabbed all the money in her wallet, thrust it into the nurse's hands, and insisted that the man be admitted to the hospital and given all necessary treatments. While they waited for news on the man's condition, my mother learned how to operate the projector. They later learned that the man was occupying my father's old room in the ICU, where he eventually made a full recovery.

After leaving the hospital, my parents moved to a Manila hotel where a large convalescent room was set up for my father. We were brought directly to the room when we arrived. My dad was sitting up in bed and looked tiny and scared and pale. I noticed a cane resting by the side of his bed. When he stood up to greet us, it was devastating to see him able to hug us with only one arm, while he used the other to steady himself. His voice was weak, which was the most alarming part. My father had always had a loud, boisterous speaking voice and an infectious laugh. It was as if the power had been drained out of him.

We kids had our own room down the hall, and at night we'd go to my parents' room to watch films with them. Charlie and I would open a canister, thread up the projector, and turn it on. We laughed many times while watching *To Be or Not to Be.* Several more comedies were added to the film library, and we were able to watch them with my father over the next three weeks at the hotel. Years later, Francis would tell James Lipton, the host of the television show *Inside the Actors Studio,* that my mother had saved *Apocalypse Now.* She probably did.

Little League was gearing up for the season back in Malibu, and Charlie, who was an avid baseball player, was missing the start of it. Sometimes he'd take my father outside in a wheelchair to toss a baseball back and forth. Throw and catch, then Charlie would move the wheelchair back a few feet, throw and catch, then move the wheelchair back a few feet more. Eventually my father became steady and strong enough to throw and catch while standing up.

Exercising outside in the sun also went a long way toward helping him heal.

Without a set to visit, and because my father wasn't yet strong enough to travel, we slowly started going stir crazy cooped up in the hotel. Charlie and I would kill time every day by walking the surrounding streets, where vendors displayed an array of balisong knives for sale — a kind of switch-blade with a handle that splits in two and flips around to conceal the blade. In the United States they were called butterfly knives and at the time were banned in some states. In the Philippines balisongs were common pocket knives with a whole art form to opening and closing them. My parents forbade us from having any, so naturally that meant Charlie and I ac-cumulated a whole mess of them. We took whatever money we could come up with, each bought one knife per day, and kept them hidden in our hotel room. I don't know how we expected to get them back to the States. I don't think we were planning ahead that far.

One afternoon, like any two kids with a collection, we spread all our knives across one of the hotel beds to sort through and admire. There must have been thirty of them lined up on the bedspread. Some had three-inch blades and some had six-inch blades, most had metal handles, and a few were inlaid with wood or bone. If you twisted your wrist just the right way, at just the right velocity, you could flip the knife open with one hand. It was a much cooler maneuver than popping open a pocketknife. Charlie and I practiced flipping the balisongs open and closing them until we started getting it right.

Only too late, I realized we'd left the hotel room door slightly ajar — a critical mistake. Charlie was standing with his back to the door, so I was the only one who could see my father's cane as it poked through the slight opening. We had only about five seconds before he limped his way into the room. I didn't want to imagine the outcome of his gaze landing on a bedspread covered with three dozen items of his underage sons' forbidden contraband. It would not have been a stellar moment in Sheen family history.

So quickly it was more of a reflex than a decision, I leapt on the bed and starting jumping on it like a trampoline. "Dad!" I whispered loudly. Charlie immediately leapt into action. As the knives started bouncing he swept them up in the bedspread in one swift move and shoved the whole bundle under the bed. I bounced off and landed hard on the floor a split second before my father stepped fully into the room. A Broadway choreographer couldn't have timed it more perfectly.

My father never had a clue what we were up to. Not a clue. Or if he did, he never let on.

As my father slowly recuperated, we received word that the special effects team would be demolishing Kurtz's compound outside of Pagsanjan. The production was required by law to remove all its sets, and Francis had worked the destruction of this one into the film. One version of the script called for Willard and Lance to call in an airstrike on the compound just before leaving by boat. The massive nighttime explosions would represent the eradication of evil. The surreal destruction footage appears at the very end of the film, as the closing credits roll.

By the end of March my father was stable enough for me to leave Manila for a night, so my parents gave me permission to travel to Pagsanjan to watch the compound be destroyed. Fishburne was still in the Philippines and wanted to see it, too, so we returned to the riverbank set together. It looked exactly as it had when I'd left it five months ago, minus the Ifugaos, who had returned to their mountain home.

The special effects team and camera crew had been preparing for the explosions all day. Bunkers had been dug out across the river for the cameras and a helicopter was prepared to capture the aerial views. Nobody knew, not even the special effects guys, how the demolition would actually play out that night. And this was definitely the kind of shot you could only do once.

Fishburne and I got into position across the river to watch the action. Everyone on set assumed their places as well, and then — "Action! Action! Explosion! Explosion! Explosion!" The call signs were shouted quick and loud into the walkie-talkies. Massive fireballs erupted in ear-splitting blasts across the water as demolition charges starting going off one after another, in a carefully orchestrated sequence. Enormous walls of adobe and cement burst apart, spurting large chunks into the air. The night sky filled with billows of thick gray smoke. It was like having a front row seat to a volcanic eruption, without the flowing lava. Fishburne and I clung to each other as the earth rocked under our tennis shoes. The explosions were so intense and so overpowering, speech was impossible.

A tech adviser looked up and cowered. Rocks and big clods of dirt came raining down.

"Hey! Everyone!" he shouted. "Here comes the cement!"

I looked up just in time to see a piece of cement the size of a couch flying toward us. Fishburne and I grabbed each other and dived under a massive tree trunk for cover. The cement landed on the ground with a deathly thud. We huddled there, shaking, until all the big pieces had landed.

Here comes the cement! It remains one of the most outrageous sentences anyone has ever shouted at me, before or since.

Production continued on the movie as my father recovered in Manila. Francis managed to keep the crew semi-busy by filming the other actors and the boat scenes from a distance. My uncle Joe, who looked enough like my father, was recruited from California to appear in wide and over-the-shoulder shots. Francis would get my father's close-ups later and insert them at editing time.

It looked possible that my father would be able to return to the set in a few weeks. He was steadily gaining strength, and my time in Manila started coming to a natural end.

There was no reason for me to stay longer, and many reasons for me to go back to school.

Just before I left the Philippines we received news of a devastating accident on an airstrip in the Canary Islands. A Pan Am 747 had collided with a KLM 747, killing 583 of the 644 people on board. Everyone on the KLM flight had died. It was — and still is — the deadliest crash in airline history. I'm a nervous flier even under the best of circumstances, and reading this news didn't help. A few days after the crash, Ramon and I boarded a plane for our flight to California. My parents had decided to keep Charlie and Renée with them until my father's work was done.

Ramon and I made our way down the aisle to our seats. I sat down, buckled in — and that's when I noticed the airline logo stitched into the back of the seat in front of me: KLM.

"Oh no," I said to Ramon. "We're doomed."

I thought of the last time I'd flown out of Manila, five months earlier. I'd been going home alone that time. Because I was only fourteen, the airline required that an adult guardian accompany me, and neither of my parents could act as chaperone. The singer-songwriter Jackson Browne was in the Philippines to talk with Francis about doing some music for the film and he was about to head back to L.A. My mother asked if he'd fly with me to Hawaii, where I'd then be allowed to continue on my own. He said sure.

I knew that Jackson Browne was a musician, but I didn't know anything about his work. My musical tastes veered toward Led Zeppelin, Jimi Hendrix, and Lynyrd Skynyrd. Back home, Jackson was a big deal and about to get even bigger. His last album, *Late for the Sky,* had gone platinum the previous year and his next one, *The Pretender,* would be released in November, rise to number 5 on the *Billboard* charts, and earn a Grammy nomination. I also didn't know that he'd just lost his wife to suicide and was raising their two-and-a-half-year-old son. To me, he was just a really friendly, laid-back guy with brown hair hanging in his eyes who smiled when I showed him the bag of mangoes my mother had given me for the trip.

"You brought mangoes! Far out, man," he said.

As the plane took off I confessed that I didn't like flying. And that in fact, the possibility of crashing terrified me. He had no fear of it any more, he said.

"Hey, man, neither of us is going to die in a plane crash," he said.

"Okay. Because?"

"Because we both have way too much work to do still," he said. "Our work here is not anywhere near done."

I can dig that, I thought. I also believed everyone was here for a reason, and that our task was to live up to that potential. Jackson talking about destiny and purpose resonated deeply with me. Which is probably why I've remembered that conversation nearly word for word for more than thirty-five years.

Jackson and I talked the whole way to Hawaii. A fourteen-year-old junior high school kid and a famous twenty-eight-year-old, platinum-selling musician: we had much more in common than I would have guessed. We got along so well that Jackson changed his connecting flight in Honolulu so we could keep traveling together to L.A. I never saw him again after that trip, but every time I get on a plane I still think about what he said.

I stared at the KLM insignia on the seat back in front of me as the plane started taxiing down the runway. My usual anxiety about flying started to bubble up. I pushed it back down. Tomorrow I'd be home in Malibu, and the day after that I'd be back at school. Soon to come were a class picnic, my ninth-grade graduation, and the annual Renaissance Faire, where I hoped to one day get a job.

Yeah, I don't think my work's done here, I told myself. *Not yet.*

CHAPTER TWELVE: MARTIN

1977–1979

I left the Philippines in June of 1977 a very different man from the one who had flown there from Rome in April of 1976. *Apocalypse Now* taught me the limits of my endurance as an actor and a man. Looking back, I wonder if the heart attack wasn't a subconscious attempt to remove myself from the craziness of the situation.

It wasn't just the grueling physical toll the film took on me, though that was surely part of it. The oppressive heat, anxiety, and sickness — fourteen months of that could have forced anyone to his limit. But the movie also extracted a psychological toll. The role of Willard had mystified me and I couldn't get a handle on who he was. I'd never been a soldier, didn't know anything about the physical or mental aspects of war, and despite Joe Lowry's assurances to the contrary, I don't believe I would have survived combat. I couldn't imagine killing anyone, for any reason, though I also couldn't deny that under extreme circumstances, such acts are possible for anyone.

"You're Willard," Francis had told me, which was both intriguing and frightening and, ultimately, impossible to accept. It seemed that to truly embody Willard I had to accept as fact that all human beings are innately hostile and aggressive, especially men. On the set Francis advocated this Freudian philosophy as a motivation, but at home Janet advocated the opposite. She believed that we are all born loving and compassionate, and that we learn how to be hostile and aggressive through fear. I agreed with her wholeheartedly, but that philosophy was hard to hold on to when the character I needed to inhabit was in the Vietnam jungle on an assassin's mission to kill.

Years later, when I read Viktor Frankl's 1946 book *Man's Search for Meaning,* I found a writer who articulated my beliefs about human nature. Frankl, an Austrian psychiatrist who survived three years in Nazi concentration camps, believed humans are innately compassionate beings and community builders. He wrote that, if Freud had seen prisoners taking care of one another at Auschwitz, he might have revised his whole philosophy. Even in Auschwitz

Frankl saw repeated proof of man's fundamental goodness. If anyone had reason or motivation to be hostile or aggressive toward his fellow men surely it would have been those inmates. And yet they *weren't*. Many of the men in Frankl's barracks were loving and compassionate despite their circumstances and did whatever was within their limited power to help one another survive.

So there I was in the Philippines, on the set for eight to twelve hours a day with Francis urging me to be more aggressive, and then bringing that back to the cabana at night, where Janet would say, "What the hell's the matter with you?" I had to learn how to come home and get mellow, then go back to the set and get crazy, then return home and get mellow, then return to the set and get crazy again. It was a completely fractured existence, a Jekyll and Hyde act, and while it sounds very funny now I wasn't laughing then. Nobody was.

After the third and final leg of the film, Janet, Charlie, Renée, and I left the Philippines and stopped off in Hawaii on our way home. I needed a few days to pull myself together before returning home and reuniting with the other boys. When we landed in Hawaii I was very thin, insecure, and emotionally fragile. I'd taken to wearing black

Vietcong pajamas everywhere because they were so comfortable, and I can only imagine the impression I must have made when I walked into the upscale hotel lobby in Honolulu: skinny, jumpy, disheveled after the long flight, and wearing what looked like last night's pajamas. Of course the front desk clerk refused to give us a room.

Exhausted and furious, I started making a scene.

"What do you mean, we can't have a room?" I shouted. "Isn't our money as good as anyone else's?" I could feel my rage threatening to get out of control.

"Calm *down*," Janet said, and that's all it took. I had only to remember that just hours after the heart attack I was airlifted to Makati Medical Center in Manila and was being raced down a corridor on a gurney with fluorescent lights streaming overhead. Suddenly, Janet's face appeared above mine like a vision. She smiled, leaned down, and whispered in my ear, "It's only a movie, babe."

Oh my God, I thought. *She's right. Yes. It* is *only a movie.* And at that moment I started to recover.

I'd already survived the physical part of the heart attack. Now Janet was helping me start to heal psychically. The bond that had formed between us when we delivered Ramon together in 1963 was solidified in Manila that day.

The desk clerk in Hawaii finally did admit us, and I spent most of that week in the room, reflecting. I was sensitive and weak and seemed to weep at the slightest provocation, sometimes from despair, sometimes from relief, sometimes from pure joy. Like a deep-sea diver coming back up to the surface I had to slow my ascent to keep from getting the bends, and come up in stages to integrate back into regular life slowly. I couldn't jump straight from Manila to Los Angeles. Hawaii was a necessary stop. I wished our soldiers returning from Vietnam had such a respite. Instead, many of them came out of combat and in less than forty-eight hours were back in what they called "the world" without any time or preparation for transition.

Soon we were back in Malibu. I gladly returned to the same neighborhood, the same trees, the same house that I'd left in January. The physical geography had remained static, yet monumental changes had occurred in the country over the half-year that I'd been gone. Jimmy Carter had become president and pardoned Vietnam draft dodgers on his first day in office; the

California state legislature had voted to restore the death penalty; and antinuclear protests were heating up all over the country, especially in New Hampshire, where 1,414 protesters had just been arrested and charged with criminal trespassing. In our family, Emilio had turned fifteen and was moving on to high school; all the boys were bigger, stronger, and seemed to need me less; and Renée was becoming an accomplished equestrian already at ten years old.

I had changed profoundly, as well. The heart attack was a serious wake-up call, but it was also a serious confidence crusher. I felt less certain about my abilities, including my ability to fully recover, but even as I went through the necessary convalescence with exercise, good diet, and rest, an insidious form of self-pity had started to snake its way into my psyche.

Self-pity is a terrible disease. Its focus is self-absorption. *What about me? Look at me!* There's no joy in self-pity. It pulls us away from our true selves into egocentricity and isolation.

But I didn't know this in 1977. All I knew then was how vulnerable I was, and how good it felt to be back home.

August arrived, and with it a publicity trip

to Paris to promote *Sweet Hostage,* a film I'd done for American TV now being released in France as a feature film. I'd be spending my birthday in Paris with Janet, who persuaded Emilio to join us. The production company put us up in a suite at the Plaza Athénée. It was the kind of hoity-toity hotel I never would have stayed in on my own, but for those few days it was Paris at its finest, all five stars of it every day.

On August 3, my thirty-seventh birthday, Emilio and I took the elevator down to the lobby and headed out for a morning walk. I stopped at the hotel registration desk as usual to pick up a copy of the *International Herald Tribune* and scanned the front-page headlines.

"Oh, my God," I said.

"What is it?" Emilio asked.

"Francis Gary Powers. He died in a helicopter crash two days ago. Oh, no."

Francis Gary Powers had been an American pilot working for the CIA in 1960 when his U-2 spy plane was shot down by a Soviet missile after it was spotted in Soviet airspace. His capture provided incontrovertible proof that the United States was spying on missile sites inside the USSR and its Warsaw Pact neighbors. The event had brought the 1960 Paris summit between the superpowers to a halt. Powers spent nearly two years imprisoned in the Soviet Union before he was released as part of a prisoner exchange between the United States and the USSR. I'd met him at a party in California a few years back and we'd stayed in touch since. He'd wanted me to play him in a TV movie about his life. "All I ever wanted to do was fly airplanes," he told me the night we met. Recently he'd been working as a helicopter pilot for KNBC doing traffic reports. That's what he was doing when he went down. Heroically, he managed to divert the helicopter away from a populated area before it crashed.

After all he'd been through and survived, now this?

I went back upstairs to call his widow in California. When she answered the phone at their house in the San Fernando Valley, it must have been the middle of the night.

"Mrs. Powers . . . it's me . . ." I said, my voice cracking. "It's Martin."

I was so broken up I must have frightened her. "Who is this?" she demanded. She must have been exhausted as well and had no doubt been taking calls all of the previous day.

"It's me, Martin Sheen, and I just wanted to say how sorry I am." But the static on the line was awful and we could barely hear each other.

"Whoever this is, please don't call here again!" she cried, and hung up.

On the street with Emilio later that day, I couldn't shake my deep feeling of sorrow. Francis Gary Powers was gone in an instant. Life could end, just like that. It could happen to me, too. It almost had. What would prevent it from happening again? I tried to explain this to Emilio, but it came out all wrong.

"You don't understand," I argued. "You've got to realize how vulnerable I am." My voice became more insistent. I wanted something from him, some kind of validation, I suppose, but I wasn't reaching him.

"I could drop dead *at any minute,* and you wouldn't have a father anymore," I went on. "One day, maybe, you'll understand."

I felt my chest start to tighten. Please — not again.

"Oh, dear, forgive me, but I have to . . ." I said, as I sank down to the sidewalk. "My heart . . ."

The way I remember the story, I sat on the curb. Emilio remembers me actually lying on the sidewalk. Either way, I was on the pavement on Avenue Montaigne and he was standing above me, looking down.

I knew exactly what I was doing. I was trying to get Emilio to show some concern. In truth, I was trying to get him to feel sorry for me. If he thought I could drop dead at any minute, he might give me the attention and appreciation I thought I deserved.

"Oh, get up and stop feeling sorry for yourself," Emilio said. He was impatient and embarrassed, a fifteen-year-old boy who didn't want to be part of a public drama.

"What'd you say?" I asked, though I'd heard every word clearly.

"Get *up*," he said, looking around to see who might be watching.

"Look at me," I moaned. "I might never work again." I pressed my hand against my chest for added effect, even though my chest pains were clearly not a heart attack. They were pains of the ego, and Emilio saw right through them.

"I've had enough of you and your crap!" he shouted, waving his arms for emphasis. "The hell with you — you're fine! You don't need me!"

And then he walked away. Just like that, he walked away.

I sat there on the sidewalk, stunned. Emilio? Walking away from me? Leaving me in the gutter by myself? *Emilio?* Of all four of the kids, he'd always been the one most willing to let me off the hook, who accepted my flaws and always forgave me, who never held a grudge. I'd known I had that going for me, and I'd been taking advantage of it, as I'd done many times before. But this time was different. He had completely had it with me. I lifted my head to see if he'd really gone. There he was, marching away down the sidewalk. He knew I'd been playing on his sympathy, trying to get something I thought I desperately needed for myself, and he wasn't going to tolerate it anymore.

I felt a rush of deep, crippling disappointment mixed with anger and resentment as I watched him disappear into the crowd — how could he *do* this to me? — and then I felt a rush of something else. Pride. I was proud of him for taking a stand and walking away. *Good for him,* I thought ruefully, as I slowly sat up and brushed myself off. I mean, what was he supposed to have done? Picked me up and carried me back to the hotel? He knew that if he got sucked into the grip of my self-pity he'd wind up there next to me on the sidewalk, feeling sorry for me. I had to hand it to him. He'd made the better choice by far.

Weak people don't realize they're weak until they're in the presence of someone strong. Emilio became the strong person for me that day. I owe him that moment in Paris when he had the courage and the strength to walk away. What later became known between us at the Paris Sidewalk Incident was a watershed moment for both of us. It marked the beginning of a new phase in our relationship.

Children instinctively know more about their parents than we think they do. They know all the colors of our characters, and they're onto us the whole time. They know when we're being dishonest, and it alters the relationship. In Paris, Emilio helped me see that I couldn't hide anything from my kids. They all knew me too well.

By walking away, he also showed that he wasn't afraid of my disapproval. Most kids are afraid to rock a parent's boat because their sense of security is wrapped up in the parent's approval and acceptance. They'll shy away from confrontation because they don't want to risk being pushed out. It takes a great deal of courage for a child to call a parent's honesty into question. That's what Emilio did to me that day. Ramon did it too, Charlie and Renée as well, all in their own time. But Emilio was the first, and when he took a stand, he forced me to look in the mirror. I realized I had to change the way I was behaving. I couldn't keep inflicting my self-pity on anyone, especially the family. Once I knew that, I started to get strong again in body, mind, and spirit. I still had a long way to go, of course, but it was a start. Thanks to Emilio, it was a start.

I may have left the Philippines in June but I hadn't left *Apocalypse Now* behind. Not by a long shot. Over the next two years I made at least three trips up to Zoetrope Studios in San Francisco to record the narration for the film and did several more such sessions in Hollywood as well. Francis hired Michael Herr, the author of the brilliant, best-selling Vietnam memoir *Dispatches,* to write the text for Willard's voice-overs and we experimented with many different interpretations to see how it sounded when it was cut into the editing process against the picture. Sometimes these sessions would go on for many hours, often stretching into the next day.

"Martin, try this now."

I'd say, "Okay," and I'd try it again . . . my way.

"Try this now? Would you do this?"

"Okay," I'd say. "Sure," and still do it my way. I could be stubborn.

"Marty, could you try this for me? Just try this."

"Okay." Same result. Francis's frustration would mount.

Sometimes I'd get it just as Francis wanted, but more often I didn't. One day I flew up to San Francisco for a Saturday morning recording session and went straight from the airport to the studio. I was sitting there in the booth when an enormous blond fellow with a bodybuilder's physique walked in from the outer room.

"He's got something for you," Francis said through the microphone.

This guy walked into the booth and looked at me. He must have been in his early forties and stood at least six foot six.

"Maybe this will help," he said. There was very little light in the sound booth and I couldn't see what he was offering. Was he giving me a cup of coffee? I reached out, and he placed an automatic .45 pistol in my hand.

I knew right away what it was from the feel of it. I'd carried one throughout the film and Joe Lowry had taught me everything a soldier needed to know about a .45. I knew that weapon better than any other. I knew how much it weighed when it was empty, and what it felt like with a full clip. And as soon as this one was put in my hand, I knew that it was loaded.

I looked down at the safety. It was off. *This is insanity,* I thought.

The guy, it turned out, was a Vietnam veteran, Special Forces, who'd come to witness this session of narration, and I was led to believe that he'd actually done some of the things that Willard had done in the film. I suppose Francis thought this guy would help me get in the proper spirit of the narration. But it only made me nervous and pushed me further away from violence in any form. Oh yes, sometimes I could be very stubborn.

Early in 1979 I was hired to play John Dean for the TV miniseries *Blind Ambition,* which would air in four two-hour segments. As special counsel to President Nixon, Dean had been at the heart of the Watergate cover-up and had written a book about his experiences. His wife Maureen had also written a book called *Mo: A Woman's View of Watergate* and the miniseries was a compilation of the two.

We filmed at CBS Studios in Los Angeles. Filming a miniseries is different than filming any other type of TV show because you usually cover long stretches of historical time on screen. The filming happens quickly, and that typically means shooting scenes out of sequence, according to location. If the beginning and end of a film take place in the same location, for example, those scenes would be filmed on the same day so that the cast and crew don't have to return to the same spot later. When you shoot the end of a film like that, you have to pretend that you've already done the whole movie by that point. Hair and wardrobe have to be intricately coordinated so they're the right style and fashion for the particular year in the first shot, and then everything has to change to be accurate for the time period of the next scene you shoot.

When Dean was arrested and charged with obstruction of justice and taken to a run-down city jail in Washington, D.C., he was perfectly coiffed and wearing a three-piece suit. The scene in our script called for me as John Dean to walk into the cell with my hair done and my clothing perfectly tailored. It was scheduled to be filmed on a day when other, unrelated scenes were also being shot on the same soundstage. I did my first scene that day, a lively one, and as soon as it was finished I walked across the soundstage to a separate set. This one recreated a little cell the size of a large closet. It had been stripped to its bare essence: just a toilet and a bed. The script called for me to walk into the cell, turn around, and have an emotional breakdown.

No one else was in the scene, just me and the cell. There was no time to fuss about anything. The gaffers were setting up the lights, and the camera crew were getting into position.

"All right, Martin," said George Schaefer, the director. "Your back is going to be blocking the camera at first so that when you walk away from us we'll realize that you've walked into the cell. You'll go all the way up against the wall, then turn around and face the cell door. I'm going to have the camera dolly right up to you for a moving close-up. That'll be it. That's the scene."

"I have to weep in this scene?" I asked.

"Oh, yes. A complete breakdown," he said.

"Easy for you to say," I replied.

I surely would have passed that cup if I could have. There are certain days when you should shoot a scene like this one, specifically days when you're already feeling bad. Not when you're still coming off the high of a previous scene.

How in heaven's name am I going to pull this off? I wondered.

While I stood there trying to figure out what to do, the wardrobe assistant called my name and said my three-piece suit was ready.

"Be right there!" I called back.

Inside the cell, a set decorator was preparing the space. He was writing graffiti on the walls with a thick marker as if prisoners had scrawled it there, counting off days, signing their names. I watched the guy scribbling, then suddenly I knew exactly what I had to do.

"Excuse me," I said. "Could I borrow that pen?"

I walked to the far wall with the marker in my hand and turned around to face the cameraman. "When you get into here, how much are you seeing?" I asked as I raised my hand midchest. "Is it here?"

"Right there," he said.

"Okay." I raised my hand with the pen above my head. "How much are you seeing above my head?"

"I'm seeing right there, where you've got the pen."

"Okay," I said. "Thank you."

I turned around. In the spot on the wall right above my head I scrawled RAMON. Then I handed the pen back to the set decorator.

"Call me when you're ready, not a minute sooner," I told the assistant director.

By the time they were ready to shoot I was, too. I walked to the set where everything was in place. The lighting was on, the cameras ready to go. We did one technical rehearsal to make sure everything was properly marked and measured, and then I came back to the starting point.

"Make sure we've got this now," I said to no one in particular, "because I'm only going to be able to do this once." Then I turned my back to the camera and waited.

"Action!" George called out, and I walked into the cell. When I looked up, all I could see was a single word on the wall: RAMON.

Only three people in my life had ever called me Ramon: the director Joe Papp, the actor Roscoe Lee Browne, and my father, Francisco Estevez. In 1979, Joe and Roscoe were still living. Francisco was not. Having missed his funeral, I'd never taken the time or given myself the license to mourn him. It occurred to me that day on that set that I'd been suppressing those feelings for more than four years. There was a deep pain within me that I hadn't expressed because I hadn't allowed it to surface. *I can do it now,* I thought. *I'll allow myself to celebrate his memory and thank him for everything he gave me.*

I had an artistic responsibility in that

scene to portray John Dean's desperate situation honestly, and I had a personal need to finally mourn my father. I looked at the name RAMON scrawled on the wall, turned around, and wept uncontrollably. That was it. In one take, thanks to my sense memory, the most invaluable emotional tool available to an actor, I was able to fulfill both requirements at the same time.

"Transference" is the term often used for this common acting technique. An actor delves into his own personal memory to conjure up an appropriate emotional state required for a particular scene. It's a form of self-hypnosis. One of the most astonishing examples of this I've ever seen was a performance by Alan Arkin in *The Heart Is a Lonely Hunter,* based on the Carson McCullers novel of the same name. Alan played a deaf-mute boarder in a southern rooming house whose best friend, also a deaf mute, had recently been institutionalized. Every week Alan would go visit his friend, until the week he arrived at the institution and discovered his friend had died. He goes to the cemetery and stands at the grave, where he's so overcome with grief, all he can do is stagger around and make signs from his heart. The character's private grief and Alan's ability to convey it without words is a stunning moment in film. He was nominated for an Academy Award for that role.

When I turned around in the jail cell, the viewers may have thought, *John Dean, look what happened to this guy. He was riding high, handsome young lawyer to the president, flying around on Air Force One, and now he's stuck in this toilet. Look at him now, alone, brought low and weeping in a cell.* But I was the only one who knew it wasn't just John Dean bemoaning his fate in that scene. It was also a boy named Ramon finally mourning his father, Francisco, in a deeply personal yet public form.

In May of that year, *Apocalypse Now* had its world premiere at the Cannes Film Festival in France, where it received a standing ovation and co-won the prestigious Palme d'Or prize. I heard that the scene in which I punched the mirror, that scene of such personal anguish, was not included in the Cannes version of the film and I was relieved. In that moment, on that set in the Philippines, I thought I'd wanted the moment captured on camera, but three years later in a more sober state I didn't want anyone to see that part of me on the screen. There's a limit to how much personal pain you can bear to take public.

But the gap between a world premiere and a U.S. premiere offers time for additional editing, and a few months later I heard that Francis had decided to open the film with that scene intact. Now I was concerned. I didn't want to see the film knowing those images would be in it so I made sure I was busy on another film at the time of *Apocalypse Now*'s U.S. premiere in mid-August. That film was *The Final Countdown,* in which I played a civilian observer aboard the aircraft carrier USS *Nimitz* on the day the ship gets caught in a vortex and travels back in time to December 1941, just before the Japanese attack on Pearl Harbor. The movie required me to be on location in Norfolk, Virginia, and offshore aboard the real USS *Nimitz.* The production ran over schedule when the ship's nuclear power source malfunctioned and it had to stay in port for nearly two months for repair. Joe Lowry had a part in the film as well, and when *Apocalypse Now* opened we were both conveniently otherwise occupied somewhere out on the Atlantic Ocean.

As soon as *The Final Countdown* finished shooting I took the family to Hawaii for vacation, a deliberate move. It kept me unavailable when everyone else associated with *Apocalypse Now* was doing publicity and the film was opening in Los Angeles, New York, and Toronto. By the time we returned, a huge ground-swell of interest had developed around the movie, particularly among Vietnam veterans, including my younger brother John, who had served four years in the U.S. Navy as a third-class hospital corpsman and done a tour of duty in Vietnam from 1965 to 1966, much of it with the Seventh Marine Regiment in Chu Lai. "You want to know what it was like for me over there?" he said. "Go see the film."

Critical reviews were mixed but popular support slowly started to grow and by mid-October, when the film was about to open nationwide, I knew I couldn't avoid doing publicity any longer. That fall I flew to New York for some interviews. The film was still playing at the Ziegfeld Theatre on Fifty-Fourth Street where it had opened and my dear friend from high school John Crane, who was both Emilio's and Ramon's god-father, urged me to see it with him.

"All right, John," I said. "We'll see it together."

The Ziegfeld Theatre seats more than 1,100 and was completely sold out for the show. We sat about three-quarters of the way back in the audience. Nobody recognized me, and I was relieved for that. I don't know how I got through the opening scenes. I must have divorced myself from any personal connection to them. It felt painful and humiliating to have been so vulnerable and to have revealed it so publicly.

During the film, I thought people were coming into the theater and talking during the show, but then I realized that the voices were coming from a new kind of soundtrack, surround sound. *Oh, my God,* I thought. *I'm engulfed! I'm right in the middle of this thing again.* I was so overwhelmed by the horrific helicopter attack on the village, the sight of all those innocent people being slaughtered, juxtaposed with Wagner's triumphant "Ride of the Valkyries," that I wept. Those scenes had been filmed long before I arrived in the Philippines so I hadn't seen them, but they resulted in one of the most powerful film sequences I have seen in any movie, ever, and still evoke the same emotional response in me when I watch the film today.

Nineteen seventy-nine became one of the most challenging years of my adult life. By that fall I was drinking heavily, and Janet couldn't bear it any longer.

"You're an asshole and a bore, and I'm not sure where this is going," she told me. "I'm not holding you back. I can't go anywhere, but you can. Why don't you take a break and give me a break for a while."

I couldn't come to grips with moving out. I couldn't see myself ever leaving the family. At that time Burt Reynolds had his dinner theater in Jupiter, Florida, and he offered me a part in *Two for the Seesaw* with Julie Kavner. "Come down and do this play," he said. "It'll keep you occupied." It seemed like a perfect solution: Janet and I would get time apart and I could go back onstage.

So I left for Florida, where I went from bad to worse.

Two for the Seesaw is William Gibson's 1958 two-character play about a lawyer on the brink of divorce and a dancer he meets at a party one night. Henry Fonda and Anne Bancroft originated the roles of Jerry and Gittel on Broadway, the part that made Anne Bancroft a star. As Gittel, Julie Kavner became my anchor on that show. Once I was separated from the family, I couldn't stop drinking and I didn't study my lines so how could I expect to know them? On opening night I was drunk and improvised most of the show. I think I even did an impersonation of Al Jolson in the middle of the second act. It was a mess. Poor Julie had to carry me through.

Afterward, I felt so disgraced and humiliated I tried to sneak out of the theater to avoid the opening-night party. Burt sent someone down to get me.

"I can't go up there now," I said. There was no way I could face all those people. But Burt dispatched a second person to try to change my mind.

"All right," I said. "I'll just come up the back steps and say hello."

Outside, I sneaked around to the back stairs, hoping no one would see me. As I started up the steps, the door at the top swung open and Sally Field appeared. Burt had invited her down to see the show. I must have looked as embarrassed as I felt. I didn't want to be noticed by another actor, especially one who might feel obliged to say something about my performance that night.

But she just smiled and said, "I know exactly how you feel. Remember, I was the Flying Nun."

I have adored her from that moment.

Burt Reynolds started his dinner theater with the help of three of his closest friends: Dom DeLuise, Charles Durning, and Charles Nelson Reilly. The three of them would come down to Jupiter, Florida, to direct plays and give classes to the college interns Burt employed. The theater became a place I knew I could go to work and be with friends who would tolerate me even when I was close to hitting bottom.

The next scheduled play at Burt's theater was *Mister Roberts*. He asked me to play the title role and asked Joshua Logan to direct. Logan had cowritten and directed the original production on Broadway and also directed the movie version with Jimmy Cagney, Jack Lemmon, and Henry Fonda. I accepted without hesitation, then headed home for Christmas. I dreaded the thought of going back to Florida alone. Then it occurred to me: This might be a good chance for Emilio to act in a professional production, so I asked if he'd like to return to Jupiter with me in January.

"Sure," he said. "But I don't want this to be a case of nepotism. I want to audition for any role the director thinks I'm right for, and we'll go from there."

"Fair enough," I said, and we were off.

Emilio was in his senior year at Santa Monica High School by then, so we had to bring his lessons down to Florida for the next six weeks. Burt set us up in an apartment near the theater. Our dear friend Joe Lowry was cast as Doc. Emilio auditioned and was cast as a sailor in the crew. It was a small role but this was a professional production, and even though he was the youngest cast member everyone treated him like an equal. We'd rehearse during the day and often socialize with the cast at night, but other nights we stayed home. We'd cook together or bring in takeout and help each other study our roles. Once the show was up and running we'd go swimming or play basketball or read books during the day and go over to the theater together at night.

Those were good weeks for us, doing *Mister Roberts.* It was great fun living and working together on an equal footing in our chosen profession for the first time. I was still drinking but far less than before, and I never went on stage drunk ever again. With Emilio I was more steady and reliable. He knew he could trust me now, which revived my confidence and self-esteem. This also paved the way for another trip together the following year, one that would take us to India for *Gandhi* and change both of our lives significantly.

CHAPTER THIRTEEN: EMILIO

1979–1980

From all the months I'd spent on sets, I understood how much planning and effort went into making a movie. After our family trip to Ireland in 1973, Charlie and I had started using the family's 8-millimeter camera to shoot short movies in Malibu with the neighborhood kids. We wrote our own scripts along the lines of *Dr. Jekyll and Mr. Hyde* and made awful, dark horror films where a killer would break into a house and wipe everyone out. Someone was always getting killed. The films that had influenced us most were *The Godfather, Taxi Driver, The Deer Hunter,* and *Apocalypse Now,* and basically everything we made was a derivative of one of those, or all four. We did a film we called *The Godbrother* about diamond dealing and the Mob, where we put the neighborhood kids in their fathers' hats and long coats. For a murder scene we threw a dummy stuffed with newspaper off the cliff at Point Dume. Without enough weight it became tangled in weeds on the way down and stayed there shedding newspaper for weeks as it slowly fell apart.

Today, any kid can make a video on a flip camera or a Mac, but homespun filmmaking in the seventies was very labor intensive, very hands-on, an incredible training ground. I had to learn how to operate technical equipment and I made mistakes and learned from them.

At the time, I was the only kid I knew with access to a movie camera. Then in 1977 my parents upgraded to an instant-movie system called Polavision, Polaroid's precursor to VHS. It was a handheld camera with a removable cartridge that popped out to be played in a special Polavision deck that looked like a portable TV with a screen but no dials. The system was very neat and self-contained, but limited. The tapes worked only in this camera and deck and there was no option for post-production editing unless you broke open the cartridge and pulled out the film. You had to edit in the camera as you shot, which meant no second takes, so you had to be very specific about what you wanted the first time. The beauty of this was it forced a discipline on us as filmmakers, but at the time we were just a bunch of stupid kids, fooling around and having fun. We didn't realize the value of what we were doing until much later, when those of us who became actors and directors realized we'd spent our teenage years attending a hardscrabble film program of our own design.

At some point I found an old cassette recorder at a garage sale, which gave me an idea. "Okay," I told Charlie. "Let's shoot with the silent camera we have, I'll record on this cassette deck, and then we'll figure out how to marry the picture and the sound together."

For this one, we decided on a story about a couple who moved into a possessed house, based on *The Exorcist,* of course. The only catch was we'd need to shoot it at night. My parents, God love them, signed off on having a bunch of kids take over the house one weekend from 8:00 p.m. to 6:00 a.m. Their bedroom was on one side of the house, and we commandeered the kids' rooms at the other side for our sets and rotated jobs as needed. Whoever wasn't on camera was directing or art directing or being the sound guy with a mic taped to a broomstick held over the actor's head.

After two nights of keeping the folks awake we'd shot only about half of the film.

I told everyone, "I'll work on this half and figure out how to put the sound and picture together and then we'll shoot the rest." But I hadn't realized the film and sound were taping at different speeds, and even after hours of trying I couldn't figure out how to get them aligned. We never finished that film. Instead, I moved on to a series of skateboarding and surfing movies that featured the local kids on their boards and I put the images to music.

In 1978 we attempted a bigger production with the Penn brothers, Sean and Chris, from around the corner. Their father Leo was a director and their mother Eileen was an actress, so like us they were familiar with minute-to-minute operations on a set. Sean was an intense, focused, creative kid two years older than I who used to drive me to high school in Santa Monica before I got my license. His younger brother Chris was working on his own Vietnam opus based on *Apocalypse Now* and was eager to be included in our films and willing to do whatever was needed. He always had his hands on M-80 and M-100 firecrackers, so he became our explosives expert. The empty field next to my parents' house became our Trinity Site, where we'd stick M-80s under a paint can or other objects and then film the explosions. When we watched our footage at the end of the day we'd sometimes see Chris's hand coming in to light the fuse. *Hmm,* we'd think. *Oh, well. Maybe no one will pay attention to that.*

For this film we chose not to work with a script. We started with a concept and just added on as ideas came to us. Sean played a disturbed neighbor who coveted our German shepherd puppy and was willing to employ any means necessary to steal him, including killing his own mother. Eileen Penn played herself as an off-camera voice. On screen all you saw was Sean sticking a gun into the Penn's kitchen and then, *blam.* From there he came over to our house and killed Charlie, and then it turned into a revenge movie where I went after Sean and blew him away in the middle of the street.

By that time I had an editing bay set up in my bedroom, which meant we could do multiple takes of each scene and choose the best ones. I'd sit at my desk with splice tape stuck to my fingers, and when I finished editing I'd call everyone over and put a reel on for feedback — or at least the kind of uniquely undiscriminating feedback teenage guys supply.

"What do you think of this?"

"It's good, man."

416

"Yeah, excellent, man."

"All right."

My mother watched it not long ago and said, "My God, it's amazing any of you ever had a career." It was *terrible.*

Making my own films meant creating opportunities for myself to act and direct, both of which had gotten harder to come by in high school. Because Malibu didn't yet have its own high school all the Malibu kids were bused to Santa Monica High, an hour-long ride each way. Malibu kids were mostly outdoors types, athletes and surfers, while the kids from Santa Monica were artsy and edgy and already had their own relationships going from the Santa Monica junior highs. My first year at SaMoHi, I ran track and played soccer, and my friends were my teammates and kids I knew from Malibu. The drama club was a separate clique, and when I joined it in my junior year, a pecking order was already in place. Two of the juniors in the club, Brent Hinkley and Lee Arenberg, were so talented and charismatic they were automatically cast in all the leading roles.

Lee was the big man on campus that year, a natural and constant performer who did our daily morning announcements over the school PA. With his oversized aviator glasses and mop of wild brown curls he was an eccentric class clown.

Lee had no problem calling attention to himself, where as the son of an actor who was often in the spotlight I always tried to deflect attention away from myself. As opposite as Lee and I were, when I saw him reading plays in his free time I earmarked him as a potential friend. I was thinking about auditioning for TV and film jobs, and I approached Lee one day in the school library.

"Hi, I'm Emilio," I said. "I know you're that actor guy. I'm just starting to go out for jobs and I really want to work on cold readings. It'd be cool if we could run lines together."

He looked surprised. Later I learned that he knew who I was and was flattered that one of the cool kids at school would approach him. Cool? I'd never thought of myself that way.

"Sure," he said.

From there, one of my closest high school friendships was born. Lee and I would get together at lunchtime to read plays and sometimes we reserved the little study rooms in the school library. That spring I went to my track coach and told him I'd be leaving the team midseason. "Summer's coming up," I explained. "A lot will be happening. I need to start getting my feet wet and going out on auditions."

"Oh, so you're going to be an actor now?" he teased.

Coach Paul Kerry was a former world-class athlete from USC. He'd always been supportive of me and his reaction was disappointing, but I wasn't surprised. Almost everyone at school gave me a hard time about the choice. I played soccer, I ran track, I got good grades, and they saw me heading down a different path. I already thought of myself as an aspiring actor, but I had to wait a while for everyone else's images of me to catch up with my own.

Pursuing acting seriously meant beating the pavement in the hopes of landing my first role. But the first, necessary step in that direction was to find an agent, someone who could get me the auditions. Even before that, I needed head shots.

Our family friend Tim Perior was a commercial photographer and a screenwriter, a very worldly, very funny, very artistic cat who'd spent some time with us in Rome in 1976. I asked him to take my pictures. The first batch I printed had the name "Emilio Sheen" at the bottom. Agents and managers who'd expressed an interest in me had encouraged me to use Sheen because it would make their jobs easier if they could introduce me as Martin's son. Also, there were enough hurdles as it was to break into acting. I figured that maybe a non-Hispanic, already-known surname would give me an edge.

Emilio Sheen. I looked at it sitting there alone in the bottom right corner of the photo.

It had seemed like a good idea, but on paper, it looked terrible. My Latin first name bumped up against my father's chosen name Sheen in an obvious, dissonant way.

Trying to be supportive, my mom suggested, "Why don't you just change both names?"

I shook my head no. "I'm going to go with it for now," I said.

I looked at the photo again. *Emilio Sheen.* Who was he? Doing my own gut check, I thought, *This doesn't feel right.*

I showed the head shot to my father. I could see his eyes dropping down to read the name along the bottom. He stared at it for an extra beat.

"You really ought to reconsider this," he said. He'd changed his name to the great sadness of his own father, and once he'd started making a living as Martin Sheen he couldn't go back.

"One of the biggest disappointments I have is that I don't own the name I use," he said. "It belongs to a fantasy. It's not me. Think about what's happening in the country now. So many Hispanics are starting to rise up. Wonderful things are happening in that community. You can be part of that movement." Then he said, actor to actor and father to son, "Don't do it. You'll regret it for the rest of your life."

I had to ask myself: Did my father really believe changing my name was unnecessary? Or did he want me to keep the family name to make up for a choice he'd regretted? Was this about helping me claim my identity or about trying to undo his own mistake?

If I'd liked the way Emilio Sheen looked I might have pushed back to an extreme and said, "The hell with it, I'm going with Sheen." But instinctively, I knew it was the wrong choice. I knew my father was right. Emilio Sheen wasn't me.

Against the better judgment of people in the industry, I said, "Okay, we're going back to Estevez." The agents and managers did the equivalent of throwing up their hands and rolling their eyes. "Okay, if that's what you want to do, fine," they said. "But it's just going to make everyone's job more difficult."

I understood their frustration. Keeping my name meant I'd have to rely on my own merit to get jobs. The work would have to speak for itself. And that was fine with me. If I was going to make it as an actor, I wanted to get there because I had talent and worked hard, not because I had the right connections. In many ways Hollywood was and still is an insider's game of handshakes and favors and personal connections, but that wasn't how I'd been raised to operate. If I felt entitled to anything at all, it was to get the same chance as any other actor trying to break in.

At the same time, I inevitably had access to agents and managers just by virtue of having grown up as an actor's son. That much would get me in the door, but once I stepped in I'd be on my own. Like every other aspiring actor, to get an agent I needed to have either film experience or prepared monologues I could perform. In effect, I had to audition. I chose a passage from William Inge's *The Dark at the Top of the Stairs* and a classic monologue from act 2 scene 2 of *Hamlet* when the Players first arrive: "You are welcome, Masters, welcome, all!" At the time I didn't realize it was the same monologue my father had used, in 1960, when he first auditioned for Joseph Papp.

I was terrified to walk into an office, stand in front of a desk, and launch into a monologue on the spot, knowing how much was riding on my performance. But if this was a hoop I had to jump through to get an agent, I was willing to do it. "I'm a young actor," I would say when I walked in the door. "This is my background. I'm using my real name. I'd like to audition for you now."

The fifth agency I approached, Dade/Rosen, was based out of a tiny office above a Jaguar dealership on Sunset Boulevard. They weren't one of the big players in town, but they were willing to meet me. I walked up a little flight of stairs and entered the reception area. When I was called back to the agent's office it was the same routine I'd been through at four other agencies: handshakes and hellos, "Let's see what you've got," one monologue followed by the other, and then "We'll get back to you." The classic neutral response. I walked out the door every time not knowing if a call would come or not.

This time, it did, in the form of Sharon Black on behalf of Mike Rosen. "Let's get some pictures and résumés together, and we'll start sending you out," Sharon said.

A few weeks later, she called back with details for an audition. It was for the British director Alan Parker, who'd recently been nominated for a Best Director Oscar for *Midnight Express.* Now he was casting for a film about students at a performing arts high school in New York. The script followed eight students over the course of their four high school years, with the. working title *Hot Lunch.* I was asked to read for the role of Montgomery Mac-Neil, a quiet, sensitive drama student who reveals he's gay during sophomore year. I picked up the lines from my agent, and Lee helped me run them to prepare.

The audition fell in the middle of a weekday. I didn't have a car at school, but Lee had his mother's Volvo that day so the two of us ditched lunch to get me over to the MGM studio in Culver City in time.

I popped a Miles Davis tape into the cassette deck as we cruised along the 10 freeway. I was nervous, but excited. Alan Parker was known as a very serious, very important director, and I was a huge fan of *Midnight Express.* I didn't want to embarrass myself, but more than anything, I wanted to feel that I'd done the best job I could. My father kept a framed quote from

James Dean on display in our living room: "Being a good actor isn't easy. Being a man is even harder. I want to be both before I'm done." I was hoping for both that day, too.

Lee drove through the white colonnades at the entrance to MGM. In those days you could take your car right onto the lot and up to the studio door. He waited outside the entrance while I walked in alone.

"Right this way," the casting director said, motioning me into a separate room.

A man in rolled-up shirtsleeves with brown hair hanging in his eyes was sitting on a chair. I tried not to let my nervousness show. The only other seat in the room was on a couch directly across from him. I sat down.

"Hello," he said, in a melodious English accent. "I'm Alan Parker." Then he picked up a video camera and lifted it to his eye.

"And . . . go!" he said, without even a word of small talk.

This is so odd, I thought. The lens couldn't have been more than two feet from my face.

"Okay . . ." I said, and delivered the lines I'd prepared. When I was done, Parker switched off the video camera and placed it back in his lap.

I waited.

"Thank you very much," he said.

I'd just had my first professional audition. And I'd be back to school before the end of lunch.

Lee was waiting in the car outside. "How'd it go?" he asked.

"I have no idea," I said as I slid back into the passenger seat. "But I got all the lines right."

Parker auditioned more than three thousand young actors and high school students for his film. The role of Montgomery went to Paul McCrane, a soft-spoken eighteen-year-old redhead from Pennsylvania who nailed it on camera. When the film was released in May of 1980, it had a new title: *Fame.*

Every morning in creative writing class, Mrs. Shackleton greeted us the same way: "How is your consciousness today?"

A petite woman with short curly hair and penetrating eyes, she would stand in front of the class and let her words hang in the air. It wasn't a question in search of an answer — more of an invitation to reflect.

The first time she posed the question, the room filled with embarrassed giggles. Mrs. Shackleton just stood there, taking it in. It was as if she'd anticipated this reaction and wasn't bothered by it. The next day she asked us again. This time there were fewer giggles. The third day, even fewer. By the end of that first week, we were all engaged.

I'm not sure a teacher could get away with this in the more cynical world we live in today. Today's parents would probably call the school in an outrage, demanding, "What the hell is this about? I sent my kid to school, not to a therapy session." But at sixteen, I thought it was a fascinating, progressive, and very bold question to lay on a room full of high school students. How *was* my consciousness today? No one had ever asked me that question in quite that way, so I'd never before stopped to ask myself.

In Mrs. Shackleton's class, I began to flourish as a writer. Her exercises challenged us to express ourselves in print and also to think in new ways. She would ask us to write an essay about what we valued most, or what we'd learned outside of school. One assignment asked us to imagine a utopian classroom. She was interested in our ideas and that was really all a class of sixteen-year-olds needed to inspire them to create.

At the end of the school year, one of our last assignments was to write letters to our unborn children from the points of view of the parents we expected to become. I produced five notebook pages in my careful school penmanship. Reading it now, I'm struck by how much of who I am today was already in place at sixteen, and also by the insight and maturity, as well as the self-criticism that I don't remember having back then.

Emilio Estevez
Per. 3 6/2/79

Letter from a Parent

Dear Son,

I'm writing to you direct from Paris, France, where I'm finishing up my new feature film that I told you so much about. I guess that's all I've ever done is tell you about ME, and I've often neglected your feelings and interests on life. I have shunned the questions you have asked me, only to avoid my own embarrassment. No amount of apologies or "I'm sorrys" will ever replace my shallowness towards you. This is the main reason why I am writing to you now. I really want you to know that I love you.

You will see that as you venture on through life, you will constantly learn more and more about yourself and your environment. I feel that there are certain things of interest that I should pass on to you, to help you to get a firmer grasp on life. I want you to know things that will help you to build up the foundations of a sound future.

I went on to write a long passage about spiritual awakenings and tried to describe my personal beliefs:

Inside each and every one of us, there is a light . . . a spiritual light that carries you through life. It eats with you, sleeps with you, and experiences all that you experience. In a sense, it is a great force of energy within us all. When you die, it leaves the body and travels on to another material body where it will do new and different duties. And no, Dad has not gone mad or flipped his wig. I'm simply relating to you what I have found and experienced. In your lifetime, you will probably search long and hard for your spiritual being and maybe even without success. Please remember that you must never abandon your spiritual search. If you do, then you basically abandon life.

After a few more paragraphs I concluded with:

I want to leave you with one last thought to remember: you may try hard, but you will never outlive your father, even after I'm dead. I'll always be in your mind, taking care of you, and making sure that everything is all right.

And then I ended with the same signature my father used in his letters to me, adding my own personal twist:

> Keep eating your greens!
> Peace & Love,
> Dad

The assignment asked us to project our current selves into the future and see what we found, but the letters were more of a reflection of who we were right then, about our core values and long-term aspirations. Having a son and being a parent were such abstractions to me in high school, maybe I was also writing the letter I imagined my own father could have written to me — or wished he had.

During senior year I landed a small role in a school production, and an even smaller role in a larger, professional play. The SaMoHi production was *Stage Door,* the

1936 play about a group of aspiring actresses living together in a New York City boardinghouse. I landed the part of Sam Hastings, a suitor from Texas. My parents came to opening night, but there wasn't much of me to see. Sam Hastings had a whopping three lines to deliver in a Texas cowboy accent. I actually spent more time building the sets for *Stage Door* than working on my performance. Still, it got me up on the SaMoHi stage for the first time.

Not long after, my father left for Jupiter, Florida, to do a series of shows for Burt Reynolds's Dinner Theater. My parents had been having trouble in their marriage, but I had chosen to remain neutral. Whatever problems they had between them were their business, and I trusted they'd figure it out.

When my father learned there would be a bunch of roles for young sailors in a revival of the play *Mister Roberts,* he asked if I'd like to go down with him and audition for a part.

"Sure," I said. I'd taken classes over the past two summers to have a lighter course load during the school year, so I didn't have a full class schedule as a senior. It wasn't hard to get a leave of absence from school and bring whatever class work I'd be missing to Florida with me.

As the leading man's son I had a little edge in the auditions, but I wanted the director, Joshua Logan, to make the decision that was best for the play. On audition day, I walked onstage with a group of other actors and stared into a cavernous, dark space. Logan was sitting in a front row wearing a white shirt, a jacket, and a tie. Always impeccably dressed, even for rehearsals, Logan was a theater legend who knew the play so well he could recite it in his sleep. He was getting on in age by then and during the audition and rehearsals he would sometimes nod off. But if you missed a single word he'd lift his head, say, "That's an 'and'!" and then fall back asleep.

For the audition he asked me to read for every possible role he thought I might be right for, and then he'd mix it up and have me try a different part while another actor read the one I'd just done. At the end of the audition he scanned the group and basically said, "You'll play this part, and you'll play that part, and the rest of you, thank you very much."

I was cast as a crew member and every night I'd swagger onto stage in a white sailor's suit and cap. I had an absolute ball for the three weeks of rehearsal and the three-week run. Dinner-theater audiences would generally be happy that actors showed up, but Burt's dinner theater was a far more professional operation than most. We played to a packed audience every night. Burt could draw well-known actors to his stage and for me it was an opportunity to be in the company of seasoned professionals. One of Burt's longtime friends, Alfie Wise, played Ensign Pulver, the Jack Lemmon role in the film, and was hilarious. The Jimmy Cagney role of Captain Morton was played by Simon Oakland, a stage, television, and film actor best known as Doctor Richman in *Psycho* and Lieutenant Schrank in the film version of *West Side Story.*

My father and I shared an apartment near the theater for the six weeks in Jupiter. I was already looking ahead to what I'd be doing after graduation and was a little self-involved. We didn't spend much time together, but I shopped to buy him food and cooked healthy meals for him. We were just two actors living together with separate interests during the day, doing our jobs together at night. They were good weeks together. No conflict and no drama, except on stage, of course. Just good weeks.

I returned to SaMoHi in February ready to appear on stage again. If the drama department wouldn't cast me, I decided, I always had the option of writing something for myself. Our drama and English teacher, Mr. Jellison, was a careful, meticulous, frighteningly thoughtful native of Maine who inspired a whole generation of SaMoHi actors, including Sean Penn, Chris Penn, Robert Downey Jr., and Rob Lowe. With his aviator glasses and brushed-back graying hair he looked like a middle-aged version of the director John Hughes.

Mr. Jellison encouraged his drama students to discover their passions by choosing their own work. That said, he had his own strong opinions. I once brought him a copy of *The Naked Hamlet,* part of my campaign to star, like my father had, in the rock-and-roll version of the play. It was a long shot, but I hoped the avant-garde, outrageous remix of Shakespeare would inspire Mr. Jellison the way it had inspired me. In 1980 it seemed like exactly the kind of play the high school should be doing.

A week later he returned the book to me, holding it out between his thumb and forefinger as if it were a turd he'd found in a swimming pool.

"Sacrilege," he said. "Please take it back."

I thought his response was hilarious, but I revered him anyway.

Soon after *Mister Roberts* ended I'd started bouncing around the idea for a two-person play about the aftereffects of the Vietnam War. In early 1980 the Soviets had just invaded Afghanistan, fifty-two American hostages were being held in Iran, and the U.S. government was talking about reinstating Selective Service registration for eighteen- to twenty-five-year-old men. It was an uncertain time to be seventeen years old: The possibility of another war and all that this implied was on everyone's mind.

I imagined a play where one character would be a hardboiled career soldier working as a military recruiter and the other a Vietnam veteran who'd been shattered by his experiences. How would each man answer the questions, "What does war mean to you?" and "Where are you now, emotionally, after the war has ended?"

I asked Lee to cowrite it and we worked together at lunchtime and after school to bang out a first draft. Ultimately we created an hour-long one-act play we called *Echoes of an Era,* which involved dual overlapping monologues exposing how both characters, despite their obvious differences, were coming from a place of pain and regret. Instead of doing a regular Friday night, Saturday, Sunday performance, we were able to do two daytime shows for English and history classes and one after-school show for anyone else who wanted to come.

Throughout February and March, Lee and I were writing, directing, and acting in the play. At one point we discovered that every writer, and every writing team, reaches a point where they need a fresh, outside perspective. The day we hit that wall we were sitting in my bedroom, stuck in a discussion about how to stage the play, when we heard a knock on my window.

The neighborhood kids were always coming and going at our house, so I was used to this. My bedroom was next to the front door with a big window that looked out over the front lawn, and some of my friends liked using my window instead of the door. Charlie had it even easier: his room had a second door that opened onto the backyard. His friends could come and go and no one in the house ever knew.

On this particular day, Lee and I looked up to see Sean Penn knocking. I opened the window to let him in.

"What's happening?" he said. He angled his left leg over the hedge and slid through the window frame.

Sean had graduated from SaMoHi two years earlier. For his senior project he'd done a film and enlisted a bunch of kids at school to help. Since then he'd had small roles in a few TV shows but his breakout roles as a cadet captain in *Taps* and as stoner Jeff Spicoli in *Fast Times at Ridgemont High* were still a year or two away. Still, Sean knew something about directing and a lot about acting, and he was a friend — a natural for us to turn to for help.

"Sean, man, Lee and I are doing this play at SaMo and we're lost," I said. "I need you to come in and help us stage it because we're completely at sea."

He read the script and agreed to come on board as director. We settled on a simple set, a facsimile of an army recruiting office on one side of the stage and a living space littered with beer cans and gin bottles on the other. The venue would be the 200-seat black-box Humanities Center Theatre on campus. I would play Richard Donnelly, the emotionally damaged veteran, who was putting his story on tape for a writer who was researching "our folly in Indochina." Lee would play the tough-talking Sergeant Collins, telling his story to the same writer over the phone. To write Richard's long passages about fighting and being injured in Vietnam I drew from Joe Lowry's story, what I'd seen in war films, and what I'd learned on and off set in the Philippines.

The play went up in April on a Wednesday and Thursday at lunchtime and right after school on Wednesday afternoon. I put advertisements in *LA Weekly* and the school newspaper ran a photo of Lee and me with a promo for the play, including a quote from Mr. Jellison: "It is inspirational to see what can be done by youthful talent."

The play was a politically charged and overly earnest attempt to create dialogue about the meaning of war, but the students responded positively. We opened at lunchtime on Wednesday to a full theater. More students came to see that play than any other one that year. We began with a slide presentation of combat shots, period photos, and close-ups of real GIs set to the Simon and Garfunkel song "7 O'Clock News/ Silent Night." Then the lights came up on Richard's apartment and on me, wearing Levi's, a stained tank top, and combat boots, holding a half-empty bottle of gin.

"What do you want from me, huh? What are you trying to squeeze outta me?" I began.

With each line, I felt the power behind the words, *my* words, increasing. I did more than play Richard. I actually became him. And Lee became a convincingly angry, pro-

American, pro-war sergeant. We shifted slowly from one long monologue to the other and back again until the very end of the act, when the script cut back and forth quickly between the two actors.

"War is not a cycle! It's a way of life!" Lee shouted into the telephone.

"I really don't see war as a cycle. I see it as an obsession," I said into the tape recorder.

I could sense the audience realizing that the two men were answering the same questions from the same interviewer. Sean's shaping and direction had worked exactly as we had hoped it would.

My parents came to the Wednesday after-school performance, but I didn't feel the impulse to pour it on because they were there. I just stood up after the slide show ended and did my part. When the script called for me to weep while I told the story of the ambush that killed the rest of my unit, it felt as natural as breathing.

Afterward, my parents came up to congratulate me. My father wore an expression I couldn't quite place. It was pride, no question about it, but there was something else mixed in. It could have been pain, but I didn't have time to dwell on that. I was riding high on the performance. I'd cowritten a play and costarred on a stage, and this time, I'd remembered every line.

In June of 1980, 1,200 high school students in Santa Monica were set to graduate and move on to college or jobs in the real world. My parents threw a graduation party for me a few days after school officially ended. A couple dozen people milled around in our backyard: friends from school, neighbors, and my uncles Mike and Al. My mother ordered a six-foot sub sandwich and bowls of coleslaw from a local deli and my father set up a cooler of beer outside. The drinking began midday, as soon as the guests arrived.

I was already a couple of beers in when the kitchen phone rang.

"Emilio! It's for you!" my mother called into the backyard. I walked in carrying my beer can and picked up the receiver.

"Emilio? This is Father Bud Kieser."

Father Ellwood "Bud" Kieser was a Paulist, a member of the Roman Catholic order that brings the messages of the Gospel to the non-Catholic world, doing outreach mainly through print media and film. Father Kieser ran Paulist Productions from a building down on Pacific Coast Highway where he produced, among other shows, a series called *Insight.* These half-hour segments that aired on Sunday mornings were dramatic shows with a moral message, teaching compassion, tolerance, and generosity without being overly preachy. My father had done a few of them, and a few months earlier I'd made my television debut, if you can call it that, with a walk-on role that involved all of dragging a suitcase into a motel and shouting, "Hello?" I looked so young I had to wear a fake mustache to appear old enough for the part.

"We're doing a show we think will be very interesting," Father Kieser said. "The director is here right now. We'd like to have you come in and audition for it." It was for one of their longer shows, sort of a clone of an *ABC Afterschool Special.* This one, Father Kieser explained, was about a troubled teenager whose drinking and drugging causes him to butt heads with his father, who essentially kidnaps him for a tough-love rehab camping weekend in the mountains.

I put my beer can down on the counter. I had a good buzz going, but I was sure I'd heard right. Father Kieser wanted me to audition for a lead role.

"Sure," I said. "When?"

"How does today work for you?"

Three thoughts galloped through my mind. First, *Today? As in, right now? During the party?* Second, *Wow. This is a great opportunity.* And third, *Uh-oh. How am I going to drive in this condition?*

"I'll be there," I said. "What time?"

I headed outside to look for my father. Spotting him across the backyard, I motioned him aside.

"Listen, Father Kieser just called me," I said. "He wants me to come in and audition but I've had a couple of beers and I can't drive. So, would you be willing . . ."

Within ten minutes, we were heading down Pacific Coast Highway in my father's orange Pacer. When we walked into the production building, everybody greeted him by name. I took the sides — the portion of a script an actor uses to prepare for an audition — looked at the pages quickly, and walked into the audition room. I didn't have time to memorize any of the lines. I'd have to do a cold reading of a scene where the character was drunk.

I learned a valuable lesson that day: If you're going to play someone who's drunk and you *are* drunk, you don't have any options. You can play the scene only one way — as drunk as you are. I managed to pull it off, but I don't recommend trying this one at home.

Afterward, we drove back to the party, where everyone was having such a good time, I'm not sure they even realized we'd been gone. Three hours later, the phone rang. It was Father Kieser again.

"You want to go to work?" he said.

"Absolutely."

The show was called *Seventeen Going on Nowhere* and it was scheduled to shoot that summer. Ellen Geer, Will Geer's daughter, was cast as my mother, and Ramon Bieri played my father. He'd appeared in *Badlands* as the ill-fated garbage collector named Cato and remembered me from back then. My role as the wayward rebel would require me to act sullen, sneak out at night in a souped-up VW Bug, have a fireside heart-to-heart with my father after trading blows, and spill out a tearful confession before the end credits rolled. Filming would take place in the San Fernando Valley and the mountains outside of Fresno. It was a plum job for a first-time TV actor, and I've been grateful to Father Kieser ever since for giving me the chance.

But high school graduation came first. A few days later, the official ceremony was held in the Greek Theater on the SaMoHi campus. My whole family was there to see me receive my diploma. I was incredibly proud and happy to have made it through. When I looked back at the past four years, I saw I'd survived the months in the Philippines, almost lost my father, learned how to shoot and edit short films, acted on a professional stage, written my first play, and landed my first television role. When I looked ahead, I saw a long, wide path of possibility.

The graduates were lined up alphabetically as the principal stood onstage and announced each of our names into a microphone. I stood amongst the E's and looked back at the line extending behind me. Twelve hundred students. *Twelve hundred.* That is not a small number, no matter how you line it up.

Aran, Arenberg, Armer.

I watched Lee walk onto the stage. He was headed to UCLA in the fall, and although we'd never intend for it to happen, we'd lose touch for many years. A true character until the very end of school, Lee scrawled in my yearbook: Echoes of an Era *was really a piece of left-wing propaganda. The more I think about it the more pissed off I get to have wasted all of my lunch time with you on that pile of shit. I wish you would get me a spot in your agency. I have already spoken to your father about being adopted. He said cool as long as I cut the lawn once a month. It's a shame that there are two people in this school with acting talent. Even more of a shame that you are not one of them. Peace, Love, and Martin Sheen forever. P.S. Emilio, if Ronald R. becomes president, you pay for gas. I'll drive.*

If there had been a category for Most Original, Lee would have won it hands down. As it was, of the 1,200 students in our class he was voted Best Actor. I won for Prettiest Hair.

Engle, Espinoza, Estevez.

My section of the line made its way onto the stage. By the time I reached the principal, nine more names had been called. Then it was a quick shake-hands-take-the-diploma-walk-off-the-stage-shuffle-back-down-the-stairs.

I opened my diploma holder. Nothing was inside. "You've got to turn in your cap and gown to get it," another graduate told me as he walked by. When I handed over the armful of fabric, a volunteer leafed through a file box until she found a stiff sheet of ivory paper with my name printed underneath the school's seal. She handed it over to me.

And that was it. I was officially done with school.

CHAPTER FOURTEEN: MARTIN

INDIA
1981

Watching Emilio perform in *Echoes of an Era* was an unforgettable experience. When he talked about losing platoon mates in an ambush and broke down weeping, his tears struck me to the core. *Oh, my*, I thought. *He has that invaluable sense-memory well that all artists draw from to share their own fear, anger, pain, and joy. And he knows how to access it publicly. He's a fellow actor, top grade.* It was a stunning revelation to watch him step out on his own and declare himself as such.

To be honest, I was relieved he was so good. But I also hurt for him. My oldest son would soon enter my profession, and I knew all too well that it would cost him dearly. Anything worthwhile has to cost you. If it doesn't, you're left to question its value. What would this choice cost Emilio? Ideally, being a committed actor or any type of serious artist is a deeply personal effort to discover one's own authenticity and then share it with others. It's about transcendence. It's not about ego, money, power, celebrity, or success, and you can take that to the bank, with my compliments.

Emilio had grown up observing me, and I suspected he knew what he was getting into on every level. As he stood up there on that stage, embodying that Vietnam veteran, he knew I was watching, but he wasn't leveraging on my name or playing off his good looks. He clearly owned his talent and it was a frightening and beautiful thing for me to behold.

In early December, Janet, Ramon, Charlie, and I traveled to Kenya, where I participated in the ABC-TV series *The American Sportsman.* The episode told the story of a young man from Washington State who purchased three retired circus elephants and returned them to their natural habitat in Africa. Our travel included an overnight stay in London before going on to Nairobi, and we awoke to the tragic news of John Lennon's murder in New York City. The song "Abraham, Martin and John" — about three heroic men, Abraham Lincoln, Martin Luther King, and John F. Kennedy, all of whom had been assassinated in their prime —

looped endlessly in my mind. When would this senseless gun violence in my country ever end?

Back home I'd been offered a role in *Gandhi,* a film about the adult life of Mohandas K. Gandhi, the father and chief architect of the Indian independence movement and the inspiration for nonviolent resistance to oppression worldwide. I admired and was very fond of the director, Sir Richard Attenborough, who for twenty years had personally pursued every effort to bring Gandhi to the screen. Now he had succeeded and was gathering an extraordinary cast in India, which included Sir John Gielgud, Candice Bergen, the South African playwright Athol Fugard, and a newcomer named Ben Kingsley to play Gandhi. Without hesitation I accepted the role of Vince Walker, a composite character of the Western journalists who were instrumental in conveying reports of India's nonviolent resistance to the rest of the world. But the vast majority of my character was based on the real-life American journalist and author Vincent Sheean, whose successful book, *Not Peace but a Sword,* had been banned in Nazi Germany. Sheean was the only Western journalist who had personally witnessed Gandhi's assassination, recounted in his book, *Lead, Kindly Light.* My scenes were scheduled to shoot in India for five weeks beginning in January 1981.

I asked the production company for extra airline tickets in the hope that Janet and the kids would come with me, but it proved impossible since Ramon, Charlie, and Renée were returning to school and Janet needed to get things back to normal after Christmas holidays and the recent trip to Kenya. That left Emilio, who had already finished school and was still living at home. I longed to share the experience of India with him, but he was reluctant at first.

"Come on," I said. "It's not going to be like the Philippines. We'll be in India five, six weeks, tops."

To my relief he agreed to join me and came to view the trip as a great adventure. We both did.

We took off for India in early January, just as the other kids returned to school. After stopovers in Tokyo and Bangkok we landed in New Delhi at night, collected our bags, and stepped outside into a sea of humanity. There were *throngs* of people, many of them wrapped or draped in colorful, traditional Indian dress. My first thought was, *Everyone's in costume!* The scene had the same electric energy and constant activity of a staged set. So many people were congregating in and around the airport that at first, I thought a celebrity or an important government official must be arriving or departing soon. But everyone was there to watch the airplanes take off and land. It was a type of free entertainment.

Emilio and I slid into the first taxi in the line, a tiny cab driven by a young driver with a turban wound around his head. I sat directly behind him, with Emilio next to me. The cab was so small the back of the driver's head was only a foot or two from my face. I could see bugs crawling around in the back of his hair, going in and out of the turban. He didn't seem to be bothered by them, or even to notice they were there.

I looked at Emilio. He'd seen it, too. *We're a long way from home,* I thought. It was a portent of what was yet to come, and I sensed that nothing we encountered on this trip would be like anything we had experienced before.

Our cab traveled through densely crowded urban streets where people lived outdoors in pup tents, cardboard boxes, lean-tos, under trees, near fountains, anywhere they could clear a space. The hotel was like a marble palace rising from the city center, with a lobby the size of three ballrooms.

The cool, pristine, spacious interior was the antithesis of life outside. *They could fit half the people on the street in here,* I thought.

The next morning when we returned to the street in daylight, we entered a kaleidoscope of action and smells and sounds. A family of five rode by on a bicycle with two flat tires. A donkey with a broken leg pulled a cart carrying three people. The air was filled with the smell of open fires and putrid smoke that stung the backs of our throats. Mules, horses, cattle, camels, donkeys, and an occasional elephant strolled down the street amid the constant stream of bicycles, motorcycles, scooters, and little cars with drivers leaning heavily on the horns. Occasionally a cow would plop down in the middle of the sidewalk.

And the *people,* everywhere the people, walking, driving, rushing, sitting, lying in the gutters, some with stubs for limbs; women with smudged *bindis* between their eyebrows; blind beggars crying out for coins; businessmen striding purposefully past cluttered storefronts; peddlers pushing wooden carts; toddlers traveling in packs, many of them pulling on the clothes of Caucasian tourists and extending empty hands encrusted with grime. This was leagues beyond whatever poverty we thought we'd seen in Mexico or the Philippines.

Disease was palpable and public. And yet this tragedy coexisted with such extraordinary beauty. The Delhi streets held so much raw, obvious need and yet there was so much *life*. It was clear to me why some of the first sproutings of intelligence in the human race grew out of this culture. It was vibrant and vital.

The horrible deprivation was nearly overwhelming, and I had to find a way to embrace both worlds of poverty and privilege and to stay conscious of the boundaries. *I'm a visitor here,* I thought, *I have a passport. I can leave any time.* But India can set any Western concept on its heels. Most of the world still suffers from a lack of basic necessities like food, shelter, health care, and environmental protection, and when you see this up close, you also see the need for justice, mercy, and love. And if you are vulnerable to these musings your life may never be the same.

In India I learned that the West spins one way, and the East the other. I had to make a conscious decision not to be pulled into cycling in reverse. If I started spinning with India, especially for such a short time, I knew I'd get dizzy and I wouldn't be able to focus on the film. Perhaps a compromise was possible.

When my scenes began filming I alternated between working for a few days and then having a few days off. At first, during my free time, I'd stay close to the hotel. But Emilio went out to explore every day with extra rupees in his pocket for the many children who swarmed around him. It was such a loving, pure, practical way to try to alleviate the suffering the only way he could, but it marked him as a Western tourist with money, and the children started to recognize him.

"You've got to go into the streets," he would tell me. "You've got to come down with me and experience what's going on there."

I followed him down on my next day off and he was right: The streets jarred me awake. Innocently, as we started giving some money, the crowds pressed into us from all sides, trapping us like a mob. On one occasion we needed the police to get us out. Another time as we were trying to get through a crowd of children, pressing a few coins into their hands, we had to escape the crowd ourselves by pushing our way into a cab. As we drove off I heard a pounding on the back window. Three little girls, maybe five or six years old, were hanging on to the back of the taxi, one with her face pressed up right against the glass a foot away from mine. They were risking their lives. "Stop the cab!" I shouted. We put them inside, turned around, and took them back.

The *people.* The poverty. The possibilities.

Emilio and I would meet many Westerners in hotels and restaurants and on the streets, sincere young men and women who had come to India on personal spiritual quests. "I'm here with Maharishi So-and-so. I'm staying at his ashram," they might say, or "I'm going to this guru." It seemed they all had gurus, but they could walk down the street and trip over people without ever really seeing them. *Just open your eyes!* I thought. *These desperate poor are your gurus.*

While I wasn't looking for a spiritual connection or Eastern mysticism, the experience in India began to reconnect me to Catholicism, which had always been my anchor. The spirituality among those ministering to the poor in India was the same type of commitment I was drawn to in the Catholic activists I admired most at home, like Dorothy Day of the Catholic Worker Movement, who embraced the command of the Gospel from the nonviolent Jesus to "feed my lambs, feed my sheep" and who, through her peace and social justice work, had embodied the voice of the poor, speaking truth to power. She had passed away only weeks before, but her dear friend, Mother Teresa, was still very much alive and living in India.

Sir Richard Attenborough and Mother Teresa had become great friends when he narrated a documentary about her after she won the Nobel Peace Prize. One day he told a group of people on the film that we'd been invited to meet her that coming Sunday after Mass at her home for the dead and dying in Calcutta. I rushed back to the hotel to share the news with Emilio.

"Who?" he said.

"Mother Teresa! We've been invited to meet Mother Teresa!"

"Why do you want to do that?"

"You're a crazy boy!" I said. "I can't believe a son of mine is asking this. We're invited to meet Mother Teresa! We can take the train Saturday night and get to Calcutta Sunday morning. We'll go right to Mass and afterward Mother will receive us."

"Why do you want to do that?" he asked again.

"What's the *matter* with you?" I said. "This is a living saint, for God's sake! Look out in the world. Who else is doing that kind of work? And we have an opportunity to meet her personally. It's an opportunity of a lifetime."

"I understand all that," he said. "And I know who she is. But why do you want to *meet* her?"

"So I can tell everybody that I met Mother . . ." and then I stopped midsentence. *Oh my God,* I thought. That was the real reason I wanted to go, so I could brag about having met her. And Emilio knew it. He'd wanted me to admit it to myself. That moment of self-discovery humbled me greatly.

In a sense, at that moment Emilio became my teacher. He helped me realize that meeting Mother Teresa for the wrong reason would be worse than not meeting her at all, and I decided to pass on the trip to Calcutta. It would be another ten years before I finally met Mother in Rome, and when I told her this story we shared a good laugh.

A few weeks into filming *Gandhi,* I gave one of our unused airline tickets to Emilio's godfather from New York, John Crane. John often joined us on our travels when he could get time off from his job with the post office in New York City. One day the three of us hired a driver to take us from Delhi to Agra to see the Taj Mahal. John was a terrific amateur photographer and he'd gotten Emilio interested in photography. At one point we were standing on the terrace behind the Taj Mahal, looking down the Yamuna River, and John was teaching Emilio how to focus with his new zoom lens. I was standing there, casually watching them, when I noticed Emilio's face turn completely white. He bent over as if he was going to be sick.

"What's the matter?" I asked, alarmed.

"Look through the lens," he said, handing me the camera. I lifted the camera to my eye, focused, and saw what he had seen: A dead body lying on the riverbank was being eaten by a pack of dogs, as vultures circled overhead. This was a burial site for a certain Indian sect, who brought their corpses to the river. For them it was a normal practice, an accepted part of their culture, but for us the sight was a terrible shock.

Death, disease, poverty: All of the social ills that were mostly kept under cover in the West were on constant display in India. Later in the film shoot, when we were staying at a hotel near the beach in Bombay, Emilio was walking on the sand when a body washed up. Nobody around him acted as if this was an unusual event.

Death was all around us on that trip, just as it seemed to be for Indians in their daily lives. They routinely lost their very old and they often lost their very young. Observing all this, I couldn't help but appreciate how precious life is, *all* life, every bit of it, and give thanks and praise for mine and my family's, every day.

Mahatma Gandhi was assassinated on January 30, 1948, and his state funeral took place the following day. Several million mourners lined the five-and-a-half-mile route from Birla House, Gandhi's home in Delhi, to the funeral pyre along the Yamuna River to pay their final respects. It took five hours for his body to make the trip.

Attenborough chose January 31, 1981, the thirty-third anniversary of Gandhi's funeral, as the day to film the funeral re-creation. He needed an excessively large crowd for this scene. Today, the computer generated imagery process known as "flocking" can take a piece of a crowd and duplicate it many times to give the impression of a much larger gathering, but CGI was just being developed in 1981. All the extras in the funeral scene had to be real people on the set, in the flesh. Advertisement fliers were placed all over Delhi inviting residents to celebrate the father of their nation by participating in the scene.

The morning we filmed the funeral, Emilio and I arrived at the Rajpath, or the "King's Way," the ceremonial boulevard that runs for a mile and a half straight from the Indian president's residence to the National Stadium. The Rajpath had been along Gandhi's funeral route and is also the site of national parades throughout the year. The sequence was supposed to start at 8:00 a.m. but kept getting delayed. Eleven cameras were in place all over the Rajpath, on top of buildings and down on the ground, to capture as many angles as possible, because with so many extras we would not be able to start over and film the procession twice. From where Emilio and I stood, it looked like thousands had shown up to participate, most dressed in traditional white for a funeral as the flyer had requested.

I was in costume, in a tailored suit and tie with my head bare to the sun, and the morning began to grow very hot. Another half hour passed, and shooting still hadn't started. To see if we could identify the problem, Emilio and I walked to the top of the steps, turned around, and looked back. A chill zipped straight up my spine. The Rajpath was *jammed* with people. That's what

459

was holding everything up. People were packed shoulder to shoulder along the boulevard. Hanging from lampposts. Dangling from trees. Standing on top of cars. People *everywhere,* far more than a million of them. The crowd was like a white living organism, moving and shimmering in the bright sun. Attenborough truly had managed to recreate the day of Gandhi's funeral. It was, and remains, the largest cast of extras ever assembled in the history of film.

Eventually I had to go back down into the middle of that crowd. I carefully made my way to the place behind the military caisson where the principal characters would walk. A wax model of Ben Kingsley lay on the caisson's open back, wrapped in a white cloth and covered with pink and yellow rose petals. The wax figure looked as much like Gandhi as Ben Kingsley did. Their resemblance was remarkable. Actors had been cast to be lookalikes of the real individuals, and Kingsley was almost a double for Gandhi, as was the Indian actor Roshan Seth for Prime Minister Jawaharlal Nehru and Athol Fugard for British general Smuts. This went a long way toward making the film feel authentic, one of its strongest points. The recreation of the funeral looked so much like the real funeral I imagine the editors could have spliced actual footage from 1948 into our scene and the transition would have looked almost seamless.

When the procession finally began, we walked slowly along the Rajpath with cameras off to the left and right capturing all our moves. The military led the procession, followed by the Bengal Lancers, all of them Sikhs on horseback, and then the caisson bearing Gandhi's body. The actors playing Gandhi's family, colleagues, and ashram devotees walked directly behind. Everyone was packed in very tight. The crowd must have been fifty deep on each side of the road.

After a short while, the procession came to a full stop while the cameramen adjusted their equipment. They needed to move everything a few hundred yards up the Rajpath to film the next segment of our walk. The extras lining the boulevard were in a festive mood or maybe just bored with the wait and they began to throw small items at the horses and shout at the mounted cavalry. The Sikhs looked fearsome up on horseback with their pointed lances and military-issue olive-green turbans. I couldn't understand what the people on the ground were saying, but from the tone of it they seemed provocative, like schoolyard bullies taking jabs at their classmates just for fun.

After ten or fifteen minutes of this, the soldiers abruptly decided they'd had enough and they ordered their horses to charge.

The collective cry of a million people is much louder than I ever could have imagined. As the crowd took off in every direction, I threw myself onto the pavement and tucked myself into a bundle. *Oh my God,* I thought. *All these people will be trampled. We're going to be killed!* And where was Emilio? He had to be down here somewhere in the crowd.

For the next few moments the only sounds I could hear were people's screams and the horses' hooves smacking down on the pavement as the stallions reared up and landed once, twice, three times. And then, as suddenly as it had broken out, the pandemonium stopped.

I opened my eyes in the eerie quiet and lifted my head. Before me, at eye level, was a sea of empty shoes scattered across the pavement. Sandals, loafers, flip-flops — every conceivable mode of footwear littered the street. People had scrambled away so fast they'd run right out of their shoes. It was one of the most astonishing sights I've ever seen.

Even more amazing was that no one had

been hurt, but the horses had scared the bejeezus out of everyone. It occurred to me that the soldiers hadn't intended to hurt the people, only to frighten them and remind them who was in power. For them, it was also a break in the monotony between takes. As I slowly stood up, I watched the soldiers guide their horses back into formation. The people reclaimed their shoes and settled back into their spectator roles. And, almost immediately, they started harassing the horses again.

This time the soldiers refused to be provoked and stared straight ahead, unmoved, like annoyed parents saying, "All right, you've had your fun. Enough's enough. We're not going to pay any attention to you anymore." None of this was caught on film, but the horsemen seemed to know exactly how to act, almost as if the exchange had been scripted. It was third world authority on display, and impressive to watch.

Later, someone explained to me that this was how the common people got their licks at authority figures. The poor in India had few chances to vent their frustration with the authorities, so they did when small opportunities like this one arose. It was a familiar cultural dance to the participants.

As I waited for the cameras to roll, I

looked closely at the extras around me, trying to commit their faces to memory. In large crowds in the third world, I'm always struck by the knowledge that, although I'm in close proximity to these particular people now, it's unlikely I'll ever see these faces again. In Delhi I'd just witnessed a profound cultural event and I wanted to remember the participants.

From Delhi the majority of the company moved more than 700 miles southwest to Bombay (now Mumbai) on the west coast of India along the Arabian Sea while a small camera crew and a few cast members went on to film a special sequence in Porbandar, the seaside town in the province of Gujarat where Gandhiwas born in 1869 and later returned to live. I was needed for a few scenes in Porbandar when Walker comes to see Gandhi in India after many years apart. In one scene they sit on a wall by the sea. "I've been all over the world," Gandhi says, "and I ended up where I started." He looks at Walker and he looks at the sea and says, "I've come home." In the film, that's when he gets the idea for the Salt March to the sea to protest the British tax on salt and invites Walker to join him. "It would have been very uncivil for me to have invited you all this way for nothing," Gandhi explains.

My favorite scene in Porbandar, and one of my favorites in the film, is what we called "the marriage scene." Gandhi and his wife Kasturba married at thirteen and remained together for sixty years until her death. In this particular scene, Gandhi and his wife re-create their wedding ceremony for Walker to demonstrate the seven vows of a Hindu wedding. The ritual involves a series of symbolic steps the bride and groom take together, to begin a journey that is not just about them, but also about their responsibility to each other and to their community.

"In every worthy wish of yours, I shall be your helpmate," Gandhi's wife says.

"Take the fourth step, that we may be ever full of joy," Gandhi says, slowly circling an imaginary fire.

"I will ever live devoted to you, speaking words of love and praying for your happiness."

"Take the fifth step, that we may serve the people."

"I will follow close behind you and help you to serve the people," his wife answers.

Watching this struck a deep chord within me. Essentially, the man is saying, "I will do this to serve the community," and the woman is saying, "You are taking the responsibility of going forward and I will make sure you don't get hit from behind. They'll have to go through me to get to you." They promise that they will be there for the community and the community can count on them. Now that they're a couple they're not interested in their own agenda. They will contribute to the community as a family.

The final vow of a Hindu wedding is "the seventh step, that we may ever live as friends." I couldn't help thinking of my own marriage vows and how selfish they'd been: "I take you to be *my* wife." The vows that Gandhi and his wife took seemed ideal to me, and also necessary for the vitality of a culture. They reminded me what it truly means to be married: the end of selfishness.

My friend Dan Berrigan, the Jesuit priest and social justice activist in the nonviolent resistance movement, once told me about a couple who asked him to marry them. "Let me ask you a few questions first," he said. "I assume you love each other?"

"Yes," they said.

"Then are you willing to promise to help each other become yourselves?" he asked.

He wanted them to understand that marriage is not about "becoming one" in the romantic sense we ascribe to it in the West but about supporting the truth in each other and being willing to risk a partner's wrath by pointing out when that partner isn't being honest. It's not about "becoming one" as a method of happiness but about helping each other become strong and authentic individuals together.

I began to realize in India that this was the kind of relationship Janet had always wanted with me. For twenty years she was quite willing to risk my wrath by telling me the truth, the whole truth, and nothing but the truth, all the time. For me, unfortunately, honesty was at best a sometimes thing. And now the consequences were becoming clear as a husband and father, and I needed to make some serious adjustments if I was ever to become my true self.

Emilio and I had already begun a new phase in our relationship when he walked away and left me on the sidewalk in Paris in 1979. It led to our time together in India, which dismantled and reassembled our ideas about poverty and humanity and survival and cemented a relationship of mutual respect and real love and support between us. Because he was eighteen and I was forty, the trip changed us in very different ways. Nonetheless, our shared experiences in India allowed us to have an equal, honest, enduring relationship that persists to this day.

Those five weeks in India had also launched me on a deeply personal spiritual quest that would culminate four months later in Paris, on the first day of May.

CHAPTER FIFTEEN: EMILIO

INDIA
1981

In India, my father observed, "All of your senses are assaulted here, especially your sense of justice." I can't imagine a better description of our time there. From the moment we got off the plane in Delhi we were surrounded by colorful, active crowds of people reaching for us. The smell of the city was multilayered, like a glass of wine. What do you smell in a Cabernet? Hints of cherries, leather, tar, ink, pencil lead? If the Philippines had been a glass of wine, I would have found the aromas of water, wet leaves, and tropical fruit. But Delhi in a glass would have been air pollution, burning garbage, and hot asphalt.

We'd observed poverty in rural Spain, Mexico, and the Philippines but India took it to the tenth power. The population density in the city created sights of unimaginable desperation. Families were living in makeshift shelters; children were begging in the streets. The city center was dusty and dry, brown and gray, a moving organism of more human beings than I'd ever seen gathered in one place. It was hard to be in the midst of Delhi and not see it, feel it, smell it, and taste it, every day. India challenged both of us at every possible level: physical, emotional, spiritual, and practical. It was, in a word, devastating.

It wasn't like my father says, that I went into the streets with pockets full of rupees to give away to children. I went out with whatever money I had on me, and I found it impossible not to give it all away by the end of the day. The suffering was so visible, it was impossible not to take it personally and want to help. I went to India with a suitcase full of my T-shirts and jeans and I came home five weeks later with just my camera and the clothes on my back. I'd given everything else away.

The way my siblings and I were raised, we recognized poverty but we never passed judgment. All the years that the four of us slept in the same room, I never thought of us as poorer than anyone else. We just lived the way we lived, with no stigma attached. Similarly, when we traveled, if a house lacked in modern conveniences, we accepted that was how people lived in that place, according to their culture and their means. India was the first time I met with situations that exceeded my comfort zone. On a day trip to Agra we stopped at a roadside restaurant to use the restroom. In the tiled floor of the men's room there were two places to put your feet with a hole between them. *Okay,* I thought. *This is a first.* This *is foreign. I don't know how I'm going to manage this one.*

As a cultural experience, the country was mind-blowing. Professionally, it was an exceptional experience, too. By eighteen I was auditioning for film roles in Los Angeles, and when I learned that *Gandhi* would have Sir Richard Attenborough at the helm and a list of phenomenal actors attached, I thought, *This is going to be something you want to see.* On set in India, I was hired to work as my dad's stand-in, which meant I'd take his place in costume while a scene was being set up. This kept him from standing out in the sun all day, especially in Bombay, where temperatures even in January hovered up in the nineties.

My dad and I were similar enough in stature and appearance for me to easily do the job. In several scenes he wore a white button-down shirt and an Irish tweed flat cap, so I was dressed in the same shirt, hat, and round wire glasses his character wore. At one point I was standing in front of the camera as the operators were setting up the shot, and Sir Richard Attenborough strode onto set.

"All right. You ready to shoot?" he asked, as he assumed his position.

Wait a second, I thought. *Somebody better tell him he has the wrong guy.* The resemblance between me and my father must have been that close. Fortunately, my dad and I managed the switch just in time.

I also had an opportunity to meet Ben Kingsley and watch him work — his discipline was extraordinary — and to see another big feature film come together. *Gandhi* was a gentle epic, whereas *Apocalypse Now* had been a bombastic one, and the energy on the Indian sets was much calmer and far less dangerous than in the Philippines. *Gandhi* was also done on a much larger scale. I'd look at the daily call sheet and see outrageous entries like "Today: Extras, 5,000." "Extras, 10,000." The funeral scene was phenomenal. The first assistant director in charge of all those extras was a British guy named Dave Tomblin who'd worked on films with large numbers of extras like *Raiders of the Lost Ark* and *The Empire Strikes*

Back. On the set of *Gandhi* he was like a rock star, communicating with and coordinating thousands of people without a hitch. Without a doubt, he was the right guy to have on that job.

The production company had reserved six airline tickets for our family, and the remaining four tickets would revert to the company at the end of the shoot. Nothing said they had to be used by family members, so we gave one to my godfather, John Crane, who joined us partway into the trip. In a conversation with my mother, our friend Roscoe Lee Browne revealed that he was going through a bout of depression. My mother innocently asked, "Would a trip to India help? We have an extra ticket." Roscoe replied, "Oh, darling, forgive me, but I only fly first class." She laughed and said, "It *is* first class."

Roscoe, who was best known as the chef in *The Cowboys* with John Wayne and as the butler, Saunders, in the TV sitcom *Soap,* had met my father in Los Angeles in the early 1970s. A poet, professor, and a former national track star, Roscoe was a brilliant, interesting, complicated cat. He and my godfather were both African-American but opposite in every other possible way. John was six foot five and weighed all of 140 pounds, while Roscoe was compact and muscular, with the build of an athlete even at the age of fifty-six.

They couldn't bear each other and seemed always at odds about something, like two warring factions my father and I constantly had to referee. We loved Roscoe like an uncle, but we couldn't deny that he was opinionated, dramatic, and never hesitated to speak his mind. One night at dinner in a restaurant in Bombay he began arguing with the South African playwright Athol Fugard — whom he greatly admired, by the way — and before long they were *screaming* at each other. The scene went from uncomfortable to excruciating when everyone in the room turned around to watch. As quickly as their argument began, it ended, to our relief. And the restaurant scene notwithstanding, we loved him so much we just took him as he was.

Roscoe was one of a kind. So was John Crane. Influenced by Roscoe and John, their manners of speech, their humor and imagination, and their profound intelligence, I'd use both of them twenty-five years later to create the character of Edward, the African-American sous chef in the kitchen of the Ambassador Hotel, for my film *Bobby*. Laurence Fishburne played the role, but only after Roscoe's death in 2007 did I discover that Roscoe had been a mentor to Fishburne for years.

The five weeks in India affected my father in a very intimate, personal way. For me, they had more of a sociocultural impact. India woke me up to everything that Americans take for granted, even things as simple as clean running water. After we came back to the United States I saw excess everywhere I turned — in how big our cars were, in the amount of clothing each person owned, even in the food we scraped off our plates, uneaten. I'd been overseas for only five weeks but I had a difficult time readjusting when we came back.

In India I'd started asking myself big questions like, *Why is there such injustice in the world? Is it a responsibility or a burden to notice the suffering?* I thought I'd be relieved to come back to the familiarity of home and the relative safety of L.A. Instead, I would drive on the Pacific Coast Highway with my windows down and inhale the clean ocean air, or turn on the tap in our kitchen and have fresh water instantaneously, and I would be flooded by a sense of gratitude. *How did I get so lucky?* I would wonder. *Was it fate? Was it karma?* Somehow, these questions were equally hard to answer.

EMILIO

The Catedral de Santa María in Burgos, Spain, commands the center of the Old City like a white limestone palace. Begun in 1221, consecrated in 1260, and completed in 1567, the Gothic-style cathedral houses the tomb of the eleventh-century Christian knight Rodrigo Díaz de Vivar, also known as El Cid. It's a significant landmark on the Camino Frances, sitting about a third of the way from St.-Jean-Pied-de-Port to Santiago de Compostela, and ranks as the third-largest cathedral in Spain after the ones in Seville and Toledo. Burgos residents have a saying similar to the Americans' "Is it bigger than a breadbox?" They ask, "Is it bigger than the cathedral in Burgos?" Not much is.

We're here today in this city of 180,000 to film a sequence in which Tom and his fellow pilgrims arrive in Burgos's Old City and reconnect with pilgrims from earlier in their travels. While we're having coffee in a local restaurant, a gypsy boy, known locally as a Gitano, steals Tom's backpack outside and runs off. Tom and his three companions give chase through the city, and while they don't catch the boy they do meet his father, who makes his son return the bag and invites them all to a community celebration that night.

My son Taylor lives in Burgos with his wife, Julia, whose family introduced us to the real-life Gitanos who appear in the film.

Today's scene, too, dates back to a Malibu morning in 2008.

Knock knock.

My father strides into my living room, full of enthusiasm after his morning yoga session and a workout on the basketball court.

"I have a great idea!" he announces. "A gypsy boy steals Tom's bag!"

I quietly close the front door behind him. "A gypsy boy?" I ask.

"Yeah, then they have to chase him through Burgos," he continues. "They run this way" — he mimes a mad dash to the left — "and they run that way" — he lunges to the right. The aspiring action hero strikes again.

This time, I like the idea right away. By losing his backpack — which holds the box of his son's ashes — Tom risks losing Daniel again. The theft allows him to discover that the items in his backpack have no real value to him, while Daniel's ashes do. Also, we have a chance here to address the public image of gypsies. The gypsy minority is discriminated against all over Europe, and Burgos is no exception. But Julia's mother Milagros has a close friend, María José Lastra, who lives in Burgos, has taught many gypsy students and has observed how close-knit and joyous their families are. My father's idea for this sequence would let us play both into and against political stereotypes of gypsies, which appeals to us both.

Burgos is a special place for our family. It was here that Taylor, traveling with my father in 2003, met Julia. At nineteen, Taylor was working as my father's personal assistant on *The West Wing.* During a six-week hiatus from the series they traveled together to Ireland for a family reunion organized by my brother Ramon on what would have been my grandmother's hundredth birthday.

My father invited Matt Clark, whom he regards as a brother, and after the three-day Irish reunion, the two of them plus Taylor flew to Spain to explore the Camino, which my father had always wanted to do. But with only a few weeks before *The West Wing* resumed production, the three of them didn't have enough time to walk the Camino, so they rented a red Mercedes with the intention of driving along the Camino Frances. From Madrid they headed north toward the nearest major stop along the Way of Saint James: the city of Burgos.

That first night, they arrived at Hornillos del Camino, a small town on the outskirts of Burgos. The local *refugio* for pilgrims was full for the night, with rows of pilgrims' hiking boots lined up along the walls to air out after hours of walking. While my dad visited the local church, Taylor and Matt visited a pub to inquire about a place to spend the night. Matt saw a sign on the wall for thermal baths that caught his interest, and he and Taylor emerged from the pub with directions to a nearby town.

That's how they stumbled upon El Molino.

El Molino ("the Mill") is what Spaniards call a *casa rural,* or rural house, sort of a cross between an upscale hostel and a bed and breakfast. It's a three-floor, six-bedroom stone inn with red tiled roofs and a canal running straight through its center. The canal was El Molino's power source, keeping the inn off the grid, and greatly added

479

to its appeal.

They booked rooms for two nights. On the second night, the host, Max and Milagros, invited them to the pilgrims' supper.

As Taylor remembers it, a beautiful girl walked into the room and joined them. It was the hosts' daughter, Julia, a student at the university in Burgos, who was visiting her parents for the evening. Taylor couldn't take his eyes off her.

After dinner, she asked, "Do you want to go outside for a cigarette?"

"Of course," he said. His Spanish was good, but limited, and she didn't speak any English, but sitting on the steps outside they managed to share the broad strokes of their life stories. After Taylor left to continue his travels they spoke by phone every day, and on the way back he convinced my father and Matt to pass through Burgos again, where he stayed with Julia for a few days. By the time Taylor met up with my father in Madrid and boarded the plane for the States, he knew what he wanted to do.

"I think I'm in love with Julia," he told my father during the flight, "and I want to go back. What do you think?"

"Follow your heart," my dad told him. "Don't ever leave it behind. You can always say you made the wrong choice afterward, but you should have the experience rather than risk the regret of never knowing. If you love this woman, find out if it's for real and if it's reciprocal."

Back in the States, Taylor applied for a visa and was back in Burgos within a few months.

My son moved to Spain because he fell in love, but as he came into adulthood he also needed to strike out on his own. It's one thing to grow up in the shadow of a famous father, and another to grow up in the shadow of a famous father, uncle, and grandfather. Expectations for his success in the United States, real or perceived, must have weighed on him heavily. In Los Angeles people in the film industry often greet one another with "What are you working on now? What have you done lately?" immediately trying to gauge their own successes relative to another's. In Spain, Taylor would be more likely to hear "How's your family?" Or "How are you feeling today?" Or "What are you doing this weekend?" It's easy to see why that kind of environment would appeal to anyone.

Taylor had been living in Burgos with Julia for two years when I paid him a surprise visit for his twenty-first birthday. I coordinated the details with Julia and my aunt

Carmen, who lives in Madrid. I called Taylor from Carmen's house on my U.S. cell phone so that the number would come up as a stateside call.

"What time is it over there?" he asked. "It must be really late for you."

Oh, no, I thought. I'd forgotten about the time change. "I can't sleep tonight," I fibbed. "I'm up late doing some writing."

The next day, I took a train from Madrid to Burgos. Julia had spun a tale for Taylor that involved an urgent visit to the post office, which is connected to the Burgos train station, and as Taylor walked out of the post office he saw me on the train platform. His face registered an expression of absolute shock and joy.

"What are you doing here?" he asked. "You're supposed to be in Los Angeles! I just talked to you on . . ."

We threw our arms around each other. Taylor remembers this day as one of the best birthdays he's ever had.

In central Burgos, clusters of pilgrims continually passed by Julia and Taylor's house, and I began inquiring about them and their journey along the Camino. But I was deep into work on *Bobby* at the time, so my interest in the Camino did not fully develop until 2007 after *Bobby* had been released and I could turn my attention to a new project.

Six years after my surprise visit to Burgos, in the summer of 2009, with pre-production for *The Way* in full swing, I flew to Spain for Taylor and Julia's wedding. My plan was to firm up the locations and coordinate the filming, go home to California, and then return to Europe in September to start production. But once I got to Spain and realized how much film prep and location scouting work there was to be done I never went home. A benefit of having grown up with a seminomadic childhood, moving from place to place as my father's career required, is that I can adapt to whatever situation presents itself. *Okay,* I thought in Spain. *I'm already here. I might as well stay. I can just buy more clothes if I need them.*

And now here we are in the autumn of 2009, standing outside the walls of the famous cathedral early in the morning. My father spots a Catholic priest from Mexico, whom we met in the small town of Torres del Rio about 90 miles back, walking with two other pilgrims.

"Padre!" My dad waves him down. "Would you please give us a blessing to begin our day of filming?"

"It would be my honor," the padre says.

The cast and crew fall silent as the pilgrim priest offers prayers and intentions in Spanish for us all. We cross ourselves when he finishes and offer him much thanks all around.

"*¡Buen Camino!*" we call out, a traditional farewell to pilgrims, as he and his companions begin their daily trek to the next town.

One of the great ironies of this production will be that this day of filming in Burgos, begun with that priestly blessing, becomes the worst day of the entire shoot. We've been looking forward to Burgos because we'll be among family, and also because the local government is excited to have us here, yet somehow almost everything that can possibly go wrong this day does. I don't know what causes it. All I know is that I'll never ask for a mortal blessing on this production again.

Today's sequence in Burgos calls for Tom, Joost, Sarah, and Jack to enter the Old City and head toward the Burgos Cathedral, where they're reunited with pilgrims they met earlier on the Camino. They gather inside a nearby restaurant, where my dad finally gets to order a *"Café con leche, por favor."* While Tom talks with a priest, played by Matt Clark, he sees the gypsy boy grab his backpack and take off. Tom and his friends chase the boy through the city, dead-ending in an isolated courtyard where the boy has disappeared.

What should be a rigorous yet straight-forward sequence is first complicated by the restaurant set. When I scouted the location back in February, the owner agreed to let us film inside. Coincidentally, a real pilgrim's backpack had been stolen outside his restaurant just the week before, he said, and he was agreeable about giving us the place for the day. We believed that by paying him we'd rented the whole restaurant, but he clearly has other plans. In the middle of filming, a busload of fifty Japanese tourists starts streaming through the restaurant en route to a private room in the back. We have to work to keep them quiet, and then to get them back onto the street when they're finished without disrupting our shots.

Outside the restaurant, crowd control has become a major problem. Our reputation as filmmakers has preceded us into Burgos, and people knew we were coming. Production assistants are dispatched to find police officers and obtain yellow tape to cordon off portions of the street.

Then the protesters arrive.

A large group of striking union workers,

armed with a bullhorn, colorful banners, and a petition with a list of grievances, march in unison onto the film set. Our first assistant director, Manu, rushes toward them to quell their minor yet very noisy demonstration. The loud shouts can't be kept off our soundtrack and we can't film unless they tone it down.

When the strikers see the film crew they see the opportunity for media attention as well, and they position themselves in the middle of the plaza where we need to shoot our next scene. Turns out it's a good strategy. Local news crews that arrive to report on our production begin to shoot street scenes that include the protesters, getting a twofer for their filming efforts. I start pulling my beard out, literally, one hair at a time.

Taylor, who's out on the street directing traffic, tries to reason with the protesters, but his pitch-perfect Spanish is drowned out by the incessant chants demanding "fairness," "higher wages," and "respect."

"This is a public street," they shout at Taylor. "And we have every right to demonstrate here!" Taylor remains calm and genteel, as is his nature. "Guys," he tells them. "I'm very sympathetic to you for losing your jobs, but if you don't quiet down,

I'm going to lose mine."

This disarms them a little

Suddenly, to my complete horror, my father, "Martin Sheen, Man of the People," breaks ranks from our crew, tosses off his backpack, and jumps into the protest. He starts shaking hands, and — I don't think I'm imagining this — takes their bullhorn to speak on behalf of the demonstrators, though he speaks very limited Spanish. Bulbs flash, video rolls, and production on our film halts while Sheen saves the day.

I turn to David. Words completely escape me. He's speechless, too. My dad takes photos with each striking worker and then with the entire group as they wave their banners and flags. He smiles for every person who points a mobile phone camera in his direction, even allowing for seconds to make sure no one is left out.

Finally, I find my voice. It has all the strength of a leaky helium balloon. "It's like he's running for president of Spain," I say.

David puts his arm around my shoulder, calming me down. "He could probably win," he agrees. "But look at it this way: People love him. And he loves them. Would you prefer it any other way? He's in his element and he's enjoying it."

"Let's see how much he's enjoying it ten

hours from now when we're in overtime and we haven't completed today's work."

Eventually, the demonstration moves to another location, after my father's intervention, which includes signing the petition.

Our next sequence, set close to the University of Burgos, involves Tom, Joost, Sarah, and Jack chasing down the gypsy boy, played by Omar Muñoz. We'll have to film all four of them running at full tilt through alleyways, around corners, and down long flights of stairs. Each shot requires multiple takes. Pounding the stones for hours is physically taxing work for them all. Even Jimmy Nesbitt, who runs every day, isn't used to this level of intensity. It's incredible that my father, at sixty-nine, manages to keep up. His strength and dedication continually surprise me, stun the crew, and inspire the other cast members. My mother, who's been on hand for the whole production and serves as an executive producer, had confided in me several times about how badly my father wants to please me with his performance and work ethic. She said she hasn't seen him work so diligently since he was a struggling starving actor in New York.

But even the most committed actors can only pound stone streets for so long. After several hours of filming, Yorick van Wageningen is in pain, Jimmy has twisted his ankle, and my dad has a pulled groin muscle on top of a pulled hamstring. Finally, we arrive at the scene where Tom and his fellow travelers land in a courtyard of a gypsy compound. Laundry lines crisscross overhead and firewood is arranged in neat stacks against the interior walls. The boy is nowhere to be seen but Tom calls out to him, hoping he can hear.

"Come out here, you little thief! Give me that bag, you little rotten . . . !" my dad shouts. His voice reverberates loudly off the stone walls. He's yelling and cursing, carrying on. It's too over the top for this scene.

"Cut!" I shout.

"What's wrong?" he asks.

I respond, "You're chewing up the scene. You're making it too big."

"It can't be small," he argues. "The boy stole the bag with the ashes . . . It's my son . . . I'm outraged!"

"Okay," I say. "Let's try it again."

More yelling and cursing.

"Cut!"

My dad wants this to be a big emotional moment, but for a scene like this less is often more. He needs to let us see Tom's private pain rather than hear his public pain.

"It's your job to inhabit the character," I tell him. "Be subtle. Trust me and the camera to do the rest."

After a few more takes, he gets the scene down to the perfect balance of emotion and restraint. In the final version he kicks at the air in frustration and calls out into the empty courtyard, his voice thick with emotion, "Can you hear me, son? I know you're here. Just give me the box! Just give me the little box. You can keep the pack! Just give me the box!" His performance is spot on, small and centered and direct yet powerful and moving at the same time. "Just give me the box!" he calls out. Then as Joost gently leads him away, the boy's father steps silently into the scene and watches Tom leave.

When David and I were casting in Madrid I had an idea of what the gypsy father should look like, and several Spanish actors who fit the bill came in to read. Then Antonio Gil, an accomplished Spanish actor, walked into the room. He was tall, thin, and intense, not at all what I'd had in mind for the character, but his reading was perfect.

"Straight to wardrobe," David whispered to me, which means, "Look no further. He's our guy."

490

It's rumored that the director John Huston was once asked, "Why don't you just be honest about it? Ninety percent of your directing is in the casting."

"Wrong, sonny," Huston responded. "Ninety-five."

It's true. If a director casts well and hires actors he or she can trust, the job is mainly to jump into scenes as an acting intervention only when necessary. The rest of the time, the actors do the work. One of our luckiest casting breaks in *The Way* is with the gypsy community in Burgos. Julia's family friend has arranged for about fifty of her former students to perform their traditional music and dancing for a scene in which Tom and his friends join a party in their courtyard compound around a blazing bonfire.

We're not carrying enough equipment in our truck to light night scenes, so Taylor helped us find this enclosed location. In the courtyard we can light the scene with a single large bonfire and three smaller fires in oil drums, using firelight that bounces off the walls.

Two *hombres de respeto* ("men of respect"), elders in the Gitano community, arrive with the group of young people. As we prepare the set they sit quietly by the bonfire and observe the action. I sense there's something they want to say, so I walk over and ask, "Are we doing this right?"

"No," they admit. "We wouldn't have the fire there. We'd put it over here. And you wouldn't have the dancers there. They'd be over here."

"Okay," I say. "Thank you." Then we rearrange the set to make it accurate.

The Spanish crew has warned us about hiring gypsies. "They're not going to show up," we heard. "If they do, they'll steal from you and they'll leave early," but this group of Gitanos is magnificent. They arrive on time and play their instruments and dance beautifully in the bone-chilling cold of an October night until the very last shot is completed at 2:00 a.m. They do it all for free and the only thing they take with them is the leftover food, which they ask for in advance.

As we pack up the last of our equipment and start heading back to our hotel, my dad and I blow on our hands for warmth. We've put in a long, hard day. At the end of it, we shake our heads in wonder. From sunup to sundown we witnessed an impossible day of filming. Then we lit the fires and the music and dancing began, and a joyous camaraderie developed between the local Gitanos and our cast and crew. The whole spirit of the day changed after the sun went down. Leave it to the Gitano community to have reversed our fortunes. They were the true Burgos blessing.

CHAPTER SIXTEEN: MARTIN

1981

While Emilio and I were still in India I'd received a phone call from my manager about a part in a film called *Enigma*. The role was to play an East German defector recruited by the CIA to return to East Berlin to steal a computer scrambler from the KGB.

"They're going to film in Paris," she said. "Are you interested?"

"Of course I'm interested," I said. "When can I read the script?"

But the overseas telephone connection was very poor and before I could get any more information the line went dead. I tried but couldn't get another connection through to the States. *Oh, well,* I figured. *I guess it can wait.* So I was caught by surprise when Emilio and I walked through our front door in Malibu a few weeks later to find an equally surprised Janet saying, "What are you doing here? You're supposed to be on the way to Paris for *Enigma.*"

"Oh, for God's sake," I said. I'd thought I was saying yes to an inquiry, not an offer. I hadn't even read the script.

"Well, the understanding is you agreed to do the film. They're expecting you in Paris tomorrow."

It had been assumed that I'd agreed to what's called a "deal memo" for the film, when an actor verbally consents to take a role. Now I had to turn around immediately and leave for France to honor a commitment I hadn't even known I'd made.

It was out of the question to take anyone with me on such short notice, so I didn't ask. But I did get a promise that everyone would come visit me during the two-week Easter vacation in April, and within days I was in Paris alone. The film wasn't particularly difficult to shoot. Locations were all in France, including Lille and Strasbourg as well as Paris, where the majority of scenes would be filmed. We worked largely during the day, with most nights off. The KGB official assigned to track down my character was played by the wonderful actor Sam Neill, long before his role in *Jurassic Park.* The production company had put him up at the Hotel Lenox in the Saint-Germain-des-Prés neighborhood on the Left Bank, and one night he invited me over for a drink.

"You ought to see my room. It's just terrific," he said. He showed me his suite on the top floors, with a little sitting room and a balcony and a cozy bedroom with a skylight upstairs.

"This is wonderful," I said. "I wish I had a room like this."

"It's yours," he said.

"Oh, no, I couldn't," I told him, but he insisted that I take it for the remainder of the shoot.

I was deeply moved by his generosity. I would not have been able to give up that room to anyone, for any reason. It was a magnificent retreat. Every morning I'd wake up to the light shining through the skylight and I'd call downstairs for a cappuccino, a freshly baked croissant, and the day's copy of the *International Herald Tribune.* We'd film during the day, and every night after dinner I looked forward to returning to my exquisite quarters. I'd brought some books back from India about Indian culture and spirituality that I was eager to read and reflect on at home. Instead, I brought them with me to Paris and read them in bed for hours every night. One of the books was a Western interpretation of Indian thought that discussed the Eastern concept of death. The author wrote that we "wake up" in death, as if awakening from a dream in a strange place, disoriented. It takes only a few seconds to remember who and where we are, but those few seconds can feel like an eternity. That's what happens when we die, the author wrote, and I thought about that possibility for quite a while. The idea was fascinating to me.

One day I was walking in the neighborhood when I saw a familiar figure heading my way. Could it really be?

"Terry, is it yourself?" I called out.

"It is, Martin!" Terrence Malick said. "What are you doing here?"

It had been nearly five years since I'd last seen Terry, when I was back in California after the typhoon in the middle of filming *Apocalypse Now* and he was in Los Angeles preparing to film *Days of Heaven.* In the meantime, he'd moved to Paris and married a Frenchwoman named Michelle. They were living on rue Jacob, close to my hotel. We were so glad to be reunited we began to spend evenings together after I'd finished work.

A true intellectual, a Harvard graduate and Rhodes Scholar with an unquenchable thirst for knowledge, Terry Malick had taught at MIT and written for the *New*

Yorker. He spoke four languages, and I couldn't mention a book he hadn't read. Conversations with him were like a tutorial. Despite a great sense of humor, he was enormously private and extremely shy. For the next few months, I became his informal education project. He taught me how to use the Paris subway system and took me on tours of Ile Saint-Louis and the Ile-de-France. He introduced me to the famous English-language bookstore Shakespeare & Company along the river Seine, where he plucked books off the shelves for me to read. Sometimes we'd meet at night at Saint-Germaindes-Prés, the oldest church in Paris, where a group of local musicians held informal, public charismatic gatherings. Filled with the spirit, they'd sing and play guitars and pray in French in a corner of the cathedral. Terry loved hearing their beautiful voices fill that space and sometimes we would sit listening for long periods, in rapture.

Terry knew me very well from our time together on *Badlands,* and I began to open up to him about what had happened in the Philippines and the experiences I'd had in India. From my journey through the last five years, it had become clear to me that we are all responsible for our own happiness — only we can choose what will make us happy, but we can't achieve that state without living an honest life.

Deeply spiritual, Terry was a devout Anglican and he recognized that I was going through a personal transition. Slowly, without either of us realizing it at first, he became my spiritual director. We talked about the need to live an authentic life and that the individual is the only one who truly knows when he or she is being honest or dishonest. "Our opinions of ourselves are the only ones that matter," Terry told me.

One day, at Shakespeare & Company, he bought me a copy of *The Brothers Karamazov*. A big fan of Dostoyevsky, and of this novel in particular, Terry said, "Read this book. I think it'll have an effect on you."

I'd never read Dostoyevsky before, and, from the start, the story of the ethical and moral dilemmas faced by Fyodor Pavlovich Karamazov and his sons fascinated me. I stayed up late reading every night. The book was nearly a thousand pages. Every character in that book is invested with equal measures of faith and flaw. It was very easy for me to relate to them, especially to the father. But most of all I was struck by the theme of love in the book, the message that love is not a sweet thing but a terribly painful endeavor because it requires total honesty. And yet, as Dostoevsky conveyed, love is valuable above all else.

The company moved to Strasbourg to film for a week, and the family joined me there for the kids' spring break. We then spent several days back in Paris before they returned home. It was a wonderful though brief reunion, and afterward I got my special room back at the Hotel Lenox for the final few weeks of filming.

Friday, May 1, was a national holiday in France similar to our Labor Day in the United States. I woke up late beneath the skylight in my attic suite of the Hotel Lenox and somehow, I knew: *This is it. Today is the day.*

St. Joseph's Catholic Church near the Arc de Triomphe on the Avenue Hoche is a parish run by Irish Passionists, serving English-speaking Catholics in Paris. In fact, it is the only English-speaking church in all of France. American embassy personnel and other expats from the United States, Britain, and elsewhere, including a large number of Filipinos, make up the congregation. The first week I was in Paris, before I moved to the Hotel Lenox, I'd stop there occasionally for Mass or to light a candle. After I moved to the Hotel Lenox I went to Saint-Germain-des-Prés often with Terry, touching the edges of Catholicism but not quite ready to step back in.

May first.

I walked the three miles from the Hotel Lenox to St. Joseph's Church as a form of pilgrimage. And when I arrived at the church around noon I banged on the front doors with urgency and purpose.

No answer.

I banged again, harder this time. Still no answer.

Well, I thought, *maybe this is* not *the day after all.* So I turned and walked back down the steps, but just as I hit the sidewalk I heard the church door swing open behind me. I turned around and there he was: the Irish priest I'd seen on my occasional visits. He was holding a napkin in one hand and he was chewing. I'd interrupted his lunch.

"Yes, what is it?" he asked. He must have thought there was a riot outside from the way that I'd been banging.

"Well, Father," I said. "I'm sorry to bother you. But I haven't been to confession in years and I'd like to come back to the church." His eyes narrowed, and from his reaction, I knew I'd come to the right place.

"Well," he said. "Come back here tomorrow morning at ten. And don't be late. I have a wedding at noon."

"I will," I said.

The next morning, when I walked into the church, I was the only one present. This confession was by appointment. I'd had the last rites after the heart attack in the Philippines and received Communion but I couldn't confess then because the priest spoke only Tagalog. I hadn't been to confession in a dozen years or so but the process was still very familiar and, when the time came, I entered the confessional box and began.

"Bless me, Father, for I have sinned."

Then I unburdened a heavy load from my soul. Father listened patiently and gave me some spiritual advice. Then he gave me a penance before absolution.

"For your penance, say one Our Father," he said.

"*One* Our Father?" I asked. "Just one?"

"Have you been gone so long," asked the priest, "that you can't remember the Our Father?"

"No, I remember it." I laughed. I just hadn't expected the penance to be so light for someone who'd been gone as long as I had, and who'd accumulated so much to confess in the interim.

I left the confessional booth and sat down in a pew to reflect. I had just confessed the whole truth about the past dozen years of my life and absolution was graciously granted without hesitation or judgment. Gradually, an overwhelming sense of freedom and familiarity consumed my whole being. I had returned whence I'd come. I imagined the Prodigal Son might have felt the same way when, as the Gospel parable tells us, he returned from his wayward travels rehearsing lines of apology, only to be greeted by a father who loved him so unconditionally the son was welcomed with open arms, no questions asked and no judgment passed.

I'd just taken the first step of a long, complex spiritual journey that would change my life. But I wasn't focused on the future now, only on this transcendent moment. Sitting alone in that church I began to weep uncontrollably with tears of sheer joy.

In my absence from the church, Vatican II had made some extraordinary changes begun by Pope John XXIII in 1962. Church dogma and canon law were still intact, of course, but gone was the Latin Mass and many of the fear-based traditions of hellfire and damnation. Gone, too, were many of the ancient barriers that separated Catholicism from other faiths and traditions. *Good riddance,* I thought.

I don't know how long I sat sobbing in the pew, but eventually I needed to blow my nose. I felt around in my pockets for a handkerchief but came up empty. Then I saw a crumpled Kleenex on the floor. I'll never forget how I felt to see that Kleenex. The simple gift of a tissue on the floor at my feet when I needed one filled me with a sense of gratitude. It seemed to assure me that from now on, all my needs would be met if I stayed the course I'd just begun.

From that day forward, everything began to change for me. Everything. I sought to follow the Gospel in its purest sense, on my own terms. I wouldn't be returning to the Catholic church of fear and guilt that I'd been raised in. None of that interested me. I chose to come back to the church of social justice and nonviolent peace activism.

It's really going to cost you something now, Sheen, I thought.

I was now part of a revitalized and more modern church that embraced the world with compassion, service, and love. Fear, guilt, and condemnation were greatly diminished by compassion, hope, and reconciliation, and simply living an honest life was celebrated as the ideal path to salvation.

504

I had no conscious choice of saving my soul or anyone else's. I came back to the Catholic church to discover who I truly was. I'd been living a confused, often selfish and unhappy life but beneath the drinking, self-pity, and anger was a person who longed to be set free. The church of the 1980s offered new possibilities and a moral compass. My reconversion was never about religion or politics. It was about spirituality and humanity. Catholicism became the door through which I began my own spiritual journey, not its final destination. At last I had found a way to unite the will of the spirit to the work of the flesh.

A few afternoons later I went to an eight-plex movie theater on the Champs-Elysées to see Martin Scorsese's new film, *Raging Bull,* which had come out in the United States around Christmastime. Robert De Niro had already won the Oscar and Golden Globe awards for his extraordinary performance as the ill-fated boxer Jake LaMotta. Now the film was playing in France and I finally had a chance to see it.

De Niro gave one of the most magnificent performances I'd ever seen, culminating with LaMotta, alone in a dark jail cell, banging his head against the wall in anguish and despair. De Niro's depiction of LaMotta was so stunning and courageous I felt enormous gratitude to know that someone from my own profession was capable of such depth. Watching De Niro in that film made me feel extremely proud to be a fellow actor and I longed to work with him.

The best films, I believe, strike a universal chord that inspires us to take action in our own lives. They invite us and challenge us to become better people. *Raging Bull* was such a film for me. The movie let out before sunset and, on the way back to the hotel, I had to fight the sudden impulse to tell everyone I saw how wonderful they were and to publicly declare how great it was to be alive. "How you doin'?" I wanted to call out to the people who passed me on the sidewalks. "I'm an American, I'm in Paris, I don't know anyone, I don't even speak your language. But I'm so happy to be alive and so grateful I'm not in a cell beating my head against the wall!"

We wind up in cells of our own making when we're not generous, loving, compassionate, and forgiving. Without love, we build dungeons in our hearts and fill them with our perceived enemies. We believe they deserve to be there for the harm they caused us, but by imprisoning them we're destroying our own spirits. When our dungeons are overflowing with these prisoners we refuse to set free, we become slaves to our self-righteousness, our anger, resentments, and self-loathing, which we let multiply until we wind up imprisoned on our own death row.

Raging Bull helped me realize how important it was to open up my own dungeons and set the captives free. If I didn't, I'd wind up like Jake LaMotta, alone and banging my head against a wall. I was amazed that an artist helped me realize this — and a fellow actor, no less. That was the power of De Niro's performance and Martin Scorsese's magnificent direction.

That night at the hotel I wrote De Niro a fan letter thanking him for what he'd accomplished with the film. I didn't know if he would read it or even get it, but I sent it off the next morning nonetheless. Five years later, when I saw him perform in *Cuba and His Teddy Bear* at Joe Papp's Public Theater in New York, I went backstage to congratulate him after the show.

"Martin Sheen?" he said, shaking my hand.

"Yeah. I'm a fan," I said.

"I know. I got your letter from Paris," he said. "Thank you."

■ ■ ■ ■

My return to the church and the awakenings it fostered were so joyful and profound that when I returned home from Paris I thought, *Surely, the whole family will want to join me!*

"You've got to follow me on this spiritual path!" I urged them. "Everything's going to be different from now on." I envisioned them all falling in line behind me, converting, with all of us trotting off to Sunday Mass together.

Well, not exactly. "He wants us to what?" the kids asked. "Why?"

Looking back, I have to laugh. No one in the house had the slightest interest in the new direction I'd chosen, and I must have driven everyone nuts with my campaign. I didn't want to travel this path without them, but they were making it clear they didn't want to travel it with me.

Then in June of 1981 another unexpected phone call came.

This one brought news that my oldest living brother, Mike, had died very suddenly. Mike had been one of my heroes, a Korean combat veteran who'd achieved a PhD on the GI bill and had lived with us in Malibu for a while when he'd been in poor health. A devout and liberal Catholic, he'd been so pleased to learn that I'd come back to the faith. The kids had been very attached to him, especially Charlie, who adored him. Losing him was a heavy blow to us all.

"It's not fair," Charlie kept saying. "It's not fair."

"It's not," I agreed. There was nothing I could say to make it right. "It's life, and it's not fair."

Losing Mike reminded me of how vulnerable we all are, and how important it is to make the most of whatever time we have. I started making choices that would determine the direction my life would take from that point forward and knew I had to commit to whatever came with taking a stand for what I believed in, even if and even when it meant getting arrested as a result. My conscience was aligned with Father Daniel Berrigan's work with nonviolent resistance against every form of institutionalized violence. Shortly after Mike died, I met Father Berrigan on the set of *In the King of Prussia,* a true docudrama by Emile de Antonio about a group of Catholic peace activists who had broken into the General Electric plant in King of Prussia, Pennsylvania, and poured their own blood onto the nose cones of two nuclear warheads.

The group called themselves the "Plow-shares Eight," and Father Berrigan along with his brother Phil were the leaders. I was asked to play the presiding judge, Samuel Salus II, in courtroom scenes to be filmed in New York City. My friendship with Dan Berrigan began on that set and grew over the years, leading to a series of arrests with him starting in June of 1986 for civil disobedience and trespassing — those were usually the charges — at nonviolent demonstrations against nuclear war, environmental hazards, and the misuse of American military intervention in Central America.

I've participated in many such demonstrations and been arrested sixty-seven times. I do it because I love my country enough to risk its wrath by drawing attention to its darker angels, but I never go to a demonstration with the intent or the hope of being arrested. On the contrary. I never know what to expect when I arrive. I often go because I cannot *not* participate and still be true to myself, but I may have gone about it too seriously in the beginning.

At first I was worried about getting physically accosted and being treated badly in jail. I was most comfortable at demonstrations when women, children, and news cameras were present. If none of the three was there it was a much riskier situation. Soldiers and police officers were less inclined to be brutal with women and children present, and above all they wanted to avoid public scrutiny from being captured on film. It wasn't until I participated in a demonstration at the Nevada Test Site in 1989 that I started to lighten up. It was spearheaded by Catholic Worker activist Kathleen Rumpf, who led a kick line of women doing the hokey pokey back and forth across the border that demarcated public and private property, finally landing on the side that led to their arrests. They completely disarmed the police in a hilarious show of protest. I'd never seen anything like this before. Even the police officers were laughing. It completely changed my attitude about protest. *You're not going to change the world, for God's sake,* I realized. *You do this for yourself, and only for yourself.*

The first few years after my return to the church and my entry into social justice activism I felt as if I were clinging to a rock in a rough sea. At the same time, it felt good to have a rock to cling to. Still, I'd ventured out into this place on my own. The rest of the family began to observe me at arm's length, as if this were a curious fad or phase that Dad was passing through. It took a while for everyone to get used to where I was going.

While I'd been in Paris filming *Enigma,* Emilio had been starting his acting career in L.A. By the summer of 1981 he'd auditioned and landed a role in his first feature film, *Tex,* based on the S. E. Hinton book of the same name. *Tex* was the story of two brothers living on their own in small-town Oklahoma after their mother died and their father left town. Jim Metzler played the responsible older brother and the hotheaded younger one, Tex, was played by Matt Dillon. Emilio was cast as Johnny, Tex's best friend.

Filming took place in and around Tulsa in the summer of 1981. On his flight to Oklahoma, Emilio sat with Terry Malick who, by pure coincidence, was traveling to visit his parents in Bartlesville, Oklahoma. After a few weeks I headed to Oklahoma, too, to visit Emilio on location for a weekend. A reporter assigned to write an article about me met me there.

On Sunday morning, I looked for a local church for Mass. I'd been going to Mass and Communion every Sunday since my reconversion in Paris and I loved the ritual and the comfort of the sacrament. The regular worship kept me anchored and grounded in a way I hadn't felt in many years.

But Tulsa wasn't like New York City where it seems a Catholic church sits waiting with open doors every few blocks. I didn't know the Sooner landscape, and it was taking a while to find a church and make a plan. Meanwhile, the cast and crew of *Tex* had the day off and most of them were going on a white-water rafting trip on a nearby river. Not being a big fan of water, and especially not being a fan of rapids, I didn't have any interest in the trip, but Emilio wanted me to go.

"Okay," I said. "I'll join you after Mass."

"They're leaving *now,* Pop."

I shook my head. "I'm going to Mass first. If you can just wait for —"

"*Mass?*" he said. "This is the only day I've got off! And you want to go to *Mass?*"

"I'm sorry. I —"

"I can't believe this!" Emilio shouted. "Are you saying Mass is more important to you than I am?"

Mass *was* more important than anything to me that summer, but Emilio wasn't having any of it. I invited him to join me for Mass, but he had no interest. And I wasn't giving in. He had his agenda, I had mine, and the argument escalated into a terrible row in front of everyone — including the reporter who was there to profile me.

Emilio was right to be upset. I'd come all that way just to see him, and yet the most important thing I had to do that morning didn't include him. I was putting him second when he wanted to be my first priority. But I was right, too. Mass had become essential to my well-being over the past few months and I thought he should accommodate that.

That morning I felt myself shrinking in stature in Emilio's perception. I'd been showing off in front of him and his friends over the years, trying to cultivate a heroic, macho image of myself to impress them. It was all about my ego, the vision that when he introduced me to his friends they'd have a certain sense of awe that *I* was his father. I longed for all my children to think of me that way. *If the only way they can see what a great man I am is through their friends' eyes,* I would think, *then, hey, have at it!*

But really: How could Emilio, or any of the kids, possibly think of me as heroic? They were too used to me. They saw me every day, at my best and my worst. Parents are never prophets in their own home. We're too familiar.

And so slowly I began to let go of the idea that I would be a hero to my kids. I'd walk onto a set and see Emilio acting, or Ramon acting, and before long I'd see Charlie and Renée acting as well, and I'd be the one filled with awe. I'd hold my head in astonishment and say, "Oh, my *God.* That's my *son.* That's my *daughter.* Those are my kids!" and I'd hardly be able to contain my pride over what they'd accomplished on their own. That gave me an understanding of where I stood in all this: not as their hero, or their prophet, but simply as their father.

As I let go of the idea of being their hero, I also let go of trying to convert them to Catholicism. That one was hard to relinquish, knowing how the church was providing me with such a moral compass, and knowing the kids would face difficulties as adults that they wouldn't be able to manage easily on their own. But I understood: Each of the kids had an individual spiritual journey of his and her own to take. Faith meant allowing Emilio and the others to find and follow their own paths.

In 1981, I was forty-one years old, barely middle-aged, and my oldest son was already becoming an adult. In letting go of my image of being his hero, it was time to sort out when to be his mentor, when to be his colleague, when to silently bear witness. I would always be his father, but the ground had shifted beneath us, and the landscape was considerably different now.

CHAPTER SEVENTEEN: EMILIO

1981–1983

If my father had just been honest with me that Sunday morning in Oklahoma, I might have handled myself differently. I knew he was afraid to go out in white water, and he didn't want to admit it. "Listen, I have to go to Mass so I'm not going to be able to go on this float trip," he told me. It had sounded like an excuse and I was terribly let down. He'd shown up for a weekend with a journalist in tow and there I was, with a solid supporting role in my first feature film, acting with Matt Dillon and Meg Tilly as my classmates and Ben Johnson, an actor whom I worshipped from his role in the 1969 Western *The Wild Bunch,* playing my father. If my own father was making the effort to visit me on set in Oklahoma I wanted to include him in what we were doing. The rafting trip had been planned for weeks, and I'd already told production that he'd be going. I'd wanted everyone on the set to meet him. To be honest, I'd wanted to show him off.

His decision to go to Mass left me with two choices: I could go on the rafting trip without him, but then we'd hardly have any time together before his flight on Monday morning. I could stay behind, but then I'd miss out on a trip we'd all been planning for weeks. Either way it was clear that my father wouldn't be rafting that day.

We got into an epic fight in the parking lot of the Ramada Inn where I was staying. We were screaming at each other. Cursing. In public. I didn't even care who saw or heard. It got so ugly that the journalist had to spend the next two hours walking me around the parking lot while I raged. While my father was at Mass I spilled everything I was feeling to this virtual stranger, and then we went out for a couple of beers. When his article came out a few months later, I got to experience the fight for a second time, this time in print. Reading his account was hilarious and mortifying and gave me my first lesson in what an actor should and should not share with the press.

I wasn't that angry at my dad. Mostly, I was disappointed. If he'd just said, "This is what's going on: I'm terrified of the river. I'm afraid to go on it in a raft," I would have said, "Okay. That's cool." Only the most inconsiderate son would pressure a father who doesn't like roller coasters to go on one. I thought my dad would have known that.

Also, I was surprised and confused by this sudden interest in Mass. *Church?* I'd thought. *Come on. This doesn't add up.* When he came home from Paris I had already moved out of my parents' house and into an apartment in Santa Monica so that I could have the kind of independence I would have had if I'd gone to college, so he hadn't shared much with me about his return to the Catholic church. I knew he'd been raised Catholic but I'd never seen him go to church before. I had no frame of reference for him suddenly becoming devout. It was as if he went to Paris for four months and when he came back I was a film actor and he was a Catholic and we had to orient ourselves to the developments that had unfolded while we were apart.

Neither of us went on that rafting trip. The punch line to all this is that, thirty years later in northern Spain, my father ran headlong, willingly, and fully clothed into a raging river for a scene he'd come up with for *The Way*. Fortunately for all of us, it wasn't a Sunday.

I celebrated my nineteenth birthday on the set of *Tex,* where I played the role of Johnny Collins, Tex McCormick's best friend. Johnny lived on the right side of the tracks in a big house with a domineering father and a younger sister, played by Meg Tilly, who became Tex's love interest in the film. Matt Dillon, who played Tex, had already achieved a measure of teen stardom as a junior high delinquent in *Over the Edge,* a summer-camp love interest in *Little Darlings,* and a high school bully in *My Bodyguard.* When word got out in Tulsa that Matt Dillon was filming in town, girls started camping out in the parking lot of the Ramada Inn. He should have had a security detail but no one had security back then, especially not a sixteen-year-old, so we would have to make our way through the crowds of girls clamoring to see Matt every time we walked in and out of the hotel.

My character Johnny rode a motorcycle in the film but I didn't, so I had to learn how. This had always been one of my mom's nightmares. Her stepfather owned a Honda shop in Ohio and for years I was obsessed with getting a motorcycle of my own. I once tried to mail a letter to my grandmother that said, "Mom and Dad said it's fine for me to have a motorcycle now. Please send one immediately," which my mother inter-cepted just in time.

One day in Tulsa I was practicing on the motorcycle and the director Tim Hunter said, "We'd love for you to do a wheelie in this shot. What do you think?"

"I'll try it," I said.

"What about the stuntman?" Susie Hinton asked.

Susie was the author of the book *Tex* and was a constant presence on set. Over time she became something of a den mother to us, the resident mom/sister/confidante with a posse of adolescent boys she'd half imagined into being.

"It's okay. I can handle it," I said. "I've been practicing."

I tossed my leg over the motorcycle seat, adjusted my helmet, said good-bye to Matt, and took off.

Riding a motorcycle is like taming a large animal that sometimes has a mind of its own. Sure enough, the bike got completely out of my control and almost hit members of the crew. When it crashed it came right down on top of my knee.

Everyone rushed over to me. "Are you okay? Are you okay?" Tim Hunter kept asking. I wasn't hurt badly, but I could have been.

Susie Hinton was furious. She thought it was completely reckless to have let me do the stunt myself. She looked at me on the ground, and she looked at Tim trying to help me up.

"Well, Emilio," she said, "If you're a good boy, maybe Tim will let you do that again."

Susie and I became very close on set. I'd read all of the books she'd published up to that point: *Tex, The Outsiders, Rumble Fish,* and *That Was Then, This Is Now.* Francis Coppola had optioned *The Outsiders* and with *Tex* already in progress I thought, *Wow, this author is going to be wildly popular. That Was Then, This Is Now* was her only book still available for a film option and I started making plans from the set of *Tex* to option it myself. At nineteen, I was already thinking about writing a script, being a producer, and securing an option on a book before anyone else could take it. It would take four years to get that film up and running, which felt like an eternity at the time. Now I know otherwise. In this industry, four years is nothing.

Back home, I discovered that living in an apartment in Santa Monica would have been a better plan if I'd had consistent funds coming in to pay the monthly rent. The apartment was on a month-to-month lease and whenever my money ran out I'd move back into my bedroom at home. After I got paid for a job and could afford to pay rent again, I'd move back down to Santa Monica. When that money ran out, I'd go through the formality of asking permission to move back home again.

"Hey, Mom, Dad, have you rented my room out?"

"No, of course not."

"How do you feel if I come back for a little while, until my next job?"

"That's fine."

I was bouncing back and forth like this in the fall of 1981 when I got an audition call for a lead role in an ABC made-for-TV movie called *In the Custody of Strangers*. It told the story of a rebellious sixteen-year-old kid from a working-class family who goes for a drunken joyride, hits a police car, and lands in jail. His father leaves him there overnight to teach him a lesson, but one mishap leads to another and the boy winds up spending six horrific weeks inside a system that renders him and his parents powerless.

The role of troubled teen Danny Caldwell was multidimensional, requiring an actor who could play angry, defiant, vulnerable, and despairing. I'd auditioned for a lot of

TV movies by that point and the final decision usually came down to a contest between me and an actor named Ike Eisenmann, who was best known at that point for playing the boy lead in *Escape to Witch Mountain*. Ike and I would show up for auditions at the same time, do our readings, and then he'd get the part. But this time I was cast. The role advanced me a rung on the acting ladder, both professionally and within the family. At the time, made-for-TV movies were treated like independent films are now, with red-carpet premieres and coverage in the industry papers. My father had been a fixture in Movies of the Week for a while during the mid-1970s as he was building his career, and when I was cast in *In the Custody of Strangers* I thought, *Okay, this is a big deal.*

Robert Greenwald was the director; he was coming off the film *Xanadu* with Olivia Newton-John. He later went on to direct or produce more than seventy television and feature films. Almost as soon as I was hired he started pairing me up with young actresses to cast the role of Danny's girlfriend. Dominique Dunne, the daughter of journalist Dominick Dunne, came in and as soon as we read together everyone knew she was the girl. Beautiful and talented, with several

TV movies to her credit, she was cast quickly, but before shooting could begin the ABC executives decided she'd done too many TV movies and they'd rather have a fresh face. I always regretted losing the chance to work with Dominique. It wouldn't come again. A year later she was murdered by her former boyfriend, at the age of twenty-two.

Another young actress was hired to replace Dominique, and attention then turned to casting Danny's parents. I went in for a meeting one day about hair and wardrobe, and Robert Greenwald approached me.

"What's your dad doing these days?" he asked.

"He's working mostly features," I said.

"You know, we'd love to have him play the father in this. Do you think he'd consider it?"

"I don't know," I said, which was true. I didn't know what my father had on his calendar for that winter. "Make him an offer," I said.

The production company didn't waste time contacting him. Before saying yes or no, my father came to talk with me.

"You said you didn't want to go back to television," I reminded him. "Are you sure you want to do this?"

"Yes, with you, I do," he said.

Wow, this will be a great opportunity for Dad and me to work together, was my first thought. The second was, *Now everyone's going to think the only reason I got this job was because of him.* I knew we'd have a better movie with him acting in it. And I knew the film would get more attention, because he had such name recognition by then. But there's a part of me that wondered, and has always wondered: Was I being used as a carrot to begin with, just to get my father on board?

The role of Frank Caldwell, an unemployed plant foreman desperately looking for work while trying to extricate his son from an unsympathetic juvenile system, was a good fit for my father. It played close to home for him on several levels: the working-class background, the family to support, the scramble to find work, the defiant teenage son. When the script called for Frank to explode in anger at Danny, shouting, "You ain't going nowhere! Long as I'm paying the bills around here and feeding your face you'll do as I tell you!" the exchange wasn't that far off the mark from ones we'd played out in real life. When Danny raged back at his father, all I had to do was tap into the anger I'd felt in dealing with my own dad over the years. It helped that I was actually looking at him when I did it for the camera.

Jane Alexander was cast as my mother, and she played tough and distraught and patient to a T. My father was brilliant as Frank. In one scene, when he answers the phone to discover he hasn't been hired for a job, it could have been any one of a number of calls he'd received himself over the years. He played the hope and disappointment and pride in that scene perfectly for his character, just as I'd remembered seeing it myself as a child.

I was living back at home during the filming, and after work each day my father and I would walk around the backyard together, away from the phones, and run our lines. "Again please," he'd suggest, "Let's go one more time. One more time," and "Why don't you try this?" and then he'd demonstrate. We became two actors helping each other out, not just father and son. On set he had a big trailer and I'd go in there and run lines with him during breaks, too.

We'd practice until we felt we'd nailed a scene. It's preferable to do this in the actual filming location, where you can attach a movement or a gesture to a specific spot or object in the room, but running lines into thin air, as we did in our backyard and in the trailer, helped us own them. The whole point of rehearsing is to learn the lines so well that you forget you're reciting them, so that each time you say them they come to you as a fresh thought. James Cagney is rumored to have said acting is a great profession, as long as you don't get caught at it. We actors interpret that to mean, *Be natural. Make it look effortless.* The actor's job is to make it look as if he's not doing any work at all.

As helpful as my dad and I were to each other in our off hours, in front of the cameras I felt fiercely competitive with him, as if I needed to out-act and out-box him in every scene. But why? And for whom? I wonder. It wasn't as if I were being tested. I'd already gotten the role. I suppose part of the reason was just my own adolescent bluster and swagger, and part was that I didn't want to disappoint my father. I wanted to prove that I was as good an actor as we both hoped I could be.

I'd made sure I was prepared for the role both physically and emotionally. By the time filming began I knew not only my own lines but the lines of everyone who shared scenes with me, and I had a great deal of confidence in myself. The movie was shot mostly in San Pedro, California, a rough-around-the-edges port city about fifty miles southeast of Malibu. My father's longtime friend Matt Clark was playing an attorney in the movie and the three of us would drive to and from the set together on the days we were all scheduled to shoot. We'd talk and run lines together in the car. One evening we were heading home after a long day on set. The two of them were trying to make sure I understood the difference between being a serious, working actor and being a celebrity.

"Don't concentrate on people knowing your name," my dad said. A curious statement, I thought, from a father who'd urged me to keep the family name just a year and a half before.

Matt agreed. "Do good work, you'll get hired, and you'll have a career as an actor," he added. "But don't do this to be famous. No one's going to know your name."

Their message, loud and clear, was, "Get over yourself. No one's ever going to know you." I remember being furious with both of them for trying to short-circuit my ambition before it even had a chance to take off. Or were they instead trying to convey their own disappointments as actors? Or giving me solid advice born from years of experience? Over time I've come to see it as the latter, having learned from my own experience that work begets work, and that doing good work that lasts is more important than celebrity. But on that evening in 1981, as I pushed myself deeper into the backseat of my father's car in defiance, I thought, *Okay, you know what? It's a different time now. People are going to know my name.*

I loved going to work every day on that film, loved the challenges I faced on the set. This was the film in which I learned to trust my instincts as an actor, and I would ad-lib from time to time and make adjustments to the character on the spot. In a scene where Danny meets with his probation officer in a prison rec room, I wandered around the room nervously touching objects and hitting a Ping-Pong ball around. On pure impulse I opened the door of a wooden coat closet, stepped inside, and closed the door behind me. The cameraman wasn't prepared for that, but to his credit, Jon Van Ness, who played the probation officer, didn't miss a beat. He leaned back in his chair, impatiently flung the door open, and kept on going with his questions. His response was so in character that the scene ended up in the film.

I'm not sure I could be that bold on a set now. At nineteen I had the sort of unselfconscious abandon you can afford to have when you're young and don't know any better. It's a time to make mistakes, when nobody holds you accountable because of your age and inexperience. I'm much more cautious now that the expectations and the stakes are both higher.

Toward the end of the filming my father left to do a play and I filmed the scenes that took place in jail. In one sequence, Danny is serving eggs in the chow line when one of the inmates picks a fight. Danny throws eggs in the guy's face and leaps over the counter to attack him. The inmate was played by Anthony Davis, a famous former football player for USC. The stuntman, Gary McLarty, walked me through how to throw a punch on screen. I'd never done staged fighting before and Gary taught me not only how to throw a punch without hurting its recipient, but also how to receive one so it looked like I'd been hit. Twenty-eight years later I would think of Gary, and what he taught me on that set, when my father and I tried to teach two police officers how to duck staged punches in the courtyard of the *bodega* in northern Spain.

Soon after *In the Custody of Strangers* finished filming I went to audition for Francis Coppola and Fred Roos. They were casting for *The Outsiders,* a film based on Susie Hinton's first book, written when she was still in high school, about a group of boys called Greasers from the wrong side of Tulsa and their run-ins with the affluent kids from the south side, the Socs (pronounced "soashes"). The story centers on a family of three brothers, Darrel, Sodapop, and Ponyboy, trying to stay together after their parents were killed in a car wreck.

Published in 1966, the book explores the social divisions Susie saw in her own school and became required reading in middle schools across the country. Almost fifteen years later, Francis received a letter from a school librarian in Fresno, California, asking him to consider making the book into a film. She included a petition signed by all her middle school students. Francis had never heard of the book but he was so moved he decided to read it and immediately realized the story would make for a compelling film.

Virtually every male actor under the age of thirty-five in Los Angeles turned out for *The Outsiders* auditions, which were held in an enormous soundstage at Zoetrope Studios in Hollywood, Francis's Los Angeles headquarters. Val Kilmer, Dennis Quaid, Scott Baio, Anthony Michael Hall, Vincent

Spano, Nicolas Cage, and a new kid named Tommy Howell — everyone wanted a shot. For the role of Cherry, the Soc girl who befriends the Greasers, a crop of young actresses that included Brooke Shields, Nicollette Sheridan, Kate Capshaw, and Helen Slater were considered. I went to audition for the role of Sodapop, Ponyboy's sweet, protective older brother who drops out of high school to help support the family with a job at a gas station.

For the auditions for *The Outsiders* Francis used a method that was different from any reading I'd done before. For starters, he kept everyone in the room together so we all saw one another read. That alone was unusual. Then, after three or four actors had read a scene together, he'd juggle the roles around to see what kind of new synergy he could create among the actors.

"Okay," he'd say to whoever was at the table. "Now we're going to switch it up. This time you're going to play Sodapop, and you're going to take Johnny, and you're going to play Darrel. Great. Let's go."

It was like watching tryouts for a football team. The actors Francis called on would jump in and do the scene, and then that group would be shuffled around before being replaced by the next one.

Francis looked much as I remembered him from the Philippines, with a thick dark beard and oversized glasses and an air of absolute authority. He knew what he was looking for, even if we didn't know how to deliver it.

"Now you . . . I want you to stick around," Francis would say when he was done with a group. "And you, thank you very much. You can leave." The process was fascinating and exciting and nerve-wracking all at once.

The auditions went on for weeks. The guys in the room were desperate to stand out, and we all came up with different quirks and styles for the characters we wanted to play. I fashioned a reverse duck's ass in my hair with gobs of grease every morning. As competitive and selective as the process was, I always thought I would be cast. Maybe it was because I'd already done a film based on an S. E. Hinton book, or maybe it was because my intuition told me I'd get a role, or maybe it was just pure, uninhibited nineteen-year-old confidence. As I sat in the soundstage and watched actor after actor go up to the table and then either get sent back to his seat or directed to the door, I thought, *I'm a natural for this. I'm going to get a role here. I don't know which one, but I'm going to be in this film.* Still, I had to go through the audition process like everyone else. If Nicolas Cage, who was Coppola's nephew, didn't have an edge, then my father's prior film relationship with Francis wasn't going to matter. If anything, having already done *Tex* with Matt Dillon and knowing my way around Tulsa seemed to help distinguish me more.

Every morning of the auditions I drove to the soundstage with an actor my age from New Jersey who was staying at our house. His name was Tom Cruise and he'd worked with Sean Penn a year or two earlier on *Taps.* Tom was driven, focused, and hilariously self-effacing. I was living back at my parents' house at the time, and Tom was looking for a place to stay during the auditions. He seemed like a nice-enough guy, and Sean vouched for his character.

"There are two beds in my room," I told him. "Just stay with us."

So Tom Cruise and I became roommates in my parents' house for a while. One night we were fast asleep when a loud *boom boom boom* woke us up. It took me a few seconds to realize someone was pounding on the window. It took me a few seconds more to realize it was Sean. I rolled over and looked at my clock: just past 3:00 a.m.

"What the hell, man?" I said, unlocking

the window. Sean angled himself over the hedge and into the room in his usual fashion. He was hammered, and he was raging because he couldn't get the audition he wanted for *The Outsiders.* He'd set his sights on the role of Dallas, the delinquent Greaser to whom the younger ones go for help. Sean was an up-and-coming actor at the time, but for some reason Francis wouldn't let him read for the part.

"I'm telling you, it's an injustice, man!" he shouted as he paced around my bedroom. "It's a missed opportunity!"

Tom and I agreed that to omit Sean from the auditions was insane. If anyone from our generation of actors should have been included, it should have been Sean Penn. He was one of, if not the most, compelling and important young actors in our group.

The more Sean shouted, the more worked up he became. I flipped on a lamp and noticed his face and his fists were covered with blood.

"What happened to you, man?" I asked.

"Ah, just some fight," Sean said, and went back to raging against Francis. He was like a living embodiment of one of the Greasers that night. I've always wondered why he wasn't asked to read.

One morning on the soundstage, a slightly

older actor came sauntering into the room to read for the role of Darrel, Ponyboy's oldest brother. Mickey Rourke was already known for his work in *Body Heat* with William Hurt and Kathleen Turner and when he read for Francis that day I thought he nailed the role. He destroyed all the props on the set, smashing them with his fists and his feet, while the rest of us sat there quietly staring at him in awe. It was staggering and inspiring to see how good he was.

When the call came, I was surprised to learn that Mickey hadn't made the cut. I was even more surprised to learn that the call was for us to go to New York, where we'd audition with the actors who'd made the East Coast cuts. We hadn't even known that a nearly identical set of actors had been auditioning for *The Outsiders* in New York.

From the whole crop of Los Angeles actors who'd auditioned, Francis chose only four to fly to New York: Tommy Howell, Rob Lowe, Tom Cruise, and me. In New York City we were mixed and matched with the actors there and met up with Matt Dillon, Ralph Macchio, and a relatively unknown actor, dancer, and gymnast named Patrick Swayze. At twenty-nine, Patrick was the mature counterpart to the rest of us, who were constantly poking one another and pulling pranks in the hotel. It was an incredibly competitive week or two as we all vied for the roles we wanted, but it was also a time of true camaraderie. We were on the brink of something big, together, and this sense of fellowship would extend throughout the entire shoot.

In the end, Matt Dillon, who'd starred in *Tex,* landed the role of Dallas. Patrick was cast as Ponyboy's older brother Darrel, and the middle brother, Sodapop, went to Rob Lowe. Tom got the part of Steve Randle, Sodapop's best friend, and Ponyboy went to Tommy Howell, a quiet, intense fifteen-year-old kid whose film experience, up to that point, was limited to a small role in a movie none of us had seen yet, called *E.T.* Ralph Macchio, a twenty-year-old actor from New York who'd had a recurring role on the TV show *Eight Is Enough,* was hired to play Johnny. I was cast in the role of Two-Bit Matthews, who rounded out the core Greasers gang.

Fred Roos, who'd done the casting for *American Graffiti* and had also cast my father in *Apocalypse Now,* proved once again to have a true gift for matching actors to roles. The casting in *The Outsiders* was spot-on. My father and Matt had been right: Good work begets good work. In that winter of

1982 in New York we had no way of knowing how well known all of the actors cast as the Greasers would become, but by the end of 1984 Tom had broken out in *Risky Business,* Ralph in *The Karate Kid,* Rob in *The Hotel New Hampshire,* and Patrick and Tommy in *Red Dawn,* which would also be my brother Charlie's first major feature film.

The seven of us Greasers, plus Diane Lane and the kids playing the Socs, arrived in Tulsa about three weeks ahead of shooting to have ample time to rehearse. Francis also had us practicing gymnastics and learning how to fight. He wanted us all to be physically fit for our roles, and able to do nearly anything he asked of us. Patrick, who'd gone to college on a gymnastics scholarship, served as our unofficial coach and taught us how to do flips and basic gymnastics. You can see Tom turning flips off of cars twice in the film.

At first, I'd been terribly disappointed to be cast as Two-Bit Matthews. I'd wanted to play Sodapop, a more substantial role. But Francis encouraged us to develop our own characters during those rehearsal weeks and all of us — Tom, Ralph, Tommy, Patrick, Rob, Matt, and me — were eager to do anything we could to stand out from the pack. Tom decided Steve should lose a tooth in the big rumble between the Greasers and the Socs toward the end of the movie, and even went so far as to have one of his teeth removed and a fake one fashioned. I came up with the idea for Two-Bit to like Mickey Mouse and started wearing Mickey Mouse T-shirts with the sleeves cut off. The reverse duck's ass stayed. Most of the boys carried blades, and I decided that Two-Bit should carry one of the butterfly knives I'd brought back from the Philippines. I'm not sure if that was an anachronism or not — could a balisong knife have found its way to a kid in 1966 Tulsa? Maybe if Two-Bit's father had fought in the Korean War? — but Francis was so charmed by the Philippines connection he let me use the knife in the film. You can see Two-Bit swinging it open at the end of the drive-in sequence as if he's very familiar with that knife, a gesture that took a lot of practice.

I played Two-Bit with a high-octane laugh, a tough-guy swagger, and a perpetual beer in his hand. The way Francis cut the final version of the film Two-Bit wound up getting the screen time Sodapop was supposed to have and then some, so getting cast as Two-Bit turned out to be a blessing in the end.

Francis's son Gio, with whom I became reacquainted on that set, had an unbelievably bright mind for emerging technology. He had dialed Francis in to what's now called "video village" for his prior film, *One from the Heart*. On most sets, video village is a tent set up with monitors, but for *The Outsiders* Francis had converted a silver Airstream trailer into his mission control. During rehearsals we would stand in front of a green screen while Francis watched us on video monitors inside the Airstream and directed us from there, with chroma-key backgrounds on his screen that the rest of us couldn't see.

"Okay," he'd tell us as we stood in front of absolutely nothing. "You're in the house now," or "All right, now this is the scene in the park." Filming that way made me feel like a weatherman standing in front of an empty background that would show up as the entire country's weather map on TV.

When filming began, we shot the movie in sequence, starting with a first reel that introduced the characters but wound up being cut, and then moving into the drive-in scenes. It must have been very expensive to film that way, since we would return to the same locations multiple times, but it helped us live our roles as much as act them. Before filming started, Francis even made Patrick, Rob, and Tommy live together for a few days in the house he was using as the Curtis brothers' home to help them feel like a real family.

On *The Outsiders,* I received a first-rate education in how accidents can sometimes be transformed into art. Francis allowed us to ad-lib and often used our impromptu lines or gestures in the final cut, and he was a genius at letting action naturally unfold. In the drive-in scene when Matt Dillon is harassing Diane Lane's character, he accidentally falls off his chair. All the other actors started laughing. Any other director might have yelled "Cut!" when Matt hit the floor — you can even see Tommy Howell looking right at the camera, expecting Francis to do just that — but Francis kept the camera rolling and used the fall to let Matt's character Dallas be a little more vulnerable and a little more likable than he might otherwise have come across in that scene.

One night we were filming outside with a couple of big Ritter fans blowing — incredibly noisy, two-thousand-pound, eight-foot-tall fans Francis used in many of the outdoor scenes to simulate wind. In this particular scene I was walking across the street with Ponyboy and Johnny when a hat came tumbling right into the frame. A Ritter fan had blown it off cameraman Elliot Davis's head, and when I saw it cartwheel past I ran over, picked it up, shouted, "Whoa! Looky here! Got myself a new hat!" and stuck it on my head. It was exactly something the rambunctious Two-Bit might have done, and Frances left that moment in the final cut, too.

But the most memorable happy accident we encountered occurred when we filmed the big rumble scene toward the end of the film, when the Greasers and the Socs call in their reinforcements to face off in a Tulsa park at night and agree to use only hand-to-hand combat, no knives or chains. This was the most physically taxing of all the scenes we shot. It was already early summer when we got to that scene but the Tulsa nights could be cold, and that one in particular was freezing. Most of us were out there in just T-shirts and jeans. Soon after the first punch was thrown for the cameras, the sky opened up and rain started *pouring* down on us. Some of the crew wanted to stop filming but a couple of the actors shouted to keep the cameras rolling. We were pumped up and really going for it in the rain and mud, wrestling on the ground, tossing one another across the screen. With all that chaos, a few real punches must have been thrown.

Francis liked the ambience of the rain and mud so much he decided to use it in the film. The only problem was that when we continued shooting that scene the next night, it wasn't raining anymore. Rain towers had to be brought in to shower down on us and keep the shots consistent from night to night. Between takes we'd get wrapped in blankets and drink hot chocolate to stay warm. It was worth it. The result was a dark, moody fight scene that viewers remember decades later. It turned out brilliantly because Francis had been willing to adapt to what nature handed him that night.

After *The Outsiders* Francis was staying on in Tulsa to direct *Rumble Fish,* also based on an S. E. Hinton book. This story was about a teenage hood who aspires to be like his older brother, a former gang leader. Francis and Susie Hinton had written the screenplay on days off from *The Outsiders,* and he'd recruited Matt Dillon to stay on in Tulsa to play the lead role of Rusty James, as well as Diane Lane to play Rusty's girlfriend Patty. Mickey Rourke was coming in to play the older brother, along with Dennis Hopper to play the father and Chris Penn and Laurence Fishburne had supporting roles. Francis asked me to stay on to play Steve, Rusty's best friend.

As much as I would have liked being reunited with Hopper and Fishburne, during *The Outsiders* I'd taken constant teasing from the vehicle drivers when I told them what I was earning per week. "Really?" they'd laughed. "We're making more than you are. We're making more than all you guys." The role Francis offered me in *Rumble Fish* came with a two-hundred-dollar per week raise, which put my salary just a bump over the Screen Actors Guild minimum but still under what the drivers earned. If I stayed for *Rumble Fish* I'd be doing the same thing I'd been doing for the past three months, without much opportunity for growth and barely a raise in pay. *I don't want to stay in Tulsa* that *much,* I thought. I decided to go home. Francis hired Vincent Spano to play Steve and I headed back to Los Angeles, where I immediately reentered the audition fray.

So much of an actor's life involves just trying to get a role, and so much of getting a role involves luck and opportunity rather than craft. In the beginning, I would go into auditions fully prepared and walk out shouting, "I nailed it! I nailed that one, man!"

but wouldn't know that a guy was already in line for the role and the producers were waiting for him to take it or pass. If he passed, there were five more guys they had in mind right behind him. Underneath those five guys were another ten guys who formed a sort of producer's B-list for the film, and underneath them was everyone else who was auditioning. I was fortunate to eventually go from being the kid in the parking lot shouting, "I nailed it!" and not getting the role to being one of the ten guys on the B-list, to being one of the five guys on deck, to being the guy with the offer while the other guys waited for me to pass. But between the ages of seventeen and twenty-five, I spent most of my time going from studio to studio, and from casting office to casting office, trying to get the next role. The movies I did then were reflective only of the parts I got as opposed to the hundreds I didn't. I didn't choose my films. They chose me.

Sometimes I could get audition sides in advance and then I'd run lines at home with my dad to prepare. But sometimes I'd have to pick them up that morning, study them in the car, and go in and read. It was always "Thank you very much," and I'd go on to the next one. The audition turnover was so fast I'd start losing track of whom I was reading for. I'd walk into a room full of people and only then realize who I was there to meet. Sometimes not even then.

Once I was up for a TV movie at Universal called *Nightmares,* an anthology of four stories that ultimately got a feature film release. The audition was straightforward and simple, nothing extraordinary or unusual. After I read we all did our "Thank you very much" exchange and I left. Later that day, I got a call saying the director really liked my reading.

"Who was the director?" I asked.

"Joe Sargent."

"No," I said. "Joseph Sargent was in the room? You're *kidding* me."

Joe Sargent had done a movie I'd loved as a kid called *The Taking of Pelham One Two Three* about a hijacked New York City subway train, starring Robert Shaw, Martin Balsam, and Walter Matthau. I must have seen it three or four times. At the audition, I'd missed the opportunity to tell Sargent how influenced I'd been by that film and what a fan I was of his work. But maybe it was for the better. I might have blown the audition if I'd known it was him. Instead I told him how much I'd liked *The Taking of Pelham One Two Three* after I got the job.

■ ■ ■ ■

A few days before *In the Custody of Strangers* aired on television it screened at the Academy of Television Arts & Sciences in Beverly Hills. I'd stayed in touch with Mickey Rourke after his audition for *The Outsiders* and invited him to the screening. He came with his wife at the time, Debra. I felt tremendously honored that he would accept my invitation. During the screening I looked back at the audience and saw Mickey sitting in the crowd. In some ways, I was happier and more proud to have him there than to have my father sitting next to me. At twenty-nine, Mickey was more my contemporary, an actor of my generation who was just a couple of steps ahead of me and whose success felt within reach. He wrote me a fan letter after the screening that said, "Hey, man, I just wanted to tell you that I loved the movie and you've really got the stuff."

That meant a lot to me, not just that he'd liked my performance, but that he'd taken the time to write. *Wow,* I thought. *I just got Mickey's seal of approval. I don't need anybody else's.*

Soon after, I auditioned for a movie at

Universal with casting director Michael Chinich. He had a roster of big films to his name, like *Dog Day Afternoon, Animal House,* and *Coal Miner's Daughter.* This one was about a boy with a rare disease that caused deformities in his head and face. It was called *Mask,* and the role of Rocky looked like an incredible part in an equally compelling film.

After my audition Chinich offered to walk me out of the office. In the hallway, he broke the news. "You're not going to get this movie," he told me.

"Okay," I said. "Well, then thanks."

"But I do want you to drive over to Venice," he continued. "Vickie Thomas is casting this little movie called *Repo Man.* Here's the address. I think you've got a real shot at getting that one."

I took his advice and drove straight there. That audition landed me the role of Otto in *Repo Man,* a film about a young punk who loses his job in a supermarket and quickly lands in the car repossession business, where he gets entangled in a repo deal involving a 1964 Chevy Malibu driven by a crazed scientist with an alien life form hidden in its trunk. It was a silly script by any standard and it wasn't a blockbuster by any stretch, but over time it became a cult favorite and I've always been grateful to Michael Chinich for sending me to the audition. Even now, people still stop me on the street to talk about Otto. In fact, I can usually tell if a stranger who walks up to me is going to say that *Repo Man* is his favorite movie before he even opens his mouth. Fans of that movie all share a similar vibe.

By the time *Repo Man* finished filming I'd strapped my bed to the roof of my truck for the last time, moved out of my parents' house for good, and started making the audition rounds again. John Hughes, a young writer-director from Illinois who'd recently done a film called *Sixteen Candles* with Molly Ringwald, was casting for another film set during the high school years, this one about five kids from different social groups randomly thrown together in a weekend detention class.

The week I auditioned for John Hughes I must have had twenty other auditions for commercials and TV shows and films. I'd become accustomed to the phone ringing with bad news or not ringing at all. The process was giving me a good education in what my dad had gone through all those years when he was trying to get his career off the ground and raising a family at the same time.

I couldn't imagine working this hard and facing so many disappointments with the additional pressure of a family to support. But soon enough, I would learn that, too.

Chapter Eighteen:
Emilio
1983–1987

Carey and I met in 1983, when she was modeling through Wilhelmina Models and I was still very much a struggling actor. She was sharing an apartment in Brentwood with a bunch of girls I knew from high school, six or seven of them living together and working as waitresses at night while trying to break through as actresses and singers during the day. Carey was dazzling, beautiful and smart, with a college degree in business. I liked her for many reasons, not the least being that she said she wasn't impressed by my family or my work. We dated steadily and had a relatively happy relationship for about a year.

Then Carey told me she was pregnant, and that she'd decided to have the baby.

A child? I was twenty-one, and the news felt like the end of my life as I knew it. I was just getting started as an actor, and I wasn't sure I wanted to spend the rest of my life with Carey. At the same time, I knew that if my parents had made a different decision about marriage and parenthood I might not have been raised by both of them, or might not have been born at all.

When my parents learned about the pregnancy my father started counseling me about "doing the right thing," meaning sticking out the relationship and raising the child with Carey, but I was terribly conflicted about committing to a long-term union with her. There was no easy solution, and a baby was very much on the way.

Soon after Carey's announcement, I auditioned for the John Hughes film about five high school students stuck in a Saturday detention session. In their nine hours together they discover they have more in common than the school's strict social categories allow them to believe. The film would be called *The Breakfast Club,* and I read for the part of John Bender, the hardened delinquent from an abusive home who provokes the other students and raises hell all day long, but when John Hughes couldn't find the right actor to play Andrew, the athlete, he asked me to take that role instead. Nicolas Cage and John Cusack auditioned for Bender but the role went to a relative newcomer named Judd Nelson, a twenty-four-year-old actor from Maine. Also cast were Anthony Michael Hall and Molly Ringwald, who'd both appeared in *Sixteen Candles,* as the class brain and the popular, spoiled prom queen. Ally Sheedy, who'd recently starred in *WarGames* with Matthew Broderick, landed the part of the school outcast.

Accepting the role of Andrew meant spending January through May of 1984 in Des Plaines, Illinois, a suburb of Chicago, where Hughes had taken over the former Maine North High School. The whole shoot would take place at the school for a budget of $1 million. Spending four months in the Midwest would mean leaving Carey during most of her pregnancy, and when I accepted the role it understandably put us on bad terms. She felt I was giving more attention to my career than I was to her and the baby and she was right, but my years of pounding the pavement and trying to get work as an actor were finally starting to pay off. The 1980s were a good time to be a young actor, and I needed to work to take care of Carey and a child, following the model I'd observed from my father throughout my whole childhood.

The day I left to film *The Breakfast Club,* Carey and my parents took me to Union

Station in downtown Los Angeles, where I boarded the Southwest Chief train to Chicago. I could have flown but I wanted to ease into the Midwest, and the past few weeks with Carey had been so dramatic and so intense I needed some time to myself. I said good-bye to the three of them at the station in Los Angeles in January, knowing I wouldn't be back until May.

The two-day Amtrak journey to Chicago took me through Arizona, New Mexico, Colorado, Kansas, and Missouri and into Illinois, where the *Breakfast Club* cast assembled in Des Plaines about three weeks before shooting was scheduled to begin. Just as with *The Outsiders,* the actors arrived early to rehearse scenes, bond with one another as actors, create a shared history for our characters, discuss our roles with the director, and do wardrobe, hair, and makeup tests. Back then our contracts would include rehearsal time for either half our regular rates or for free, depending on the film's production budget. Often today, if a director tries to get actors to show up in advance of the first day of production they'll roll their eyes, but in the 1980s we never questioned the practice.

The day we arrived at Maine North High School, which doubled as Shermer High for the film, we were led onto the main set. The art department had transformed the school's large gymnasium into an exact replica of a two-floor high school library. The majority of our scenes would be shot in that room, and we rehearsed there sometimes for ten hours a day. John Hughes gave us wide latitude with our characters and encouraged us to improvise during rehearsals to make the parts our own.

One day, he told Judd and me that he'd written the first draft of the script in a single weekend. "How many drafts did you write?" we asked.

"A couple of them. Why?"

"Can we read the others?" we asked. The earlier drafts he showed us had such good material we asked him to put some of it back into the shooting script. John was always willing to discuss our ideas and often made the changes we suggested.

Though we were playing high school seniors, Judd, Ally, and I were already in our twenties. Molly Ringwald and Anthony Michael Hall, who went by Michael, were real-life high school students. Both of them turned sixteen during filming and had to attend classes on set for a few hours each day during the school week. The film was shot mostly in sequence, and with one main set, the same five characters in nearly every scene, and very little action other than conversation, filming often felt more like performing a play than shooting a movie. Outside the school building the Illinois winter was bitter, but inside we were insulated both from the weather and from Hollywood, and the double remove helped us travel deeply into our characters and stay there, without the pressures or the distractions of home.

I returned to Los Angeles in the middle of May, just after my twenty-second birthday, to a girlfriend who was eight months pregnant and parents who were now adjusting to the idea of a second grandchild. While I'd been gone, Charlie's high school girlfriend had also become pregnant, and so at the age of forty-three my parents were facing grandparenthood twice over, with neither of their sons moving toward marriage. Still, even though my father had been pressuring me to marry Carey, I never felt any judgment from either of my parents about her pregnancy. My mother had been born out of wedlock and never knew her biological father, and I knew both my parents would embrace the baby after he or she arrived.

A month later, on the twenty-first of June,

a Thursday, I got a call about a screen test. Joel Schumacher was casting a film about a tight-knit group of seven friends in Washington, D.C., making their way through their first few postcollege years. The film's title was *St. Elmo's Fire* and I was asked to test for the role of Kirby Keger, a law student by day and waiter by night who becomes obsessed with an emergency-room doctor and goes to great lengths to earn her affection. The casting director wanted me to come in the next day.

"I'd like to, but my girlfriend's pregnant and she could go any minute," I said. Carey and I were barely on speaking terms at that point, but I was trying not to schedule anything unless it was absolutely critical.

"Well, that's when we're doing the screen test, and that's when we need you to be there."

This was how the system worked. You either made yourself available when the casting director and director needed you, or you didn't get the job. So I went in the following day.

Carey went into labor in the middle of my screen test. When our son, Taylor Levi Estevez, was born a few hours later, my parents were there to cut his umbilical cord. I was still at the audition when he arrived.

As awed and as grateful as I was to hold Taylor for the first time, I knew by that point that Carey and I could not live together. Still, there was now a child to consider and I was committed to supporting him, even as work took me in and out of town, more out than in. The month after Taylor was born, I left for Minnesota for three months to film *That Was Then, This Is Now*, a script I'd adapted from the S. E. Hinton novel of the same name. I came home for three weeks and then left for Washington, D.C., to film *St. Elmo's Fire*. Throughout that time I was also writing *Men at Work*, about two garbage collectors who get involved in a murder cover-up, and *Wisdom*, a road story about two lovers on the run. In retrospect, I was looking for as many distractions for myself as possible, to keep from having to focus on the difficulties at home.

In Washington, D.C., the production of *St. Elmo's Fire* reunited me with Ally Sheedy and Judd Nelson, in roles that couldn't be more different from the social outcast and the delinquent they'd played in *The Breakfast Club*. This time Judd had been cast as an aspiring politician who crosses the aisle from Democrat to Republican to further his career. Ally played his live-in architect girlfriend who keeps putting off his offer of marriage. The core cast also included Rob Lowe, who'd gone on after *The Outsiders* to star in *Class, The Hotel New Hampshire,* and *Oxford Blues;* Andrew McCarthy, who'd costarred with Rob in *Class;* Mare Winningham, who'd been doing television work for almost ten years; and an actress named Demi Moore, who had been a regular on the soap opera *General Hospital* for two years. On-set romances are usually as ephemeral as they are predictable, but this one was neither. By the time *St. Elmo's Fire* finished filming that fall, Demi and I were a couple.

My father thought she was smart, level-headed, and classy but kept up the pressure for me to try family life with Carey and Taylor. "This is your son," he would say. "This is the woman who loves you. You've got to raise your son together."

Selfishly, I wanted to be a movie star more than I wanted to be a father, and as a result I was a better movie star than I was a father at that time. But I don't want to have any place for regret in my heart. I made mistakes in my twenties, a lot of them — who hasn't? — but each one helped shape who I am today, and today I have an extraordinarily close and loving relationship with both of my children. Still, I had to achieve that as a part-time father who was working nearly all the time, and that wasn't always easy.

The Breakfast Club was released in February 1985 to positive reviews from the media and a huge reception from teenagers nationwide. The film grossed more than $5 million on its opening weekend and more than $35 million in its first three months, an enormous margin for a film that had cost only $1 million to make.

Film critic Roger Ebert praised the film for creating fictional teenagers who seemed plausible to real teenagers. That's exactly what John achieved. By reaching so far beneath the superficial stereotypes of his five characters — the jock, the brain, the hood, the prom queen, and the outcast — he stepped into the realm of archetypes where viewers could identify with children struggling to become adults in a complex world and recognize the mask each character wore as a form of self-protection.

The Breakfast Club was my first commercially successful film and my performance as Andrew established me as one of a group of up-and-coming actors. Every twenty years in Hollywood a new cycle of young talent emerges, and I was fortunate to be part of that mid-1980s group. In addition to acting, I'd also decided to write and direct and in June of 1985, just before the release of *St. Elmo's Fire, New York Magazine* sent a journalist to Los Angeles to profile me as an emerging young actor-filmmaker.

At least that was the original plan.

Most of my film roles to that point had been ensemble work — *The Outsiders, The Breakfast Club,* and the upcoming *St. Elmo's Fire* — and I didn't feel right about an article focusing exclusively on me and denying the others the spotlight we'd shared on screen. The films we'd made had succeeded because they were a sum of all their parts. They didn't live or die by a single actor's work. Also, I didn't want any of the others to think I saw myself as different from them or better in any way, because that wasn't true. So I called up the other cast members from *St. Elmo's Fire* to see who was in town and who wanted to go out for an evening when the journalist came to L.A. Judd and Rob both agreed to join us.

The journalist met us at the Hard Rock Cafe, a loud, boisterous restaurant in Hollywood. Afterward we went out to a couple of clubs. Then the journalist spent a few more days traveling around L.A. with me and meeting several other young actors in my circle of friends.

Whatever the journalist observed or thought he observed that week then went through the mysterious alchemy that only journalists with their own agendas can explain. The result was a June 10, 1985, issue of *New York Magazine* with a photo of Rob, Judd, and me on the cover and the title "Hollywood's Brat Pack." Even worse than the condescending term was how the writer described me as the group's "unofficial president," which had no truth to it whatsoever. He also dubbed me the group's "unofficial treasurer" when he misconstrued me picking up the bill that night — which I did because I'd invited the others to join us — as evidence that I regularly paid everyone's way.

I could have lived with those jabs, and even with the way some of the other actors turned on me anyway because of the article's focus and tone, but what stung me most was how the writer lumped eleven male actors together as entitled, attention-seeking, womanizing playboys and painted us all with the same broad strokes. This might have been true for some of the actors, but it wasn't true for me. I was the only one in the group with a child to support, and while some of the others may have been out sleeping with royalty or doing lines of coke I was at home writing scripts. Yet somehow I was associated with all that and it was a bummer, to put it bluntly, because it wasn't who I was. I'd already done all of that stuff in the Philippines when I was fourteen. By twenty-three, I felt long past it.

The *New York* article coined a phrase that would stick to those eleven actors to this day. Privately, it ended an era for our formerly tight-knit group. The camaraderie and support we'd enjoyed on the sets of *The Outsiders, The Breakfast Club,* and *St. Elmo's Fire* became tarnished after we were slapped with the derogatory label. We started feeling uncomfortable around one another, carefully measuring what we said or did out of fear that it would be misinterpreted or misreported. Even after the name "Brat Packer" had lost its negative connotation and become just a shorthand method for describing any successful actor under the age of thirty in the 1980s, the sense of healthy competition and collaboration between the original ensemble members was gone.

The year 1985 was the most prolific of my acting career thus far, with *The Breakfast Club, St. Elmo's Fire,* and *That Was Then,*

This Is Now all released between February and November. But at home, my personal life had become increasingly difficult. My parents now had two grandchildren, whom they adored, and I know it was hard for my father to see me keeping Carey and, by extension Taylor, at arm's length. My relationship with Demi was off and on, and my father pleaded with me to give Carey another chance. Family meant everything to him, and as my father he wanted me to be involved in raising my own son.

He thought I was being stubborn. I thought he didn't understand the complexities of my relationship with Carey. Still, I did want to raise Taylor. So partly to appease my father and partly because I knew it was the right thing for Taylor, I put my tie on and committed to trying one more time. In the spring of 1985, between the releases of *The Breakfast Club* and *St. Elmo's Fire* I parted ways with Demi and bought a condo in Malibu to share with Carey and Taylor.

It was a halfhearted attempt at best, disastrous at worst. Carey and I wanted different things and our desires rarely overlapped. And then she became pregnant, again unplanned, at a time when it was evident to both of us that I was more focused on my career than on being a parent and that our relationship as partners would never work.

Twenty-three years old, on the brink of acting success, and soon to be a father of two: This was never how I'd imagined my life unfolding, yet it was practically a mirror image of what had happened to my dad. At twenty-three he had two sons and was appearing in *The Subject Was Roses* on Broadway, his breakthrough theater role. I had to wonder: Does a father pass down more through his DNA than just hair and eye color? Does he pass down memory? Does he pass down patterns of behavior? Or was it just some strange coincidence that my father and I both became fathers and actors simultaneously, and so young?

With the release of *St. Elmo's Fire* in June 1985 and its immediate commercial success, the acting careers of all seven of its stars were firmly established. For the first time I now had the freedom to pick my own projects rather than waiting and hoping for one to pick me. I decided to take a role in a film called *Maximum Overdrive,* for no other reason than the author Stephen King was directing and I thought it would be cool to work with Stephen King. The movie was billed as an action/horror/science-fiction/adventure film, which offers an idea of both its ambition and its silliness. Loosely based on the Stephen King short story "Trucks," *Maximum Overdrive* featured machines that come to life and go on murderous rampages across North Carolina. A carving knife cuts a waitress of its own volition, a soda machine shoots cans into a customer's stomach, cars drive themselves into crowded buildings. All this, set to a soundtrack by the heavy metal band AC/DC.

"Why did you do that film?" my mother asked when she saw it.

"I wanted to work with Stephen King," I explained.

"You couldn't just help him paint his house?"

When I shared her comment with Stephen later, he laughed out loud. "Oh my God! You could have!" he said.

We both might have been better off. The film was absolutely trashed by critics and Stephen chose never to direct again. Still, I meet fans of *Maximum Overdrive* even now who ask, "When are you making part two?" Which only goes to show, there's something out there for everyone.

By the end of 1985 I'd finished the screenplay for *Wisdom,* a film about two lovers on the run. Demi and I were back together and had recently gotten engaged, and *Wisdom* was meant to be a vehicle for us to act in together. One day I got a phone call from my agent Mike Menchel at Creative Artists Agency, known as CAA.

"David Begelman read your script. He's put a deal together and they want to meet with you tomorrow," he said.

I knew David Begelman mainly as the former head of Columbia Pictures who'd been busted for forging the actor Cliff Robertson's signature on a check. Now he and his partner Michael Nathanson were running a production company called Gladden Entertainment that distributed its films through Twentieth Century Fox. When we met they were both friendly and enthusiastic about *Wisdom*'s script. Begelman particularly liked the main character, John Wisdom, a recent college graduate with a past felony conviction that prevents him from finding a job.

"I love the idea that this guy doesn't get a break," Begelman said. "He made one mistake in his life, and he can't shake it." *Maybe he's feeling a personal connection to this character,* I thought.

"We want you to direct," Begelman continued. "But it's a five-million-dollar budget and we're not comfortable with handing you that amount of money as a first-time director unless you have an executive producer on set."

"You mean like a babysitter?" I asked.

"You can call it a babysitter if you want, but it's more of an insurance policy for us. Will you consider meeting with a few guys?"

"Okay," I said. "How about you put a list together, and I'll put a list together, and we'll compare?"

On their list was Robert Wise, who had edited *Citizen Kane* in 1941 and gone on to win Best Director Oscars for *West Side Story* and *The Sound of Music* in the 1960s. On my list was Taylor Hackford, who'd directed *An Officer and a Gentleman.* On their list was Burt Reynolds, who was Burt Reynolds. On my list was James L. Brooks, who'd just won three Oscars for Best Director, Best Screenplay, and Best Picture for *Terms of Endearment* with Debra Winger, Jack Nicholson, and Shirley MacLaine.

If my father had been directing by that point, would I have put his name on the list or gone to him for advice? Maybe. But this was professional territory in which, for the first time, my father couldn't advise me. As long as we were both acting he was the experienced elder I could turn to for guidance, but as a first-time director I would have to reach beyond our relationship to find the mentoring I needed. It would be another five years before my dad would sit in a director's chair for a feature film and by then he would be coming to me for advice.

I met with each of the directors in very different settings. Early on I realized I was auditioning them instead of auditioning for them, which was at first a disconcerting turn of events. At barely twenty-four I knew I was swimming in the deep end with this list, so to speak, but at the same time, I felt I was staying afloat. I'd written the script for *Wisdom* and I felt able to convey my vision for the film.

James Brooks and I sat for a few hours at his office at Sony Pictures, where we talked about story, character, themes — the elements that Brooks handles so well in all his films. Burt Reynolds and I already knew each other from the months I'd spent doing *Mister Roberts* at his dinner theater in 1980. He invited me to his house in Los Angeles for dinner, where we sat down with his girlfriend (later his wife) Loni Anderson at one end of an elegant dinner table that must have been thirty feet long for a meal of spaghetti and meat sauce. This was long before anyone asked if guests had any dietary restrictions, and I was a strict vegetarian, but after a moment of inner debate I decided to break from my principles for one night and eat meat rather than risk coming across as difficult while interviewing one of my father's friends for a job.

After dinner, Burt led me into his private screening room and gave me a gift: a book on the films of Japanese filmmaker Akira Kurosawa. He was very supportive about my decision to direct, but he wasn't interested in functioning as an executive producer for the film.

"You don't need anyone with you on set," he said.

Next I sat with Taylor Hackford at the swimming pool on his estate. He'd just finished directing *Against All Odds* with Jeff Bridges and Rachel Ward and was dating the actress Helen Mirren, who would later become his wife. He was also encouraging and knowledgeable, but when we shook hands good-bye I think we both knew we wouldn't see each other again for a while.

The last director I met with was Robert Wise, who'd by then directed thirty-nine films in his career, including one of my longtime science-fiction favorites, *The Andromeda Strain*. He was serving as the current president of the Academy of Motion Pictures Arts and Sciences and had by far the most experience of anyone on our lists.

From the start, Wise was different from the other directors I'd just met. He didn't want to speak about the script. Instead, Wise talked about the technical aspects of filming and impressed upon me the importance of going into a project prepared.

"The movie will live or die by your prep," he explained, "especially if you're doing three jobs at once." By this he meant if I was going to be the writer, the director, and the male lead I had to do as much of the pre-production work as possible before we started to film, to minimize the amount of work I'd be responsible for on set.

With a full head of gray hair, oversized black glasses, and an easy, friendly smile Wise looked and acted the part of experienced mentor. He was already in his seventies when we met but he was very strong and energetic, and something about mentoring a first-time director must have appealed to him.

"I'm excited to be on this journey with you if you want me," he said before we parted, and then reminded me again, "but if you don't prep properly you're going to be shooting yourself in the foot."

All the directors I met had encouraged me, but Wise was the one who seemed to take me most seriously as a director. His advice had already been valuable and helped me feel, as a first-time filmmaker, that I had the skill to direct a film.

After I left Wise's house I called David Begelman. "Even if Robert Wise doesn't come and do the film, just meeting him has given me an extra boost," I said. "But if you guys are willing to write the check I'd love to have him on board."

So Robert Wise joined us on *Wisdom.* Early on, he told me that the film's editor is a director's best friend and that I needed to choose one wisely. Michael Kahn, who edited Steven Spielberg's films and coincidentally also edited *Rage,* the 1972 film my father had done with George C. Scott in Arizona, had a small hole in his schedule and joined us when he heard that Robert Wise was on board. I couldn't have asked for a better editor at that point in my career.

For the film's score, I'd set my sights on Danny Elfman, the lead singer and songwriter of the band Oingo Boingo. Even before Wise signed on to help I stood outside the back door of the Hollywood Palladium after an Oingo Boingo concert with a copy of the script in my hand.

"Mr. Elfman, someday I'm going to direct. I'd like for you to do the score for this script," I said.

"I've never done a movie score," he said.

"I know you haven't. But I'd really like you to do this one."

By the time I approached him again, he'd already scored *Pee-Wee's Big Adventure* for director Tim Burton, who'd had the same idea. We were fortunate to get Elfman before he became one of Hollywood's most sought-after film composers. He later went on to score *Men in Black, Good Will Hunting,* and most of Tim Burton's films, including *Alice in Wonderland.*

Rounding out our crew for *Wisdom* was production designer Dennis Gassner, who lent a unique style to the look of the film and later went on to do *Field of Dreams, Barton Fink,* and *Bugsy;* director of photography Adam Greenberg, who had recently shot *The Terminator;* and producer Bernard Williams, who had worked with the director Stanley Kubrick on *Clockwork Orange* and *Barry Lyndon.* It was an extraordinary brain trust for a first-time director.

Too bad I didn't listen to them more.

When I look back now at the production of *Wisdom,* I see a very young writer/ director who had the aesthetic sensibility to pull off some good shots but didn't yet have strong storytelling skills. I would think, *This crane shot would look cool* or *This transition into the next scene would be bitchin'* as opposed to *This makes sense* and *This is good storytelling.* At twenty-three I was one of the youngest Hollywood directors ever to write, direct, and star in my own film, and I was too inexperienced and too ambitious to slow down, admit what I didn't know, and ask for help. I'd had such a bad experience with my first script, *That Was Then, This Is Now,* that I was hell-bent on not letting a project get away from me again. On that film, the producers actually came into my apartment, commandeered my computer, and rewrote the script. I'd let it happen because they were writing the checks, but once it was out of my hands the film became somebody else's vision, and the movie suffered for it.

Wisdom became a classic example of letting my past dictate my present. Instead of leaning more on the incredible talent that had assembled to do the film, I didn't let myself trust them. I was too afraid they would conspire to take the movie away from me.

Had I listened to them, had I let their wise counsel penetrate, would I have wound up with a better movie? I'll never know. I know only that at the time I was neither a collaborator nor an experienced enough filmmaker to do an excellent job on my own.

Nothing could have prepared me for walking onto a set and facing a hundred people asking, "Where do you want the camera?" and "Where do we stand?" and waiting for me to make the decisions that would determine their next moves. Nothing prepares you for that experience except the experience itself. Some days I would go into my trailer and wring my hands while I worried about which choice to make next, and then I'd walk back out and make a decision, because I was the director and I had to. Having Robert Wise on the set helped me understand what worked and what didn't. He would sit in front of the video monitors and watch scenes in real time as they were being filmed. I'd look over and he'd be laughing or giving me the thumbs-up. Whatever criticism he gave was always constructive, which to me is the mark of a true mentor.

I'd worked with my brother Ramon on *In the Custody of Strangers* when he played one of Danny Caldwell's derelict friends but *Wisdom* marked the first time I cast a family member in one of my films. It was the start of a practice I'd go on to use in nearly every film I've made. I could count on my family members to do good work, and if the film was low-budget I knew they'd help me out for cheap or even for free. For *Wisdom* I asked my brother Charlie to take a small role as the manager of a burger joint who has to fire my character. Charlie was leaving for the Philippines the next day to shoot *Platoon.* "Before you go, can you just come in and play this? We won't even hear what you're saying," I said. As Charlie's character fires John Wisdom, Elfman's score drowns out most of his lines, but his angry gestures and expression of fury convey the manager's sentiments perfectly. You don't need to hear Charlie's voice to guess what he's saying.

The film had an obvious part for my father in the role of John Wisdom's father, but I chose to meet with other actors, including Dennis Hopper. I wound up casting Tom Skerritt in the role even though Hopper had wanted it. Years later he told me, "Hey man, you know, I'm really mad you didn't cast me in that film. I thought I was more right for that role than Tom Skerritt." There was nothing to say at that point except, "I'm sorry." I'd made a choice that I felt was right for the film, but it could have been fun to work with Dennis Hopper as my on-screen father, given our history together.

Wisdom was released in January 1987, and of all the reviews in the media the one I looked forward to most was from the *LA Weekly,* which functioned as my entertainment bible. I liked reading it so much I would have friends send copies to me on location. In the 1980s, F. X. Feeney and Michael Wilmington were cool, progressive film critics writing for the *Weekly* and I valued their opinions above all.

The *LA Weekly*'s review of *Wisdom* was titled "Ain't No Rosebud." It was a reference to *Citizen Kane,* which Orson Welles had written, directed, and starred in at age twenty-six. From there, the review went from bad to worse.

Even though I still had to believe the film was good, in retrospect the reviewer was spot-on when he explained why the movie was weak. On the other hand, he took two whole pages of valuable *LA Weekly* real estate to do it. Ultimately I was left with respect for him for making a thoughtful effort to deconstruct the film instead of writing up the usual dismissive single paragraph films often receive.

My salvation during that week of harsh reviews was the *Los Angeles Times,* where

Michael Wilmington called the film a weak attempt to revive the mix of violence, social context, and lyricism of *Badlands* and *Bonnie and Clyde.* But he also said that the film showed more promise than Ron Howard's first film, *Grand Theft Auto,* which Howard also wrote, directed, and acted in at age twenty-three. And we all know how that career story turned out.

My father, who'd had his own share of film highs and lows — with one of the highs being *Badlands,* also a film about two lovers on the run — became both a voice of reason and a source of emotional support for me at that time. He waxed philosophical about the reviews.

"Imagine they were singing your praises," he said. "Where would you go from there? Now you've got somewhere to go."

It was hard for me to see his point back then, but he was right. I did have room to improve. I'd jumped into directing without being ready for it, driven by ambition and the desire to tick a new box earlier than I was ready to. I'd wanted to learn a new skill set but instead of going to film school I chose to learn on a public stage where everyone could watch me stumble. My experience with *Wisdom* was the epitome of taking a risk and not doing it safely. Or maybe it was that in my twenties I had such a measure of fearlessness I didn't realize the extent of the risks I was taking. Or maybe I was just too stupid to know or to care. Probably a combination of both.

It may be a cliché to say that over time we learn more from our mistakes than we do from our successes, but that doesn't make it any less true. The *Los Angeles Times* critic had been right when he described *Wisdom* as a poor derivative of *Badlands* and *Bonnie and Clyde.* I was writing a script and making a film about something that wasn't personal. I didn't know anything about bank robberies or helicopter chases. It would take me another movie about two garbage men (*Men at Work*) before I fully understood that a personal connection to one's material makes for a much better film. Then I would give myself license to direct and act in *The War at Home,* a Vietnam War–era drama about a son who returns from the military and a father who can't see his pain; to direct and act in *Rated X,* about the contentious relationship between two brothers who helped launch the adult film industry; to write, direct, and act in *Bobby,* about the night of Bobby Kennedy's assassination at the Ambassador Hotel; and, most recently, to create *The Way,* the most personal of my films by far.

Once I let go of the capers and the chase scenes, when I stopped trying to provide what I thought Hollywood wanted and started focusing instead on human relationships and all of their corresponding joys and disappointments, I felt myself shift from being a maker of films to being a filmmaker. I believe the work reveals the same.

Paloma Rae Estevez was born on February 15, 1986. Sadly, by the time she arrived it was clear to everyone that Carey and I couldn't live together again. My father still thought I was stubborn, and he was right, but over time, he became resigned to my position and readjusted his expectations of me. "You don't have to be a full-time father," he told me, "but you still have to welcome these children into your life."

He and my mother tried to fashion their own relationship with Carey so as not to be cut off from Taylor and Paloma. They rented a house in Malibu for her and the kids and welcomed the kids into their own home whenever she wanted to bring them over. Their motto was that all differences had to be checked at the door, and while at first I objected to them jumping over my relationship with Carey to forge their own, over time I came to recognize it as the best choice for everyone involved. They wanted to have access to their grandchildren, and as a result my kids' connection to my parents has been one of the most rewarding in their lives.

The mid-1980s was a tumultuous time for my dad and me. I was becoming as well known as an actor, perhaps even more well known than he was at the time. I was also choosing to separate from the family, not out of anger or animosity but out of a desire to assert myself as an independent artist. Charlie was acting by then — *Platoon* was released just a week before *Wisdom* — and the media had already started talking about our family as a sort of acting dynasty. I didn't want to arrive at every screening, premiere, or party and have it look like a family function. Also, by making the decision to keep my name I'd discovered that my individuality was important as well. I didn't want to be thought of as the parenthetical guy in the family who was described as Emilio Estevez (Martin Sheen's son), or Emilio Estevez (Charlie Sheen's brother), or Emilio Estevez (Brat Packer). I wanted my name and my work to stand on their own merit. The choice to step out on my own wasn't a personal rejection of the family, but rather a separation from the professional connections between us.

And so I backed away from the family and became less available. I'd bought a little prefab house on some land near Whitefish, Montana, where I started spending more time, and when I came home to California I acted like less of a family team player. This didn't always go over well with my parents.

"Oh, come on," they would say.

"Come on what? Give me my moment here," I'd tell them.

It's clear to me now that I had to pass through this stage to assert myself both as an artist and a man. The historical father-son struggle for power and dominance that's practically encoded in our DNA took place, for my dad and me, in the professional arena. Most of the time it was driven by fear that I wouldn't get the credit I deserved for my work. I was afraid to appear as if I were riding on his coattails, especially when, as a father now myself, I was committed to making my own career choices and not to be influenced by his.

Growing up, I'd watched him make decisions that weren't good for his career but that he felt were necessary to feed his family. In the years before *Apocalypse Now* he'd been a journeyman actor, experienced and talented but never distinguished from the pack. *Apocalypse Now* had given him the potential to become a movie star, but he never saw himself that way. His self-image remained that of a struggling actor who answered the phone each time his agent called and thought, *I have to take this role; it could be my last job.* Rather than looking at the bigger picture and asking, "Is this a movie that I want to be part of?" he would dial back into actor mode and say, "This is a great role." I heard him say that a lot. Not "This is a great movie" but "This is a great role." The problem with that? If it's a great role but a shitty movie, no one's going to see it.

My father never saw himself as a movie star, and therein lay the heart of his professional dilemma: Because he didn't see himself as a star, other people in the industry didn't see him as a star either, and actors who aren't seen or treated as stars don't get starring roles.

I didn't want that to happen to me, and when I first started out as an actor, it didn't. But then, at the age of twenty-four, I was supporting two children, an ex-girlfriend, two households, and trying to keep everything up in the air. Before long, I found myself doing exactly what my father had done all those years: taking jobs for the money. *Another Stakeout; D2: The Mighty Ducks; Loaded Weapon 1; Judgment Night:* these films were neither career moves nor creatively challenging roles for me but they paid the mounting bills. For the first time, I could empathize with the source of my father's past dissatisfaction and rage.

By my late twenties I truly understood what my father had managed to pull off for all of my growing-up years. I learned about the struggle between balancing the anxiety that comes with being a provider with the pride in being a father and had to figure out how to reconcile the resentment over having to support a family at such a young age with a fierce and selfless love for the children who made those responsibilities necessary.

My dad and I were both so young when fatherhood took us by surprise. Like him, I felt like more of a contemporary and a friend to my children than like their parent, as if we were only half a generation apart instead of a full one. My children and I grew up together and had to figure out a lot of things simultaneously. It would take ten years of parenthood before I felt that I was a good father. By then my kids had matured enough to understand the choices I'd made, and I'd matured enough to be able to understand and explain them myself.

I give thanks every day now for Taylor's birth, and for Paloma's, too. As unexpected and as challenging as those first ten years were, early fatherhood changed my life and shaped my view of everything that followed. Everything.

CHAPTER NINETEEN: MARTIN

1984–1989

In director Oliver Stone's 1987 film *Wall Street,* Charlie and I played a father-son scene that perfectly dramatized the characters' father-son struggle. In the movie Charlie plays Bud Fox, an ambitious young stockbroker who comes under the tutelage of the ruthless corporate raider Gordon Gekko, played by Michael Douglas. I played Bud's father, Carl, a hardworking blue-collar foreman and union president at Bluestar Airlines. In this particular scene we've just come from a meeting where Gekko reveals his plan to take over Bluestar, provided I can get the workers to agree to work longer hours for less pay. As Bud and Carl ride the elevator down to the street together, I tell my son that Gekko is using him but that he's too blind to see it.

"What I see is a jealous old machinist who can't stand that his son has become more successful than himself," Bud says.

"What you see, son," Carl says, "is a man who never measured success by the size of a man's wallet."

"That's because you never had the guts to go out in the world and stake your claim," the son responds.

"Boy, if that's what you think," the father says, "I must've really screwed up my job as a father."

Oliver Stone got that one right. The upstart young Turk, the aging patriarch, and all the misunderstandings between them: a variation of that scene could play out in nearly any adult father-son relationship on the planet. The Irish have a proverb that says, "A craftsman's son may grow up in ignorance of his father's skills." How often do sons and fathers see each other for who they really are, and how often do they see what they need to, ascribing wrongful motivation to each other to justify their own beliefs?

In my forties, some part of me couldn't let Emilio own his own success. In some ways, I still expected the family spotlight to shine brightest on me. Now, as a grandfather of seven, I shy away from attention. I want the grandchildren to bask in their own light. But in the 1980s, when Emilio was the oldest and the first of the kids to move out and forge his own career path, I found myself standing there and wondering, *When did this happen? Why wasn't I informed? Why wasn't I asked for permission?* Like Tevye, the patriarch from *Fiddler on the Roof,* I was still living with a sense of Old World tradition. I wasn't resentful toward Emilio. I just felt left out. Plain and simple.

I was still just a kid when my own children were born, but when Taylor, Cassandra, and Paloma arrived I was in my early forties. I finally felt old enough to be a father yet I was still young enough to chase the grandchildren around in the backyard and jump in the pool with them. They brought me a sense of renewal and a tremendous feeling of liberation. I could still have an influence on my own children through my grandkids, and I could make up for a lot of things I had or hadn't done as a young father, but I didn't have the full weight of responsibility I had as a parent. I've never met a grandparent who doesn't feel the same way. We become attached to our grandchildren in ways we never could have imagined with our own children, with whom the responsibilities and the risks always felt so huge. It's as if we've already made our parenting mistakes and learned from them, and now that we know how to do it better, maybe we can even do it right.

Janet and I loved having the grandchildren come over to our house. We often had all three of them spend weekends with us and they became close. Our backyard had a huge pit trampoline where they would bounce for hours, then sit on it and eat picnic lunches. In 1982 we had a lagoon-style pool put into our backyard and the grandkids loved to come over to swim. They'd race straight through the house and jump right into the pool, and the backyard would be filled all day with the splashes and squeals of children having fun.

Our house was a neutral zone where the grandkids and their mothers were always welcome. We told both boys, "This is what we've chosen. The children are welcome and their mothers are welcome. You don't have to come but if you choose to, you all have to park your differences at the door." I even put a sign out front that read "All Are Welcome Here" to drive the point home. And so everyone agreed to set aside their quarrels, at least when at our house, for the sake of the children, which was its own form of grace.

The pool in particular was instrumental in breaking down barriers. When the kids frolicked in the water with absolute glee, we would all react in the fun of the moment, without regard for what had been said last week or what might happen tomorrow. Everyone shared in his exhilaration the first time Taylor jumped off the big rock into the water, and together we witnessed Paloma's astonishment when she discovered the underwater tunnel in the middle of the pool.

The summer Taylor learned to swim was the summer I saw Emilio start embracing fatherhood. He would go in the water with his children and let go of everything except the pure joy of being with them. I sat on the patio and watched with gratitude, thinking, *All right, now. This is the way it should be.*

When Emilio began directing in 1986 I had very little advice to offer. I had no experience directing feature films. I generally knew a scene was good when I saw it, but I didn't always know how to make it happen. Emilio took to directing very early, at twenty-three becoming one of the youngest directors to do a studio feature. By the time I tried my hand at directing a feature film, I was nearly fifty, and of course by then he had far more experience in the director's chair than I did.

The film I directed was called *Cadence,*

based on the novel *Count a Lonely Cadence* by Gordon Weaver. It was a military drama about an army private who goes AWOL after his father's death and winds up as the only white prisoner in a military stockade in Germany in 1965, where he finds himself torn between the angry, racist white sergeant Otis McKinney in charge of the prison and the community of African-American prisoners. The film was a difficult sell to studios until Charlie agreed to play the leading role of Private Bean. He was an emerging star by then and with his name attached we were able to get funding and hire other actors, including Laurence Fishburne, to play fellow prisoners. My son Ramon also joined us to play the young guard Corporal Gessner, McKinney's sycophant.

I brought as many of my close friends and family members into *Cadence* as I could. "Come to Canada with me!" was my invitation. In addition to Laurence and Ramon, I also recruited Matt Clark to play Private Bean's father; Joe Lowry, my technical adviser on *Apocalypse Now,* to play McKinney's drinking buddy; and a close friend from childhood, Eunice Augsburger (known professionally as Samantha Langevin) to play a small role at the funeral in the beginning of the film.

We all headed north to a former air force radar station outside Kamloops, British Columbia, in June of 1989 for a two-month shoot. Kamloops was way up in the Okanagan Valley, the heart of Canadian lumber country, bucolic and peaceful except for the nearby lumber mill that made the valley smell of sulfur. The base was perfect for the purposes of our story because it was isolated and small, removed from civilization and surrounded by nature. It looked exactly like the kind of place no one would want to get sent to, so for a young army private, it would surely have looked like the middle of nowhere. To me, it was the center of the universe for the next two months. I shared a rental house with Ramon, Joe Lowry, and a talented newcomer named Harry Stewart. I couldn't have picked a more beautiful location or a better cast for the film, or so I thought.

The filming would have progressed smoothly and as planned if not for complications that developed with the story's leading antagonist. About ten days into the forty-day shoot we parted ways due to creative differences with the actor who'd been hired to play the abusive Sergeant McKinney. This left us with a gaping hole in the cast and no way to fill it in time to finish the film.

"You have to play McKinney," Charlie told me. "Otherwise, we'll be throwing the money away."

"How am I going to do that?" I said. "I'll have scenes with both you and Ramon in them and none of us are related in the film. How are we not going to look like a family?"

"Don't worry," Charlie said. "Nobody's going to care. It's the only way to finish the film."

I knew he was right. There was no other solution. Before then, I'd been planning to play a small role as a JAG military officer and that role would now need to be filled by another actor. We didn't have time to fly actors up to Canada to audition for the part. I'd have to rely on an actor I already knew and could trust to do the job. Charlie, Ramon, Matt, and Joe were already in British Columbia with me, which significantly decreased the number of people whom I could call. In fact, it left only one who I knew for sure would help me.

I picked up the phone and called Emilio.

"I'm in trouble up here," I explained. "We just lost the lead antagonist and I have to take his place in order to keep the film from going under. So I need you to come up here and play the role I was going to do."

"I'm sorry," Emilio said. "I can't do it." He was in Tucson, Arizona, at the time, shooting *Young Guns II* during the day and editing *Men at Work* at night.

"Please," I said. "I need your help."

"I'm sorry," he repeated. He was sympathetic to my plight, but he wasn't willing to bend his schedule to accommodate me. As a professional I respected that choice, but as a father the refusal was painful and disappointing. I was up in the woods of Canada with a full cast and crew, trying to save a movie. Emilio knew what a jam I was in. It honestly hadn't occurred to me that he'd give me a flat-out no.

Much later Emilio told me the real reason he'd said no was because he thought I'd lean on him to help me direct, and he wanted the film to remain my vision. He was probably right about that. Without a doubt, I was looking to him to get me off the hook. However, as I stood in the production office in British Columbia holding the telephone in my hand, I was astonished to discover Emilio's loyalty was to his work, not mine.

What? I thought. *You're refusing me in my hour of need?*

Afterward I called my friend F. Murray

Abraham and asked him to come up to play the JAG attorney, and he agreed on a moment's notice. After *Cadence* was completed, I could look back and feel gratitude that Emilio had turned me down. He'd made the only choice he could have made and he'd been honest with me: he simply wasn't free, and he couldn't let family loyalty or feelings of guilt bring him up to Canada and compromise his own work back home. We were father and son but we were also working professionals and he had kept those boundaries clear.

When I made that phone call from British Columbia, our roles as father and son had reversed. I'd been the frightened child looking for someone to fix my problem and he'd been the parent who knew I was able to handle the situation myself. He'd essentially told me, "I can't swim for you. You've got to swim on your own, and you know how. Just go and do it."

I thought I'd raised Emilio to always come to the aid of family, and I'd been disappointed that he hadn't. That wasn't true at all. Emilio had been raised to be honest, even when he knew that honesty would cost him. He knew his own mind and he followed it, and I admired that in him. I hadn't had that quality at his age. I'd been too easily swayed by external factors in my family and my career, mostly out of fear. When I understood Emilio's refusal to come to Canada as an assertion of his own strength rather than as rejection of me, my admiration, respect, and pride for him increased a thousandfold.

With my return to the Catholic church, I'd committed to a personal path of honesty and social justice activism. It would have been tidy and convenient if all my behaviors had immediately followed suit, but lives never change in an instant, for good or ill, except in novels and films. In real life, change is often gradual and slow, if at all. That was the story with my drinking. After my reconversion in Paris, I drank a little less although with a much better attitude.

I still drank a lot of beer, but my drink of choice in the 1980s was Irish coffee, which is essentially a cappuccino mixed with a couple of shots of whiskey. It was an upper and a downer at the same time, strong enough to get me drunk but caffeinated enough to keep me alert for driving home. The coffee masked the taste of the alcohol, and sometimes I would down six or eight Irish coffees back to back without realizing how much whiskey I'd consumed. I would have terrible hangovers the next day, of course.

In 1985 I played the father in *Shattered Spirits,* a TV movie for ABC about an alcoholic named Lyle Mollencamp whose drinking and domestic violence spiral out of control, to the point where he loses his wife and three kids and is forced to join Alcoholics Anonymous to regain the privilege of seeing them. The job happened to come along at a time when I was drinking heavily, but I couldn't see myself in that character. Talk about denial. I was drinking for every scene, and a couple got more than usual. For a scene where Lyle gets swacked and mows the hell out of his front lawn in the middle of the night I really had a fun time out there with the lawn mower. I wasn't out of control or falling down. I was just being my alcoholic self.

Vincent Canby of the *New York Times* said I portrayed Lyle with "chilling conviction," which may well have been true. Doesn't it often take one to know one? Still, when I saw that film on TV a few months later it didn't motivate me to quit drinking.

A few years later, I was filming at Universal Studios and at the end of the work day I stopped at a bar with a few friends for a drink on my way home. Afterward I got in my car and took the Ventura Freeway, heading to Malibu.

I don't know how long the sheriff's cruiser was following me, but at some point I noticed the flashing lights in my rearview mirror and pulled over to the shoulder of the highway. A young deputy sheriff got out of his car and approached my driver's window.

"Officer," I said.

"Your license, please."

I fumbled around in my pocket for my wallet. My driver's license has my real name, Ramon Estevez, which sometimes causes confusion or problems. I handed the license to the officer, who took it back to his car. When he returned he said, "This is your real name, but you're that actor. You're Martin Sheen, aren't you?"

"Yes, I am," I said.

He stared at me for a long moment, and when he spoke, his voice was thick with disappointment.

"I used to admire you," he said. He spit the words out with such disgust. "But I don't want to see you ever again. You know you're drunk. Get the hell off the road and get some coffee. And don't ever do this again."

As he walked back to his car, I rested my

forehead on the steering wheel. I was a man in my forties, a husband, a father of four, a grandfather of three, a successful actor. What was I doing? The disappointment and shame the officer conveyed became my own.

That brief encounter gave me a shocking look at who I'd become and what I didn't want to be. Regrettably, I didn't stop drinking that night and wouldn't stop for another few months, but the officer's personal outrage was a pivotal moment that helped push me in that direction. I never forgot it and I never drank and drove again.

I finally stopped drinking in December of 1989. With the holidays approaching I couldn't bear the thought of going through another Christmas with alcohol stirring up the sad memories and battles it always stirred up at that time of year. I didn't want to put my family through it again, and I had no great desire to go through it myself, either.

Drinking no longer gave me the feelings of bravado and invulnerability it once had. Instead of lifting me up, it had begun to drag me down. I was reminded of the line in Eugene O'Neill's play *The Iceman Cometh,* when the saloon owner Harry Hope tosses down the drink Hickey the traveling salesman offers him and then complains, "What did you do to the booze, Hickey? There's no damn life left in it." By 1989, I'd arrived at the same point. Alcohol didn't have the effect on me that it once had, and what it did give me, I wanted less and less of. The difference between Harry Hope and me was that I knew it wasn't the booze that had changed, it was me.

Christmas arrived and I thought, *This is a good time to go without a drink,* so without making a big deal of it, I just didn't drink. I'm not sure anyone even noticed. January came and I went a week without drinking, and then it was a month, and one month built on top of another and another. Before long it was the summer of 1990 and I'd been sober for half a year. But by then it had become clear that my son Charlie was in trouble with alcohol and drugs.

I knew a few things about drinking but I had no insights into drugs, and Charlie was struggling with both. We planned an intervention for early August but I knew I didn't have the skills to help Charlie get through this to the other side. My friend Matt Clark, who'd gotten sober many years earlier, had been encouraging me all along to join Alcoholics Anonymous. "You've got a problem," he would tell me. "You're an alcoholic." When he learned about Charlie he insisted I join Al-Anon, the program for family members of alcoholics. "You've got to get in there and learn some skills to help him," he said. That's finally what brought me into a Twelve Step program: the desire to help my son.

At my first Al-Anon meeting I sat on a folding chair in a room filled with people. I was astonished that so many relatives and friends of alcoholics were there to seek help, and to help one another. I was equally surprised to discover the program, which was nondenominational, had a spiritual component and freely used the word "God." *How do they get away with that?* I wondered. They also talked about the existence of a Higher Power, a force greater than ourselves that guides and protects us no matter how far from grace we've fallen, which was also my long-held belief.

When a member of the group read the Twelve Steps out loud, I was struck by how similar some were to practices I followed in the Catholic church. The step about taking a searching and fearless moral inventory of oneself: That's what Catholics call an examination of conscience. The step in which we admit the exact nature of one's wrongs to another person? That's confession, or the Sacrament of Reconciliation. The step to

make amends wherever possible is the C[...]
olic concept of penance. Example: I[...]
steal money you have to pay it back; that's
both your penance and amends.

When I heard the steps I thought, *I can do this. I'm* already *doing this. Catholicism's got this down.*

At the end of the meeting, the group held hands and said the Serenity Prayer: *God, grant me the serenity to accept the things I cannot change, the courage to change the things I can, and the wisdom to know the difference.* I've grown to love that prayer for its implicit message that we are not asking for advice about how to act or what to do. It's assumed that we already have the power, and that if we can tap into it the answers will become known. That prayer is really saying, "God, give us the courage to unleash our power," but first we have to accept the responsibility for knowing our strength, and that's often when fear comes in. We have to get over the fear of living up to our own potential.

I joined AA about eight months after I stopped drinking. Though I was already sober, I hadn't yet addressed the core issues that had led me to drink. There's an old saying in AA that if an alcoholic horse thief gets sober, he's a sober horse thief. If you don't understand why you steal horses in the first place, you've got a lot more work to do. The Twelve-Step Program is what helped me stop stealing horses.

A good guest knows when to leave the party. In my case, I left the drinking party late. I was forty-nine years old. Alcohol had been my companion of default and a reliable partner for almost thirty-five years but it was no longer a friend. It had caused rifts in family relationships and diverted my energies away from what mattered to me most. One of the many beauties of the Twelve Step program is that it helps us release the negative judgment about ourselves and others that prevent us from healing. There is never a bad time or a wrong time to stop drinking. Neither is there a best time. There is only the day you stop, and everything good that follows.

CHAPTER TWENTY:
EMILIO
1990–1994

In January 1990, the Bill Moyers television special *A Gathering of Men* aired on PBS. In the ninety-minute segment Moyers interviewed the poet Robert Bly about the workshops he was leading for men around the country. Using mythology, poetry, tribal stories, chanting, and drumming, Bly was taking participants on three-day explorations of manhood, men's roles in society, and their inner lives.

The Industrial Revolution, Bly explained, had removed fathers from the homes and the fields where sons had once learned by their sides and sent them into factories and offices during the day to return exhausted, irritable, and disconnected from their families at night. Soon after the special aired, Bly published the book *Iron John: A Book About Men,* which became an instant bestseller and established him as the leader of what became known as the mythopoetic

Men's Movement of the early 1990s.

At the time, I was living in a house on the beach in Malibu with my dog, Rowdy, a big, friendly Rhodesian ridgeback I'd adopted from a pound in northwestern Montana in 1987. Demi and I had ended our engagement a few years back, and I looked forward to Wednesdays and every other weekend when I got to spend time with my kids. The year 1990 had been crazily busy for me. *Men at Work* had been released in early August and *Young Guns II,* the sequel to a film in which I'd played a fictional version of Billy the Kid, came out just a few weeks later. I'd also just finished filming the futuristic thriller *Freejack,* about a race-car driver catapulted into the future.

That September I was taking a breather to think about what would come next, when my mother called to say she had a VHS tape for me to watch. It was a tape of the Bill Moyers special, and she thought Ramon, Charlie, and I would all get something out of seeing it. She'd been concerned for years that our father hadn't passed down the coping skills his sons needed to be men. She thought Bly's work might offer some insights and explanations that could help us all.

I watched the tape and was profoundly

moved by Bly's message. Standing and working beside their fathers all day had once given sons vital knowledge and awareness, a special type of male nourishment, he said. Now that fathers went to a workplace outside the home, the average American father was spending only ten minutes a day with his son. When sons and fathers interact only at the end of a work day, Bly said, a son is exposed only to his father's temperament — which has been shaped by stress at work, humiliation from his boss, and competition with other men — and not his teachings. Modern men were grieving that loss but didn't have a language or forum for talking about it.

This all made a lot of sense to me.

My mother learned that Bly was coming to Ojai, California, to lead a weekend workshop in late October. "You guys need to go," she said.

Many times during my childhood, my parents had made me attend events I wasn't keen on or was too immature to appreciate. The Krishnamurti lecture immediately comes to mind. My mother presented the Bly workshop the way she'd presented other ideas to me in the past: "It'll be good for you," she said. "It'll be chicken soup for the soul." This was one of the few times I said,

"I think you're onto something. I connect with these ideas, and I'll go." My father was a fan of Bly's poetry and also of Bill Moyers's work and, though he was unsure about what the three days would hold, he was intrigued and agreed to try it. So my mother signed up all four of us — me, my father, Ramon, and Charlie — for the workshop, hoping it would teach us something about fathers and sons.

The Friday afternoon we were supposed to leave for Ojai, Ramon, my father, and I waited for Charlie at the house for hours. He was supposed to meet us there so we could all drive together. When it became clear he wasn't coming, the rest of us got in the car and drove there without him. We arrived at the workshop almost at dusk and the event had already begun.

An enormous white revival tent had been set up on the grounds of the Ojai Foundation, the nonprofit educational organization sponsoring the event. Tucked away in the Upper Ojai Valley east of Santa Barbara with the Topatopa Mountains rising in the distance, the location is so picturesque that an aerial view had been used in the 1937 movie *Lost Horizon* to depict the utopian Shangri-La.

By the time we parked and walked up a

gentle hill to the event site, the tent was packed. There must have been three hundred men inside. We took three chairs in the back and turned our attention to the far end of the tent, where Robert Bly and his colleague, Michael Meade, were sitting on a small elevated stage.

"We are leaving our time now . . . we are leaving our time now . . ." Bly began. Thoughtful and soft-spoken, in his midsixties with a shock of white hair, Bly wore a button-down shirt, a flowered vest, and an ascot. He strummed on a bouzouki, a slender-necked stringed instrument from Greece, as he spoke. "There are places where time moves more slowly than here."

I felt a kinship with Bly's coleader, Michael Meade, right away. He was younger than Bly, probably in his early forties, and communicated with us mainly through stories and myths. He broke his stories into segments and would pause after each one to ask questions of the audience and tap out rhythms on his *djembe,* a chalice-shaped African drum he gripped between his knees. He seemed genuinely interested in what the audience had to say. Many of the men in the tent had brought their own drums and most of the participants seemed to have come there alone.

"How many of you came here today with a son?" Bly asked at one point.

A few men in the audience raised their hands.

"How many of you are here with more than one son?"

My father's was the only hand that went up.

"You're a very brave man," Bly said, and the tent erupted in laughter.

Bly told us that night that we men were not only grieving the loss of our fathers' knowledge but also the loss of our male initiators, the older wise men who once guided a boy into manhood. "Something has to die for a man to be born," Bly said. "What has to die is the boy, but that doesn't happen anymore in our culture." Without formal initiation rituals, he said, contemporary men were being left in a state of eternal childhood, like modern-day Peter Pans. Then Bly presented us with another idea: that the natural tension between fathers and sons makes fathers a poor choice for initiating their sons into manhood. This should be the job of tribal elders, he said, family friends, uncles, grandfathers, or other older, unrelated males. I thought of the men who'd helped and guided me along my way: my godfather, John Crane, whom we had lost only a year before; Mr. Thacker, the drama club director at Malibu Park Junior High; Mr. Jellison, the English and drama teacher at Santa Monica High; and film director Robert Wise. But these men had mostly given me artistic and professional mentoring. Who had taught me the fundamentals of being a father and a man?

Maybe my mother was right. Maybe my father hadn't given me the male knowledge that I needed. And if he hadn't, how would I be able to pass the proper teachings down to Taylor? He was only six, but already I knew that he needed things from me that a mother couldn't provide.

That night, most of the men at the retreat camped in a grove of walnut trees down the hill. Ramon, my dad, and I had taken a room in a motel nearby, and we reconvened with the other men the next day at 9:00 a.m. Overnight, our group seemed to have grown exponentially. Word of mouth must have gotten around. There weren't enough seats for everyone and the overflow spread onto the dry grass outside the tent. When Meade told his stories from the stage, he would pause for longer periods between sections as the men in the back row of the tent relayed his words to the men standing outside. It really did feel as if we had stepped back into an era of oral tradition, a place where time moved more slowly.

The night before, we'd been divided into three groups coded by color: red for fire, blue for water, and yellow for earth. I'd been assigned to the red group and as the day progressed and the groups splintered off for their own activities, I noticed my father standing apart from the other men.

"What's going on?" I asked.

"I won't be part of any group," he said.

This again? I thought. *Oh, give me a break.* It was his old excuse of not wanting to align himself with a particular group or a label, dating back to his days as a caddy working at the exclusive Dayton Country Club.

"Well, you kind of have to join a group if you're here," I said. "You signed on for this. How are you not going to participate for three days?"

"No, I'm not going to be part of any group," he said.

I suspected that, once he'd seen what the workshop was about, he'd decided it was a bunch of sissy men sitting around crying. Granted, the weekend did have moments of men breaking down, but for the most part it was about storytelling and connecting to ritual, and about the processes by which boys become men. At first my father's response disappointed me. I thought he could have gotten something important from the workshop if he'd been willing to jump in. Part of the day was spent drumming and dancing around a bonfire, which was an incredibly freeing experience when I let go of self-consciousness and allowed myself to participate fully. If anyone there recognized me from film, they didn't make an issue of it. I felt free to drum and dance like any other man at the workshop, and I tried to make the most of the experience for as long as I was there.

As the day wore on and my father remained on the sidelines, I found myself getting more and more irritated with him. Hadn't this workshop been partially his idea? Wasn't encouraging Ramon, Charlie, and me to accompany him just a newer version of dragging us to Ojai fifteen years ago to hear Krishnamurti talk endlessly in a hot room while he sat in awe of every self-important gesture? And now here we were, in the presence of two incredible, renowned storytellers and suddenly my father was above it all and relying on the lame excuse of not wanting to belong to a group?

His was the most recognizable face in the tent and we were obviously father and son, which made his refusal to participate all the more embarrassing for me. Even worse, whenever the men clustered in their color groups to perform tasks, my dad repeatedly told the volunteer organizers — and anyone who'd listen — why he didn't want to belong to a group. I shook my head in frustration.

Come on, I thought. *These red, blue, and yellow groups are hardly exclusive or elitist.*

He was completely missing the point. By refusing to identify that weekend with an exclusive group, didn't he realize he was actually representing the pinnacle of elitist snobbery? We all possess oppositional forces within ourselves, but sometimes, when my father stubbornly digs in and then offers an explanation for doing so, his explanation seems to be at odds with the reason why he dug in in the first place. I suspected that, beneath his stubbornness, was a shyness about letting go of inhibition in front of other people, especially as a publicly known figure, but if that was the case I wished he'd just been honest with me about that. Or was he too embarrassed to let me know?

The irony of my situation wasn't lost on me. Hundreds of men at the gathering were trying to understand and forgive their fathers and there I was, so damn angry at my father for being who he'd always been.

In the tent that weekend, Bly introduced us to the myth of Iron John, a story based on a tale by the Brothers Grimm that has ancient roots in many other cultures. As Bly tells it, the story takes place in a troubled medieval kingdom. Every time the king sends a hunter into a mysterious forest, the hunter vanishes, never to be heard from again. This goes on until all of the hunters in the kingdom have disappeared and the king and all his people have shut themselves up in the castle, isolated by their fear. One day a young hunter shows up with his dog, looking for adventure, and asks for and receives the king's permission to explore the forest. After walking a short distance through the trees, he comes to the edge of a pond, where a hand reaches straight up out of the water and snatches his dog.

Very calmly, the hunter says, "This must be the place."

He returns to the castle for more men and some buckets and together they drain the pond. At the bottom they find a naked man with long hair the color of rust — Bly called him the Wild Man — who goes by the name Iron John. He's taken back to the castle and imprisoned in a cage, until the king's son sets him free and accompanies him back to the woods, where the prince learns the male secrets of survival in the world. Mishaps ensue, and a beautiful princess is involved, but the important point is that Iron John remains the boy's protector and, at the end, we learn he's really a king himself whom the mature prince has freed from an enchanted spell.

The Wild Man, Bly told us, represents the primitive male energy deep inside the psyche of all modern men that connects us to the earth. The Wild Man is the warrior, the leader, the iconoclast who resists corporate America's attempts to mold us into replicas of one another. The chanting and drumming, whooping and hollering we did outdoors that weekend helped us connect with that source of primal energy. When we drummed together, we were communicating without words, using a rhythm we all intuitively understood.

If a Wild Man lived inside me, I thought, he was being nurtured that weekend. But as I watched my father standing quietly on the sidelines, refusing to dance or chant with the group, I couldn't help wondering, was he completely out of touch? Or was he actually more in tune with the Wild Man than I gave him credit for? When he took risks as an activist railing against corporations and military establishments and shouted lines from Tagore's poem as police officers led him away in handcuffs; when he steadfastly refused to suck up to studio heads in favor of befriending only people he knew he could trust — my father might say these were acts of social justice, or merely the response to his fears. But were they not also peaceful acts of conscience against what Bly called "the civilized world" that the Wild Man opposes by nature?

It was worth considering.

This must be the place. That line, when the young hunter sees the hand reach out of the pond and take his dog, made a lasting impression on me. Not just because of the surprise or because of the poor unlucky dog, but also because of the calm, knowing way that the hunter responds to such an unexpected, unwelcome event. That type of deep inner knowledge has always appealed to me. I've met Vietnam vets who talk about walking through the jungle and knowing exactly when to step to the left or the right to avoid an incoming shell that otherwise would have taken their lives. *This must be the place I need to move away from* or *This must be the place I need to move toward,* they would know, just in time.

Several times I've found myself standing still, filled with a similar awareness that I'm suddenly in a place of great personal importance that will affect me for the rest of my life. I try to keep my high beams on all the time so I don't miss those moments, which signify a kind of deep, calm knowing, a connection to the spiritual that keeps us aware, alert, and alive. When we get thrown off our personal axis by the distractions and noise of daily life, we get disconnected from everything that keeps us grounded and from knowing whether this is the place or not. Because *This must be the place* can be referring to the right place or the wrong place, and we need as much clarity as possible, as often as possible, to be able to discriminate between the two.

That line in the myth has been so memorable and so poignant for me, I've been trying to find the right place for it in a film ever since. For *Bobby* I wrote a scene for Elijah Wood's character, a high school boy staying at the Ambassador Hotel that fateful night with a young woman, played by Lindsay Lohan, who had offered to marry him to keep him out of the draft. The camera was following Elijah closely through the hotel. He turned one way and the camera revealed Tony Hopkins and Harry Belafonte sitting in the lobby. He turned another way and we saw other characters in the lobby. When he stopped walking, the camera pulled back and he whispered to himself, "This must be the place."

It was meant to be a magical moment of self-awareness, where the boy couldn't quite put his finger on what it all meant but knew something important and profound was taking place. But in the editing process the scene came across as too self-conscious, and I had to take it out.

I tried to insert the line again at the end of *The Way*, when Tom and his three traveling companions arrive at Muxia, along the coast of Spain, to scatter the remainder of Daniel's ashes. As they stare at the crashing ocean waves before walking down to the rocks by the shore, I had the character of Jack say, "This must be the place." Again, it felt too self-conscious when I saw it on film. Eventually, I found a place for the line to live organically on *The Way*'s soundtrack. I gave track 6 the title "This Must Be the Place." It's the piece of music playing when Tom's character finds the cross in the Pyrenees marking the place where his son has died.

■ ■ ■ ■

Saturday's workshop schedule alternated between outdoor activities with our groups and storytelling sessions in the tent, with a break for lunch spread out on long tables in the shade. At one point Michael Meade shared an African story with us called "The Hunter and His Son." Meade's method of teaching through story had been resonating with me as a writer, and I leaned forward in my chair to make sure I could hear him clearly.

"The hunter and his son went into the bush one day to pursue their occupation," he began. "They hunted all morning and found nothing to sustain them but one small rat."

He paused while the men in the back of the tent relayed the opening lines to the others standing outside. In the past few hours, our group had grown even larger. Men must have been driving in from miles around.

"The father gave the rat to the son to carry," Meade continued. "It seemed of no consequence to the son, so he threw the rat into the bush. The rest of the day they saw no other game. At dusk the father built a fire and said, 'Bring the rat to roast, Son; at least we will have something to eat.' When he learned that the son had thrown the rat away, he became very angry. In an outburst of rage, he struck the son with his ax and turned away. He returned home, leaving his son lying on the ground."

The son, Meade went on, went home later that night, packed up his belongings, and traveled to a nearby village where the local chief had recently lost his son. The boy and the chief devised a plan by which the chief would pass him off to the villagers as his son returned from battle, and the boy went through various tests to prove his authenticity, all of which he passed. He lived in the village as the chief's son for years thereafter, until one day his real father came looking for him. In a final test of loyalty, the king, the hunter, and the son rode off into a clearing with three horses and a sword.

"The king gave the sword to the son," Meade continued, "and said, 'We are here unarmed. You hold the sword. Either you must slay me and return to your village with your father, or you must slay your father and return with me and live in my village as we have been.' The son did not know what to do."

There was a long pause as the story was passed back to the men outside, and as the men inside the tent considered the son's dilemma.

"What would *you* do?" Meade asked us.

The tent was filled with the silence of four hundred men thinking. What *would* we do? Choose the real father who had struck us and left us lying on the ground, or choose the false father and place material riches ahead of blood ties? These were matters of loyalty and fidelity that probably any man in the tent could imagine facing, maybe had even faced at some point in his life.

What would *I* do? It was a good question. Blood being thicker, I would have struck down the false father, I thought.

It's easy to interpret "The Hunter and His Son" as a simple tale of loyalty, but Meade encouraged us to interpret it in another light. He brought us back to the beginning of the story, when the father and son were hunting and caught the rat. The son, he explained, who was young and full of potential, believed more game would be caught that day and that he and his father would share in the outcome. In his confidence he tossed away what seemed like an inconsequential catch. But the father, in his maturity, understood that some days brought good hunting and others not and had been trying to teach the son something about the uncertainties of life and the practice of accepting what is given. If they were to catch bigger game, they would celebrate. If not, they would at least have the rat to eat. The expectations of father and son were at odds, and each had wound up disappointed in the other.

"If we look at this story one way, the father is seen as a very limited and limiting person," Meade explained. "But look at it another way, and he can be seen as the king who gives royal gifts. Where are each of you with your fathers?" he asked. "Do you feel limited by him or do you feel that you've received some gifts?"

I looked over at my father, sitting attentively on his folding chair. He, too, was listening to the story. Was he thinking of his own father, who'd raised him mostly on his own while working long days in a factory? Or was he thinking about how he'd raised his three sons and his daughter, and what he did or didn't teach us?

That night after dark, in a field beside a massive oak tree, Meade and Bly created an altar out of a pile of rocks and set up a wooden doorway nearby for the men to pass through. This was based on a Sufi tradition of building a doorway without walls in the middle of the desert as a reminder that even the most adverse environment contains a threshold to another world, whether it's the world of imagination, the world of art, the world of spirit, or the world of the soul. We were asked to each select an object from nature — a small bunch of dry grass, a flower, a rock, a piece of fruit, a clod of dirt — to represent something in our lives that was keeping us from moving forward. Then we were to carry it through the doorway while imagining the next steps of our lives and lay the item to rest at the altar on the other side.

I found a stone in the field and got in line. In the stone I held in my hand I felt the weight of a burden I'd been carrying for the past six years: the guilt I felt for not having married my kids' mom. The line inched forward toward the door. There must have been a hundred men ahead of me and just as many behind. I couldn't see my father in the crowd but it didn't matter. He would participate or not; it was his choice, not mine.

One by one the men stepped through the doorway and approached the altar. By the time I reached it, the pile included hundreds of flowers and rocks and pieces of fruit. I placed my stone on the top. And with it, I committed to laying down my burden and moving forward as a father without a place for that guilt in my life.

Almost twenty years later, I would see a similar symbolic pile of rocks while on a location scout for *The Way,* when I saw the Cruz de Ferro ("Cross of Iron") outside the city of Ponferrada on the Camino in northwest Spain. Cruz de Ferro is a simple iron cross on Monte Irago, the highest point on the Camino, and a place where pilgrims ritually lay down a stone they've carried with them the whole way to represent a relinquishing of their burdens. The pile is enormous, taller than two men, maybe even three. In *The Way,* the character Sarah pulls a stone from her pack with a note wrapped around it, but she's unable to read it without her voice breaking up. She hands it to Tom, who steps in as a father figure to read it out loud for her: *Dear Lord, May this stone, a symbol of my efforts on the pilgrimage, that I lay at the foot of the cross of the Savior, weigh the balance in favor of my good deeds some day, when the deeds of my life are judged. Let it be so. Amen.*

In 1990, I had no way of knowing I would make a film about a father and son, or about the Camino de Santiago, or that my six-year-old boy would grow into a man who would seek his future in a country 6,000 miles away. I knew only that it felt good to symbolically lay down a small personal burden with a group of men committed to doing the same.

From the altar, we were guided into a field where Bly and Meade led us in a group song, and then we lay on our backs side by side. Several of the myths we'd heard that day involved descent and going down into the earth and the hard ground and small pebbles pressing into my back felt solid and right, a firm reminder that we all came from the earth and we'd all return to it one day. The stars overhead were spectacular without interference from ambient city lights. A half moon cast a faint glow on the field.

"Imagine that these stars live inside us, that a speck of stardust exists in each and every one of us," Meade said. "We may be earthbound beings, but we have imaginations that reach from the earth all the way to the stars, and part of the purpose of humanity is to unite heaven and earth."

Bly read us some poems, and then the field fell silent until, off to my right, a man started quietly weeping. Another one started sobbing off to my left. And then another. In a short while, the field was filled with the sound of men crying, but it wasn't uncomfortable to lie in the midst of it. Everyone there felt moved for a different, personal reason.

I lay on my back and looked up at the stars, feeling the firm, stable ground under my shoulders and my head. I was part of this earth, part of my family, part of a lineage, part of this group of men. I was an actor and a writer and a filmmaker, a storyteller and a storymaker, a son and a father and a man.

Do you feel limited by your fathers? Meade had asked us. *Or do you feel that you've received some gifts?*

That's when I realized: My mother might have been wrong about my father and me. He may not always have been available to me emotionally because of his work but he *had* passed down some very valuable knowledge. He hadn't gone off to a nameless factory to build widgets. He'd done something personal and artistic, and he'd always included us in his life and shared his experiences. He'd insisted on keeping the family together and had taken us to places where we could observe him creating a character in a different time and place. I did get to learn at his side, as much as his profession would allow. I learned how to conduct myself on a set and how to treat everyone on a crew with equal respect, from the director right down to the interns. He'd led me through whatever rites of passage he knew how to share, from helping me prepare for auditions to teaching me that good work is more valuable than fame to insisting that my relationships with my children were more important than any other relationships in my life. Where he may have failed in the eyes of others, maybe even in his own, he hadn't failed in mine.

Three or four mornings a week I'd pick up my kids at their mom's house and drive them to their schools. I had the kind of cookie-cutter arrangement that weekend dads were often awarded through the California family court system, meaning I saw the kids every Wednesday and on alternate weekends, but I knew I needed to be more present to them than that schedule allowed. The drives to school gave us extra time together to connect. It meant spending almost two hours in the car every morning just to be with them for forty minutes, but it was worth it to see them regularly, and I tried to make the most of our time together.

The Monday morning after the Ojai retreat, Rowdy, my Rhodesian ridgeback, leapt into the back of the car — he loved any kind of road trip — and we drove off to pick up Taylor and Paloma as usual. My head was still buzzing from the weekend. I'd never experienced the power of narrative quite that way before and I wanted to share it with my kids.

We've got to tell stories, I thought. *We'll either make them up as we drive along or we'll breathe new life into old stories and myths.*

I could hardly tell them, "Your grandfather and I just went into the woods with four hundred men to hear stories" and expect them to understand what that meant. They were much too young, only four and six. Instead, I started tapping on the steering wheel, the same rhythms that four hundred men had pounded on their drums in the dark just a few nights earlier. When I had the beat going, I started telling them a story.

"There once was a young prince named Taylor," I would begin, or "There once was a young princess named Paloma."

Storytelling in the car became our morning tradition. Some days Charlie's daughter Cassandra rode with us, and she'd listen, too. I'd tell serious stories and silly ones, trying to engage them and make them laugh, and on mornings when I couldn't think up a new story I'd fall back on old ones I remembered from childhood, or simplified versions of ones that Bly and Meade had told over the weekend. Some stories were true and some made up. They were all a way to help me connect with the kids, to share values and teach them life skills, and to help them parse out fact from fiction. Most of all, they were a way to help them learn from me, by my side.

I've always loved road trips. Give me a car, a full tank of gas, and a long stretch of open road and I can be happy for days. When I had a little house in northwestern Montana about fifty-five miles from the Canadian border, I used to drive there straight from L.A., stopping only at a rest stop outside of Salt Lake City to catch a few hours of sleep. The ride took a full twenty-four hours and with no cell phones, Internet, or GPS, the biggest decision I'd have to make was, "Is it going to be I-15 or I-5?"

In 1992, I married the pop star Paula Abdul and we bought a bigger house in Montana on a lake. Paula wasn't a big fan of long road trips, so we would usually fly to Montana rather than drive. Two years later, as the marriage was ending in divorce, the last thing I wanted to do was spend a summer at home feeling sorry for myself. I had the kids to myself for a month, and I thought, *Let's get out of town.*

Long road trips were a large and memorable part of my childhood, whether we were driving from Mexico to Los Angeles; Malibu to Colorado; or to other locations in the West for my father's work. Sometimes we'd stop along the way to see sights like the Grand Canyon but we were always destination oriented and never camped. My father didn't know how to start a fire or pitch a tent and I wanted to make sure my kids had the experience of sleeping in the woods, hiking, and connecting with nature. Most of their travel to that point had involved airplanes, not the open road.

I was determined to show them the national parks because, one, I wanted them to know the natural beauty of the West and, two, I hadn't seen a lot of them myself. Rowdy and I had made the trip between Los Angeles and Montana many times, but we rarely stopped along the way. So that summer of 1994 I rented a Winnebago and planned a two-week road trip for the kids and me through the southwestern and mountain states, leading us all the way north to the house in Montana.

My parents thought I was out of my mind. Taylor was ten that summer, Paloma was eight, and their favorite pastime was fighting. They would constantly push, poke, kick, shout, shriek, hit, and scream at each other. Sometimes I wasn't sure if I were their father or their referee. Sibling rivalry is a rite of passage; I knew that from all the years that Charlie and I had fought like animals as kids, and now as adults we made movies together and took care of each other on set. I knew Taylor and Paloma would eventually grow out of this phase, and I also knew that much of their rivalry was a competition over me. By doing a long road trip together, I figured, they wouldn't have to fight for my attention. They'd have it all the time. I wouldn't be on the phone or in the middle of a film.

"Let's do this," I said. They seemed game. So we loaded up the Winnebago and headed out toward the I-10 East, the same highway that had carried my family west into Los Angeles in 1969.

My mother had made a promise to Taylor and Paloma. "I'll give each of you a thousand dollars cash if you manage not to fight for the whole trip." That was an enormous amount of money in 1994. It's still an enormous sum today. "Okay, Grandma," they'd said. She must have known her chances of having to pay up were slim. We weren't even out of Malibu before the yelling and kicking in the back of the Winnebago began. I gripped the steering wheel and took a deep breath in and out. The Winnebago was less aerodynamic than I'd bargained for and I had to keep both hands firmly on the wheel to keep from getting blown all over the road. I couldn't let myself get distracted.

"Move *over!*" Taylor shouted.

"Stop touching me!" Paloma screamed. "Stop looking at me! *Daaaaaaad!!!"*

It was going to be a very long drive.

Our route took us to the Grand Canyon and then over to the Anasazi ruins at Bandelier National Monument in New Mexico before heading up to Yellowstone National Park in Wyoming; Mount Rushmore in South Dakota; and the site of General Custer's Last Stand and Glacier National Park in Montana. It was an ambitious itinerary, but we were prepared. The Winnebago was a self-contained unit, with a shower, a toilet, and some beds. It even had a television for Taylor and Paloma to watch on the long desert drives.

It was a miserable trip. *Miserable!* The kids fought the entire way while I tried to navigate an RV the size of a small bedroom through mountain passes buffeted by wind, screaming at the top of my lungs, "Sit down and stop fighting or we're all going to die!" They knew how to push my anger buttons just as I'd known how to push my father's, and they pushed every one of mine on that trip. I took the most striking photo of Paloma standing at the site of Custer's Last Stand. I'd physically pulled her and Taylor off of each other to get her to pose for the shot. In the photo she's in front of the most extraordinary Montana sunset, with a historical marker visible in the background, and she's standing there scowling with her arms crossed tightly, completely unaware of anything but her own anger. It was an awful moment but it made for a hilarious photo.

And me? My most vivid memory of our Winnebago adventure is the drive back. My father had flown up to Montana for our last four or five days at the house. I might have sent up a flare to say, "I can't handle this by myself!" or he might have just wanted to spend time with me and the grandkids. Probably both. He decided to drive back to Los Angeles with us, so we all packed up the Winnebago together. Our route this time was to take US 93 in Idaho all the way down through Nevada until it hit I-15 outside of Las Vegas, and then cut over to L.A. I estimated it would be three full days of driving.

On the road, I thought we should try to hit I-15 sooner than Las Vegas, which meant taking a minor two-lane road along the Salmon River in Idaho for a while. This would have been fine had the road not been under construction, which I hadn't known. Without a shoulder on either side, the road was narrow and the river ran right up against one side. We hadn't been on it long when the rain and wind began.

By then, I'd spent enough time at the wheel of that enormous vehicle to know how to maneuver it pretty well. Even on a narrow road with two kids fighting in the back, I was all right, though I was struggling against the winds. My father, on the other hand, didn't have any experience riding in a box on wheels that was getting blown around. He's never comfortable in precarious driving conditions, and this situation was making him nervous. It didn't help that the kids had started fighting again in the back.

"Come on, guys," he said to them. "Come on, come on. Keep it down back there."

A strong gust hit the side of the Winnebago, making us swerve slightly toward the side of the road. I struggled to regain the vehicle's stability. My father glanced at me nervously.

"You okay?" he said.

"I'm okay."

"Gimme that!" Taylor shouted in the back, and Paloma let loose with the piercing scream of a child who'd just had an object ripped from her hand. It would be mere seconds, I knew, before she tried to grab it back.

"Keep it down!" my father shouted over his shoulder. "Your father's trying to concentrate!"

Another gust hit the camper, this one threatening to push us closer to the river. It took most of my strength to keep us in our lane. In the rearview mirror, I could see Paloma heading for Taylor in the back.

"Sit down!" I shouted.

"Get away!" Taylor shouted at Paloma.

"Idiot!" Paloma screeched. "Stop touching me! *Daaaaaaaad!"*

That's when my father lost it. He spun around in his seat.

"STOP IT!" he screamed, as loud as he could. *"STOP. IT!"*

It was effective. They stopped fighting, immediately. It was probably necessary, too. The kids were completely unaware of the stress I was under trying to keep the Winnebago on the road, and of the consequences if I couldn't. My father was unloading a dose of what I probably should have given them earlier in the trip. At the same time, hearing him yell like that made me shrink emotionally until I felt the size of a ten-year-old, too. A ten-year-old driving an enormous Winnebago. It dialed me right back to the scene of many crimes.

I learned a valuable lesson on that trip, which was never to take my kids in a Winnebago for two weeks by myself ever again. I also learned that these are the kind of experiences from which childhood memories are made. Taylor and Paloma, now in their mid-twenties, still remember our Winnebago trip in great detail and, somehow, they remember it fondly. They remember hiking down the rim of the Grand Canyon on a diabolically hot day and running into an Australian tourist who shouted at them to stop feeding the squirrels. They remember spending a night in animal-skin teepees along the Rio Grande at the home of the artist Mark Rendleman, the friend of a friend, who was diving into the river, naked, as we drove up. For years afterward, they referred to him as "Naked Mark." And they remember white-water rafting on the Flathead River in Montana, where we stayed at our house for ten days, the longest leg of the vacation.

They also remember me yelling at them in the Winnebago, and they remember my father exploding at them on the road in Idaho, but they laugh about that now. Fortunately, their good memories far outweigh the difficult ones. I'm grateful to have been able to give those good memories to my kids and for my father to have shared in so many of them with us.

I may have gone off to work every day when my kids were young, and sometimes gone on location for months, but, just as my father did, I took my kids with me whenever I could. Taylor flew up to Vancouver in 1993 when I was shooting *Another Stakeout* and spent time with me on the set. He and Paloma traveled with me to London in 1995 when I had a small part in the first *Mission: Impossible* movie, and that year Paloma was also with me in Austin, Texas, for *The War at Home,* in which she appears in a scene at the end. And in 1999 Taylor, then fifteen, flew to Toronto where Charlie and I were shooting *Rated X,* a film I wrote and directed, to play my character as a boy when the actor we'd hired had to back out at the last minute. Taylor was terrified to be on film and kept forgetting his lines, but he ultimately did a terrific job and I felt enormously proud of him for facing his fear.

Knowing what my father gave me, I can see what I've been able to pass on to Taylor: courage, determination, kindness, gratitude, curiosity, love for family, and a passion for everything we do. This may not have been the kind of male knowledge Bly was talking about, but it's the kind that works for us.

Chapter Twenty-One:
Emilio
2000–2012

Four events occurred in quick succession in the spring of 2000: I celebrated my thirty-eighth birthday; I sold the house at the beach; *Rated X* aired on Showtime; and I lost Rowdy, my faithful canine companion of thirteen years.

I was heartbroken by his death. Since the day I'd found him in a Montana animal shelter when he was just two years old, Rowdy had been my road trip copilot, my running partner every morning, and a quiet friend when I needed to be left alone. Everyone had loved him. A friend once said Rowdy was such a civilized dog I could probably take him to the movies, put a bucket of popcorn and a drink next to him, and no one would object. I couldn't bear the thought of long drives without Rowdy or of running alone the following morning. I buried him under a young plum tree on my new lawn.

My new home was a spec house on the same street where I'd grown up and where my parents still lived — "spec house" meaning that a builder had gutted and remodeled one of the original 1950s ranch homes, hoping to find a buyer who'd like the new design. I'd had only thirty days to vacate the beach house because the new buyers wanted it for the summer season, and the readymade Mediterranean villa for sale on my parents' street came at a good price. I closed the deal and moved in quickly.

I'd traded an expansive ocean view for a landlocked property with an enormous lawn, where a landscape architect had designed the front and back yards with plants that required large amounts of water to maintain. In the months that followed I replaced them with drought-tolerant varieties and capped off most of the sprinklers. Then I turned my attention to the house's interior. *I'll do a little work here and a little staining there,* I thought, *and I'll just move these piles over here,* and before I knew it I was spending most of my days driving to Home Depot and the old Malibu lumberyard for supplies.

This was all just a way to distract me from what I really needed to be doing, which was finishing the script for *Bobby,* which I'd started a few months earlier, after Charlie and I had been asked to do a cover shoot for *TV Guide* at the Ambassador Hotel in downtown Los Angeles.

The Ambassador had shut its doors to guests by then and was primarily being used as a location for films, commercials, and music videos. In between setups for the *TV Guide* photo shoot, Charlie and I wandered around the gardens. The hotel groundskeeper offered to take us on a tour inside.

"Would you like to see the kitchen where Bobby Kennedy was shot?" he asked.

"Of course," we said. "Let's go."

He led us through the Embassy Ballroom. As soon as I saw the arched, coffered ceiling I remembered that this hotel had been our family's first stop in Los Angeles in 1969. I remembered standing next to my father as he gazed at an empty wall in the ballroom and said, "Kids, a great man, Bobby Kennedy, once spoke here."

As Charlie and I toured the hotel, I started imagining what had occurred there the day Bobby was shot. What else was going on when everyone had seats on the *Titanic,* so to speak, and didn't know it yet? Aside from the famous people, who were the regular people who'd been in the hotel that night?

"What would a movie about that day look

like?" I wondered out loud to Charlie. "Who would these people have been?"

That night I went to the screening of a World War II submarine film called *U-571*. I hardly ever went to film premieres or Hollywood parties anymore, but the actor and singer Jon Bon Jovi, who had a role in it, was a close friend and he'd asked me to come. I went to the theater straight from the photo shoot and arrived early. After walking the red carpet into the theater I sat down in a mostly empty row. While I was waiting for the film to start, someone plopped down next to me. I looked over. It was Bobby Shriver, an attorney, film producer, philanthropist, and a nephew of Robert Kennedy.

What were the chances of that?

"How are you doing?" we said. We'd met a few times before, so we chatted for a while. After the movie, I went home and thought about the random encounter. Had it really been by chance? I didn't particularly believe in signs, but still, the coincidence was startling.

To research the time period around Bobby Kennedy's assassination, I spent hours down at L.A.'s Central Library poring through newspaper articles on microfiche. I wanted to learn what had happened in sports, entertainment, and the news on and around the night of June 4, 1968. I discovered that Don Drysdale of the L.A. Dodgers had pitched a no-hitter earlier that night and Andy Warhol had been shot by Valerie Solanas the day before. Five other people had also been shot in the kitchen along with Bobby. *What if those five other people were characters that we get to know in the course of a movie?* I thought. *Viewers would have an investment in the story that's not just about Bobby, but about the lives that he touched, really touched.*

Over the next few weeks I wrote thirty pages, starting with the assassination and the famous image of the busboy who'd knelt at Bobby's side after he fell to the floor and pressed a rosary into Bobby's hand. The rest of the film would be told in flashback.

And then I got stuck. What came next?

I carried those thirty pages around in a briefcase for about a year. I couldn't figure out who the main characters were and what they needed to say and do. And so I let my new house become my distraction to keep me from feeling anxious about a screenplay whose spine I couldn't crack. Every day I'd wake up thinking, *Today I'll write!* and then I'd get in the car and make another Home Depot run. I started hosting parties and salons at the house, surrounding myself with people and distractions.

My folks started getting nervous about my lack of focus. They mentioned their concerns to Charlie, who showed up at my house one day that summer. "Can I see the thirty pages you've been talking about for the last eight months?" he asked. "I want to make sure they even exist."

"Sure," I answered.

He sat in my backyard and read them. "You're onto something," he said. "But I think you need to get away from this house. You need to change your environment and stop throwing parties. All these people will be here when you get back. Just pack up a bag with all your research and get the hell out of town."

"You're right," I said. "No more excuses."

I took off the next day in the car with my computer, my notes, and a storyboard. All I knew was I was heading for Pismo Beach, a coastal town about a three-hour drive north of Malibu. I'd passed it before on my way up the coast and had thought, *Someday I'm going to come here and write.* But it was summer now, peak tourist season, and none of the hotels or inns had any vacancies. Around dusk I started heading north on Highway 1 toward Shell Beach, where I saw a semi-dilapidated motel with some prewar charm and a neon vacancy light glowing.

The woman at the registration desk recognized me when I walked in.

"What are you doing *here?*" she asked.

"I'm trying to get away from everything," I said. "I'm here to work on a script."

"Can you say anything about it? Or is it a super-secret project?"

"It's about the day Bobby Kennedy was shot," I told her.

The woman looked like she'd just received an electrical shock. "I was there," she said.

"What do you mean?"

"I was there that night. I was a Youth for Kennedy volunteer. I was in the ballroom when the shots rang out."

What were the chances of *that?* The coincidences were starting to pile up.

"Do you have a room here I can dig into?" I asked. "And if you do, would you talk to me about that night?"

She said yes to both. I checked in and stayed for three weeks. Her name was Diane, and she told me her whole story, including the part where she'd married twice, both times to keep the boys from going to Vietnam. Each one had shipped off to Germany instead of Asia after his classification changed. Diane became the inspiration for the character Diane in the film, who was played by Lindsay Lohan. I finished the script later that year and the movie went into pre-production a few years after that.

Back home, I took a long, appraising look at my lawn. The monthly water bills were still huge. *I can't eat it, I can't cultivate it, I don't have kids who want to play soccer on it, and it's an enormous expense,* I thought. What could I do with it?

A family friend, an architect named Carl Volante, was living in a guest house in Malibu on a piece of land where he'd designed and built a house. The house's owners had allowed a vineyard to be planted on a piece of their land and Carl now found himself the caretaker of a field of overgrown grapevines.

"I haven't figured out what I'm going to do," he told me. "I've got all this fruit growing and I'm up here by myself. Why don't you come up and take a look at it?"

We sat outside at his house drinking glasses of wine, looking out over the vineyard he'd inherited. Rows of green grapevines always unlocked a feeling of nostalgia and yearning in me, a familiar feeling of something lost and also something found.

"I have the romantic notion of having my

own vineyard someday," I said to Carl. "But I've never had the land before. I always thought it would have to be up in the hills where the Malibu vineyards are, but here you're doing it right near the ocean."

I looked out past the vines where the Pacific stretched for miles like a vast blue field. Off the coast, a gray whale arced out of the water and landed with a huge splash. Then it breached a second time. And a third.

Again, I'm not the kind of guy who goes looking for signs. But I am the kind of guy who recognizes one when it smacks him in the face. This felt like one of those times.

"I think I need to plant a vineyard," I said.

Carl laughed. "Where are you going to do that?" he said.

"Where the lawn is now." As soon as I said it, I knew it was possible. Why not? I had a big, flat space in back and another one in front. "Do you know a vineyard consultant I can talk to?"

"I'll get some names for you," Carl said.

Back home, I started pulling up the lawn. A friend of mine had a little Caterpillar front loader tractor and he said, "If you pay for gas and beer I'll come over and do the lawn for free." So on April 18, my mother's birthday, we got off to a start.

One of my mother's friends, an interior designer, heard I was going to rip up my lawn. "You're going to ruin your view!" she exclaimed.

"What view?" I asked. "I don't have a view. I'm going to create one."

Hers was a common response during those weeks, but the more naysayers I encountered, the more empowered I felt. I pushed the project through out of sheer determination, not out of skill. To be honest, I didn't really know what I was doing. I was just following instinct and banking on luck. *The yard would look pretty good with this orientation,* I would think, and then I'd plan for rows of grapevines in that spot. When a vineyard consultant suggested that I have the soil tested I said, "Okay, I'll get around to it," but I never did.

Vineyards don't come fully assembled; you have to put them together, piece by piece. Another friend, a plumber, came over to help lay out the drip irrigation system. That was right around the time my parents came over to survey the work.

"You're out of your mind!" my father said. "What are you doing? You've destroyed your yard. All the money that the builder and landscape architect spent on plants, and you just pulled them up. You could have repurposed them!"

He was right, and then I felt guilty. I started going from door to door in the neighborhood, asking if anyone wanted the piles of sod stacked by my driveway. I went to construction sites and asked there, too. No one was ready to lay down their lawns yet, and unfortunately, all of that beautiful, water-intensive grass had to be hauled away as trash.

Those were months of hard physical labor in the sun, and I relished them. Nothing felt better or more natural to me than being outside and sticking my hands into the earth. I'd never had such a tactile connection with dirt before, at least not since I'd played outside in it all day as a kid, and I felt an enormous respect for its possibilities. Progress in the yard was slow, but I could feel and see the results of my work. If I put in the time and the effort, the land responded. Simple, perfect cause and effect.

By June all the vineyard infrastructure was in place and I was ready to order the vines. The best choices for a cool coastal climate are Pinot Noir and Chardonnay. I don't drink a lot of white wine, so I figured that if Pinot was the only red variety I could grow, that's what I would grow. I ordered the same rootstock and clones that Carl had on his land, mostly Dijon clones named after their origin in the Burgundy region. In the coming months, I decided, I'd learn as much about Pinot as I reasonably could.

Winemakers call Pinot the heartbreak grape because it can be so difficult to grow. It's fickle about weather and soil, and its thin skin is susceptible to fungus and mold. Beautiful but temperamental, Pinot vines require constant maintenance to produce a decent yield. Luck helps produce a fine one.

On the Saturday afternoon before the rootstock arrived, I walked into a flower shop in Malibu to buy roses for my daughter Paloma's high school graduation ceremony. The blond woman working there was someone I'd seen around town at the farmer's market and the local grocery store. We sometimes passed each other on our morning jogs as we ran in opposite directions on the beach and we'd shared friendly greetings — "Good morning; nice to see you!" — but I realized I didn't even know her name.

I was horribly sunburned from the past few days I'd spent preparing the vineyard. The woman looked up from the flowers and smiled.

"Hey, buddy," she said. "It's called sunscreen. You live in Malibu. You should know better."

"I know," I said. "I'm building a vineyard. Sometimes I wear sunscreen, sometimes I wear a hat. Sometimes I forget and wear neither."

"A vineyard?" She looked interested. "Where?"

I told her where I lived.

"I live near there."

"I know. I see you around."

"Well, if you ever need any help, I'd love to know more about vineyards."

"As a matter of fact," I said, "I have four hundred vines coming to my house on Monday. I've burned all my relationships with my family and my friends asking them to work in my yard. Now when I call them they run or don't pick up the phone. If you're game, you can come around noon on Monday and help me plant."

I figured if she worked in a flower shop, she must know something about planting. She figured if I was building a vineyard, for God's sake, then I must know what I was doing. We were both in for a few surprises.

Sonja arrived at my house that Monday a few hours after the plants had been delivered. We opened a big cardboard box and there was the rootstock, lying inside in tightly packed rows. I'd turned on the drip emitters over the weekend to loosen up the ground and the soil was soft and pliable. Sonja and I spent all afternoon working in the backyard. I dug a hole under each emitter and then she came up behind me and planted a bare root. Slowly and steadily we made our way down the preplanned rows. It was an incredibly efficient system.

By the end of the day, we'd planted half of the rootstock. "Would you be willing to come back tomorrow?" I asked.

"Sure," she said. "I'll be here."

On Tuesday we followed the same routine and finished all the planting. Afterward we opened a bottle of Pinot to celebrate the completion of our work and sat outside talking. It was an amazing two-day first date: sweaty and self-effacing, nothing pretentious or cool about it. We were both covered in dirt and spent long portions of time in a comfortable silence. I hadn't been looking for a relationship and neither had she, but ours fell perfectly into place. Eight years later, we're still together.

Soon after we finished the vineyard, Sonja said, "Let's plant some vegetables."

"Sure," I said.

Not "Why?" but "Of course." A garden felt like the natural next step.

"Let's put in a chicken coop," she said next.

"Of course." There was never any question. It felt like what I was meant to do. Recently, we've added bees and Sonja goes out in the yard suited up in her white beekeeper suit to harvest honey. Little by little, we've added elements to the land in which we have no formal training, and yet our modest enterprise thrives. Somehow I know how to do the right things. I'll be out in the vineyard pruning the vines by instinct, and then I'll stumble upon a book about pruning and discover I was right on the mark.

How do I have this knowledge? It didn't come from my father, for whom farming was never on the agenda. He laughs out loud when I even joke about this. And yet the skills do filter down through him, I believe. When I visited our relatives in Galicia during the production of *The Way,* nearly every house I saw had a backyard vineyard, a backyard garden, and chickens running around. The yards in Galicia looked just like my yard in Malibu, and I realized I'd unconsciously created a place that honored my family's ancestral home.

If there is such a thing as ancestral memory, I feel it at work at my home in the guise of my grandfather, Francisco. I never had a chance to develop a close relationship with my father's father, who died when I was ten. Yet I feel his influence in my vineyard and my garden each time I pull a vegetable from the ground or check the progress of the vines. The relationship we're having now, removed from the trappings of time, echoes back to generations of men before us who lived off their land. Unlike my father, I never chose a formal religion to follow, but the connection to the earth and this connection to my grandfather are my form of spiritual sustenance. They aren't things I asked for but things that just seemed to happen, that slowly revealed themselves to me.

I can feel these connections and I know they're real, but I struggle to explain exactly how they work. Language is often a poor vehicle for communicating the unknown. By trying to define the experience I run the risk of being ridiculed, so I don't. Or maybe I don't want to define it. Maybe the mystery is part of the point.

MARTIN

During the Middle Ages, cathedrals were often the final destination for pilgrims all over the world. The magnificent spires could be seen from miles away, and sometimes stayed in view for days' worth of travel. The very first glimpses of their cherished goals heightened the pilgrims' anticipation and assured their spirits that their long and difficult journeys were nearly over. At last, they were within sight of the gates of heaven.

Some modern-day pilgrims who arrive at the Cathedral of Santiago de Compostela after long and difficult journeys may not experience that same level of anticipation and transcendence, but a great many do. I am no exception.

Santiago is not journey's end for *The Way* but it is a significant milestone for our production. Even though sequences in Muxia and Morocco still need to be filmed, for all intents and purposes Santiago is our goal. We arrive in the Plaza del Obradoiro on a cold, overcast morning in November. Pilgrims mill around the square, admiring the grandeur of the towering Romanesque cathedral as they wait for the Pilgrim's Mass that is celebrated every day at noon.

I've been in the cathedral twice before, once in 2003 when I drove the Camino with Matt Clark and my grandson Taylor, and again on August third of this year. It was my sixty-ninth birthday and church officials honored me by lighting the Botafumeiro at the end of the Pilgrim's Mass.

At 176 pounds and almost five feet in height, the Botafumeiro — which means "smoke expeller" in Galician — is the largest censer on the planet. A select group of men in pilgrim costume reverently pull on its long, knotted ropes, causing it to swing in a wide arc from one side of the cathedral to the other, from floor to ceiling. The first time the magnificent silver capsule came whizzing by me overhead at fifty miles per hour, depositing thick, fragrant clouds of incense in its wake, I ducked. Then I watched it swing up and away, descend rapidly back down again, and continue like this for a full five minutes.

The spiritual image, we were told, is that the Botafumeiro goes all the way up to heaven, comes down to collect us, and then carries us back up. Whatever its symbolism, the process was mesmerizing and drew thunderous applause from the pilgrim congregation at its conclusion. Emilio also was inspired by the Botafumeiro and planned to include it in *The Way*. But four months later, as we're preparing to film inside the cathedral, we are keenly aware that our presence here can't be taken for granted. Until forty-eight hours ago we were officially denied permission to film inside the cathedral. In fact, we learned that no production has ever been permitted to film there: Only an occasional documentary and some news coverage have been allowed.

It seemed that church officials had some concerns about how we were depicting Catholicism and the Catholic church in general. The provincial government of Galicia also was concerned about how our film would depict the Camino and Spain. This was a critical situation, with an importance that could not be underestimated. If we were forbidden from filming interiors in the cathedral, our film would suffer a critical blow. Not only would one of the most critical sequences of the film have to be eliminated, but it would also preclude the very goal of every pilgrimage and destination of every pilgrim: the cathedral itself.

Fortunately everyone in the cast, crew, and production unit of the film rose to convince both church and state that the concerns were unfounded. Emilio offered to rework any part of the script that either entity found objectionable. David worked hard to assure the local and national government that we intended to celebrate the Camino as a national treasure and honor the Spanish culture. Taylor, Carmen, and I assured the local bishop of our sincere respect for Catholicism and the sacredness of the cathedral. In the final analysis, it didn't hurt our cause that Carmen and I are practicing Catholics as well as first generation Galicians, and that Taylor was a resident of Spain and married to Julia, a Spanish citizen.

Deeply grateful and greatly relieved that permission has been granted, we now turn to the conditions that come with it. We've been given a total of only three hours — and not a minute more — to film the entire sequence inside the cathedral. *Okay,* I think, *Beggars can't be choosers.* Yet in those three hours, some of the most extraordinary moments of the film occur, from the moment when the four of us arrive at El Pórtico de la Gloria (The Portico of Glory) where

Joost drops to his knees in front of the statue of Saint James in a moving gesture of innocent faith and adoration; to Sarah's acceptance of grace and forgiveness; to Jack's profound emotional release; to Tom's visitation at the tomb of Saint James beneath the main altar; to the solemn Pilgrim's Mass and the final blessing of Daniel's ashes; to the extraordinary Botafumeiro spectacle filmed for the first time for any movie. And all of this is achieved without a single word of dialogue.

Any pilgrim who has walked at least one hundred miles of the Camino is entitled to receive a *compostela,* an official document or diploma of sorts (suitable for framing) that confirms their efforts. In the story, our seasoned "gang of four" has walked the entire five hundred miles and has the scars to prove it. They proudly present themselves to the upstairs office next to the cathedral for the pilgrim's final ritual.

The office is staffed by volunteers who ink each pilgrim's passport with the official stamp of the cathedral. Then, before receiving the personalized *compostela,* they are required for the record to answer the standard question: "What is your reason for walking the Camino?"

The answers are as varied as the pilgrims themselves. After walking for weeks, sometimes even months, much of it in solitude, many pilgrims begin to reveal deeply personal information they've never expressed before. Some even break down and weep as they recount their experiences along the way. Often the volunteers remain late into the night listening like skilled therapists or priestly confessors. It's almost as if the pilgrims are being asked, "What is the reason for your life?" and respond with, "I thought you'd never ask."

But Tom is a rare exception. He's caught off guard and isn't inclined to share his deep personal feelings or insights despite the life-changing experience of his pilgrimage. Put on the spot, he tries to summon up an answer.

"Ah . . ." he says. "Well . . . I mean . . ." He stammers on, "I guess . . ."

He can't find the words to explain why he's there in place of his dead son, Daniel. In fact, until that moment Tom has hardly considered the reason for his journey. Back in St.-Jean he'd decided to walk the Camino on impulse, perhaps in a desperate effort to understand the mystery of his son's sudden death while on a personal quest in a strange place, and also to understand the deep regret he felt about their estrangement. In truth, he may have had his son's remains cremated and carried the ashes with him to hold on to Daniel for as long as he could. Any explanation is possible, Tom realizes, but how can he articulate such possibilities to a complete stranger?

Instead, he manages a simplistic response to satisfy the questioner: "I thought I should travel more." But we're left to wonder about his true motive, and the question lingers for the remainder of his journey, as well as for my own. It will accompany both of us to Muxia along the coast, where we surrender Daniel's ashes to the raging tide of the North Atlantic and then south to Morocco, where the final sequence suggests that Tom has embraced Daniel's spirit and sense of adventure and by doing so, becomes his true self.

As expected, the same question — "What is your reason . . . ?" — is waiting for me back in Malibu when I return from Spain. Indeed, this question has been the one constant throughout my journey since May 1, 1981, in Paris and I suspect that it will accompany me to the end, or so I hope.

There's an old saying: If you arrive at the Kingdom alone you must answer just one question: "Where are the others?"

We are made so that we must travel alone, yet we cannot do so without community. No one can live our lives for us or carry our inner burdens, yet we can come to know ourselves only through our compassion for others. "I may not feel your pain or understand your situation, but I will stay with you so that you never feel alone or forgotten." This, I believe, is the basic understanding and purpose of community, and the simplest form of love.

Our first concept of community is family, the one into which we were born or adopted and where we learn to forge our own life, and then the family we create as we enlarge the original one. As we have been formed, so we form, and so on. As I age I can hardly believe how much I have become like my father, for good or ill. I suppose that my children will come to the same realization about me, if they have not already.

I've loved all of my children equally, always, but I've also loved them differently, each one according to his or her needs, which has always seemed quite natural to me. While this shared memoir has involved my personal and professional relationship with Emilio, I trust that Ramon, Charlie, and Renée understand and rest assured that their stories with me are forthcoming.

The Way has been described as a film inspired by a grandson, dedicated to a grandfather, and created by a father and son in between. Taylor is that grandson, Francisco was that grandfather, and Emilio and I are that father and son. We are part of a community that spans four generations and three continents, and we continue to grow and challenge the best in one another. But maybe the best is yet to come. If the road ahead is anything like the one we've already traveled — and I suspect it will be — I welcome every positive gain and painful loss, with a renewed sense of gratitude and joy.

The Irish tell the story of a man who arrives at the gates of heaven and asks to be let in.

"Of course," Saint Peter says. "Just show us your scars."

"I have no scars," the man replies.

"What a pity," Saint Peter says. "Was there nothing worth fighting for?"

Epilogue:
Emilio
2000–2012

The sun sets quickly in Malibu, descending behind the ocean like a bright coin slipping into a distant slot. The sky offers a stunning display of pinks and oranges and reds. Especially in the fall and winter, after a day out working in the yard, the sunset feels like a reward from the heavens. The day's labor is finished, the job well done, and Sonja and I can sit outside with a bottle of our estate Pinot Noir, its grapes grown on the vines in front of us. As the sun goes down, we admire the awe-inspiring streaks across the sky as the vineyards slip into dusk. We're home.

This must be the place.

Our vineyard has become a communal effort, bringing friends and family together for pruning and harvests. Some days a dozen people populate the yard, each working in quiet, individual contemplation. It's meditative, peaceful work once you get into the rhythm.

My father likes to walk over, pull on a set of work gloves, and pick up a pair of pruning shears. The man who hasn't had a drink in more than twenty years has come to understand what Sonja and I have learned, and what my grandfather Francisco and his family must have known as well: that winemaking is not about wine drinking. It's about community. It's about growing and harvesting the plenty together, about creating and engaging in a common activity that at some level is familiar to us all. It's not about getting drunk. It's about sharing an experience. And that we can all do, in abundance.

After fifty years my father and I have arrived at a place of comfortable peace with each other, despite our divergent views about faith. When he talks about scripture he still speaks as if he just witnessed the events last night on *Dateline.* My argument is always, "How do you take the Gospels as fact? When you say 'Jesus said . . .' how do you know he did? Or is that an interpretation of what he may have said? In which case, the Bible is the greatest story ever told." I know my skepticism frustrates him and that he still holds out hope I'll become a Catholic one day, but for now skepticism suits me. I need the tactile experience of verification. I'm always looking for a measure of proof, and even as proof reveals itself, I still want more. It keeps life interesting.

I've come to recognize my father's connection to faith and his devotion to attending weekly Mass as his form of sustenance, akin to a sobriety meeting, and I respect that. I used to question it, but I've had enough sober people in my life by now to know how vital that sustenance is. We each have our own form of spirituality, and that's how it should be. As my father says, "Faith is deeply personal. If it's not personal, it's impersonal, and if it's impersonal, who cares?" Twenty years ago, I wouldn't even have entertained a discussion about spirituality or faith, but as I get older and more in touch with my own mortality, I'm more open to the dialogue. That's been a surprise for me, but one that I welcome.

An even bigger surprise, perhaps, has been the relationship my father and I now share as adults. Whenever we embark on a personal journey we never know if we'll encounter people on our travels, if someone will be at our side to help us along, or if we'll arrive at our destination alone. For much of my life I thought it unlikely that my father and I would end up on this path together. It's been a wonderful surprise for me to discover him right here beside me.

The public mythology of our family is that we all grew up blessed, with silver spoons in our mouths. The spoon part isn't true at all, though I do feel blessed. Every day I feel as if I've won the lottery, though not in the traditional sense. Certainly not in the way others might expect.

Success to my grandfather was not measured by what a man achieved in his career or how much money he made but by the state of his health, his relationships with his children, and the strength of his marriage. I think that's how my father always defined success as well. Instead of chasing fame he chose to compile a vast body of work, share a fifty-year marriage, and raise four children, all of whom he's worked with over the years. Now he gets to reap the benefits of those choices. Making *The Way* together, as a family effort, created an art form that celebrates us all. *The War at Home* and *Bobby,* too — these were experiences we shared together. For a father and son to share this level of collaboration is very special, even in this town.

Our family is not unique in terms of dealing with alcoholism or competition or arguments about faith. But we may be unique, at least by Hollywood standards, in that we're still together. So many families around us have fragmented and dismissed and abandoned one another. That's something my father has never done. He always hung in there, with each one of us, through everything we've faced, and he always finds the will to forgive.

That, I think, is his greatest lesson of all.

Reliving our relationship in its entirety for this book wasn't always easy. It required painful, honest gazes backward, whereas I prefer to always look forward. But it was well worth the time. My father and I learned things about each other we'd never known, and we shared stories we'd forgotten or never told before. We spent time again with people who are no longer with us, people who meant a great deal to us over the years: the actors Marlon Brando, Dennis Hopper, George C. Scott, Chris Penn, and Patrick Swayze; the director Robert Wise; our dear friend Roscoe Lee Browne; my godfather John Crane; my grandfather Francisco; my aunt Juaquina; and my uncles Mateo, Lorenzo, Manuel, Conrad, Mike, Al, and Carlos.

Remembering them and missing them all over again has made me all the more grateful for the people who are still here. I think specifically of Matt Clark; Joe Lowry; Laurence Fishburne; Jimmy Keane; Lee Arenberg; my aunt Carmen, and, most of all, my partner Sonja, my mother Janet, my siblings Ramon, Charlie, and Renée, and my children, Paloma and Taylor.

And of course, first and foremost, my dad. Ramon. Otherwise known as Martin. The man who for so many years walked ahead of me, who briefly walked a separate path, and who now walks by my side.

ACKNOWLEDGMENTS

The authors would like to thank the following people for their help and support with this book from the very start: Leslie Meredith, our smart, thoughtful, and very patient editor at Free Press; our tenacious agents, Elizabeth Kaplan and Scott Waxman; Donna Loffredo and Carisa Hays, our champions at Free Press; and David Alexanian of Elixir Films, who helped nurture this book into being.

We're also very grateful to Taylor Estevez; Ramon Estevez; Charles Laughton; Matt Clark; Jimmy Keane; Lee Arenberg; Joe Brinkmann; Michele Cofield; Mark Ortiz at Paulist Productions; Michael Meade; Diana Kelly, Joe Provisor, and the Ojai Foundation; Fatah Evans; Melissa Nykanen at the Malibu Historical Archives at Pepperdine University Libraries; the staff of the Malibu High School library; Jewels Nation; Belen Ricoy; Cree Miller; and Jackson Browne.

Special thanks to Renée Estevez for extensive help with photographs and archival information; CarolLee Streeter Kidd for transcribing hundreds of hours of interview tapes; and April Fitzsimmons for research assistance. We couldn't have pulled this together without you.

Most of all, our deepest thanks go to Janet Sheen, Sonja Magdevski, and Uzi Eliahou — for everything, and more.

ABOUT THE AUTHORS

Martin Sheen was born (and still is) Ramon Antonio Gerardo Estevez. Sheen is perhaps best known for his unforgettable performances in *Badlands* (1973), *Apocalypse Now* (1979), *Wall Street* (1987), and as President Josiah Bartlet on television's *The West Wing* (1999–2006). A longtime activist for social justice and human rights, in 2008 he received the Laetare Medal from the University of Notre Dame for his humanitarian work. He holds an honorary arts doctorate from the National University of Ireland. He lives in Malibu, California, with his wife of fifty years, Janet.

Emilio Estevez is known for his roles in *The Outsiders* (1983), *The Breakfast Club* (1985), *Young Guns,* and *Young Guns II* (1988, 1990), and as Coach Gordon Bombay in *The Mighty Ducks* films (1992, 1994, 1996). More recently, he's made a mark as a writer and director willing to tackle complicated social subjects (*The War at Home, Bobby*). With his partner, Sonja Magdevski, he is coproprietor of Casa Dumetz vineyards in Malibu, which produces organically farmed Pinot Noir as well as Viognier, Grenache, and Syrah from Tierra Alta Vineyards in Santa Ynez, California. Their microfarm also produces eggs, honey, and organic vegetables.

Hope Edelman is the author of five prior nonfiction books, including the international bestseller *Motherless Daughters* and the national bestsellers *Motherless Mothers* and *The Possibility of Everything*. She lives with her husband and two daughters in Topanga Canyon, California.

The employees of Thorndike Press hope you have enjoyed this Large Print book. All our Thorndike, Wheeler, and Kennebec Large Print titles are designed for easy reading, and all our books are made to last. Other Thorndike Press Large Print books are available at your library, through selected bookstores, or directly from us.

For information about titles, please call:
  (800) 223-1244

or visit our Web site at:
  http://gale.cengage.com/thorndike

To share your comments, please write:
Publisher
Thorndike Press
10 Water St., Suite 310
Waterville, ME 04901